Cape Town

www.timeout.com

Guides

Time Out Digital Ltd
4th Floor
125 Shaftesbury Avenue
London WC2H 8AD
United Kingdom
Tel: +44 (0)20 7813 3000
Fax: +44 (0)20 7813 6001
Email: guides@timeout.com
www.timeout.com

Published by Time Out Digital Ltd, a wholly owned subsidiary
of Time Out Group Ltd. Time Out and the Time Out logo are
trademarks of Time Out Group Ltd.

© **Time Out Group Ltd 2016**
Previous editions 2004, 2007, 2009.

10 9 8 7 6 5 4 3 2 1

This edition first published in Great Britain in 2016 by Ebury Publishing.
20 Vauxhall Bridge Road, London SW1V 2SA

Ebury Publishing is part of the Penguin Random House group of companies
whose addresses can be found at global.penguinrandomhouse.com

Distributed in the US and Latin America by Publishers Group West
(1-510-809-3700)

For further distribution details, see www.timeout.com.

ISBN: 978-1-84670-361-4

A CIP catalogue record for this book is available from the British Library.

Printed and bound in China by Leo Paper Products Ltd.

MIX
Paper from
responsible sources
FSC® C018179

Contents

110

86

135

227

Time Out Cape Town

Editorial
Editor Lisa van Aswegen
Copy Editor Ros Sales
Listings Editor Lateefah Williams
Proofreader Marion Moisy

Editorial Director Sarah Guy
Group Finance Manager Margaret Wright

Design
Art Editor Christie Webster
Group Commercial Senior Designer Jason Tansley

Picture Desk
Picture Editor Jael Marschner
Deputy Picture Editor Ben Rowe
Picture Researcher Lizzy Owen

Advertising
Managing Director St John Betteridge

Marketing
Senior Publishing Brand Manager Luthfa Begum
Head of Circulation Dan Collins

Production
Production Controller Katie Mulhern-Bhudia

Time Out Group
Founder Tony Elliott
Executive Chairman Julio Bruno
Chief Executive Officer Noel Penzer
Publisher Alex Batho

Contributors
Revised and adapted from previous editions of *Time Out Cape Town* by Lisa van Aswegen, with additional writing by Lisa van Aswegen, Bianca Coleman, David Engelbrecht and Mark van Dijk.

Maps JS Graphics Ltd (john@jsgraphics.co.uk)

Cover Photography Stephane Frances/Onlyfrance/SIME/4Corners

Back Cover Photography Clockwise from top left: Juburg/Shutterstock.com; Courtesy Shimmy Beach Club, Cape Town; Neil Bradfield/Shutterstock.com; Courtesy African Pride 15 on Orange Hotel, Cape Town; Andrea Willmore/Shutterstock.com

Photography pages 10/11 meunierd/Shutterstock.com; 16/17 Grobler du Preez/Shutterstock.com; 18/19 Ollyy/Shutterstock.com; 20 Magdalena Paluchowska/Shutterstock.com; 22/23 (top), 217 NegativeC/Wikimedia Commons; 22/23 (bottom), 56 Claire Gunn Photography; 24, 30/31, 34/35 (bottom) Wesgro; 26 Go2africa/Wikimedia Commons; 26/27, 100/101, pull-out map Jurie Senekal; 27 (bottom left) Kolesky/Nikon/Lexar; 28/29, 110, 114 Kirstenbosch NBG; 29 Halden Krog/Gallo Images/Getty Images; 30, 42/43, 136, pull-out map Neil Bradfield/Shutterstock.com; 32 HelenOnline/Wikimedia Commons; 33 InnaFelker/Shutterstock.com; 37 Nicky Schrire; 38 Michelle Petrie; 39 Peter Larkin; 48, 50, 51 Carina Beyer; 58, 59, 169 Jesse Kramer; 61 Laura McCullagh; 81 Cape Town Diamond Museum; 88 (bottom) Karin Schermbrucker; 91, 126 Lisa Burnell; 106 Jason vd Merwe; 109 Hayden Phipps; 115 Adam Harrower, Kirstenbosch NBG; 116 (bottom) Mark Williams; 118, 119 Montebello & studios at Montebello; 121 Andries Joubert; 126/127 Stefan Schäfer, Lich/Wikimedia Commons; 128/129, 131 Allan McCreadie; 130 Simon Scarboro; 138 Lionel Besterfield; 140, 141 Troy Goldie Photography; 143 Jacques Marais; 144 Hamlin Jansen van Vuuren; 145 Yolande Snyders; 148 © Two Oceans Aquarium; 155 Troy Davis; 156 Moviestore/REX Shutterstock; 160 © Synergy Exposure; 161 Samantha Marx/Wikimedia Commons; 164 Jonx Pillemer; 170 Helena Fagan; 182 Vergelegen; 183 Cape Canopy Tour; 196/197 Gimas/Shutterstock.com; 198/199 Anna Zieminski/AFP/Getty Images; 201 Andrew Hall/Wikimedia Commons; 203, 205 Wikimedia Commons; 210/211 © Africa Media Online/Alamy Stock Photo; 214/215 © Realimage/Alamy Stock Photo; 218 Tinus Potgieter/Shutterstock.com; 219 Circumnavigation/Shutterstock.com

The following images were supplied by the featured establishments: 4, 5 (top and bottom), 12, 12/13, 25, 27 (top right and bottom right), 34/35 (top), 36/37, 38/39, 40/41, 55, 62, 63, 70, 71, 72, 73, 74, 76, 77, 78, 84, 86, 88 (top), 92, 94, 98, 100, 105, 107, 108, 110/111, 112, 113, 116 (top left and top right), 120, 122, 123, 132, 133, 146/147, 150, 154, 157, 158, 162, 163, 168, 171, 172, 174/175, 177, 180, 190, 191, 192, 194, 195, 220/221, 222, 223, 224, 226, 227, 234

About the Guide

GETTING AROUND

The Explore chapters covering central Cape Town include street maps of the area, marked with the locations of sights and museums (❶), restaurants and cafés (❶), pubs and bars (❶) and shops (❶). There are also street maps of Cape Town at the back of the book, along with an overview map of the city. In addition, there is a detachable fold-out street map.

THE ESSENTIALS

For practical information, including visas, disabled access, emergency numbers, lost property, websites and local transport, see the Essential Information section. It begins on page 220.

THE LISTINGS

Addresses, phone numbers, websites, transport information, hours and prices are all included in our listings, as are selected other facilities. All were checked and correct at press time. However, business owners can alter their arrangements at any time, and fluctuating economic conditions can cause prices to change rapidly.

The very best venues in the city, the must-sees and must-dos in every category, have been marked with a red star (★). In the Explore chapters, we've also marked venues with free admission with a FREE symbol.

PHONE NUMBERS

The area code for Cape Town is 021. You need to use this area code, even when dialling a local call within the city. From outside South Africa, dial your country's access code (00 from the UK, 011 from the US) or a plus symbol, followed by the South African country code (27), then 021 for Cape Town (dropping the initial zero) and the number. So, to reach the Iziko South African Museum, dial + 27 21 460 8242. For more on phones, see page 236.

FEEDBACK

We welcome feedback on this guide, both on the venues we've included and on any other locations that you'd like to see featured in future editions. Please email us at guides@timeout.com.

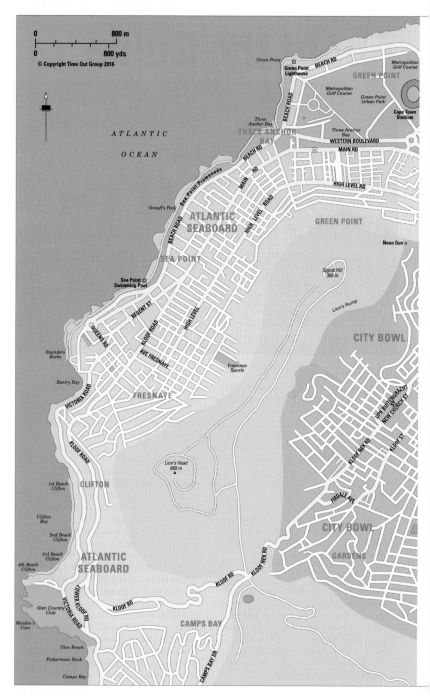

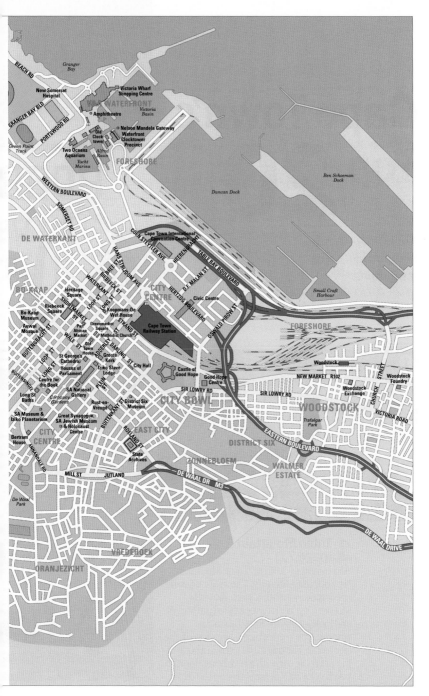

Cape Town's
Top 20

*From awe-inspiring
nature to hip
restaurants.*

ROBB
WE
WI
ONS DIE

1 Table Mountain
(page 77)

At a height of 1,067m, Table Mountain
tops our list – literally. The awe-inspiring
sandstone monolith towers above the
Mother City. With fynbos-filled pathways
and lookout points dotted about the
summit, you'll get a bird's-eye view of the
city below. The ride to the top is in a state-of-
the-art cable car with a revolving floor, so
you'll get a 360° perspective on the trip.

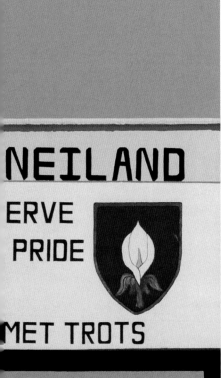

2 Robben Island
(page 86)

Infamous as the location of the maximum security prison where Nelson Mandela was incarcerated for 18 years, Robben Island is a sparse and desolate place. A ferry takes visitors to the island, where they can see the tiny cell where Mandela was imprisoned for rebelling against the apartheid regime. On the tour, you'll find out more about the island's 500-year history.

3 Constantia Valley Winelands
(page 119)

At the heart of these winelands – the closest to Cape Town – lies Groot Constantia, founded in 1685. Today the area is home to eight wine estates, many of which produce some of the world's top wines. You can visit historic wine estates, or try a boutique winery or two for a modern approach. Excellent restaurants round off the Constantia winelands experience perfectly.

4 V&A Waterfront
(page 85)

This eating, drinking, shopping and leisure hub is an essential port of call. Not only will you find top fashion retailers, original crafters and high-end jewellery stores in this harbourside hub, but there are plenty of activities too. The Two Oceans Aquarium will delight the little ones, while the Cape Wheel offers fantastic views of the city.

5 Bree Street
(page 44)

Urban, hip, artisan, cool – just a few words that describe über-trendy Bree Street. This is where those in the know converge for boutique shopping, artisan food retailers and an array of restaurants and bars. It's the perfect base for a day-into-night experience, with eateries serving gourmet tapas and craft beers.

6 Green Point Urban Park
(page 91)

The new green lung of Cape Town, the Green Point Urban Park showcases indigenous flora alongside expansive lawns and two playgrounds, making it a wonderful escape from the city for an hour or two. Interactive displays and open-air gym equipment provide activities, there are shaded picnic spots and little people will love splashing in the pebbled stream.

7 Two Oceans Aquarium
(page 87)

There's entertainment for all age groups at this underwater world. After posing with clownfish and gazing at luminescent jellyfish, head to the predator tank, where

health-boosting smoothies. There's a good range of baked goods, charcuterie and cheeses as well as plenty of fresh fruit and veggies. The design market showcases clothing, jewellery and leather accessories.

a glassed half-tunnel allows incredible up-close views of sharks, rays and other marine creatures. Watch the penguins being fed before heading to the restaurant.

8 Neighbourgoods Market (page 108)

The place that put Woodstock on the map, the Neighbourgoods Market at the Old Biscuit Mill is a weekly gathering of artisan producers and cool designers. Get there early, before the crowds descend, for gourmet sandwiches, dim sum, single origin coffee and

9 Boulders Beach (page 133)

Where else can you go swimming with penguins? The 2,000-odd jackass penguins that call Boulders Beach home provide entertainment with their noisy antics. Either stroll along the boardwalk to see their nests and view them waddling towards the sea; or spend the day splashing about with them in between the rocks and coves of the beach further along.

10
Kirstenbosch National Botanical Garden
(page 115)
These expansive gardens in the Southern Suburbs are a haven for nature lovers and popular for family days out. Vast lawns, indigenous plants, ponds and streams are interlinked with pathways. These lead visitors to spots like the Bath in the Dell, a wild almond hedge planted by Jan van Riebeeck in the 17th century, and a range of gigantic yellowwoods. The Boomslang Tree Canopy Walkway provides views from 12 metres high in the treetops, and modern and traditional sculptures punctuate the natural surrounds, from African stone pieces to bronzes by Dylan Lewis.

11 Bo-Kaap
(page 65)
The historic Malay Quarter is a vibrant hub characterised by steep, cobbled streets and brightly painted houses on the slopes of Signal Hill. Join a walking tour to find out more about the place and its people before stopping to buy aromatic spices and see the Noon Gun in action.

12 Kalk Bay
(page 130)
Fashionable boutiques, antiques dealers and bohemian shops rub shoulders in this seaside village. Once you've explored the retail opportunities, head to the harbour to watch the catch of the day being unloaded. There are plenty of seafood restaurants, from haute to rustic, many with dramatic locations at the ocean's edge, and it's easy to spend a lazy afternoon drinking in the view – and some top wines too.

13 Art galleries
(pages 61, 65, 67, 89, 90, 109, 119, 131, 132)

Cape Town is the place to find contemporary South African art, in venues ranging from hole-in-the-wall galleries in the centre of the city to vast warehouse exhibition spaces in Woodstock. There's a distinct street edge to pieces by local artists, with graffiti, multi-media and pop art also getting a look in.

14 Cape Point
(page 135)

Head to the southernmost tip of the Cape Peninsula for a day out in nature. Cape mountain zebra and buck roam in the Cape of Good Hope Nature Reserve and whales frolic in the ocean in spring. The funicular is a fun way to get to the top of the pinnacle where the lighthouse is situated, and there's a decent restaurant where you can revive your flagging energy and keep admiring the views.

15 Company's Garden
(page 48)

This is where it all started… The Dutch East India Company established a vegetable garden in the Cape in 1652 to provide fresh produce to ships sailing to India from Europe. Today the gardens provide a quiet haven, with tree-lined walkways, lawns and cultivated beds. The restaurant has been recently revamped and many of the city's museums can be accessed from the gardens.

16 Chapman's Peak Drive
(page 99)

One of the world's iconic drives, Chapman's Peak is etched into the cliff face linking Hout Bay and Noordhoek. You'll need strong nerves to face the 114 twists and turns on this precipitous pass, but the views are worth it. If you can't face looking down, look up at the feats of engineering holding up the cliff face above.

17 Sea Point Promenade
(page 91)

Having recently undergone a R17-million upgrade, the Promenade snakes all along the Atlantic coast from Mouille Point to the end of Sea Point. It's always busy with joggers, dog-walkers, kids on bikes and those out for a gentle stroll. The adjoining lawns, with outdoor exercise equipment and jungle gyms, and the small beaches dotted along the way add to the appeal. The Sea Point Swimming Pool is right at the end, with four pools where locals love to cool off.

18 Castle of Good Hope
(page 45)

This pentagonal fortification was completed in 1679 and is home to a military museum and collection of 17th-century paintings and furniture. See the daily key ceremony and take a ride in the horse-drawn carriage while you're there. The castle also hosts contemporary exhibitions.

19 Cape Winelands
(page 176)

While not actually in Cape Town, the Winelands are a quintessential part of the visitor experience. The historic towns of Stellenbosch and Franschhoek ooze charm, with tree-lined avenues, mountains in the distance and – of course – all those wine estates. Many wineries now offer tastings paired with canapés or chocolate and some of the country's top restaurants are here.

20 Lion's Head full-moon hike
(page 77)

Locals hike up Lion's Head during the day – and at night. When the moon is full, masses of intrepid walkers head up the steep mountain track. It's a classic Cape Town experience, and the views from the 669-metre summit over the city and harbour are spectacular. Just make sure you go with someone who knows the twists and turns.

Cape Town
Today

Gateway to South Africa? Cape Town feels – and acts – like a country of its own.

TEXT: MARK VAN DIJK

Sitting, as it does, at the toe of Africa, Cape Town serves as the gateway to Africa. At least, that's what countless visitors have believed – from early explorers (like Bartolomeu Dias in 1488) to early settlers (like Jan van Riebeeck in 1652) to the almost 1.5 million foreign visitors recorded in the summer of 2014/15.

But don't walk through those arrival gates at Cape Town International Airport expecting an instant immersion into what those early colonists called 'The Dark Continent'. Cape Town, the Mother City, is more likely to ease you slowly into your safari adventure. See, while it's unmistakably a part of Africa, Cape Town does things differently from the rest of the continent… and the rest of the country.

THE CAPE TOWN DIFFERENCE

In Cape Town the summers are warm and the winters are wet (it's called the 'Cape of Storms' for a reason), while up in Johannesburg the winters are dry and the summers bring thundershowers. In Cape Town the seas are cold (you can thank the fresh-from-Antarctica Benguela Current for that), while up the coast in Durban, where they have the warm Agulhas Current, you can surf and swim in the ocean without needing a wetsuit or a long lie in the sun. And while the Fairest Cape enjoys the bounty of vineyards and orchards, in the interior they're far more interested in the minerals that lie buried deep below the soil. Even politically the Western Cape can't seem to agree with the rest of the country: provincial election results down here invariably run in opposition to whoever's in power in the rest of South Africa.

THE FACE OF THE CITY

Cape Town's deep sense of difference goes beyond climate (political or meteorological). The mix of people you'll meet in Cape Town is quite different from the rest of Africa. The most recent government census (2011) has 'Black Africans' making up 32.9 per cent of the provincial population, compared to a national average of 79.2 per cent; while 'Coloureds' (48.8 per cent provincially, against 8.9 per cent nationally) and 'Whites' (15.7 per cent versus 8.9 per cent nationally) make up the majority of the rest. These numbers are useful for two reasons: firstly, they tell you that Cape Town has wide ethnic diversity; and secondly, they tell you that 'Coloured' is by no means a derogatory term here (which can come as one of many culture shocks for unsuspecting foreign visitors). That diversity might take some getting used to.

Walking across the City Bowl today – and it'll only take you about half an hour if you don't stop to look around – you'll brush up against an African Union of continental cultures, hearing languages from English to French to Afrikaans to Shona to isiXhosa and Portuguese. On Greenmarket Square you'll encounter Zimbabwean or central African stallholders, some of them refugees, some of them documented. Walk up to Long Street – with its boutiques, barbershops, bars and mosques – and you'll pass foreign tourists checking their street maps alongside Asian sailors, fresh from the docks. In Bree Street, you'll find a proliferation of local and international hipsters – the moustache and beard is fast becoming a lingua franca. And when you park your car, you'll meet a parking guard – Congolese, Tanzanian, or from anywhere across the African diaspora – engaged in deep discussion with the bearded hipster, armed with his skateboard and his craft beer. It's a cosmopolitan collection of people that makes it hard to believe that Cape Town could ever – let alone as recently as 20 years ago – have been part of such a racially divided, Apartheid-torn society.

That hipster's beard and artisanal coffee beans are by no means the most ironic things you'll find here. For a city where an ill-conceived, unfinished highway flyover stands as one of the city's most prominent landmarks, it looked like a monumental achievement when Cape Town was named World Design Capital in 2014.

But, ever since Nelson Mandela looked hopefully across the bay from his cell on Robben Island to Table Mountain ('To us,' he

Long Street.

once remarked, 'Table Mountain was a beacon of hope.'), Cape Town has had a knack for reinvention and renaissance. From the District Six Museum to the Houses of Parliament, from the reclaimed land of Paarden Eiland to the sprawl of its suburbs, it has been designing – and redesigning – itself for generations.

On that theme, Cape Town – superficially, at least – looks very different now from how it looked ten, or even five, years ago. The glowing silver bowl of Cape Town Stadium is the most obvious legacy of the 2010 Fifa World Cup). In the achievement of its more positive goals, world sport's showpiece event left the city with a vastly improved transport system, ranging from smarter roadways to the efficient new MyCiti bus network. (Ignore what the locals say about traffic jams. Capetonians love to complain about traffic, the weather, and the currency exchange rate.)

'With the property boom has come the gentrification of old neighbourhoods.'

For the past decade or so, the city seems to have been in a constant state of improvement: across town, and in the City Bowl especially, the skies are dotted with cranes, with new buildings popping up (and old ones coming down) at regular intervals. Sparkling new edifices like the Cape Town International Convention Centre, the Icon building, Wembley Square and Portside Tower (which, at 139 metres, set the record as the city's tallest skyscraper) now cast long shadows over the CBD's established Edwardian and art deco structures. The result is an eclectic architectural mix that reflects the city's many faces.

But with that property boom has come the gentrification of old inner-city neighbourhoods like the Bo-Kaap, where charming old homes are being converted into expensive new offices. This gentrification is a discomfiting echo of the forced removals of the 1970s, when apartheid laws sent coloured residents out of areas like District Six and into the sandpits of the Cape Flats, on the far side of the Cape Peninsula. Today, at least, when the residents move out

of their homes it's to leafier suburbs and with money in their bank accounts.

TOP OF THE LIST

Scratch the surface, though, and beneath the prosperity and the property boom you will still find a city with problems. In a modern-day twist on Van Riebeeck's early trading station, Cape Town has become a 'Gateway to Africa' for human trafficking (one related study ranked South Africa among the ten worst nations in Africa for trafficking) and drug smuggling (several United Nations studies describe South Africa as a regional narcotics hub).

But that, sadly, is what comes with being a modern trade hub. Cape Town also tops a few other, far more positive, lists. Citing the city as 'a place to meditate on freedom, and the creative life that followed', the *New York Times* rated Cape Town as number one on its list of '52 Places To Go in 2014'. Calling Cape Town 'The African capital of cool', *National Geographic* ranked Clifton as the second-best beach on the planet, while ranking beginner-friendly Muizenberg as one of the world's '20 best surf towns'. And in 2015 Cape Town's Test Kitchen ranked 28 in the World's 50 Best Restaurants.

Of course, the locals would like to see Cape Town's sports teams improve their rankings… but while the Stormers remain perennial under-achievers in the international Super Rugby rugby union championship, and soccer fans wait for local sides Ajax Cape Town and Santos to end their respective trophy droughts, cricket fans can at least console themselves with Newlands Cricket Stadium, which – surprise, surprise – ranks among the most beautiful cricket grounds in the world.

Sport (along with traffic and the weather) will never keep Cape Town's people completely satisfied. But the truth is, they're spoiled. And those locals – whether they call the place Cape Town, Kaapstad, iKapa or Le Cap – seldom let modern-day realities interfere with their enjoyment of their beautiful city. Seasons change. Buildings go up and come down. And people pass through the Cape, as they have been doing for centuries. Sure, the Mother City can be a little crazy sometimes. And, undoubtedly, it's different. But, even at its worst, Cape Town is always a charming, beautiful mess. After all, a city that's slowly being nudged into the sea by a flat-topped mountain can't afford to take life too seriously, now, can it?

Itineraries

The Mother City in a single weekend.

7AM

10AM

Day 1

7AM Rise and shine! We know it's early, but you're heading up Table Mountain today and it's a good idea to get an early start to beat the queues. To really wake up, head to Truth Coffee Roasting (p75) for a perfect cup of coffee before going to the Aerial Cableway (p77). Once at the top, take a walk around to spot cute dassies (also known as rock rabbits or hyrax), see wild fynbos and marvel at the views of the city spread out below.

10AM Once you've come back to earth, head to the city centre for a late morning of browsing and shopping. Start off in Kloof Street (p67) for boutique buys, before heading down to Greenmarket Square (p63) to barter for souvenirs and crafts. If you feel like a historical perspective on the city, join a walking tour to the colourful Bo-Kaap (p65).

1PM After all that fresh air and exercise, you've no doubt worked up an appetite. The

Clockwise from left: **Table Mountain Aerial Cableway**; **Greenmarket Square**; **Culture Club Cheese**.

1PM

top of Bree Street is your best bet: choose from cheese-filled delights at Culture Club Cheese (p57), a Mediterranean harvest table at Sababa (p58), Bacon on Bree's porky pleasures (p54) or crammed sourdough sandwiches at Jason Bakery (p57).

3PM More retail therapy awaits, so head down to the V&A Waterfront. If you need some respite from the merchandise, spend an hour at the Two Oceans Aquarium (p86) before popping in to the newly opened Watershed (p90) next door. Here you'll find a warehouse space dedicated to arts, crafts, fashion and accessories: everything is locally made and curated so you'll be bound to find something beautiful to take home. Then head back to your hotel to stash all your purchases, and get ready for a night on the town.

6PM A visit to Cape Town just isn't complete without a sundowner at Camps Bay:

8PM

3PM

take a stroll on the beach or head to the Grand (p87), Café Caprice (p96) or any of the myriad bars that line the palm-fringed beach, and enjoy a beverage as you watch the sun sink into the ocean.

8PM Your best bet for a delicious dinner is to head back into town. Bree Street, again, is where it's at. First up, a glass of wine and Spanish tapas will fill the gap at La Parada (p58). Afterwards wander up the road to Bocca (p54) for delicious pizzas and more bites to share.

10PM Decision-time: a nightcap at hipster-central Black Ram (p71) on Kloofnek Road will do you well; alternatively, head down to Long Street (p217) where the many clubs are just starting to warm up…

Day 2

8AM This morning it's time to explore the South Peninsula, so head straight to Kalk Bay for breakfast at Olympia Café & Deli (p131) – the pastries

are delicious. After a quick browse around the antiques shops and fashion boutiques, head further south to Simon's Town and the lovely Boulders Beach (p126).

10AM Watch the African penguins' antics from the elevated boardwalks, before enjoying some beach time of your own. Either chill out between the rocks at Boulders or go to Muizenberg beach (p126) with its warm waters and epic surfing. You can even get a surfing lesson while you're there.

1PM A lazy lunch at Tiger's Milk Restaurant & Bar (p129) at Muizenberg beach is a winner: burgers, ribs and steaks hit the spot, as do the craft beers on tap.

3PM Meander back to the city via the Constantia Winelands. The leafy surrounds will bring a lovely cool respite after the morning at the seaside. If you're after history and classic wines, head for Groot Constantia. Steenberg (p120) has a big-hitting selection of wines and a modern tasting

room; alternatively, try the boutique winery Beau Constantia (p119) with its contemporary decor and valley views.

7PM Tonight, dinner is a high-end affair. Take your pick from La Colombe (p121) for classic French dining or Greenhouse at the Cellars-Hohenort (p122) for contemporary cuisine – both are located in Constantia so you can head there after your wine-tasting (remember to

CAPE TOWN FOR FREE
Who doesn't love free stuff?

GREAT OUTDOORS
Table Mountain (p77), Devil's Peak (p69) and Lion's Head (p77) are an uphill hop from the city centre and have a variety of walking trails, from the mild to the manic. All you need is good walking shoes, a hat, sunscreen, plenty of water, a snack or two and some good friends, and the day is yours to explore.

CULTURE VULTURES
The Iziko museums (p49) offer free entry on public holidays, of which South Africa has plenty. The diversity of the museums means you can get your history, art, science or culture fix for free. While you're here, there's more free enjoyment in a stroll in the nearby Company's Garden (p48) under the shaded oak lanes.

GOOD TASTE
There are so many food markets in and around Cape Town that you won't know where to go first. Head to any one of them for free tastings of delicious foods, from olives to cheese, sausages and ice-cream. *See p108* **Market Forces** for information.

pack heels and lipstick). And if you want a sea view, head to Azure (p96) at the Twelve Apostles Hotel and Spa. The expansive deck has one of the best views in town, and the cuisine is seasonal and makes the most of South African produce.

10PM
If you can muster another venue, Planet Bar (p71) at the Belmond Mount Nelson Hotel is the perfect place to round off a perfect day.

Left to right:
Bree Street;
Constantia Winelands.

PARK LIFE
Green Point Urban Park (p91) has no entrance fee, and besides all the lovely lawns inviting you to stretch out and relax, there are jungle gyms for the kids, plant life galore, and an outdoor gym space and labyrinth to explore. The same goes for the Promenade that stretches from Mouille Point all the way along the coastline to Sea Point.

Cape Town food tour

Capetonians are food obsessed: many of the country's top restaurants are in the city, there's an abundance of excellent local produce, and artisan food producers are wholeheartedly supported.

If it happens to be a Saturday, the place to start is the Neigbourgoods Market (p108) in Woodstock. Rösti with smoked salmon, poached eggs and hollandaise, authentic French crêpes, delicious dim sum or freshly baked pastries are but some of the delights that await. Add to that a fruity smoothie and espresso from Espresso Lab (p104) next door, and you're pretty much set.

For more foodie treats, the V&A Food Market (p108) at the V&A Waterfront is a good option. Here you can stock up on dried fruits, enjoy a bubble tea or wonderful ice-cream from the Creamery's stand. And while you're in the Atlantic Seaboard area, a quick coffee at Giovanni's Deli World (p93) will keep you buzzing for the afternoon. While you're there, browse for imported foodstuffs and stock up on cheeses and charcuterie.

There's nothing more South African than a braai. And nowhere better to buy your meat

than at Frankie Fenner Meat Merchants (p62) in Church Street. While you're waiting for the butcher to cut your meat selection, enjoy a glass of wine at in-house Publik wine bar. They specialise in interesting wine finds.

In Wale Street, you'll find Bean There Coffee Company (p62), where you can buy Fairtrade coffee. Next door is Honest Chocolate (p63): not only is the raw, organic chocolate delicious, but the arty packaging turns the slabs into excellent gifts as well.

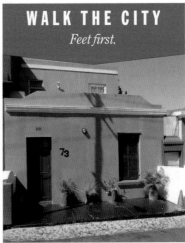

Clockwise from top left: **Neighbourgoods Market**; **Frankie Fenner Meat Merchants**; **Bean There Coffee Company**.

WALK THE CITY
Feet first.

Unless you booked six months ahead, it's unlikely you'll get a table at Luke Dale-Roberts' the Test Kitchen (p104). But with a little bit of forward planning you can book dinner at the Pot Luck Club (p104), its stylish sister restaurant, also located in Woodstock. Take the lift to the top floor of the old silo building and take in the sparkling city lights before sitting down to a multitude of tapas-style plates. Our favourites are fish tacos and smoked beef fillet with truffle café au lait.

Tours are a great way to explore the city's bustling, ever-changing streets, squares and hotspots. **City Sightseeing** (www.citysightseeing.co.za) and **Nielsen Tours** (076 636 9007, www.nielsentours.co.za) offer free walking tours of the city. There are also many specialist tours that delve into various aspects of the Cape's history, such as **Cape Town on Foot** (021 462 4252, www.wanderlust.co.za) and **Footsteps to Freedom** (021 671 6878, 083 452 1112, www.footstepstofreedom.co.za). And for a high-tech tour download the VoiceMap app – *see p134* **In the Know**.

Diary

A year-round guide to the Mother City's best events and celebrations.

Kirstenbosch Summer Sunset Concerts.

Whether you're a foodie or a sporty type, there are plenty of events in and around Cape Town that'll keep you entertained all year long. Major sporting happenings, such as the Old Mutual Two Oceans Marathon and the Cape Town Cycle Tour, are highlights in the calendar. Thanks to an abundance of food and drink festivals, as well as music events such as the Kirstenbosch Summer Sunset Concert series, and design exhibitions from Fashion Week to Design Indaba, the problem will be choosing what to do. In typical laid-back Cape Town style, many events aren't completely confirmed until the last minute, so it's a good idea to keep an eye on social media. Tickets are usually available via Computicket (http://online.computicket.com/web) and Webtickets (www.webtickets.co.za). Do also check the Arts & Entertainment section, starting on p146, for more events.

Cape Town International Kite Festival.

Spring

Cape Town International Kite Festival

Zandvlei, Muizenberg, South Peninsula (www. capementalhealth.co.za/kite). **Date** late Oct.

A magical sight awaits on vast Muizenberg beach, as kites of all shapes and sizes take to the skies. There's also a kite-making competition and food and craft stalls to add to the convivial atmosphere.

Kirstenbosch Summer Sunset Concerts

Kirstenbosch National Botanical Garden, Rhodes Drive, Newlands, Southern Suburbs (www.sanbi. org/events). **Date** late Nov-early Apr.

There are few better ways to end the weekend than with a picnic basket, good friends, the stunning Kirstenbosch gardens as a backdrop and hot music on the stage. The lawns get packed at this deservedly popular institution. Crowd favourites such as Goldfish, the Parlotones, Freshlyground, Johnny Clegg and Mi Casa have all performed here.

Cape Town Minstrel Carnival.

Old Mutual Two Oceans Marathon.

their painted faces, bright suits and joyous music. There are also contests for the best dressed team, drum major and minstrel song.

J&B Metropolitan Handicap

Kenilworth Race Course, Rosmead Avenue, Kenilworth, Southern Suburbs (www.jbscotch. co.za). **Date** end Jan/early Feb.
Parade around in your most extravagant outfit at this swish equestrian extravaganza. It's not all about sipping champagne and posing for the paparazzi, though: don't forget to place your bets and shout for your filly.

Summer

Cape Town Minstrel Carnival

City Centre, City Bowl (www.capetown-minstrels. co.za). **Date** 1-2 Jan.
Celebrating the traditional Tweede Nuwejaar (Second New Year), when slaves were given a holiday on 2 January, the Minstrel Carnival culminates in highly contested choir competitions. You can view the colourful parade that snakes through town from the Bo-Kaap, as minstrels entertain the crowds with

Design Indaba Expo

CTICC, Convention Square, 1 Lower Long Street, City Centre, City Bowl (www.designindaba.com/ expo). **Date** mid Feb.
An inspiring range of work from local designers, decorators, architects and other creatives is on show at this expo. It's part of the annual Design Indaba Conference, which brings together forward-thinkers from across the world. It's a must for a peek into the future of SA design.

Autumn

Infecting the City
Locations throughout the city centre (www. infectingthecity.com). **Date** early Mar.
This cutting-edge art experience investigates how art and audiences engage in public spaces around the city. A diversity of happenings sets this festival apart, with performances, installations and impromptu participatory events making it a vibrant addition to the city centre's arts' calendar.

Cape Town Cycle Tour
Cape Peninsula (www.cydetour.co.za).
Date early Mar.
The Cape Town Cycle Tour is the world's biggest timed cycle race, with some 40,000 cyclists racing the 109km route, is probably one of the most scenic too. Raging fires in the South Peninsula just days before the 2015 race saw a shorter route being implemented for the first time.

Old Mutual Two Oceans Marathon
Newlands, Southern Suburbs (www. twooceansmarathon.org.za). **Date** late Mar.
There's more to this Easter event than the 56km (35 mile) ultra-marathon that sees ultra-fit competitors from all over the world converge on the Mother City. There are also children's fun runs, a half marathon,

GET OUT OF TOWN

There's plenty of festive fun outside Cape Town.

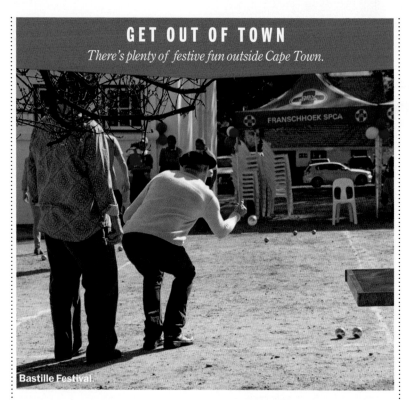

Bastille Festival.

Capetonians love going out for a drive, and the many annual festivals hosted in the Winelands and further afield provide more than enough reason for an excursion. Some are great for a day out, while others are best enjoyed over the course of a weekend.

Top of the list for animal encounters is the **Hermanus Whale Festival** (www.whale festival.co.za) in early October. As well as the excitement of spotting southern right whales from the clifftops of this Overberg town, you'll be entertained with live music, crafts and arts stalls and sporting events.

The West Coast comes alive with a magnificent display of wild flowers during spring. The **Clanwilliam Wild Flower Show** (www.clanwilliamflowerfestival.co.za) in late August is a marvellous opportunity to see 400 species collected in one venue. Make a weekend out of it and take a meandering drive through the Cederberg or West Coast.

Despite such natural bounty and beauty, food and drink festivals are by far the most popular pursuits, with the focus falling on the Cape Winelands. Oenophiles will enjoy

Wacky Wine Weekend (www.wackywine weekend.com) in Robertson in early June, where local wineries provide fun activities along with delicious tastings. Franschhoek offers two wine fests: **Franschhoek Uncorked** (www.franschhoekuncorked.co.za) in September, and **Franschhoek Cap Classique & Champagne Festival** (www.franschhoek mcc.co.za) in December. Both provide numerous opportunities to taste local wines, with gourmet food to match.

There's plenty more for foodies to enjoy, including the **South African Cheese Festival** (www.cheesefestival.co.za) in Stellenbosch in late April. Franschhoek is the setting for the **Bastille Festival** (www.franschhoekbastille. co.za), around 14 July, which provides ample opportunity to sample French fare and engage in a game of boules or two.

And who could resist the **Winelands Chocolate Festival** (www.winelands chocolatefestival.co.za)? Pure heaven for those with a sweet tooth, it takes place at the beautiful, historic Lourensford wine estate in Somerset West.

a trail run and a mini marathon series that ensure everyone, whatever their running ability, gets a chance to don their trainers.

Taste of Cape Town
Green Point Cricket Club, Green Point, Atlantic Seaboard (www.tasteofcapetown.com). **Date** early Apr.
At this foodie fest you can taste your way through delicious dishes prepared by some of the hottest restaurants in Cape Town. Along with produce, wine and craft beer stalls, there are cooking demos too.

Cape Town International Jazz Festival
CTICC, Convention Square, 1 Lower Long Street, City Centre, City Bowl (www.capetownjazzfest.com). **Date** early Apr.
A star-studded line-up has jazz aficionados jiving at this prestigious two-day event. Local musos and international names grace the stages, and there is also a number of free community concerts. The fun vibe spills out on to the streets of Cape Town for the duration of the festival, which has the city buzzing.

Good Food & Wine Show
CTICC, Convention Square, 1 Lower Long Street, City Centre, City Bowl (www.goodfoodandwineshow. co.za). **Date** late May.
Chefs from home and abroad showcase their culinary prowess at this massive exhibition. There are cooking demos, stalls selling produce, treats and kitchen gadgets aplenty, as well as wine tasting.

IN THE KNOW
HISTORY ON THE HOUSE

If you want to visit lots of museums but are on a budget remember that entry to some city museums is free on commemorative days: Human Rights Day (21 March), Freedom Day (27 April), International Museum Day (18 May), Youth Day (16 June) and Heritage Week (around 24 September). Visit www.iziko.org.za to find out more.

Winter

Cape Town Funny Festival
Baxter Theatre, Main Road, Rondebosch, Southern Suburbs (www.facebook.com/ capetownfunnyfestival). **Date** June-July.
Get your giggle on at this festival where local and international comedians vie for belly-laughs. The 2015 event not only showcased stand-up acts, but also comedic clowns, music and multimedia shows.

Mercedes-Benz Fashion Week
CTICC, Convention Square, 1 Lower Long Street, City Centre, City Bowl (http://afi.za.com). **Date** early Aug.
Local designers get their moment in the limelight at this fashion event. Everyone from big names to up-and-coming designers can be seen at the shows.

Cape Town International Jazz Festival.

Cape Town's
Best

*There's something
for everyone with our
hand-picked highlights.*

Imhoff Farm.

Bloubergstrand.

Sightseeing

HISTORY

St George's Cathedral p51
This historic church was
pivotal during the anti-
Apartheid movement.

Noon Gun p65
The big bang that get's
everyone's attention at noon.

District Six Museum p75
A community's forced
displacement brought
to vivid life.

**Cape Town Diamond
Museum** p85
It's a bling thing.

**Robben Island
Museum** p86
See where Mandela was
incarcerated for 18 years.

**Newlands Rugby
Stadium** p115
Shout for the Springboks at
this scenic stadium.

Constantia Winelands p119
History, wine, great views
and delicious food.

Township tours p125
Experience the vibrant world
of Cape Town's townships.

**Cape Town Holocaust
Centre** p44
A South African perspective
on the Holocaust.

Iziko National Gallery p49
Old masters and cutting-edge
contemporary art.

ANIMAL ENCOUNTERS

Boulders Beach p152
Penguin antics up close.

Two Oceans Aquarium p87
Dive into the underwater world
– the shark tank is a favourite.
**Cape of Good Hope
Nature Reserve** p136
Spot antelope, zebra, birds
and even whales.

OUTDOORS
Company's Garden p48
Cape Town's historic tree-
lined garden is a haven
of tranquillity.
Table Mountain p77
Tick this New7Wonder off
your bucket list.
Green Point Urban Park p91
Indigenous plants, vast lawns
and two kids' playgrounds
make this a top family choice.
Clifton's beaches p94
The water may be cold, but
these beaches are hot.
**Kirstenbosch National
Botanical Gardens** p115
A dazzling display of
indigenous flora.
Surf in Muizenberg p129
The top spot to learn to surf –
just keep an eye out for sharks.
Bloubergstrand p140
For a perfect photo op of
Table Mountain.

CHILDREN
**Cape Town Science
Centre** p151
Budding scientists will be
entertained for hours here.
**Sea Point Swimming
Pool** p93
A kids' pool and splash
pool make this a popular
oceanside spot.
Zip-Zap Circus School p173
See children from all walks of
life perform amazing acts.
Imhoff Farm p137
Snakes, farm animals and
even camels get a look-in at
this family-friendly venue.
Jolly Roger Pirate Boat p151
Be a pirate and sail out to sea
for a day.

Eating & drinking

GLOBAL EATS

Carne SA p56
Local meats, masterfully prepared with Italian flair.
El Burro p91
Fresh, authentic Mexican fare in a bright, friendly setting.
Foodbarn p137
Watch a cooking demo with the award-winning chef before indulging in French fare.
Moyo p74
A pan-African food treat, with music and face-painting too.

BLOWOUTS

Afternoon tea at Belmond Mount Nelson Hotel p116
Plush sofas, a table laden with goodies, loose-leaf teas and piano music.
Nobu p87
Japanese and South American cuisine combine at this global superstar.
Roundhouse Restaurant p96
Historic setting home to classic refined food.
Test Kitchen p106
Book six months ahead for the gastronomic experience of a lifetime.
Greenhouse at the Cellars p123
Classics get a contemporary twist in this exquisite setting.
La Colombe p122
French-inspired dishes make the best of seasonal produce.
De Grendel Restaurant p144
A big hitter in the Durbanville wine valley with breathtaking views to match the food.

CAFÉ LIFE

Hemelhuijs p57
Comfort food in an arty setting.
Power & the Glory p70
Hang with hip locals and watch the world go by.

Nobu.

Truth Coffee Roasting p75
Voted best in the world by the *Telegraph*. Who are we to argue?
La Petite Tarte p80
A slice of Paris life in the heart of Cape Town.
Kitchen p102
Moreish salads, 'love sandwiches' and the friendliest staff in Cape Town.
Four & Twenty p123
The prettiest cakes and delicious eats.

ARTISAN EATS

Bacon on Bree p54
Bacon is the new black. And on cool Bree Street, you can taste the best pork products.
Creamery p116
The best ice-cream in Cape Town, if not South Africa. The salted caramel is sensational.

Roundhouse Restaurant.

Culture Club Cheese p57
Taste and buy lovingly sourced South African cheeses.
Jason Bakery p57
Amazing bread, moreish mains and bacon croissants are all part of the package at this cool hangout.

Creamery.

TAPAS

Bocca p54
Italian-inspired nibbles and the thinnest pizzas imaginable.

Chef's Warehouse & Canteen p56
The chef's whim and seasonal produce take centre stage.

Pot Luck Club p104
Perched on top of a silo building in trendy Woodstock, this stylish place is all about explosions of flavour and sharing bites (if you must).

La Parada p58
Authentic Spanish tapas take centre stage at this busy restaurant and bar.

SEAFOOD

Harbour House p130
The freshest linefish with ocean views.

Live Bait p130
Relaxed harbour spot for a seafood feast.

DINER TREATS

Royale Eatery p58
More than 50 burgers to choose from. Wash one down with a giant milkshake.

Olympia Café & Deli p131
Laid-back fare, chilled vibes and the best bread in town.

Bistro Sixteen82 p122
Delicious eats in a stylish wine estate setting; a favourite brunch spot.

Tiger's Milk Restaurant & Bar p129
'Dude food' comes to town with ribs, burgers and steaks, plus a hip, welcoming vibe.

Clarke's Bar & Dining Room p56
This diner ticks the boxes with mac'n'cheese, tasty burgers and a cool vibe.

Hudson's – the Burger Joint p68
Succulent burgers in every shape and size.

SUNDOWNERS

Shimmy Beach Club p165
Hot young things congregate here for day-night partying.

Grand Café & Beach p87
Dip your toes in the sand and enjoy a decadent cocktail.

Café Caprice p96
The view of the sun setting over the ocean on Camps Bay beach is unsurpassed.

BARS

Bascule Bar p89
Every whisky you could ever wish for in a five-star setting.

Abode.

kirsten goss

Missibaba & Kirsten Goss London.

Orphanage Cocktail Emporium p60
Glamorous cocktails on hip Bree Street.
Village Idiot p60
This hot spot has games, great food, live music – and a stuffed ostrich named Oskar.
Lefty's Dive Bar p76
Grungy hangout with a menu of ribs, burgers, and chicken with waffles.
Brass Bell p131
Local institution located right on the rocks next to the sea.

Shopping

GIFTS & SOUVENIRS
South African Market p64
Locally designed homewares and clothing.
Present Space p73
Present ideas galore at this unique emporium.
Africa Nova p80
Curated crafts and original art set this shop apart.
Victoria Wharf p85
One-stop spot for all your shopping needs.

Made in SA p90
Souvenirs get a contemporary twist.
Watershed p90
Top crafters and designers under one roof.
Heartworks p107
Support local enterprise at this colourful shop.

HOMEWARES
Stable p65
Local design meets contemporary flair.
Baraka p80
Funky, ethnic finds.
Abode p106
Cute and quirky, this shop will brighten your home.

FOOD & DRINK
Honest Chocolate p63
Raw chocolate and arty packaging: a delicious combination.
Vaughan Johnson's Wine Shop p90
Top up your cellar from this vast selection.
Caroline's Fine Wine Cellar p125
Local and international wines.

Bay Harbour Market p108
Grab a bite to eat while browsing the clothing and homeware stalls at this harbourside market.
Neighbourgoods Market p109
This place put artisan produce on the map.

BOOKS
Book Lounge p76
Knowledgeable staff, book launches galore and children's story time.

FASHION
Klûk CGDT p63
Haute couture from Cape Town's top design duo.
Merchants on Long p64
Shop here for a highly covetable collection of fashion and accessories.
Missibaba & Kirsten Goss London p64
This shared store showcases fineleather bags and modern fine jewellery.
Cape Union Mart p89
Every outdoor scenario is catered for – and then some.

Club 31.

tribal masks and jewellery, plus ethnic fabrics and homewares.

De Waterkant p80
Cape Town's pink district is awash with charming historical buildings and gay-friendly hangouts.

Astore p72
Hip streetwear for urban guys.
Tsonga Shoes p125
These locally made leather shoes have a loyal following.
Big Blue p132
T-shirts with cool slogans, printed dresses and gimmicky toys are part of the fun here.

GALLERIES
AVA Gallery p61
A springboard for many up-and-coming local artists.
Erdmann Contemporary p73
View and buy contemporary
Goodman Gallery p102
Big-hitting gallery displaying top contemporary artists.
Stevenson p102
Local and international artists exhibit at this cutting-edge warehouse space.

MARKETS
Greenmarket Square p63
A quintessential shopping experience: head here for souvenirs and African crafts.
Pan African Market p64
A series of nterconnecting rooms reveal a collection of

Nightlife

LIVE MUSIC
Crypt p165
The best jazz in Cape Town, beneath St George's Cathedral.
Waiting Room p168
With a vibey lounge, roof deck and balcony overlooking Long Street, this is the spot for DJs and live music.

CLUBS
Club 31 p162
Sky-high smart clubbing.
Dragon Room p162
The hottest place to go for big events.

Gay & lesbian

MCQP – Mother City Queer Project p161
This annual festival with themed dressing-up is a must for party people, gay or straight.
Beulah Bar p158
Boys and girls will feel welcome at this fun bar.

Arts

FESTIVALS
Kirstenbosch Summer Sunset Concerts p29
Top performers in a breathtaking natural setting.
Cape Town International Jazz Fest p33
The city buzzes with top jazz stars from around the world.

MUSIC
City Hall p172
Wonderful venue for classical music and home of the Cape Philharmonic Orchestra.

FILM
Labia Theatre p155
Lovely retro cinema.

THEATRE
Fugard Theatre p170
Historic, renovated space showing top musical and theatre productions.
Maynardville Open-Air Theatre p172
Get your annual dose of the Bard in this sylvan setting.

Explore

City Bowl

Flanked by Devil's Peak, Table Mountain, Lion's Head and Signal Hill and hugged by the Atlantic Ocean, City Bowl is not only a geographical concept, but a psychological one too. Encompassing the commercial centre, working harbour and sloping residential suburbs, the City Bowl is the heartbeat of Cape Town. The arteries of Adderley, Long, Loop and Bree streets provide ample opportunities for shopping, eating and partying. It becomes hipper the closer you get to the top (mountain side) of Bree Street, with plenty of artisan food producers and cool eateries. Meanwhile Company's Garden provides verdant respite from the city buzz. Around this area, you'll also find most of Cape Town's museums. Heading west, historic Bo-Kaap beckons exploration with its steep cobbled streets and colourful houses. Heading up the slopes of Table Mountain you'll encounter Kloof Street and its surrounds, a buzzing home to uncountable bars and boutiques. The gritty East City is a must for any serious city explorer: here you can delve into the troubled history of District Six in between stopping at cool cafés and edgy stores.

EXPLORE

Table Mountain Aerial Cableway.

Don't Miss

1 Company's Garden Cape Town's green lung (p48).

2 Bo-Kaap Colourful houses, cobbled streets and history aplenty (p65).

3 Bree Street Artisan eats and hipster-spotting (p44).

4 Table Mountain Aerial Cableway Spectacular views from the top of a natural wonder (p77)

5 District Six Museum A look into South Africa's past (p75).

Castle of Good Hope.

CITY CENTRE

Nucleus of the city's business district, the city centre is home to an immense diversity of commerce and cultures. It's also a party hub, with action centred on **Long Street**. The name starts making sense should you decide to meander the length of the one-way 20-block stretch. Dotted with fast-food joints and discount furnishing stores, the harbour side of the mile isn't exactly thrilling, but things start getting interesting from the Wale Street intersection up towards the mountain, with an eclectic collection of shops, restaurants and hangouts. And when the lights go down, the party people come out to play: night owls of all persuasions will find a spot to flaunt their feathers here, be it at an Irish pub, gritty pool bar or svelte cocktail lounge. Bear in mind, though, that there have been recent incidents of violence near clubs and bars so best to keep your wits about you. There are plenty of places to sleep too, from stylish boutique hotels to bustling backpackers' hostels.

Off Long Street, between Shortmarket and Burg streets is **Greenmarket Square**. This frenetic hub of stalls selling predominantly African curios used to be a market where farmers sold fruit and veg. Once you've worn out the phrase 'No, thank you, I'm just looking,' head over to one of the pavement cafés where you can watch the commerce unfold from a distance over a cappuccino – all the while keeping an eye out for any sticky-fingered pickpockets, of course.

About three blocks down is **Waterkant Street**, much of it pedestrianised for the 2010 Fifa World Cup, connecting the city with a bridge to Green Point and ultimately Cape Town stadium. The **Portside building**, on the corner of Buitengracht and Hans Strijdom Avenue, was completed in 2014 and is now the tallest building in town, adding to the modernist edifices such as the **CTICC** that grace the Foreshore area.

Running straight as an arrow down the leafy haven of the **Company's Garden** is the oak-lined pedestrian strip of Government Avenue, providing access to Adderley Street, the **National Gallery**, **Houses of Parliament**, the **Iziko Museum** and **Planetarium**, and the **Slave Lodge**.

There's retail of a different kind at St George's Mall, an open-air strip starting at Thibault Square and ending at **St George's Cathedral**. It's a lively stretch, usually resounding to the sound of drum beats, and is home to lots of cafés and fast-food outlets as well as a weekly food market.

Westwards, parallel to Long, lie Loop and Bree streets. Here the venues, and the people, get less grungy, more hip. The pinnacle of hipsterdom is the top (mountain) end of **Bree Street** with its artisan food producers, cool bars and boutiques.

Sights & Museums

FREE **Cape Town Holocaust Centre**
88 Hatfield Street (021 462 5553, www.ctholocaust. co.za). **Open** 10am-5pm Mon-Thur, Sun; 10am-2pm Fri. **Admission** free. **Map** p53 G3 ❶

EXPLORE

By showing us the faces of some of the six million Jews – as well as gypsies, homosexuals and others – who were murdered during the Holocaust, the Cape Town Holocaust Centre has succeeded in giving an identity to some of those killed. Exhibits consist of text, photos, film, artefacts and recreated environments. They follow the course of the holocaust from the early days of the Nazi Party and its espousal of antisemitism, to the Third Reich and the development of the concentration camp system, and the adoption of the Final Solution. The Centre also focuses on wider issues of racism, with sections on apartheid and the South African experience.

Castle of Good Hope

Cnr Buitenkant & Darling streets (021 787 1260, www.castleofgoodhope.co.za). **Open** 9am-4pm daily. *Tours* 11am, noon, 2pm Mon-Sat. *Key Ceremony* 10am, noon Mon-Fri. **Admission** R30 adults; R15 reductions. **No credit cards. Map** p53 F6 **②**

The Castle of Good Hope is South Africa's oldest surviving colonial building. Completed in 1679, the moated, five-pointed fortress was initially built by Commander Zacharius Wagenaer of the Dutch East India Company to ward off possible attacks from the British, and later served as the hub of the Cape's civilian and military activities. It's still the seat of the Cape Town military today, and if you time it right, you can catch the key ceremony, performed by the Castle Guard. The military museum showcases several impressive pieces, interspersed with display cases filled with glassy-eyed mannequins kitted out in their military best. The Anglo-Boer War section features a coin-operated model armoured train huffing and puffing past series of block houses and through hostile British territory. The William Fehr collection gives a peek into the opulent 17th-century heyday of the Dutch East India Company. The grounds of the Castle have recently been put to use hosting diverse events such as concerts as well as Kamersvol Geskenke (Rooms Filled with Gifts) – an innovative retail concept showcasing a range of arts, crafts, clothing and accessories.

FREE Central Methodist Mission

Cnr Longmarket & Burg streets, Greenmarket Square (021 422 2744). **Open** 9am-2pm Mon-Fri; 9.30am-1pm Sat; 10am-noon Sun. **Admission** free. **Map** p52 D4 **③**

Resembling a location from a Tim Burton movie, this grey Gothic revival church, with its needle-like spires, looks a tad out of place amid the noisy colour explosion of informal stalls in Greenmarket Square. The contrast of the outside bustle with the quiet calm inside the church is intense, and it's worth a visit to marvel at the impressive architecture of pointed arches and flying buttresses, and to find out more about the erstwhile Methodist Church in Buitenkant Street – which served as a haven for activists during the struggle years – from the leaflets that you can pick up here.

FREE Centre for the Book

62 Queen Victoria Street (021 423 2669). **Open** 8am-5.30pm Mon-Fri. **Admission** free. **Map** p53 F2 **④**

EXPLORE

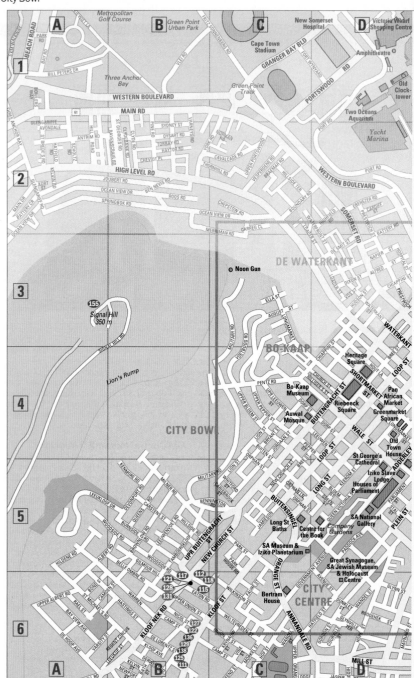

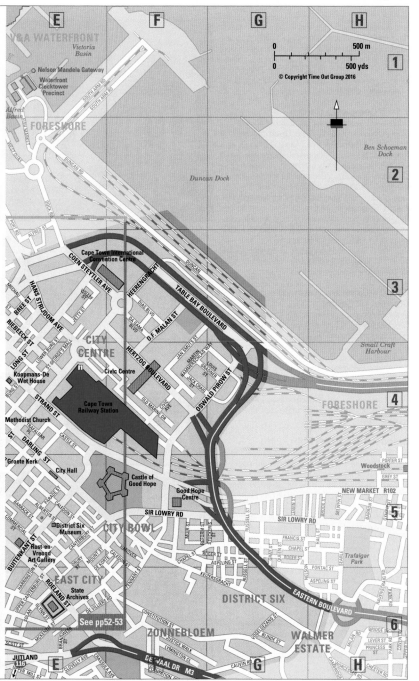

EXPLORE

Just down the road from the Planetarium, stands another eye-catching, domed beauty. This Edwardian building dedicated to all things bookish was created to cultivate a love of reading and writing among young and old, well-read and illiterate. Apart from its involvement with disadvantaged communities, it hosts writing workshops for budding talents.

★ FREE Company's Garden
Government Avenue, enter via Adderley Street, Orange Street or Victoria Street. **Open** dawn-dusk daily. **Admission** free. **Map** p53 F/G3 ❺
A symbolic bell silently stands testimony to the slaves who tilled and toiled away in what was once a vegetable garden providing sustenance for scurvy-stricken sailors of the Dutch East India Company. The cabbage patches have since made way for grassy lawns and park benches, with a few fish ponds and statues thrown in for good measure. It's an accessible oasis and smack in the middle of a culture cluster including the Iziko South African Museum, Iziko South African National Gallery and Iziko Slave Lodge (for all, *see p49*). The Company's Garden Restaurant (*see p56*) has undergone a recent makeover.

CTICC – Cape Town International Convention Centre
Convention Square, 1 Lower Long Street (021 410 5000, www.cticc.co.za). **Open** according to exhibitions. **Map** p52 B6 ❻
An arresting site on the city's foreshore, this colossal modern building has become an iconic Cape Town landmark. The centre houses some of the most sophisticated conference facilities in the country. Apart from the state-of-the-art auditoriums, it is also synonymous with the many expos held there every year, including Design Indaba and Cape Town Fashion Week.

Grand Parade & City Hall
Cnr Buitenkant & Darling streets. **Map** p53 F5 ❼
R21 million was forked out to repave and upgrade the previously run-down Grand Parade in time for it to serve as a fan park during the 2010 FIFA World Cup. Overlooking it is the sandstone City Hall, with its elaborate Renaissance-style columns and slightly out-of-place clock tower. The place is a landmark when it comes to South African history: one of the biggest multiracial protests against apartheid culminated here on 14 September 1989, and the following year Nelson Mandela made his first public speech from the City Hall balcony, just hours after his release from prison. More recently the City Hall has served as a conference and exhibition space.

FREE Great Synagogue
88 Hatfield Street, entry via Jewish Museum gate (021 465 1405). **Open** *Tours* 10am-4pm Mon-Thur, Sun. *Services* 7am Mon, Thur; 7.15am Tue, Wed, Fri; 8.30am Sat; 8am Sun. **Admission** free. **Map** p53 G3 ❽

Iziko Slave Lodge.

Referred to by its members as the Gardens Shul, Cape Town's oldest functioning synagogue was consecrated in 1905, the same year the city appointed its first Jewish mayor, Hyman Liberman. The 1,400-seater Baroque-style structure features stained-glass windows and an interior richly embellished with gold-leafed friezes and mahogany woodwork. When Cape Town's population boomed after World War II, the temple saw many of its members relocating to the synagogues in the suburbs, but the completion of the Jewish Museum and the Holocaust Centre in 1998 breathed new life into the dwindling congregation.

FREE Groote Kerk

39 Upper Adderley Street (021 422 0569, www. grootekerk.org.za). **Open** 10am-2pm Mon-Fri. *Services* 10am, 7pm Sun. **Admission** free. **Map** p53 E4 ❾

Originally a Cape Dutch building, the church underwent so much work over the years that the only remnants of the original are the old tower and the ornate pulpit carved by sculptor Anton Anreith. The construction of this, the country's first Dutch Reformed Church and the oldest in South Africa, commenced in 1678; it was finally consecrated in 1704. Interesting highlights include the country's largest organ and the biggest unsupported domed ceiling in the southern hemisphere.

Heritage Square

Cnr Bree & Shortmarket streets. **Map** p52 C3 ❿
Bordered by Buitengracht, Hout, Bree and Shortmarket streets, this block of Dutch and Georgian buildings was probably the closest thing Capetonians had to a mall back in the 18th century – gunsmiths, bakers and cigarette-makers all conducted their businesses from here. The historical site was once slated to make way for a multi-storey car park, but luckily it was given a new lease of life in the 1980s, becoming the largest private conservation project ever seen in the city. Miraculously, the country's oldest vine, dating from 1781, made it through all the ructions in one piece, and can still be spotted in the courtyard today. You'll find a hotel, gallery and restaurants sharing the space here today.

FREE Houses of Parliament

90 Plein Street (021 403 2266, 021 403 2911, www.parliament.gov.za). **Tours** 10am, noon Mon-Fri; advanced booking essential. **Admission** free. **Map** p53 F4 ⓫

Back in 1878, Charles Freeman won the grand sum of £250 prize money for his proposed design of the Houses of Parliament, but things went horribly pear shaped (costs ended up double what the government had bargained for) and Harry Greaves ended up finishing the job in 1885. These buildings have seen their fair share of action through the years, one of the most memorable events being when former prime minister and apartheid devotee, Hendrik Verwoerd,

was stabbed to death during a parliamentary session by Dimitri Tsafendas, who later explained that a tapeworm had instructed him to do it. These days, you can watch a parliamentary sitting from one of the gallery seats, or take a guided tour through the building. You'll need to bring ID such as a passport and you'll need to book at least a week in advance.

Iziko Slave Lodge

49 Adderley Street (021 460 8242, www.iziko. org.za/slavelodge). **Open** 10am-5pm Mon-Sat. **Admission** R30; R15 reductions; free public holidays. **Map** p53 E4 ⓬

Completed in 1679, this building at the north-east end of the Company's Gardens was built by the Dutch East India Company to house up to 9,000 slaves, convicts and the mentally ill; it continued to do so until the early 19th century. With no windows apart from tiny slits with bars, and a stream running beneath the Lodge, living conditions were wet, dark and dank. Visitors can retrace the steps of German salt trader Otto Menzl as he is given the guided tour through the corridors of the slave lodge by a proud VOC official in the 1700s on an audio set. Through his comments you get a pretty good idea of the squalor these slaves had to live in – the horrible stench, lack of ventilation, no view of the outside world and bedding so wet that slaves preferred to sleep on the floor.
▶ *Around the corner from the Slave Lodge lies a commemorative plaque set into the pavement of Spin Street, marking the spot of the old fir tree under which the slaves were sold.*

Iziko South African Museum

25 Queen Victoria Street (021 481 3800, www. iziko.org.za/museums/south-african-museum). Open 10am-5pm daily. **Admission** R30; R15 reductions. **Map** p53 G2 ⓭

All creatures great, small and slightly ridiculous get their moment here, whether it's the pesky tsetse fly, the duck-billed platypus or the great blue whale. One definitive South African Museum experience is sitting in the yellow submarine-like sound booth and listening to whale cries while looking out over their stuffed counterparts. The suspended whale skeleton is quite a remarkable sight. The Shark World section, where you get to examine the business end of a megatooth shark, the world's largest apex predator, will have the kids squealing. The social history section includes artefacts from prehistory, including stone tools from up to 115,000 years ago, as well as objects from the ancient world, plus furniture, glass, weaponry and much more.

★ Iziko South African National Gallery

Government Avenue (021 481 3970, www. iziko.org.za/sang). **Open** 10am-5pm daily. **Admission** R30; R15 reductions. **No credit cards. Map** p53 F3 ⓮

The permanent collection dedicates plenty of space to British, Dutch, Flemish and South African art

EXPLORE

spanning the centuries, interspersed with traditional African beadwork and contemporary South African works such as Jane Alexander's hauntingly realistic trio of beastly men, *The Butcher Boys*. The temporary exhibitions are the biggest draw, however, featuring both young and established local artists: from photographic essays to an accessible Irma Stern exhibition and a hard-hitting William Kentridge installation.

Koopmans-De Wet House

35 Strand Street (021 481 3935, www.iziko. org.za/koopmans). **Open** 10am-5pm Mon-Fri. **Admission** R20 adults; R10 reductions; free under-5s. **No credit cards. Map** p52 D4 ⑮
Set amid the hustle and bustle of Strand Street, this Cape Dutch building designed by the architect Louis Thibault was the first privately owned townhouse to be opened as a public museum – in 1914. Once belonging to the wealthy socialite Marie Koopmans-De Wet, it is furnished to recreate an 18th-century residential home and showcases an exquisite collection of Cape furniture, eastern and Dutch crockery, and red quarry tiles imported from Batavia.
▶ *Thibault also designed the Groote Kerk (see p49).*

Long Street Baths

Cnr Long and Orange streets (021 400 3302). **Open** *Pool* 7am-7pm daily. *Turkish bath* Women 9am-6pm Mon, Thur, Sat; 9am-1pm Tue. Men 1pm-7pm Tue; 9am-6pm Wed, Fri; 8am-noon Sun. **Admission** *Turkish baths* R70; R35 per hr. *Pool* R11; free-R7 reductions. **No credit cards. Map** p53 F2 ⑯
The Long Street Baths have been around for 100 years (they were built in 1908), so don't expect a contemporary spa experience. The indoor pool attracts a diverse crowd of swimmers. Or, if you prefer something a little less labour intensive, head over to the traditional Turkish baths for a soothing steam without an inflated price tag. During school holidays the pool tends to get overrun with kids.

FREE Michaelis Gallery

UCT Hiddingh Campus, 31-37 Orange Street, Gardens (021 480 7170, www.michaelis.uct.ac.za). **Open** 10am-4pm Mon-Fri during exhibitions. **Admission** free. **Map** p53 G2 ⑰
This cosy gallery on UCT's Hiddingh Campus is part of the Michaelis School of Fine Arts, which has been around since 1925. Apart from serving as an exhibition space for its students (the fourth-year final exhibition is an annual highlight in the art community), it's also seen its fair share of local and international artists through the years.

Old Town House & Michaelis Collection

Old Town House, Greenmarket Square (021 481 3933, www.iziko.org.za/museums/michaelis-collection-at-the-old-town-house). **Open** 10am-5pm Mon-Sat. **Admission** R20; R10 reductions; free under-5s. **Map** p53 E4 ⑱
The first two-storey building ever to grace Cape Town's cityscape, this ornate 1761 Cape Rococo-style construction must have elicited quite a few oohs and

Iziko South African National Gallery. See p49.

aahs back in the day. Originating as a Burger Watch House and later used as a magistrate's court, police station and town hall, it was declared Cape Town's first art museum in 1914 after a very generous donation of 17th-century Dutch and Flemish art by Sir Max Michaelis. The esteemed Michaelis Collection features paintings by Dutch Golden Age masters including Rembrandt van Rijn, Jacob Ruisdal and Frans Hals. When you've had enough art but find the thought of braving Greenmarket Square too tiring, step into the calm courtyard.

Palm Tree Mosque

185 Long Street (021 444 4613). **Open** by appointment only. **Admission** free. **Map** p53 E3 ⑲

When Tuan Guru, the father of the Islamic faith in South Africa, died in 1807, he left his imamship of the Auwal Mosque (*see p65*) to Abdulalim, much to the dismay of two of his congregation members, Frans van Bengalen and Jan van Boughies. The two resigned from the mosque and started a *langgar* (prayer room) in the upper storey of Jan's house in Long Street, which received mosque status in 1825. Legend has it that Jan wasn't exactly the easiest person to get along with, and so, within a year of the mosque's existence, Frans left the country, and the majority of the congregation returned to the Auwal Mosque. A century and a few decades later, the name of Jan van Boughies Mosque was changed to a rather more succinct one, alluding to the towering palm out front, which is said to have been planted by Jan himself.

Planetarium

25 Queen Victoria Street (021 481 3900, www. iziko.org.za/planetarium). **Shows** 2pm Sat, Sun. **Admission** R40; R20 reductions. **Map** p53 G2 ⑳

The sky is perpetually clear in the domed auditorium of the Iziko Museum's Planetarium. Features vary from live interactive lectures on spotting the constellations to pre-recorded shows covering topics such as the legitimacy of astrology and celestial clouds. During school holidays there's a children's show that'll have them begging for their own telescope.

Rust & Vreugd

78 Buitenkant Street (021 481 3903, www.iziko. org.za/museums/rust-en-vreugd). **Open** 10am-5pm Mon-Fri. **Admission** R20; R10 reductions. **Map** p53 G5 ㉑

This tranquil house – considered to be the finest surviving example of an 18th-century Cape Dutch farmhouse – is set away from the central museum area. Behind the peach-coloured walls lies a secret garden landscaped according to its original 1798 design, with hedges, walkways and a gazebo. The impressive William Fehr art collection provides a glimpse into life in the early Cape colony.

★ FREE St George's Cathedral

5 Wale Street (021 424 7360, www.stgeorges cathedral.com). **Open** 8.30am-4.30pm Mon-Fri. **Admission** free; donations appreciated. *Services* 7.15am, 1.15pm Mon-Fri; 8am Sat; 7am, 8am, 10am, 7pm Sun. *Evensong* Sept-May 7pm Sun; June-Aug 6pm Sun. **Map** p53 E4 ㉒

EXPLORE

EXPLORE

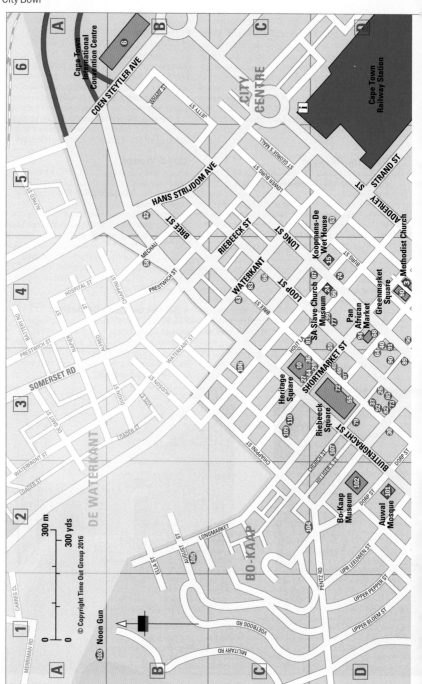

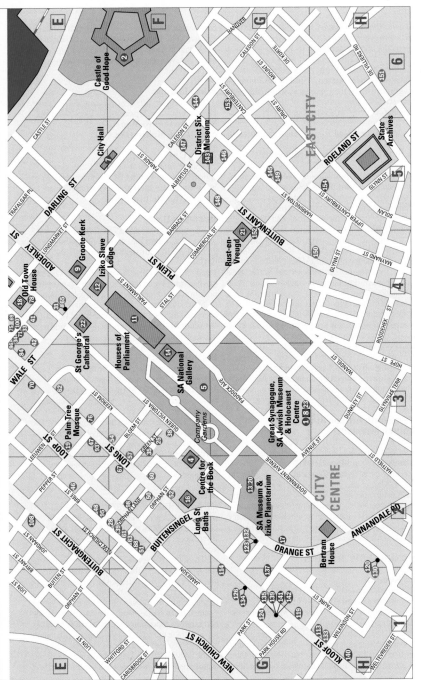

EXPLORE

Even to the non-religious, this beautiful Victorian structure inspires a bit of silence and contemplation about the human condition. Its elaborate stained-glass windows depict not only a lily-white Jesus figure, but also a black Christ and a panel dedicated to Mahatma Gandhi. Known as the People's Church, it was central in the fight against apartheid. Its members openly rejected the rules of the government, opening its doors to all races and regularly drawing huge crowds of protesters to listen to emeritus Archbishop Desmond Tutu and other speakers.

★ South African Jewish Museum

88 Hatfield Street (021 465 1546, www.sajewish museum.co.za). **Open** 10am-5pm Mon-Thur, Sun; 10am-2pm Fri. **Admission** R50; R30 reductions; free under-12s; photo ID required. **Map** p53 G3 ㉓
Built according to the same proportions as King Solomon's temple, the beautiful Old Synagogue (South Africa's first) was built in 1863, and serves as the entrance to the rest of the Jewish Museum, which was founded by Mendel Kaplan in 2000. It traces the history of South African Jewry from the first Lithuanian settlers who arrived in the 1800s to the present day. Large amounts of information are made accessible through interactive displays, films and installations. On the top floor are exquisite Judaic artefacts such as a solid silver replica of the Kimberley Synagogue; you can also discover interesting titbits about the diamond rush and ostrich feather boom and learn more about the South African Jewish community's active involvement during the struggle. A serpentine staircase takes visitors to a re-created Lithuanian shtetl. Also worth a look is the room housing Isaac Kaplan's impressive collection of delicate Japanese *netsuke* figurines.

FREE South African Slave Church Museum

40 Long Street (021 423 6755). **Open** 9am-4pm Mon-Fri. *School holidays* 9am-noon daily. **Admission** free. **Map** p52 D4 ㉔
Founded by a certain Reverend Vos in 1799, the South African Missionary Society was formed in an effort to convert slaves to Christianity, and this inconspicuous structure in Long Street was built in 1804 as the first official slave church in the country. Today it houses a tiny museum depicting the history of South African missionary work.

Restaurants & Cafés

95 Keerom

95 Keerom Street (021 422 0765, www.95 keerom.com). **Open** 6.30-10pm Mon-Wed, Sat; noon-2.30pm, 6.30-10pm Thur, Fri. **Main courses** R100. **Map** p53 F3 ㉕ **Italian**
This stylish, historic space has exposed bricks, wooden seating and even an olive tree growing on the first floor. Italian dishes are pared down and simple, relying on the freshest ingredients to speak for

themselves. Just-seared beef or linefish carpaccio, tuna with olives, capers and tomatoes or silky handmade pastas are all excellent choices. Meats such as beef fillet, veal and springbok are simply prepared and succulent.

Addis in Cape

41 Church Street, City Centre (021 424 5722, www. addisincape.co.za). **Open** noon-10.30pm Mon-Sat. **Main courses** R90. **Map** p52 D3 ㉖ **Ethiopian**
See p74 **The Melting Pot.**

Africa Café

108 Shortmarket Street (021 422 0221, www. africacafe.co.za). **Open** 6.30-11pm Mon-Sat. **Set menu** R260. **Map** p52 C3 ㉗ **African**
See p74 **The Melting Pot.**

Bacon on Bree

217 Bree Street (021 422 2798, http://bacon onbree.com). **Open** 7am-4pm Mon-Fri; 8am-2pm Sat. **Main courses** R75. **Map** p53 E/F2 ㉘ **Café**
Bacon is king in Cape Town, and there's no better place to sample and buy it than at this purveyor of pork products. From sandwiches to salads, burgers to breakfasts, bacon features prominently. Craft beers make a good accompaniment and you can sit outside on hip Bree street and watch the world go by in your bacon-induced glow.

Bistrot Bizerca

98 Shortmarket Street (021 423 8888, www. bizerca.com). **Open** noon-10.30pm Mon-Fri. **Main courses** R150. **Map** p52 D3 ㉙ **Bistro**
Set in charming Heritage Square, Bizerca serves classic French bistro fare to loyal patrons. The menu is small, but supplemented by a range of daily specials that rely on fresh and seasonal ingredients. It's a good place to go if you're keen on offal – the calf's liver is exceptional. The space is modern inside and there's a courtyard that's ideal for drinks and food on a fine day.

★ Bocca

Cnr Bree & Wale streets (021 422 0183, www. bocca.co.za). **Open** noon-10pm Mon-Sat. **Main courses** R110. **Map** p52 D3 ㉚ **Mediterannean**
It's all about sharing at this modern space on two levels – but the food's so good you'll want to keep it all to yourself. Tapas-style bites include arancini, courgette fries, meatballs in fresh tomato sauce and spicy pork ribs. The pasta is handmade and hearty, but it's the pizzas that stand out. Made in a bright orange pizza oven all the way from Naples – which takes centre stage – they're cooked in seconds: they're impossibly thin, with quality toppings, some of them unusual. Try the *di mare* with tomato sauce, just-cooked prawns, calamari and chilli aïoli; or the Lady Zaza with kimchi and ginger pork sausage. Larger platters of pork belly or grass-fed beef

sirloin are served on boards, again encouraging sharing. You can't book, but they'll be sure to find you a spot where you can enjoy a glass of wine while you wait and the service is snappy.

Bombay Brasserie
Taj Cape Town, Wale Street (021 819 2000, http://tajcapetown.co.za/dining/bombay-brasserie). **Open** 6-11pm daily. **Main courses** R175. **Map** p53 E4 ㉛ **Indian**
A meal is an opulent affair at this hotel restaurant with blue glass chandeliers and peacock-bedecked upholstery. The Indian cuisine on offer is utterly authentic. Set menus are a good way to sample the best dishes, while the à la carte offers an array of curries: from masala to tikka and biryani, as well as less-known starters including *bhallas*, lentil dumplings topped with yoghurt and mango chutney, and *jwala mirch* – spicy paneer (soft cheese). There's a good range of vegetarian options among the mains too.

Borage
Ground floor, Portside Building, cnr Buitengracht & Hans Strijdom Avenue (021 418 0992, borage. co.za). **Open** 8am-4pm Mon-Wed; 8am-4pm, 6.30pm-late Thur, Fri; 8am-noon Sat. **Main courses** R140. **Map** p52 B5 ㉜ **Contemporary**
Accessible, seasonal lunchtime fine dining, with evening openings a couple of times a week, is what this restaurant at the tallest building in Cape Town aims to provide – and locals are loving it. Borage also opens for breakfast, with its own upscale take on the likes of eggs benedict and french toast. Aside from light sandwiches, salads and herbal teas, diners can expect risottos, linefish, seared tuna and pork belly on the small but well-formed menus. Monthly supper clubs are proving popular.

Bukhara
33 Church Street (021 424 0000, www.bukhara. com). **Open** noon-3pm, 6-11pm daily. **Main courses** R150. **Map** p53 E4 ㉝ **Indian**
Fragrant curries and flavoursome tandoori dishes await you at this stalwart establishment. Study the extensive menu of Indian classics while nibbling on poppadoms and, once you've ordered, watch the chefs work their magic through the frosted kitchen glass as they prepare the legendary butter chicken, tandoori lamb chops and lamb rogan josh.

Café Mozart
37 Church Street (021 424 3774, www.themozart. co.za). **Open** 8am-3.30pm Mon-Fri; 9am-3pm Sat. **Main courses** R70. **Map** p53 E4 ㉞ **Café**
Sit outside under the trees shading Church Street to watch the passing parade of antiques shoppers, or head inside to the charming bric-a-brac filled interior. Hearty breakfasts, gourmet sandwiches and a harvest table heaped with salads are complemented by the likes of burgers, chicken pie and fish and chips.

Bocca.

★ Carne SA
70 Keerom Street (021 424 3460, carne-sa.com).
Open 6.30pm-10.30pm Mon-Sat. **Main courses**
R180. **Map** p53 F3 ⑯ Steakhouse
Calling this a steakhouse is a bit of a misnomer:
rather, think of it as a contemporary space dedicated to serving the best meats with minimum fuss.
Restaurateur Giorgio Nava is famously passionate
about provenance and the result is a farm producing
his own beef and lamb, which he serves at Carne
SA, the sister to his stylish flagship Italian restaurant 95 Keerom (*see p54*) across the way. The menu
features plenty of cuts not always seen on steakhouse menus, from ribeye to hanger steaks, and
includes a 1.2kg Fiorentina beef steak for two. And
for offal lovers, there are veal sweetbreads and calf's
liver on the menu.
Other locations Carne Kloof, 153 Kloof Street,
Gardens (021 426 5566); Carne Constantia, 114
Constantia Main Road, Constantia (021 761 0247).

★ Chef's Warehouse & Canteen
*92 Bree Street (021 422 0128, www.chefs
warehouse.co.za).* **Open** *Lunch* noon-2.30pm
Mon-Fri. *Tapas* 4.30-8pm Mon-Fri; noon-2.30pm
Sat. **Main courses** R80. **Tapas for two set
menu** R410. **Map** p52 C3 ⑯ Tapas
This establishment has two main draws: the cook-
book and kitchenware shop beloved of foodies; and
the outstanding tapas platters produced by chef
Liam Tomlin. No two days are the same, as the tapas

are based on seasonal availability and the whim
of the kitchen. You can supplement your eats with
deli staples of duck rillettes, chicken liver parfait or
some fresh oysters. If you're in a rush for lunch, head
to the basement street food outlet.

Clarke's Bar & Dining Room
*133 Bree Street (021 424 7648, www.darkes
dining.co.za).* **Open** 7am-5pm Mon; 7am-late
Tue-Sat; 8am-3pm Sun. **Main courses** R60.
Map p52 D3 ㊲ Diner
The spot that put US diner-style food on the Cape
Town map, Clarke's is famous for its burgers (served
on a rich brioche bun) and other comfort food staples
such as mac 'n' cheese, pulled pork sandwiches with
kimchi and baked oysters with black forest ham,
artichokes and hollandaise. There are classic cocktails too and a happy hour from 5pm to 7pm.

Company's Garden Restaurant
*19 Queen Victoria Street (021 423 2919,
thecompanysgarden.com).* **Open** 7am-6pm
daily. **Main courses** R70. **Map** p53 F3 ㊳
South African/café
A major revamp has recently transformed the much-
loved Company's Garden Restaurant. Under new
ownership, it still serves traditional treats such as
scones, toasted sarmies and burgers. In addition
there is a selection of South African inspired eats:
the likes of calamari salad and bobotie roti as well
as generous platters – including the Fisherman's

Culture Club Cheese.

platter, feauturing pickled fish and calamari, snoek pâté, home-made preserves, salad and bread. The adjoining children's area has some giant wooden animals and swinging nest pods in the trees that will delight the younger generation.

★ Culture Club Cheese

215 Bree Street (072 428 9572, www.cultureclub cheese.co.za). **Open** 8am-5pm Tue-Fri; 9am-4pm Sat. **Main courses** R65. **Map** p53 F2 ❸ **Café**
Say cheese! This bright yellow cheese café and shop was recently opened by British cheesemaker and cheesemonger Luke Williams and his wife Jessica. After spending a year travelling through South Africa to find small-scale artisan cheeseries, they opened this little gem to share their love with like-minded folk. Not only can you buy a variety of cheeses and accompaniments, but you can also stay for a fresh, seasonal breakfast and lunch menu featuring salads, risottos and sandwiches. They also produce their own fermented-milk drinks, *kefir*, which are delicious and good for you.

★ Dear Me

165 Longmarket Street (021 422 4920, www. dearme.co.za). **Open** 7am-11am, noon-3pm Mon-Fri. **Main courses** R70. **Map** p52 D4 ❹ **Brasserie**
With a focus on sustainable eating, as well as catering for just about any allergy or dietary requirement, this bright brasserie and café simply oozes wholesomeness. Home-made mueslis and porridge offer a healthy start to the day, while shakshuka – eggs poached in a spicy tomato sauce – adds zing to the menu. Freshly pressed juices, smoothies, herbal infusions and milk drinks are original additions. At lunchtime, the fresh approach continues with gravadlax on rye, roast beetroot risotto or sweet potato and ginger soup.

★ Deluxe

25 Church Street (072 569 9579, www.deluxe coffeeworks.co.za). **Open** 7am-5pm Mon-Fri. **Map** p53 E4 ❹ **Coffee shop**
You go to Deluxe for coffee. That's it. This is a masculine, no frills space where staff roast beans from Brazil, Guatemala and Ethiopia in-house to brew some of the best coffee in town. It has a fervently loyal following by those who are equally obsessed with the bean.
Other locations throughout the city.

Haiku

58 Burg Street (021 424 7000, bukhara.com). **Open** noon-2.30pm, 6-11pm Mon-Sat; 6-11pm Sun. **Main courses** R150. **Map** p53 E4 ❹ **Asian**
The diverse range of Asian dishes served tapas-style here includes dim sum, sushi, robata, stir fries and wok dishes. The dark interior is moody but the ambience enhanced by the open kitchen where you can see the experts hard at work. The range of

ingredients is impressive – from crayfish to wagyu beef. The difficulty will be choosing your dishes.

★ Hemelhuijs

71 Waterkant Street (021 418 2042, www. hemelhuijs.co.za). **Open** 9am-4pm Mon-Fri; 9am-3pm Sat. **Main courses** R120. **Map** p52 C4 ❸ **Café**
This poetically beautiful space gets a makeover every few months. What remains, though, is exquisite styling, bespoke crockery – and the stuffed springbok head on the wall. Food is seasonal, big on comfort and interesting combinations. Kidneys and mushrooms on toast or an Indian-inspired seafood curry could be on the cards. Or simply pop in for an orange-infused chai latte and slice of cake.

HQ

Heritage Square, Shortmarket Street (021 424 6373, www.hqrestaurant.co.za). **Open** noon-11.30pm Mon-Sat. **Steaks** R170. **Map** p52 C3 ❹ **Steakhouse/bar**
Sirloin with salad and chips are on the menu. And that's it. This spot has made a name for itself by just serving one thing, and doing it well – although lunchtime sees the addition of fish and chips and a burger. The secret is out, though, that the happening bar and lounge area does a mean list of cocktails and a vast array of sophisticated bar snacks, making it a popular stop-off point for nights on the town.

IYO Burgers

103 Bree Street (021 422 1313, www.iyoburgers. co.za). **Open** 5-10pm Mon; noon-10pm Tue-Sat (kitchen closed 3.30-5pm). **Burgers** R86. **Map** p52 D3 ❹ **Burgers**
At Inside & You're Out (what IYO stands for... don't worry, we're a bit confused too), upscale burger toppings like smoked cheddar and pulled pork are actually inside the patty. The guys behind the concept are passionate about locally sourced ingredients and environmentally friendly practices. Accompany your burger with craft beers, shakes and juices.

★ Jason Bakery

185 Bree Street (021 424 5644, www.jasonbakery. com). **Open** 7am-3.30pm Tue-Fri; 8am-2pm Sat. **Map** p53 E2 ❹ **Bakery**
What started as a small hatch serving coffee and the eternally popular bacon croissants to a loyal following has grown into a must-visit food destination. You can still order your takeaway pastries and heaving sarnies on sourdough and other breads at lunchtime. But grab a seat if you can and enjoy daily specials: the pie of the day could be roast chicken and chorizo, beer-braised wild boar with truffled mushrooms or mac 'n' cheese.

Mama Africa

178 Long Street (021 426 1017, www.mama africarestaurant.co.za). **Open** 7am-11pm Mon,

EXPLORE

Alexander Bar, Café & Theatre.

Sat; 12.30-4pm Tue-Fri. **Main courses** R110. **Map** p53 E3 ㊼ African
See p74 **The Melting Pot**.

Odyssey Gastropub

199 Bree Street (021 422 4084, www.theodyssey.co.za). **Open** noon-late Mon-Fri; 4pm-late Sat. **Main courses** R75. **Map** p53 E2 ㊽ Gastropub

Spread over two levels, the Odyssey serves modern pub fare in a relaxed setting. Light bites include Scotch eggs, sliders and platters that are good for sharing. If you need something heartier, there's a range of burgers, as well as classics like fish and chips or steak. A good selection of wines, craft beers as well as regular gigs make this a convivial spot.

★ La Parada

107 Bree Street (021 426 0330, http://laparada.co.za). **Open** noon-10pm daily. **Tapas** R65. **Map** p52 D3 ㊾ Tapas

Headed up by Spanish chef Andres Condé, who worked at El Bulli for six years, La Parada serves authentic tapas in a convivial setting. With colourful tiles, wooden tables and leather couches on the pavement, it's a great spot for drinks and nibbles that turn into dinner. Tapas burst with flavour from the likes of home-made chorizo, grilled peppers with anchovies on toast, prawns wrapped in bacon, and calamari with garlic mayo. If you're after something more substantial, mains include lamb rump and beef fillet.

Other location 140 Main Road, Kalk Bay (021 788 3992).

★ Royale Eatery

273 Long Street (021 422 4536, www.royaleeatery.com). **Open** noon-11.30pm Mon-Sat. **Burgers** R80. **Map** p53 F2 ㊿ Burgers

Bright walls decorated with musical instruments and hats, snug booths and melamine tables create a quirky diner feel at this long-standing burger joint. And it is burgers all the way: beef, lamb, pork, fish, chicken and veggie; modest or massive; simple or loaded. If you can't find a burger you love from the extensive list, well, then you could order a salad or a pizza. Finish off with a decadent milkshake.

Sababa Kitchen and Deli

231 Bree Street (021 424 7480, www.sababa.co.za) **Open** 7am-4pm Mon-Fri. **Main courses** R65. **Map** p53 F2 (51) Middle Eastern

Sisters Nirit and Tal Saban have created a deli eaterie filled with good food and good vibes. Wholesome is the byword here, with Middle Eastern flavours dominating a vast array of salads, plus meze dishes and quiches. The lunchbox takeaway is very popular, and filled pitta breads burst with flavour. Main dishes include chicken or lamb kofte in tomato sauce, alongside Indian or European dishes (curries, pasta and casseroles). Take home a decadent sweet treat or two.

Other location Piazza St John, Sea Point (021 433 0570).

South China Dim Sum Bar

289 Long Street (078 846 3656, www.facebook. com/SouthChinaDimSumBar). **Open** 12.30-3pm, 6.30-10pm Tue-Fri; 11am- 3pm, 6.30-10pm Sat. **Dim sum** R60. **Map** p53 F2 ❷ **Dim sum**
Capetonians have only fairly recently cottoned on to the deliciousness of dim sum. At this unassuming spot, with its chalkboard menu and mismatched furniture, you can expect wontons, dumplings and buns filled with goodness. The *char siu bao* (bun with sticky barbecue pork) is always a good way to start. Branching out from dim sum, prawn and pork dumplings in a noodle broth make for a perfect lunch, and there are unusual Asian specials such as calamari laksa.

Pubs & Bars

Alexander Bar, Café & Theatre

76 Strand Street (021 300 1088, http:// alexanderbar.co.za). **Open** 11am-1am Mon-Sat. **Map** p52 D5 ❸
Mostly a conversation bar, there's usually a mixed crowd of interesting locals, young and old, as well as a smattering of tourists. The functioning antique rotary dial telephone system encourages you to chat to people all over the bar. And you can also dial 9 to ring the bartender. Background music ranges from jazz and world music to funky lounge, soul and jazzy disco on busier nights. There's also a tiny theatre upstairs (*see p171*).

Beerhouse On Long

223 Long Street (021 424 3370, www.beerhouse. co.za). **Open** 11am-2am daily. **Map** p53 F3 ❹
Situated on Cape Town's bustling and vibey Long Street, Beerhouse On Long has no less than 25 taps and 99 bottles of the finest local and international beers, as well as a gastropub menu for soaking up all those ales. There's an upmarket, contemporary beer hall vibe, and knowledgeable staff are on hand to make suggestions. If you're not a beer lover yet, you soon will be.

Bierhaus + Weingarten

110 Bree Street (021 422 2770). **Open** 3pm-midnight Tue-Thur, Sat; noon-2am Fri. **Map** p52 D3 ❺
Formerly known as &Union – one of the first places to hop on to the craft beer bandwagon in Cape Town – this bar has a large undercover outdoor area with tables and benches, and a small interior. Order your beer (or wine) from the counter and have it served at your table. There are also moreish meaty dishes cooked on an open grill and regular free live music.

Daddy Cool & Sky Bar

Grand Daddy Hotel, 38 Long Street (021 424 7247, www.granddaddy.co.za). **Open** *Daddy Cool* 3-11pm Mon-Thur; 3pm-1am Fri, Sat. *Sky Bar* Summer noon-8.30pm Mon-Sat. Winter 4-8.30pm Wed-Sat. **Map** p52 D5 ❻
The rooftop bar is in an Airstream trailer park – the only one of its kind in the world; you can spend the night here as a cool, quirky alternative to a conventional hotel room. In summer they show movies up here, and have live music. Down in Daddy Cool, which it has repositioned itself as a gin bar (a very trendy spirit in Cape Town at the moment), there are salsa dancing evenings every Friday.

Dubliner

251 Long Street (021 424 1212, www.thedubliner. co.za). **Open** 11am-4am daily. **Map** p53 F3 ❼
It's billed as an authentic Irish pub – though possibly by people who've never set foot in Dublin. Nevertheless, it does have a raucous and welcoming Irish-style atmosphere, with lots of beers on tap (including Guinness and Kilkenny), singalong music, sport on the television and pub food served until 2am.

Fireman's Arms

Corner of Buitengracht & Mechau streets (021 419 1513, www.firemansarms.co.za). **Open** 11am- 2am Mon-Sat. **Map** p52 B4 ❽
Established in 1864, this is one of Cape Town's oldest pubs. We love that it refuses to budge despite all the high-rise development going on around it. It's massively popular, especially with sports fans – there are nine 46-inch TVs and two big screens. There's pizza or pub fare such as burgers, ribs or *eisbein* (pickled ham hock) if you're hungry.

EXPLORE

★ House of Machines

84 Shortmarket Street (021 426 1400, www.thehouseofmachines.com). **Open** 7am-late Mon-Fri; 9am-late Sat, 9am-2pm first Sun of mth. **Map** p52 D4 59

Housed in a historic workhouse, House of Machines fuses a prohibition-styled cocktail and bourbon bar, café, custom motorbike workshop (hence the name) and purveyor of essential menswear and accessories. Things are not cheap here but you get live music or DJs six nights a week for no cover charge, which is a great support for the local music industry. Grab a Deluxe coffee and Jason Bakery croissant if you're here in the morning.

Julep

2 Vredenburg Lane (off Long Street) (021 423 4276, www.julep.co.za). **Open** 7pm-2am Wed-Sun. **Admission** varies according to live entertainment. **Map** p53 F2 60

When it first opened – and first appeared in *Time Out* – this was a secret little bar, but it's been there several years now so it's not so secret any more. Famous for its cocktails, it's small and intimate, so a great place for semi-private parties. There is usually entertainment of some kind – music, burlesque, DJs, or simply the antics of the patrons.

EXPLORE

Mother's Ruin Gin Bar

219 Bree Street (082 681 6601, www.facebook.com/mothersruincpt). **Open** 4pm-1am Tue-Sat. **Map** p53 F2 61

Gin is without a doubt the spirit *du jour*, with artisanal gins being distilled with diverse and interesting botanicals, herbs, and spices from all over the world. These form the basis of the ever-growing collection of gins (currently more than 100) that are available here, which are paired with unique tonics and garnishes. Look out for special events like foraging sessions held every third Saturday, where three gins, at least one local, are served in unique ways with freshly foraged ingredients.

★ Neighbourhood Restaurant, Bar & Lounge

163 Long Street (021 424 7260, www.goodinthehood.co.za). **Open** noon-late Mon-Sat. **Map** p53 E3 62

A popular meeting place since 2007, Neighbourhood has firmly established itself as a one of the most popular spots in the city. It has a long balcony with tables and seating overlooking the famous Long Street, as well as an interior den of warmly furnished interconnected rooms. An eclectic crowd keeps the place constantly abuzz, sipping cocktails on the balcony or relaxing in snug armchairs and booths inside.

★ Orphanage Cocktail Emporium

Corner Orphan & Bree streets (021 424 2004, www.theorphanage.co.za). **Open** 5pm-2am Mon-Thur, Sat; 3pm-2am Fri. **Map** p53 F2 63

Cape Town is, we have to admit, a very trend-driven social city. There are the places that are casual and unpretentious, and there are those that require a deeper pocket and a better wardrobe. Orphanage fits the latter category: it's all about creative cocktails and DJ beats for an upmarket crowd. It's in a part of Bree Street that has never been cooler; this hub of bars and restaurants is even busier on the first Thursday of every month when art galleries stay open late, and the streets come alive (*see p67* **In the Know**).

★ Tjing Tjing

165 Longmarket Street (021 422 4920, www.tjingtjing.co.za). **Open** 4pm-2am Tue-Fri; 6.30pm-2am Sat. **Map** p52 D3 64

A small warning: there is a very steep staircase up to this rooftop bar, which can be all right to negotiate on the way up but coming down after a few drinks could be hazardous, so watch your step. The indoor/outdoor bar is stylish and comfortable, and being hidden away so high in a historic building lends a particular appeal. There are free wine tasting evenings during the week, and you can supplement your drinks with excellent tapas. A small restaurant, Tjing Tjing Torii, has just opened below in an elegant space decorated in deep blues and Louis Ghost chairs. It serves Japanese style tapas: pork hot dog with kim chi, tempura oysters or tuna tataki.

Twankey Bar

The Taj, Wale Street (021 819 2000, www.tajcapetown.co.za). **Open** 7am-11pm Mon-Fri; 2pm-midnight Sat. **Map** p53 E4 65

Champagne and oysters are a thing here, but not the only thing. Elegant yet casual and open all day, there is a fine menu with small plates and global mains, and free Wi-Fi. You'll also find a good selection of local craft beers from Devils Peak, Darling Brew, Jack Black Brewing Co, Robsons and Boston Breweries, as well as Everson's cider, which is the real deal.

Village Idiot

32 Loop Street (021 418 1548, www.facebook.com/thevillageidiotct). **Open** 3pm-midnight Tue-Thur; noon-2am Fri-Sun. **Map** p52 C4 66

Insanely popular from the minute it opened its doors, the Village Idiot is owned by the same people who made Aces 'n' Spades such a success. The huge corner space has a wraparound balcony, a massive bar overseen by a stuffed ostrich named Oskar who is the bar mascot, pool tables, board games, a fireplace and booths for discreet assignations. They serve great food – including a Sunday spit braai or roast – and there is a stage for live music and DJs.

Shops & Services

210 on Long

210 Long Street (021 481 1820, www.210onlong.co.za). **Open** 8am-7pm Mon-Fri; 8am-4pm Sat. **Map** p53 F2 67 **Mall**

This edgy emporium hits the mark for those who like some consciousness with their consumerism. Stop in at Hemporium for clothes and accessories manufactured from the wonder plant, check out the collection of cool threads at No Manga Manga and finish your visit with Korean barbecue at Galbi.

Afraid of Mice

86 Long Street, corner Longmarket (021 423 7353, www.afraidofmice.com). **Open** 9.45am-5pm Mon-Fri; 10am-2pm Sat. **Map** p53 A3 **⑥ Fashion**
This vintage shop's tagline is 'the clothes you wish your mother had kept for you', and it's utterly fitting. Expertly sourced second-hand and vintage dresses, shoes and bags, many with covetable labels (Chanel, anyone?), are set up in an uncluttered, organised display with lovely shop windows luring in fashionistas.

African Image

52 Burg Street (021 423 8385, www.african-image.co.za). **Open** 9am-5pm Mon- Fri; 9am-2pm Sat. **Map** p53 E4 **⑥ Art & crafts**
African Image has come to define the juxtaposition of antique Africana (trade beads and southern African beadwork) with modern transitional pieces that make novel use of contemporary and recycled materials. An amusement park of pattern, print, colour and visual rhythms, it's perfect for both local collectors and visitors.

African Music Store

134 Long Street (021 426 0857, www.facebook. com/TheAfricanMusicStore). **Open** 9am-6pm Mon-Fri; 9am-2pm Sat. **Map** p53 E3 **⑩ Music**
A unique doorway into the music of this continent, which plays a seminal role in so many of the sounds that make up our aural wallpaper. The atmosphere is relaxed and upbeat, and the music's all here: from world-music crossovers (Ali Farka Touré, Youssou N'Dour, Salif Keita) to local luminaries (Freshlyground, Judith Sephuma and the lamented Lucky Dube). The golden oldies catalogue is also full of nuggets: Sipho Hotstix Mabusa, Stimela and Cesaria Evora to name a few.

★ AVA Gallery

35 Church Street (021 424 7436, www.ava. co.za). **Open** 10am-5pm Mon-Fri; 10am-1pm Sat. **Map** p53 E4 **⑪ Gallery**
This non-profit gallery provides an exhibition space for art in all mediums, with shows changing every four weeks. Since its inception in 1971, with a variety of sponsors on board to support its endeavours, many up-and-coming artists have exhibited here.

Avoova

97 Bree Street (021 422 1620, www.avoova. com). **Open** 9am-5pm Mon-Fri; 9am-1pm Sat. **Map** p52 D3 **⑫ Homewares**
Who knew an ostrich eggshell could have so many uses? A far cry from a cheesy souvenir shop, Avoova

EXPLORE

Village Idiot.

Ebony.

has products that are stylish and understated. Think bowls, frames, *objets*, jewellery and inlaid furniture with fine mosaic patterns.

★ Bean There

58 Wale Street (087 943 2228, beanthere.co.za). **Open** 7.30am-4pm Mon-Fri. **Map** p52 D3 **73** **Food & drink**

This roaster of Fairtrade African coffees not only promotes sustainability, but serves a damn fine cup too. Beans are sourced from as far afield as Burundi, Kenya and Ethopia to create single-origin roasts. The light and airy space, with pops of colour from lampshades, is a good place to learn more about your favourite brew and buy some coffee and accessories to take home too.

Boaston Society

55 Long Street (076 923 4426, www.facebook. com/BoastonSociety). **Open** 9am-5pm Mon-Fri; 9am-1pm Sat. **Map** p52 D4 **74** **Fashion**

Streetwear from local and international designers. Brand launches and a coffee bar keep things buzzing, and there are regular social evenings with ping pong, foozball and darts on the cards.

Church Street Antique Market

Church Street, between Long & Burg streets. **Open** 9am-4pm Mon-Sat. **No credit cards**. **Map** p53 E4 **75** **Antiques**

This small cobbled stretch is a trove of vintage garb, rare coins, plastic jewellery, twee porcelain doggies and rows of empty perfume bottles. Even more interesting than the wares are the people that frequent the pedestrianised area of Church Street, who range from coffee-sipping arty folk and stealthy antique hounds to stylists.

Clarke's Bookshop

199 Long Street (021 423 5739, www.clarkes books.co.za). **Open** 9am-5pm Mon-Fri; 9.30am-1pm Sat. **Map** p53 E3 **76** **Books**

The gold standard among the city's book vendors, Clarke's is to the local literati what the Shakespeare & Company bookstore is to Paris. Clarke's is wonderfully laden with new, second-hand and rare books, maps and other published material. A long-time champion of local authors, this is one of Cape Town's most esteemed resources.

Ebony

67 Loop Street (021 424 9985, http://ebonydesign. co.za). **Open** 9am-5pm Mon-Fri; 9.30am-1pm Sat. **Map** p52 D4 **77** **Homewares**

Combining fine art, furniture and interiors accessories, Ebony manages to showcase a holistic approach to interior design. Bespoke, contemporary pieces are its hallmark and the impressive range of art from well-known artists, in various media, adds to the distinct appeal of the space.

Food Lover's Market

Newspaper House, 22 St Georges Mall (021 424 0294). **Open** 7am-6pm Mon-Fri; 9am-3pm Sat. **Map** p53 E4 **78** **Food & drink**

A food emporium, where you can do the week's grocery shop or simply stop by for fresh-as-can-be canteen-style eats to enjoy in the store or to take away. Build-your-own salads are popular, as is the freshly made sushi.

★ Frankie Fenner Meat Merchants

81 Church Street (021 424 7204, www.ffmm. co.za). **Open** 10am-6pm Mon-Fri; 10am-2pm Sat. **Map** p52 D3 **79** **Food & drink**

Sustainable and ethically reared meats, treated with care, are what sets Frankie Fenner apart. Staff are passionate about meat, and have many suggestions about how to get the best out of a specific cut. The in-house butchery will prepare to order, or you can buy from the deli counter.

▶ *In-house Publik Wine Bar (http://publik.co.za) sources wines from sustainably farmed vineyards and lesser-known estates, and is a happening spot on weekday evenings.*

★ Greenmarket Square
Cnr Shortmarket & Burg streets. **Open** 9am-4pm Mon-Sat. **No credit cards. Map** p52 D4 ⑳ **Market**
Given that this has to be one of the most beautiful and architecturally interesting city squares in the southern hemisphere, it would be a mistake to take a trip to Cape Town without spending some time at this historic gem. A lively market occupies the square: you'll find a full range of African folk art plus well-priced CDs and souvenir clothing. An added bonus is the pan-African character of the vendors (who welcome bargaining), especially on Fridays, when they don traditional garb.

Hendrik Vermeulen Couture
79 Hout Lane, corner of Hout and Bree streets (021 424 1686/7, www.hendrikvermeulen.com). **Open** 9am-5pm Mon-Fri. **Map** p52 C4 ㉛ **Fashion**
Precocious young designer Hendrik Vermeulen sold his first evening dress at age 15. It's no surprise that he has gone on to great things, with flamboyant, colourful gowns being a signature look. You'll find ready-to-wear men's and women's clothing at his boutique as well as accessories, but it's his haute couture that will quicken any fashionista's heart.

★ Honest Chocolate
64A Wale Street (076 765 8306, www.honest chocolate.co.za). **Open** 9am-5pm Mon-Sat. **Map** p52 D3 ㉜ **Food & drink**
What do you get when you combine passionate chocolatiers, organic cacao and arty wrapping? Some of the hottest chocolate on the block… This boutique chocolaterie only uses unroasted cacao beans, which means the taste and texture of its chocolate are different from that of standard chocolate bars (it's also said to be higher in antioxidants). The original artworks adorning the bars are worth collecting in their own right, but what's inside makes it even more worthwhile: dark chocolate with flavourings such as coffee, Kalahari desert salt, and orange.
Other location Woodstock Exchange, 66 Albert Road, Woodstock (021 447 1438).

Klûk CGDT
43-45 Bree Street (083 377 7780, http://klukcgdt. com). **Open** 9am-5pm Mon-Fri; 9am-2pm Sat. **Map** p52 C4 ㉝ **Fashion**
Formidable design duo Malcolm Kluk and Christiaan Gabriël du Toit create some of the most talked-about wedding gowns in the country. Their headquarters is situated in a historic house, painted stark black, with beautiful dresses displayed in the shop windows. In addition to a ready-to-wear collection, they produce couture pieces, which are all about feminine lines and luxurious fabrics. A must for any serious fashionista.

Long Street Antique Arcade
127 Long Street (021 423 2504). **Open** 9am-4.30pm Mon-Fri; 9am-2pm Sat. **Map** p53 E3 ㉞ **Antiques**
A rabbit warren of small and varied dealers where you can browse for all kinds of collectibles, including jewellery, militaria, china, crystal and silver. The atmosphere is relaxed and the shop owners are knowledgeable. Bear in mind that not all dealers will accept credit cards.

★ Luvey 'n Rose
66 Loop Street (081 031 4527, www.luveynrose. co.za). **Open** 8am-4pm Mon-Fri; 9am-2pm Sat. **Map** p52 D3 ㉟ **Gallery**
This gallery space invites patrons to pop in and browse contemporary and classic South African artworks, sit on the antique furniture that's for sale and enjoy coffee, soups and sandwiches, all in a warm and welcoming atmosphere. You'll feel like you've stepped into a friend's home – one with very good taste, that is.

★ MeMeMe
117A Long Street (021 424 0001, www.mememe. co.za). **Open** 9.30am-5.30pm Mon-Fri; 9am-3pm Sat. **Map** p53 E3 ㊱ **Fashion**
This bright space welcomes shoppers keen to explore the vast talents of local designers. It hosts

EXPLORE

over 30 labels, with clothing, shoes, bags and accessories that have been lovingly curated for the store.

★ Merchants on Long
34 Long Street (021 422 2828, www.merchants onlong.com). **Open** 10am-6pm Mon-Fri;10am-2pm Sat. **Map** p52 D4 ⑰ **Fashion**
Exquisite collections of clothing, art and artefacts awaits at this historic building. Founder and owner Hanneli Rupert uses the space to showcase her own handbag brand, Okapi, with its signature springbok horn, as well as a range of African designers' work. You're likely to find anything from highly embellished beaded dresses to batik surf shorts, tribal-print cushions and wooden sunglasses.

★ Missibaba & Kirsten Goss London
229 Bree Street (021 424 3453, www.missibaba. com, www.kirstengoss.com). **Open** 9am-5pm Mon-Fri; 10am-2pm Sat. **Map** p53 F2 ㉘ **Accessories**
Two covetable accessories brands are under one roof here. Chloe Townsend's Missibaba range has creative and colourful leather bags, from easy shoulder bags to design-driven peacock clutches and weekend hold-alls. Jewellery by internationally renowned Kirsten Goss includes an array of styles, from signature woven, beaded earrings to contemporary geometric rings and chunky cuffs.

Mungo & Jemima
108 Long Street (021 424 5016, www.mungo andjemima.com). **Open** 9.30am-6pm Mon-Fri; 10am-5pm Sat. **Map** p52 D3 ㉙ **Fashion**
A collaborative space spearheaded by designers Marian Park-Ross and Kirsty Bannerman, this shop showcases not only their labels (Good and Coppelia respectively), but also the ranges of like-minded creatives. This is the place to find feminine, easy-to-wear pieces with eye-catching details.

Olive Green Cat
76 Church Street (021 424 1101, www.olive greencat.com). **Open** 8am-5pm Mon-Thur; 8am-7.30pm Fri. **Map** p52 D3 ㉚ **Jewellery**
The jewellery on offer at these premises – shared by three creatives – is original and much-coveted by lovers of a contemporary, cutting-edge look. Expect unusual pieces such as rings with diamonds set in resin and Perspex cuffs with suspended golden floral designs. They offer a bespoke service too.

★ Pan African Market
76 Long Street (021 426 4478). **Open** *Summer* 8.30am-5.30pm Mon-Fri; 8.30am-3.30pm Sat. *Winter* 9am-5pm Mon-Fri; 9am-3pm Sat. **Map** p52 D4 ㉛ **Market**
A grand old Victorian building is the unlikely home for African artefacts from all over the continent. You can easily get lost here in the three floors of craft-crammed rooms among the art, antiques and jewellery, fertility figurines and masks. You can also order custom-tailored garments. When the relentless bartering gets you down, enjoy an Ethiopian coffee ceremony on the first-floor terrace.

Paul Smith
137 Bree Street (021 424 0354, www.paulsmith. co.uk). **Open** 9am-6pm Mon-Fri; 9am-2pm Sat. **Map** p52 D3 ㉜ **Fashion**
A bright-blue corner premises lures Paul Smith fans to shop for clothing and accessories from this iconic British designer. Signature shirts, tailored suits, urban workwear and covetable sneakers make for a distinctive look.

Second Time Around
196 Long Street (021 423 1674, http://secondtime around.co). **Open** 9am-5pm Mon-Fri; 9am-2pm Sat. **No credit cards. Map** p53 E3 ㉝ **Fashion**
Though it's become more and more difficult to find real vintage clothing these days, the owner of this second-hand clothes pitstop has a knack for ferreting out real finds. There are loads of clothes and accessories that are purely for fun, but now and then you might unearth a real gem.

Shelf Life
167 Longmarket Street (021 422 3931, www. shelflife.co.za). **Open** 10am-5.30pm Mon-Fri; 10am-2pm Sat. **Map** p52 D4 ㉞ **Fashion**
Super-cool skater- and hip hop-inspired urban streetwear can be found at this achingly hip store. T-shirts, hoodies, sneakers and – yes – an encyclopaedic range of spray cans for graffiti are for sale. This fresh local label has cult-status kudos.

Skinny Laminx
201 Bree Street (021 424 6290, www.skinnylaminx. com). **Open** 10am-5pm Mon-Wed, Fri; 10am-7pm Thur; 9am-1pm Sat. **Map** p53 E2 ㉟ **Homewares**
Heather Moore is a designer and printmaker, and at this tiny store you can see her latest fabrics. Always playful, they transform anything from a scatter cushion to a frock into a delightful original piece. Bags, scarves, aprons and tea towels make sweet gifts.

Smith
56 Church Street (083 270 8008, 021 422 0814, http://.smithstudio.co.za). **Open** 9am-5pm Tue-Fri; 10am-1pm Sat. **Map** p52 D4 ㊱ **Gallery**
New to the Cape Town gallery scene, Smith is all about making art, from both established and emerging names, accessible to buyers. The handful of artists represented cover a variety of styles, and exhibitions have been well received. The exposed stone walls and uncluttered space are inviting.

★ South African Market
1st Floor, 107 Bree Street (021 422 2898, www.facebook.com/SouthAfricanMarket). **Open** 10am-7pm Mon-Fri; 9am-3pm Sat. **Map** p52 D3 ㊲ **Accessories**

A host of pretty things for boys, girls and the home from a variety of designers await at this stylish first-floor shop, a favourite of Cape Town's fashionable young things. Objects include wallets and handbags, delightful necklaces and rings, scatter cushions and funky T-shirts.

Spaghetti Mafia

199 Loop Street (021 424 0696, www.facebook. com/pages/Spaghetti-Mafia). **Open** 9.30am-6pm Mon-Fri; 10am-3pm Sat. **Map** p53 F2 ⓼ **Fashion**
Italian designers and a smattering of European labels make this the go-to menswear store for the discerning urban man. The fact that this store has been going for a decade is testament to the owners' clear style direction and spot-on quality tailoring.

★ Stable

65 Loop Street (021 426 5094, http://stable. org.za). **Open** 9am-5pm Mon-Fri; 10am-3pm Sat. **Map** p52 D4 ⓽ **Homewares**
You'll find plenty of inspiration for your home at Stable, a space for South African designers to showcase furniture, lighting and decor items, Contemporary, cutting-edge and functional pieces sit next to items with distinctly South African elements. Bags, watches and stationery round off the high-end selection.

Worldart

54 Church Street (021 423 3075, www.worldart. co.za). **Open** 10am-5pm Mon-Fri; 10am-1pm Sat. **Map** p53 E4 ⓾ **Gallery**
A tiny, bright gallery space in the heart of the CBD, Worldart is firmly focused on South African contemporary artists, with a special affinity for urban and pop art. Peruse works such as Kilmany-Jo Liversage's massive female portraits with graffiti overlay or Khaya Witbooi's pop art with a political edge.

BO-KAAP

Characterised by its steep cobbled streets and multi-coloured houses, this area used to be known as the Malay Quarter in the apartheid years and is still home to a flourishing Muslim community. A handful of cool restaurants and craft spaces ensure that not only tourists flock here. If you're keen to stock up on local spices, head to **Atlas Trading** at 94 Wale Street: you'll be inspired by a vast array, from cumin and saffron to cinnamon sticks or ready-made curry mixes.

Sights & Museums

Auwal Mosque

43 Dorp Street (082 551 7324, www.auwal masjid.co.za). **Open** daily for prayer. **Map** p52 D2 ⓵⓪⓵
The Auwal Mosque (South Africa's oldest) was established in 1798 by Iman Abdullah Kadi Salaam.

Once an Indonesian prince, he was banished to Robben Island for conspiring with the British against the Dutch. During his incarceration he was said to have written out several copies of the Quran from memory, and upon his release in 1793, he established a *madrasa* (Islamic school) in Dorp Street. Five years later one of his students, Achmat van Bengalen, gave one of his properties to him, which became the Auwal Mosque. The building looks very different today, with only two of the original walls remaining intact after it collapsed back in the 1930s.

★ Bo-Kaap Museum

71 Wale Street (021 481 3938, www.iziko.org.za/ bokaap). **Open** 10am-5pm Mon-Sat. **Admission** R20; R10 reductions. **No credit cards**. **Map** p52 D2 ⓵⓪⓶
Through the years the Bo-Kaap has been known by many names, ranging from Malay Quarter and Slamse Buurt (Islamic neighbourhood) through to Schotscheskloof and Waalendorp. The area, with its multicoloured houses and steep cobbled streets, was developed in the 1760s by Jan de Waal (hence the name Waalendorp); the museum is the only structure built by him that's remained more or less unchanged through the years. It tells the story of the area's Cape Malays, a culturally rich community descended from East African and South-east Asian slaves and responsible for the introduction of Islam to South Africa.

Noon Gun

Military Road, follow the signs from cnr Bloem Street and Buitengracht. **Map** p52 A1 ⓵⓪⓷
How do you tell a tourist from a local? When the noon gun booms, the locals look at their watches while the tourists look around in sudden panic. Head to the cannon just shy of 11.30am to watch this traditional ritual (begun in 1806). A member of the South African Navy loads two cannons (in case one doesn't fire) with gunpowder, and then the gun is fired. The guns were initially housed in the castle, firing to aid passing ships check the accuracy of their on-board chronometers. As the city's population grew, the noise grew too much, and so the guns were moved to their current location in 1902.

Restaurants & Cafés

Biesmiellah's

2 Wale Street (021 423 0850, www.biesmiellah. co.za). **Open** 9am-10pm Mon-Sat. **Main courses** R110. **Map** p52 D2 ⓵⓪⓸ **Cape Malay**
See p74 **The Melting Pot**.

Bo-Kaap Kombuis

7 August Street (021 422 5446, www.bokaap kombuis.co.za). **Open** 8am-10.30pm Tue-Thur; 8am-11.30pm Fri, Sat; 9am-3pm Sun. **Main courses** R80. **Map** p52 B2 ⓵⓪⓹ **Cape Malay**
See p74 **The Melting Pot**.

EXPLORE

LOCAL IS LEKKER
An A-Z of South Africans' favourite foods.

Beskuit (Rusks): Bone-dry rectangular biscuits that are best enjoyed dipped into a piping hot cuppa and then slurped heartily.

Biltong The preferred snack of sports enthusiasts, these dried, salty strips of beef are perfect when washed down with liberal lashings of beer.

Bobotie This fragrant, slightly spicy Cape Malay dish is comprised of curried mince with dried fruit such as raisins, topped with an egg custard, which is then baked.

Boerewors No self-respecting braai (barbecue) should be without this beef sausage spiced with aromatic coriander seed. Slap on a long bread roll, slather with tomato sauce or chutney, and hey presto, you have a *boerie-roll*.

Bunnychow Hollow out half a loaf of white bread, fill with curry and dig in. Elegant it ain't, but damn it's good.

Chakalaka Ranging from a bit-of-a-bite to hot-as-hell, this tomato-based vegetable relish is usually served with *pap* (mealie-meal porridge) and meat dishes.

Gatsby A local favourite of chips, meat, gravy and more piled into a roll.

Koeksisters Sinfully sweet plaits of dough, which are deep-fried before being drenched in a cinnamon-sugar syrup.

Koesister Not to be confused with *koeksisters*, this sweet Cape Malay snack is more like a small, fragrant doughnut, soaked in syrup and dipped in coconut.

Potjie The key components to preparing the perfect *potjie* stew are simple enough: you need a cast-iron pot known as a *potjie*, a decent fire, a little stirring and an awful lot of patience. The choice of ingredients relies very much on the *potjie* master, but stews usually include meat and vegetables.

Smiley Describing this township delicacy as an acquired taste would be a definite understatement. It's actually a boiled sheep's head.

Walkie talkie There's no getting around this one. Chicken feet are a favourite township snack.

EXPLORE

Marco's African Place

15 Rose Lane (021 423 5412, www.marcos africanplace.co.za). **Open** noon-11pm Tue-Thur; noon-midnight Fri, Sat; 3-11pm Sun. **Set menu** R200. **Map** p52 C3 ⑩⑥ **African** *See p74* **The Melting Pot.**

★ Spasie

97 Church Street (021 422 1492, www. spasie.co). **Open** 7pm-late Wed- Fri. **No credit cards. Map** p52 D3 ⑩⑦ Contemporary South African

One of the coolest culinary kids on the block, Spasie (meaning 'space' in Afrikaans) is an underground eaterie and events space. Twice a week, dinners are cooked by rising stars of local gastronomy. Pocket Watch Wednesdays (#PWW) are an invitation-only night of streetfood and board games (email from the website for an invitation); and during the day they serve seasonal, ethically sourced ingredients turned into light and fresh breakfasts and lunches. Definitely a *spasie* to watch...

Shops & Services

Gallery MOMO

170 Buitengracht (021 424 5150, www. gallerymomo.com). **Open** 9am-5pm Mon-Fri; 10am-2pm Sat. **No credit cards. Map** p52 E2 ⑩⑧ Gallery

Newly opened in Cape Town, Gallery MOMO, with its sister gallery in Johannesburg, has a strong focus on video art. The Cape Town space has a dedicated video room, and in addition hosts exhibitions by cutting-edge young South African and international artists.

Monkeybiz

43 Rose Street (021 426 0145, monkeybiz.co.za). **Open** 9am-5pm Mon-Fri; 9am-1pm Sat. **Map** p52 C3 ⑩⑨ Homewares

More than 400 beaders in the townships of Cape Town supply their creative crafts to this studio, assuring them a much-needed income. The quirky, colourful and original beadwork figurines have been sold all over the world. Animals, dolls and Christmas decorations make for unique souvenirs and decor items.

Streetwires

77 Shortmarket Street (021 426 2475, www. streetwires.co.za). **Open** 9am-5pm Mon- Fri. **Map** p52 C3 ⑩⑩ Homewares

Visit the studio of this Fairtrade organisation where over 60 people are hard at work making colourful – and original – bead and wire objects. You'll find everything from animals to shoes, jewellery, baskets and Christmas tree ornaments on display. It's a worthwhile stop for souvenir shopping as you know your money is being spent supporting talented local people.

KLOOF STREET & SURROUNDS

Leading up from Long Street, you'll start heading into the suburbs at the slopes of Table Mountain. **Gardens** is the hub where you'll find bustling **Kloof Street** with its myriad cool boutiques and restaurants. To the west lies **Tamboerskloof**, with **Kloof Nek** (which leads between Table Mountain and Lion's Head to Camps Bay) fast becoming a hip spot for young urbanites who are buying up its Victorian homes (at a price). To the east lies residential **Oranjezicht**, with mostly mid-century architecture; exclusive Higgovale boasts fantastic millionaire pads hidden in the crook of Table Mountain; and on the slopes of Devil's Peak is **Vredehoek**, which has a vast number of apartment blocks making it the more affordable option for city living.

Restaurants & Cafés

Black Sheep

104 Kloof Street, Gardens (021 426 2661, 021 426 2753, www.blacksheeprestaurant.co.za). **Open** 6-10.30pm Mon; noon-3pm, 6.30-10.30pm Tue-Sat. **Main courses** R140. **Map** p46 B6 ⑪⑪ Bistro

This local neighbourhood eaterie boasts an interesting multilevel space with wooden elements and a great view of Table Mountain. The blackboard menu changes all the time and complements the à la carte offerings nicely. Dishes are globally inspired, and you'll see sticky char siu ribs sitting comfortably next to tagliatelle with rabbit, gemsbok with celeriac mash and cumin-roast butternut salad. A highlight, which needs to be ordered three days in advance, is the slow roast leg or shoulder of lamb for six people.

El Burro Taqueria

12-16 Kloof Nek Road, corner of Kloof Nek & New Church Streets, Tamboerskloof

---

EXPLORE

(021 422 3554). **Open** noon -11.30pm Mon-Fri; 10am-11.30pm Sat. **Tacos** R30. **Map** p46 B6 ⑫ **Mexican**

Handmade *masa* tortillas are not the only thing that sets El Burro (81 Main Road, Green Point) and its new sister Taqueria apart. Deliciously fresh and zingy fillings are the order of the day at this bright spot: pulled pork and fried fish are but two of the delish fillings you can expect. The corner, with windows overlooking the buzz, is the place to be while digging in to well-priced tacos and a tequila or two.

Hudson's – The Burger Joint

69A Kloof Street, Gardens (021 426 5974, www.theburgerjoint.co.za). **Open** noon-11pm daily. **Burgers** R65. **Map** p53 H1 ⑬ **Burgers**

It's burgers all the way at this modern diner with a cool and always friendly vibe. Choose from 180g or 250g beef patties, as well as chicken, lamb, ostrich and vegetarian options. Toppings are big: pulled pork, egg and cheese; bacon, feta and avocado; or blue cheese, mushrooms and rocket – to name but a few. Milkshakes, craft beers and classic cocktails are good accompaniments. If you really don't want to tuck into a burger, the nachos, salads or ribs are pretty tasty too.

Other locations throughout the city.

★ Kloof Street House

30 Kloof Street, Gardens (021 423 4413, www. kloofstreethouse.co.za). **Open** noon-11pm daily. **Main courses** R150. **Map** p53 G1 ⑭ **Global**

This eclectic space houses a myriad dining and drinking options: cocktails in the garden; a gourmet meal in the dining room; whiskies on leather couches in the lounge area. Candles, plants, portraits, cushions and chandeliers create an opulent feel, and the menu has touches from around the world. You can enjoy a light lunch of chicken chimichurri flatbread, say, with a Karan beef fillet or beefburger with truffled mushroom sauce for dinner.

Kyoto Garden Sushi

11 Lower Kloofnek Road, Tamboerskloof (021 422 2001, kyotogardensushict.com). **Open** 5.30-11pm Mon-Sat. **Main courses** R150. **Map** p46 B6 ⑮ **Japanese**

It's not only sushi and sashimi on the menu at this stylish, minimalist Japanese restaurant – although it does offer some of the best raw fish dishes in town. Delicacies such as clams steamed in sake, tempura scallops and crayfish miso soup are expertly prepared. Leave space for some house-made ice-cream (the black sesame seed is a favourite) and pair your meal with an original cocktail.

Lazari Food Gallery

Cnr Upper Maynard Street & Vredehoek Avenue, Vredehoek (021 461 9865, www.lazari.co.za). **Open** 7.30am-5pm Mon-Fri; 8am-4pm Sat, Sun. **Map** off p47 E6 ⑯ **Café**

Sink back into one of the retro armchairs of this small and vibey Vredehoek nook and watch the world go by. Breakfasts are hearty, with eggs Benedict a popular choice. Lunchtime sees global influences in dishes such as Thai chicken wrap or falafel pita, but the burger and chicken pie are local favourites. No visit is complete without a pink cupcake.

Maharajah

Corner Kloof Nek and Woodside Roads, Tamboerskloof (021 424 6607). **Open** 12.30-3pm, 6.30-10.30pm Mon-Fri; 6.30-10.30pm Sat. **Main courses** R110. **Map** p46 B6 ⑰ **Indian**

This Indian restaurant attracts a fair following of curry devotees. The menu is extensive, with curries ranging from mild to singeing. The tomatoey fish curry has just the right touch of spice and the lamb on the bone is amazing. Just be sure to keep those soft rotis coming to mop up every last drop.

Miller's Thumb

10B Kloof Nek Road, Tamboerskloof (021 424 3838). **Open** 6.30-10.30pm Mon, Sat; 12.30-2pm, 6.30-10.30pm Tue-Fri. Closed July. **Main courses** R117. **Map** p46 B6 ⑱ **Seafood**

This cosy neighbourhood hangout serves the freshest linefish in several ways: try spicy Cajun style, perhaps, or sweeter Cape Malay. Meat lovers can opt for the espetada and there are always curries on offer. Family-run, this is a welcoming spot that keeps locals and visitors happy.

Molten Toffee

45B Kloof Street, Gardens (021 422 2885). **Open** 7am-5pm Mon-Sat. **Main courses** R55. **Map** p53 G1 ⑲ **Café**

This cute new spot with communal table and copper lamps has quickly garnered a loyal following. Easy and delicious eats are on the menu and treats are sinful or good-as-gold: so are you going to choose the peanut butter cups or coconut and goji berry raw chocolate brownies? The freshly pressed juices will add a bounce to your step.

★ Planet

Belmond Mount Nelson Hotel, 76 Orange Street, Gardens (021 483 1948, www.belmond.com/ mount-nelson-hotel-cape-town). **Open** 6.30-10.30pm daily. **Main courses** R180. **Map** p53 H2 ⑳ **Haute cuisine**

Planet – at the equally stellar Belmond Mount Nelson Hotel – greets diners with opulent decor. Chandeliers, carpets and ceilings are adorned with stars, galaxies and twinkling lights, while the plush velvet and chrome armchairs invite an evening of relaxation. Classic dishes get a refined, modern approach. The beef en croûte – with slow-cooked sirloin with duck liver, spinach, mushroom and bacon wrapped in puff pastry for two – is a highlight. The wine list is phenomenal and the sommelier will happily offer pairing suggestions.

EXPLORE

MOUNTAIN BY THE SEA
Myths and legends surrounding iconic Table Mountain.

The iconic mountain has been the subject of many myths and legends through the ages and forms an integral backdrop to the city's identity, history and culture. Up until the 16th century the indigenous Khoikhoi people dubbed it Hoerikwaggo (Sea Mountain).

When Portuguese seaman António de Saldanha came ashore in 1503, he came up with the ingenious name of Taboa do Cabo, or Table of the Cape, and marked this christening by carving a cross into the rock face, traces of which can still be found on Lion's Head today.

The sandstone colossus is still very much in the spotlight – a string of four floodlights bathe the mountain in a celestial glow each festive season, and hundreds of thousands of people visit it each year. The **Table Mountain Cableway** (*see p77*) will take you straight to the top – with minimal sweat.

The mountain's plateau top is three kilometres long, and its highest point, marked by Maclear's Beacon, towers at 1,088 metres, making it visible from as far as 200 kilometres at sea. The summit can be reached through a multitude of beautiful, albeit exhausting, trails, giving you the chance to meet the mountain's furry mascot, the rock rabbit, more commonly known as the dassie – a little creature that is said to

be the closest living relative to the elephant – and brush up against some of the 1,470 species of fynbos that blanket the mountain.

Flanking Table Mountain to the east is **Devil's Peak**, said to derive its name from the Van Hunks and the devil legend. The story goes that during the 18th century, a pipe-puffing pirate called Jan van Hunks was approached on Table Mountain by a stranger wanting to borrow some tobacco. This set Van Hunks off on a boastful tirade about his unequalled smoking abilities, and when the newcomer took him up on his challenge, the two embarked on a puffathon that lasted several days. Despite Van Hunks transpiring to be the toughest toker, the joke was very much on him when a gust of wind blew off the stranger's hat, revealing a pair of horns. Not one to accept defeat gracefully, the devil proceeded to make them both disappear – quite aptly – in a puff of smoke. Whenever the south-easterly wind howls and covers Cape Town's flat-topped mountain with a thick cloak of clouds, locals still whisper that the two old cronies are at it again.

On the opposite side are Lion's Head and **Signal Hill** (*see p77*). Lion's Head is a favourite spot for walkers and hikers, and during full moon it can be positively packed with people.

EXPLORE

★ Power and the Glory

13D Kloof Nek Road, Tamboerskloof (021 422 2108). **Open** 8am-late Mon-Fri; 10am-late Sat (kitchen closes at 11pm). **Map** p46 B6 **121** Café

Hip young things congregate from early morning for a caffeine fix and a chance to watch the world go by from this corner café. Fresh juices, craft beers, hot dogs and sandwiches go down a treat. At night it transforms into space for the adjoining Black Ram bar (*see p71*).

Saigon

Cnr of Kloof and Camp streets, Gardens (021 424 7670/7669). **Open** noon-2.30pm, 6-10.30pm Mon-Fri; 6-10.30pm Sat. **Main courses** R130. **Map** p46 B6 **122** Vietnamese

This restaurant has been around for ages, and is still as popular as ever. Dishes burst with zingy flavours. Try the crystal spring rolls and DIY lettuce wraps with noodles, prawns and chilli sauce to start. Follow with mains like sizzling seafood hotplate (flambéed dramatically in front of the diner) with creamy curried peanut sauce and barbecue duck with chilli sauce. The duck and butternut red curry deserves a special mention. There's also plenty for vegetarians and good-quality sushi in generous portions.

Societi Bistro

50 Orange Street, Gardens (021 424 2100, www.societi.co.za). **Open** noon-11pm daily. **Main courses** R130. **Map** p53 G2 **123** Bistro

Located in a historic Georgian home with a beautiful garden, Societi Bistro has a loyal following. Exposed brick walls and an open fireplace add to the homely feel. Seasonal produce is at the heart of what Societi does – and it does it well. Many dishes are playfully named after regulars, but among them you're bound to find pasta and risotto, crisp salads and hearty mains with an emphasis on sustainable fish and free-range meats, classically prepared.

Takumi

3 Park Road, Gardens (021 424 8879, www. takumi.co.za). **Open** 6-10pm Mon, Sat; noon-2pm, 6-10pm Tue-Fri;. **Main courses** R85. **Map** p53 G1 **124** Sushi

For a pure sushi experience, this is where those in the know go. Fresh, interesting and original sushi is served in a refined, pared-down dining area and inviting courtyard. Exposed bricks, a fireplace and quirky prints on the wall add a quietly playful touch. Enjoy a lunchtime bento box or a house special at dinner. The sushi platter served in a boat is a highlight.

Tamboerswinkel

3 De Lorentz Street, Gardens (021 424 0521, www.tamboerswinkel.com). **Open** 7am-10pm Tue-Fri; 7am-4pm Sat. **Main courses** R60. **Map** p46 B6 **125** Café

Simplicity is key at this teeny tiny rustically styled deli and café. Grab a seat and enjoy coffee and farm-style eats of French toast, chicken pie or a steak roll. Chicken and salads takes you back to your mother's kitchen. Alternatively, simply enjoy a charcuterie platter with a glass of wine. Wednesday evenings see regular wine-tasting events.

Vida e Caffè

Mooikloof Centre, 34 Kloof Street, Gardens (021 426 0627, www.caffe.co.za). **Open** 7am-5pm Mon-Sat; 8am-5pm Sun. **Map** p53 G1 **126** Café

Vida e Caffè arguably kicked off Capetonians' obsession with coffee back in the day. Regulars enjoy the friendly vibe, and you'll be greeted with a loud '*obrigado*' once you order at this Portuguese-inspired café. Signature bright red accents, lots of seating along with easy eats of filled rolls, muffins and custard tarts make it a good stop during a busy day.

Pubs & Bars

Asoka

68 Kloof Street, Gardens (021 422 0909, www.asoka.za.com). **Open** 5pm-2am Mon-Sat. **Admission** varies. **Map** p46 B6 ⓲

Sitting near the top of bustling Kloof Street is this plush and colourful eastern oasis. Asoka is renowned for its legendary cocktails, with fresh fruit, herbs and juices whipped up right in front of you. Inviting couches, a tree in the centre of the courtyard and delicious bar bites make this a high-end spot.

Black Ram

13B Kloof Nek Road. Tamboerskloof (021 422 2108). **Open** 5pm-late Mon-Sat. **Map** p46 B6 ⓲

The Power & The Glory is a cool hipster hangout for great coffee and light meals during the day. At the appointed hour, the adjoining bar opens. It's a tiny space but super cosy and you'll soon be treated like a regular. Don't believe all that nonsense about Capetonians being unfriendly; this is such a small bar you won't be able to help but make new mates.

★ Blah Blah Bar

84 Kloof Street, Gardens (072 356 7056, www.blahblahbar.co.za). **Open** *Summer* 3pm-late Tue-Sat; *Winter* 5pm-late Tue-Fri; 3pm-late Sat. **Admission** varies for live music. **Map** p46 B6 ⓲

Located under Erdmann Contemporary (*see p73*), this venue was founded on the premise of providing a sophisticated yet unpretentious space for art lovers to sit and chat about art. The bar provides a space for up-and-coming artists to show their work, and also hosts poetry readings, comedy shows and live music. As for drinks, there are happy hours with specials on cocktails and selected drinks from 5pm to 7pm in summer, and 6-7pm in winter.

Planet Bar

Belmond Mount Nelson Hotel, 76 Orange Street, Gardens (021 483 1000, www.belmond. com/mount-nelson-hotel-cape-town). **Open** noon-late daily. **Map** p53 H2 ⓲

Spilling out from a contemporary, plush and cosy fireside lounge on to a chic conservatory area and then large outdoor terrace overlooking the magnificent hotel gardens, Planet Bar feels right for any mood, season or occasion. The urban-chic decor has a timeless elegance, which suits its setting at the iconic Belmond Mount Nelson Hotel. The drinks menu features a superb selection of the Cape's finest estate wines, along with an extensive classic cocktail list and a large variety of local and international spirits, whiskies and brandies. There's also a thoughtfully planned snack menu created by executive chef Rudi Liebenberg.

Rafiki's

13B Kloof Nek Road, Tamboerskloof (021 426 4731, www.rafikis.co.za). **Open** 11am-late Mon-Sat; 4pm-late Sun. **Map** p46 B6 ⓲

Societi Bistro.

IN THE KNOW HAPPY SNAPPY

A South African innovation has made shopping at markets and with more informal traders far easier. SnapScan is an app where you load your credit card details on to your phone. You simply scan the merchant's code, confirm payment, and you're done. It's making waves in informal and market trading, cutting the need to carry cash around as well as avoiding high credit card fees.

If you haven't worked it out by now, South Africans are sports crazy. This is another place you can head to if you want to catch a big game on a big screen. However, Rafiki's is on the corner of a busy intersection so the balcony is a great place to hang out if you want to watch the world instead of the rugby. There's a series of interconnected rooms and a fireplace. There are pocket-friendly meal deals almost daily.

Snug

Societi Bistro, 50 Orange Street, Gardens (021 424 2100, http://thesnug.co.za). **Open** *Winter* noon-11pm Mon-Sat. *Summer* noon-midnight daily. **Map** p53 G2 ⓬

An intimate space that embraces you with leather wingback armchairs, transporting you back to a time when gentlemen could enjoy a drink and a puff at leisure. This 'secret' space has a fireplace, and the bar opens on to the outside terrace. There's a reasonably priced, well-conceived wine list with everything available by the glass.

Yours Truly

73 Kloof Street, Gardens (021 426 2587, www. yourstrulycafe.co.za). **Open** 6am-11pm Mon-Fri; 7am-11pm Sat; 7am-2pm Sun. **Map** p53 H1 ⓭

Yes, it opens early in the morning but don't let that scare you. This restaurant and bar services the three-star backpacker hotel Once In Cape Town upstairs (which also has its own very cool bar but it closes at 9pm) and you've got to get breakfast somewhere, right? Later in the day and into the evenings it's a bustling, vibey place to hang out and meet people from all over the world. There are occasional music gigs.

Shops & Services

★ Astore

Mooikloof Centre, 34 Kloof Street, Gardens (021 422 2888, www.astoreisgood.com). **Open** 9am-6pm Mon-Fri; 9am-3pm Sat; 10am-3pm Sun. **Map** 276 G4. **Map** p53 G1 ⓮ **Fashion**

Specialising in limited-edition and unusual sports footwear, small-run T-shirts and cult literature on design and popular culture, this achingly trendy and pared-down store is a shrine for the urban cowboy.

Bluecollar Whitecollar

Lifestyle on Kloof, 50 Kloof Street, Gardens (021 422 1593, www.bluecollarwhitecollar.co.za). **Open** 9.30am-6pm Mon-Fri; 9am-3.30pm Sat; 10am-2pm Sun. **Map** p53 G1 ⓯ **Fashion**

The place to go for a well-cut, retro-inspired men's shirt. Textiles are sourced from all over the world before being turned into funky and very wearable items in local factories. The owners are seasoned local designers and this brand has grown, with stores in Joburg, East London and Pretoria.

EXPLORE

Snug.

★ Erdmann Contemporary

*84 Kloof Street, Gardens (021 422 2762, www.
erdmanncontemporary.co.za).* **Open** 10am-8pm
Mon- Fri; 5pm-8pm Sat; or by appointment. **Map**
p46 B6 **136 Gallery**

Owned and curated by renowned art dealer Heidi
Erdmann, this new location is home to contemporary art by South African and some international
artists. There's also a strong emphasis on photography. Head along to the Blah Blah Bar (*see p71*) for a
drink afterwards.

Mabu Vinyl

*2 Rheede Street, Gardens (021 423 7635
www.mabuvinyl.co.za).* **Open** 9am-8pm Mon-
Thur; 9am-7pm Fri; 9am-6pm Sat; 11am-3pm
Sun. **Map** p53 G1 **137 Music**

As charming as the frayed LP covers, Mabu Vinyl is
the aficionado's choice for pre-played records, CDs
and even cassettes. Root around for vintage press-
ings of 1960s favourites (Jimi Hendrix, Carole King,
Janis Joplin, Motown), local nostalgia (Springbok
hits, Gallo Africa) and a wide selection of dance, hip
hop, electronica and trance.

Mr & Mrs

*98 Kloof Street, Gardens (021 424 4387,
www.mrandmrs.co.za).* **Open** 9am-6pm Mon-
Fri; 9am-4pm Sat. **Map** p46 B6 **138 Fashion/
accessories/homewares**

A lovingly curated collection of beautiful things
invites browsing at this hidden-away store. Clothing
from local designers, the owners' own jewellery
range, exquisite throws and cool clutches will have
you whipping out your credit card and kitting out
yourself and your home in exotic new finds.

Present Space

*Lifestyle on Kloof, 50 Kloof Street, Gardens (021
422 2462, www.facebook.com/PRESENTspaceCT).*
Open 10am-7pm Mon-Wed, Fri; 10am-8pm Thur;
10am-6pm Sat; 10am-4pm Sun. **Map** p53 G1 **139
Accessories/homewares**

Magpies, fashionistas and decor mavens can't
help but be drawn to this store that showcases all
things pretty. It's ideal for a gift or housewarming
present, and you'll be sure to leave with something
for yourself too. Bags, pendants, quirky ceramics
and scatter cushions are displayed in minimalistic
wooden boxes.

★ Salon91

*91 Kloof Street, Gardens (082 679 3906,
www.salon91.co.za).* **Open** 10am-6pm Tue-Fri;
10am-6pm Sat; or by appointment. **Map** p53 H1
140 Gallery

Owner Monique du Preez has created an intimate
gallery space with a unique personality. She is on
hand, curating works and arranging exhibitions for
the space, which promotes lesser-known and young
South African artists. New art is continuously being
added, so you're likely to discover interesting works
every time you pop in.

Wellness Warehouse

*Lifestyle on Kloof, 50 Kloof Street, Gardens
(021 487 5454, www.wellnesswarehouse.com).*
Open 8am-7pm Mon, Tue, Thur, Fri; 9am-7pm
Wed; 9am-5pm Sat; 10am-3pm Sun. **Map** p53 G1
141 Health & beauty

This enormous store focuses on natural and organic
products for body and home. Along with a café and
food store, there is a pharmacy, baby section, alternative medicines and small beauty salon.
Other locations Throughout the city.

Wine Concepts

*Lifestyle on Kloof, 50 Kloof Street, Gardens
(021 426 4401, www.wineconcepts.co.za).*
Open 10am-7pm Mon-Fri; 9am-5pm Sat.
Map p53 G1 **142 Food & drink**

Well laid out, with attractive displays and passionate staff too, the Wine Concepts brand is a growing
one, thanks to the excellent wine choices, ranging
from popular big hitters to little-known boutique
offerings. A strong emphasis on food pairing is a big
advantage for those determined to wow their guests,
and it often hosts wine tastings late afternoons.

EAST CITY

Previously a derelict part of Cape Town, the East
City– as it is now known – houses more and more
cool spots in between warehouses and mechanics
shops. Bordering Buitenkant Street, the area
heads eastwards on the lower slopes of Devil's
Peak where it borders on **District Six**, the area
from where the coloured community was forcibly

EXPLORE

THE MELTING POT

A beachside development that's become a magnet for food fans.

If you're keen to experience local flavours, there are few places more authentic than **Biesmiellah's** (see p65) for Cape Malay food. Characterised by the use of aromatic spices, dishes such as samoosas, lamb *denningvleis* and chicken *kalya* are wonderfully moreish. You'll see influence from Indonesia and India in dishes such as lamb Penang curry, dhal and roti at **Bo-Kaap Kombuis** (see p65).

For something intrinsically African, try the **Africa Café** (see p54), where you'll have your pick of everything from Xhosa spinach patties and Mozambican peri-peri prawns to Ethiopian lamb. **Mama Africa** (178 Long Street, 021 424 8634, www.mamaafrica restaurant.co.za) is another pan-African treat, boasting a live (and loud) Congolese band and as much meat as you can eat, all served with a side of samp and pap (mealie meal porridge). There's more African food at **Marco's African Place** (see p67). Popular with tourists as well as locals, the menu includes specialities like local game meat.

You can taste the food of Ethiopia at the beautiful and authentically decorated **Addis in Cape** (see p54), where you are encouraged to eat with your hands, mopping up every drop of sauce with pieces of *injera* (flatbread).

For an all-out extravaganza, head to one of the two **Moyo** restaurants (Kirstenbosch National Botanical Gardens, Rhodes Drive, Newlands, 021 762 9585; Eden on the Bay Shopping Centre, Corner of Otto du Plessis & Sir David Baird Drive, Blouberg Strand, 021 554 9671, www.moyo.co.za). Before the meal you'll be treated to traditional hand-washing and face painting as well as live music. The buffet reads like an African Union of food with *potjies*, curries, fish and vegetables.

Another destination African experience restaurant is **Gold Restaurant** (15 Bennett Street, Green Point, 021 421 4653, www. goldrestaurant.co.za) with a gamut of authentic food choices. The Mali puppet show and Djemba drumming add to the magical atmosphere.

removed during the apartheid years. Their story is told in the **District Six Museum**. The Cape Peninsula University of Technology is on its outskirts so there are a good few unpretentious bars and clubs in the area.

Sights & Museums

★ District Six Museum

25A Buitenkant Street (021 466 7200, www. districtsix.co.za). **Open** 9am-4pm Mon-Sat. **Admission** R30 (self-guided visits); R45 (with guide); R5-R15 reductions. **Map** p53 F5 ⓭

This award-winning community museum lays bare the time in South African history when the ruling government declared District Six a 'whites only' area and over 60,000 of its residents were forcibly taken from their homes and shipped out to the Cape Flats, before their houses were reduced to rubble. The museum includes a memorial hall and a sound archive, and many of the exhibits are interactive, created with the help of former residents; they rely heavily on the medium of storytelling to reconstruct the time of the forced removals and the devastating repercussions it had on the once-vibrant community. A haunting map of District Six painted on the floor of the museum invites evicted residents to indicate with chalk where they once lived.

Restaurants & Cafés

Dias Tavern

15 Caledon Street (021 465 7547, www. diastavern.co.za). **Open** 11.30am-10.30pm Mon-Sat. **Main courses** R85. **Map** p53 F6 ⓮ Portuguese

A local institution, Dias is all about frill-free Portuguese eats and watching the sports on big screen TVs. It's packed to the rafters with regulars enjoying espetada, chorizo, spicy chicken livers and peri peri chicken. The atmosphere is convivial and welcoming, and you're sure to leave with a few more friends than you started with. If you didn't book, it's not a big deal: wait at the bar and shout for the winning team.

Downtown Ramen

103 Harrington Street (021 461 0407). **Open** 5-10pm Mon-Sat. **Main courses** R65. **Map** p53 G5 ⓯ Asian

Atop a steep staircase leading up from Lefty's Dive Bar (*see p76*), you'll find simple benches, classic Japanese posters and a blackboard menu with a handful of flavoursome ramen options. It's pared down, easy eating: vast bowls of steaming noodles in broth are served with pork belly, a soft-boiled egg, spring onion and chilli. Vegetarians can choose a tofu option and a fiery laksa is on the list for the brave. Tasty *bao*-style flat buns are a good way to start. If you're not keen on wine, beer or saké grab a drink from the downstairs bar.

Field Office

37 Barrack Street (021 461 4599, www.field office.co.za). **Open** 7am-4pm Mon-Fri. **Map** p53 G5 ⓰ Café

What was born of a need of the furniture design duo behind Pedersen+Lennard to have a communal space in which to work, meet and showcase their work, is now is a successful café chain with five locations around the city. Wi-Fi, great coffee, good food and a communal vibe is the order of the day at this, the original space, as well as the newer ones. **Other locations** Throughout the city.

★ Haas Collective

19 Buitenkant Street (021 461 1812, http:// haascollective.com). **Open** 7am-5pm Mon-Fri; 8am-3pm Sat, Sun. **Map** p53 F5 ⓱ Café

A recent relocation from the Bo-Kaap to the East City has given Haas bigger premises to showcase art, accessories, homewares and furniture in a striking Victorian building painted its signature dark charcoal. It does a mean coffee and light eats and treats keep regulars happy.

★ Truth Coffee Roasting

36 Buitenkant Street (021 200 0440, www. truthcoffee.com). **Open** 7am-6pm Mon-Thur, Sat; 7am-late Fri; 8am-2pm Sun. **Main courses** R80. **Map** p53 G5 ⓲ Café

You can't argue with the *Guardian* or *Telegraph* naming this coffee roastery one of the top in the world… Behind the hip steampunk interior lies an unmistakable core passion about coffee. The vintage Probat roaster fills the air with the smell of roasted beans that have been meticulously sourced from around the world and there are good things to eat too: egg dishes and pastries for breakfast; burgers, salads and retro hot dogs for lunch. On the first Wednesday of the month, it hosts the Truth Night Market for interesting buys and live music.

EXPLORE

Charly's Bakery.

Pubs & Bars

Lefty's Dive Bar
105 Harrington Street (021 461 0407).
Open 4pm-11pm Mon-Sat. **Map** p53 G5 **149**
The clue is in the name, but it's a compliment, not an insult. Lefty's is one of the coolest spots in Cape Town. There's a small restaurant with a courtyard serving ribs, burgers and even chicken with waffles to soak up the booze. The bar is in a separate room, decorated with vintage collectibles, and it's always packed.

Perserverance Tavern
83 Buitenkant Street (021 461 2440, www. perseverancetavern.co.za). **Open** noon-late Mon-Sat. **Map** p53 H4 **150**
Steeped in history, this is the spot where sailors arriving in the Cape of Good Hope in the early 1800s would head to. In fact, the hugely popular Perseverance Tavern got its malt and liquor licence in 1836, which makes it the oldest still-operating pub in Cape Town. You can watch sport, drink beer, and fill your belly with comforting pub grub. There's indoor and outdoor seating.

Shack
45 De Villiers Street, Zonnebloem (021 461 5892). **Open** noon-4am daily. **Map** p53 H6 **151**
One shouldn't toss the word 'legendary' around lightly, but it certainly applies to this place. In Cape Town, we say 'when all else fails, go to the Shack'. It's not fancy by any means, but it's a super cool place to hang out. There are several bars, an outside area, pool tables, shooters (lots of shooters), and you're likely to bump into interesting people. OK, maybe a few crazies as well, but it's all part of the fun.

Shops & Services

★ Book Lounge
71 Roeland Street (021 462 2425, www. booklounge.co.za). **Open** 8.30am-7.30pm Mon-Thur; 9.30am-6pm Fri, Sat; 10am-4pm Sun. **Map** p53 G4 **152 Books**
A real book-lovers' bookshop. While all the predictable departments are represented, it is the median quality of all the books on the shelves that convinces one of this. No pulp fiction here; rather plenty of comfy seating and even coffee and cakes in the basement. Informed staff are on hand for recommendations and will assist in ordering books too. Regular launches and Saturday morning children's storytime has ensured loyal support from authors and book-lovers alike.
► *Book Lounge is also in charge of organising the Open Book Festival, a celebration of diverse writing attracting an array of local and international authors, which takes place in September every year. Check out http:// openbookfestival.co.za for more information.*

Charly's Bakery
38 Canterbury Street (021 461 5181, www. charlysbakery.co.za). **Open** 8am-5pm Tue-Fri; 8.30am-2pm Sat. **Map** p53 G6 **153 Bakery**
Known for its 'mucking afazing' cakes, this brightly adorned bakery was founded in 1989 and recently gained an international following from its reality baking show *Charly's Cake Angels*. Apart from crazy cakes made in every shape and size to order, you can also get some wonderfully quirky cupcakes as well as delicious quiches and cookies, to eat in or take home.

EXPLORE

Orms

Roeland Square, cnr Roeland & Canterbury streets (021 465 3573, www.orms.co.za). **Open** 8am-6pm Mon-Thur; 8.30am-6pm Fri; 8am-1pm Sat. **Map** p53 H5 **154** **Electronics**

This photography store has everything from the biggest megapixel digicams to top-of-the-range SLR cameras, tripods, camera bags, albums and photography paper. Staff will also help you troubleshoot. Orms Print Room & Framing (66 Roeland Street, 086 166 6767, www.ormsprintroom.co.za) across the road offers excellent photographic printing services.

TABLE MOUNTAIN

The distinctive flat-topped mountain has several hiking trails snaking through a spectacular array of fauna and flora, making it well worth your while to explore up close. Maps are available from the Information Centre at the V&A Waterfront (Dock Road, 021 408 7600) and the Kirstenbosch National Botanical Gardens *(see p115).* You need to respect the mountain: gale force winds can cover it in thick mist, and it's easy to lose your way and become disorientated. Never hike on your own, don't take short cuts and no matter how stable the weather seems before the ascent, take a waterproof windbreaker, map, compass, torch, spare food and enough water, and tell someone where you're going and when you're expected back.

Sights & Museums

Lion's Head & Signal Hill

Follow directions to Signal Hill from top of Kloof Nek Road. **Map** p46 A3 **155**

Rain or shine, day or night, Capetonians love tackling the 40-minute hike up Lion's Head. On full moon nights it's packed with picknickers heading up for an unforgettable experience. While it's a relatively easy hike, it is steep in places with loose rocks, and at the top you'll have to climb up a vertiginous chain ladder. Once at the top you'll be rewarded with sensational views over the City Bowl and Atlantic Seaboard. To the east lies Signal Hill, which offers a far more leisurely experience where you can park and take in the views.

★ Table Mountain Aerial Cableway

Lower Cable Station, Tafelberg Road (021 424 0015, www.tablemountain.net). **Open** Nov-Apr 8am 1st car up daily. May-Oct 8.30am 1st car up daily. Last car up and down vary according to month and weather conditions. **Admission** R240 return; R115 reductions.

Opened in 1929, the Cableway has transported over 24 million visitors to the iconic flat summit. As you head to the cable car embarkation point, you'll see the flimsy contraptions people used to go up in way back when. Today, luckily, two state-of-the art revolving cable cars take visitors 1,067m above sea level to the top in about four minutes. Table Mountain was named one of the New Seven Wonders of Nature in 2012, and it's easy to see why. Meander along the pathways dotted with endemic fynbos leading to the various jaw-dropping vantage points for views of Table Bay, Robben Island and Cape Point, and then head to the café for some nosh. Keep an eye out for rock rabbits or dassies: these cute small furry mammals are said to share DNA with elephants. South Africans get a free ride on their birthdays.

EXPLORE

Atlantic Seaboard

The stretch of coastline that begins moments away from the city centre is a haven for shopaholics and sun-worshippers. De Waterkant's historic cobbled streets are lined with eateries and trendy boutiques. The megalith that is the V&A Waterfront houses a collection of shops that would exhaust the most committed fashionista; it's also a working harbour and home to big sights like the Two Oceans Aquarium. Cape Town Stadium and Green Point Urban Park have become landmarks, while the suburbs that stretch out along the coast become more exclusive the further south you go: from Sea Point's eclectic vibe to the exclusivity of Bantry Bay and Clifton on to trendy Camps Bay. Sundowners with a sea view are a must here. And, for a relaxing coastal drive, head out to Hout Bay with the Twelve Apostles mountains behind you and the sea spray in your hair. Yup, life is pretty good here.

V&A Waterfront.

Don't Miss

1 Clifton's beaches White sand and secluded bays make all those steps down (and up) worthwhile (p94).

2 V&A Waterfront For shopping with a view (p85).

3 De Waterkant Historic buildings, boutiques and a gay vibe (p80).

4 Camps Bay For scenic sundowners (p96).

5 Hout Bay harbour For great fish and chips (p98).

DE WATERKANT

Built in the 19th century by slaves and convicts, this gay-friendly cobbled quarter on the edge of the city centre has undergone a major overhaul, with renovations on historic Somerset Road. Art galleries and boutiques are interspersed with an array of cafés, restaurants and cocktail bars, many in the Cape Quarter open mall buildings, making it an ideal area to explore on foot.

Sights & Museums

Prestwich Slave Memorial
St Andrew's Square. **Open** 8am-5pm Mon-Fri; 8am-1pm Sat, Sun. **Map** p83 F6 **❶**
This modern rectangular ossuary houses the remains of more than 2,500 exhumed bodies that were discovered on a building site in Green Point in 2003. The unmarked graves are believed to have been those of slaves, servants and other underprivileged Cape Town inhabitants from the 17th and 18th centuries, and the memorial pays tribute to these forgotten people and the contribution they made to building the city into what it is today.

Restaurants & Cafés

Beefcakes
Sovereign Quay, 34 Somerset Road (021 425 9019, www.beefcakes.co.za). **Open** 6pm-midnight Mon-Sat. **Burgers** R75. **Map** p83 F5 **❷ Burgers**
Scantily clad waiters showing off their six-packs and drag shows – what's not to love! This over-the-top pink spot has become a favourite for bachelorette parties and fun-loving folk relishing the festive atmosphere. Oh, and it does a mean burger too. If you're not in a meaty mood, there are salads, wraps and moreish nibbles like chilli poppers or nachos.

Beijing Opera
3 Rose Street (021 418 1127, www.facebook.com/TheBeijingOpera). **Open** 11am-3pm, 6-10pm Tue-Sat. **No credit cards.** **Map** p83 F6 **❸**
Dim sum
This teeny tiny spot has already won over locals with its tasty dim sum offerings. While the selection is not huge, Capetonians are getting a taste for these traditional Chinese bites. Alongside the typical variety of steamed dumplings and friend wontons there are bowls of slurp-worthy noodles and daily specials.

★ Loading Bay
30 Hudson Street (021 425 6321, http://loadingbay.co.za). **Open** 8am-5pm Mon-Wed, Fri; 8am-5pm, 6.30pm-late Thur; 8am-4pm Sat; 9am-2pm Sun. **Main courses** R75. **Map** p83 F6 **❹ Café**
This stylish industrial space is kitted out in concrete and wood and features a trendy boutique on its mezzanine level. The food is stellar: all-day brunch dishes run from traditional eggs and bacon to a burger with truffle-salted fries. Salads and sandwiches are fresh and bursting with flavour. On Thursday Loading Bay stays open for dinner and takes things up a notch with the likes of sirloin tagliata, tuna tartare and osso buco.

★ Origin
28 Hudson Street (021 421 1000, www.origin roasting.co.za). **Open** 7am-5pm Mon-Fri; 9am-2pm Sat. **Map** p83 F6 **❺ Coffee shop**
Coffee junkies flock to this converted tobacco house for their daily bean fix. The artisan roastery stocks coffee from across the African continent as well as some of the prime coffee producers in South and Central America and Asia. Single-origin and blended coffees are roasted on site and baristas will suggest the best flavours for your tastes – you can even attend a barista course if you're a real aficionado. And if you're a tea-lover, head to Nigiro tea at the back of the space for a tea ceremony and wide selection of loose-leaf teas.

La Petite Tarte
Cape Quarter, Dixon Street (021 425 9077). **Open** 8am-4.30pm Mon-Fri; 8am-3pm Sat. **Main courses** R55. **Map** p83 F6 **❻ Café**
A most charming corner of Paris awaits at this bijou café, serving Mariage Frères teas, oozingly delicious croque-monsieurs, quiches, pies and salads. Do leave room for a baked treat – the flourless chocolate cake deserves a special mention, while the fruit tarts are seasonally inspired. The owners are on hand to add to the warm welcome and the general sense of bonhomie and *joie de vivre*.

Shops & Services

Africa Nova
Cape Quarter, 72 Waterkant Street (021 425 5123, www.africanova.co.za). **Open** *Summer* 9.30am-5pm Mon-Fri; 10am-5pm Sat; 10am-3pm Sun. *Winter* 10am-5pm Mon-Fri; 10am-3pm Sat. **Map** p83 F6 **❼ Homewares**
This encyclopaedic treasure chest of pan-African objets, local ceramic art and high-end indigenous craft sets the gold standard far above the common curio. Weaving an intoxicating mix of contemporary and tribal design, here you can find original textiles and jewellery. The perfect destination for special and unique pieces for interior designers, international visitors and collectors.

Baraka
Cape Quarter, Dixon Street (021 425 8883, www.barakashop.co.za). **Open** 10am-5.30pm Mon-Sat; 11am-3.30pm Sun. **Map** p83 F6 **❽ Homewares**
This eclectic shop should be your first port of call when going gift-hunting – for yourself or a friend. The owners source everything themselves, from homewares and art to jewellery and accessories. Pick

IT'S A BLING THING
Cape Town has enough gold and diamonds to melt your credit card.

Two big-hitting jewellers have opened museums adjoining their showrooms: at **Shimansky** (Clock Tower, V&A Waterfront, 021 421 2788, www.shimansky.co.za) you can view the history of diamonds in South Africa at its high-tech **Cape Town Diamond Museum** (*see p85*), while the **Museum of Gems and Jewellery**, housed in an 18th-century manor house, provides great insight into the world of diamonds, and forms part of **Prins & Prins** (Cnr Loop and Hout Streets, 021 422 0148, www.prinsandprins. com), a renowned family jeweller in town.

The V&A Waterfront makes an excellent one-stop shop for quality diamonds, tanzanite and other gems: **Olga Jewellery Design Studio** (021 419 8016/7, www.olga jewellers.co.za) creates interesting bespoke pieces; head to **Christoff** (021 421 0184, www.christoff.co.za) for contemporary pieces, while **Charles Greig** (021 418 4515, www.charlesgreig.co.za) also showcases design pieces, along with watches; **Tanzanite International** (Clock Tower, 021 421 5488, www.tanzanite-int.com) specialises in this

coveted blue stone and **Uwe Koetter** (021 421 1039, www.uwekoetter.com) is a well-known, reputable local jeweller.

If you're keen on exploring bling in and around the city as opposed to in a mall, the **Diamond Works** (7 Walter Sisulu Avenue, City Bowl, 021 425 1970, www. thediamondworks.co.za) will customise your jewellery, while **Afrogem** (181 Buitengracht, City Centre, 021 424 0848, www.afrogem. co.za) offers a tour and is a great spot to choose individual gems for your own design. **Jewel Africa** (170 Buitengracht, City Centre, 021 424 5141, http://jewelafrica.com) offers gems and jewellery as well as African art and artefacts, and head to **Destinée Jewellers** (45 Buitengracht, City Centre, 021 426 6789, www.destinee.co.za) for a look at the diamond-cutting process before purchasing tanzanite or diamonds, jewellery or African crafts. **Coeval** (96A St George's Mall, City Centre, 021 424 1183, www. coeval.co.za), meanwhile, is notable for classic pieces as well as interesting, more modern collectibles.

EXPLORE

EXPLORE

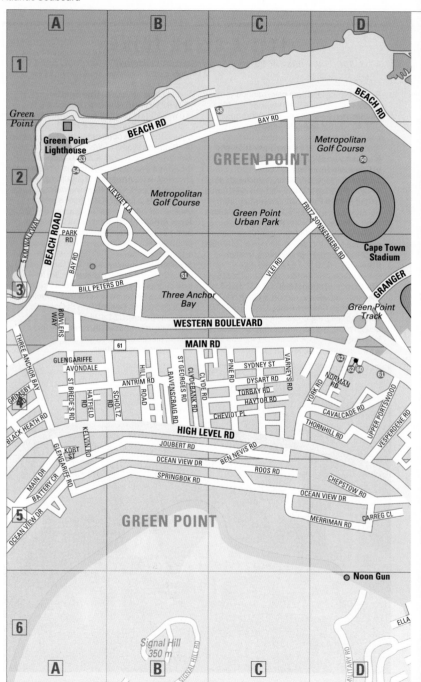

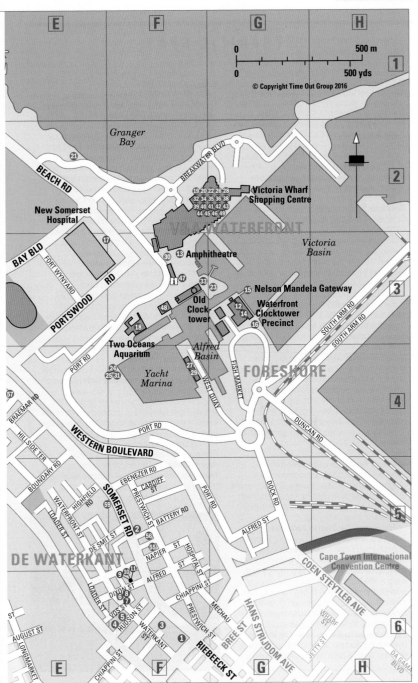

© Copyright Time Out Group 2016

Granger Bay

BEACH RD

New Somerset Hospital

BAY BLD

PORTSWOOD RD

FORT WYNYARD

BREAKWATER BLVD

19 20 22 26 28
32 34 35 36 38
39 40 41 42 43
44 45 46 49

Victoria Wharf Shopping Centre

V&A WATERFRONT

Victoria Basin

30

13 **Amphitheatre**

47

i

33

23

15 **Nelson Mandela Gateway**

12

48 **Old Clock-tower**

14

16 **Waterfront Clocktower Precinct**

Two Oceans Aquarium

18

Alfred Basin

FORESHORE

SOUTH ARM RD

SOUTH ARM RD

PORT RD

24
25 31

Yacht Marina

27
29

WEST QUAY

FISH MARKET

57

DUNCAN RD

BRAEMAR RD

HILLSIDE TER

WESTERN BOULEVARD

PORT RD

PORT RD

DOCK RD

ALFRED ST

BOUNDARY RD

EBENEZER RD

CARDIFF ST

WATERFRONT ST

HIGHFIELD RD

PRESTWICH ST

BATTERY RD

59

LOADER ST

DE SMIT ST

SOMERSET RD

2

56

Cape Town International Convention Centre

COEN STEYLER AVE

WHARF

55

NAPIER ST

HOSPITAL ST

DE WATERKANT

ALFRED

9 10 11

DIXON ST

6

5

CHIAPPINI ST

PRESTWICH ST

MECHAU

HANS STRIJDOM AVE

AUGUST ST

LONGMARKET

LOADER ST

VOS ST

7
8

4

HUDSON ST

WATERKANT ST

3

1

BREE ST

JETTY ST

6

DA GAMA BLVD

CHIAPPINI ST

RIEBEECK ST

EXPLORE

E   F   G   H

SYBARITIC SPAS
Lie back and relax.

After all that sightseeing, eating, drinking and shopping, you need a place to unwind. Luckily Cape Town has some excellent spas to choose from. Newly opened **Camelot Spa Cape Sun** (Southern Sun Cape Sun, Strand Street, City Centre, 021 426 2644, www. camelotspa.co.za) is a sophisticated place of pampering, with a couples treatment room as well as an indoor splash pool, steam shower and a relaxation area.

Another new spa in town is **Mangwanani Boutique Spa** at the Southern Sun The Cullinan (1 Cullinan Street, Foreshore, 0860 55 00 55, 021 415 4075/6, www. mangwanani.co.za), with its original African therapies. The signature Korean Scrub with African Rituals treatment begins with a soak in a glass spa bath followed by an extensive full-body exfoliation. And a pedi by the pool with a glass of bubbly is pure indulgence.

Earning top marks for the most spectacular spa location – on the 19th floor of the Westin Cape Town – **Heavenly Spa** (Convention Square, Lower Long Street, 021 412 9999, www.heavenlyspa.co.za) offers body wraps, facials and massages in its pared down, modern setting. The Africology products provide an authentic touch. Swim a few lengths in the lap pool or relax in the sauna – both with views of the harbour from floor-to-ceiling windows; then wind down in the relaxation room with more stunning views!

Set by the seaside, the **Ginkgo Health & Wellness Spa** (Winchester Mansions, 221 Beach Road, Sea Point, 021 434 2351, www.winchester.co.za) provides classic therapeutic treatments encompassing modern and ancient practices. The signature Elixir massage with melting shea butter will leave you in a sure state of bliss. Dr Babor facials are another highlight.

The **Spa at The Twelve Apostles** (Victoria Road, Camps Bay, 021 437 9000, www.12 apostleshotel.com), which is built into the mountain rock, boasts some of the city's most unusual spaces to enjoy pampering. A dip in the indoor, cave-like hydrotherapy pools is the perfect way to begin a visit. There's also a Rasul chamber (for mud cleansing treatments) as well as mountain gazebos overlooking the ocean for massages – you'll be pampered to pieces here. The in-house B|Africa products use African plant extracts that are said to calm, energise or detoxify.

For more all-out indulgence, try the **One&Only Cape Town Spa** (One&Only Cape Town, Dock Road, V&A Waterfront, 021 431 5888, http://capetown.oneandonlyresorts. com). Set on its own spa island, it's an easy place to while away a day amid the Zen-like vibe. Guests are treated to herbal teas, smoothies and snacks in the relaxation room before being whisked away to treatment rooms filled with flowers. Treatments are aimed at unwinding, restoring or elevating body and soul with scrubs, wraps, facials, massages and various other pampering treats. The male and female steam rooms, saunas and jet pools are the cherry on top.

The bold, floral design and tranquil surroundings of the **Librisa Spa** (Belmond Mount Nelson Hotel, 76 Orange Street, 021 483 1550, www.belmond.com/ mount-nelson-hotel-cape-town) ensure an unparalleled sense of being spoiled, while Dermalogica and Africology products ensure top-quality pampering. Housed in three converted Victorian buildings, Librisa Spa also has a wonderful conservatory for a relaxing herbal tea after your treatment.

Part of an internationally renowned Thai spa group, **Angsana Spa Vineyard Hotel** (Colinton Road, Newlands, 021 674 5005, www. angsanaspa.com) offers a true taste of the Orient. Specialised face and body treatments use wonderfully aromatic ingredients such as ylang ylang, jasmine and frangipani. Thai therapists are renowned for their firm pressure and each last knot will succumb to their professional touch. Afterwards, relax on the treatment room's verandah overlooking the gardens and mountain while enjoying fresh fruit and ginger tea.

up a real Panama hat, hand-woven Zulu basketry or a quirky retro poster or two. New stock constantly arrives, so you'll be freshly beguiled at every visit.

★ Cape Quarter

27 Somerset Road (021 421 1111, capequarter. co.za). **Open** 9am-6pm Mon-Fri; 9am-4pm Sat; 10am-2pm Sun. **Map** p83 F6 ❾ **Mall**

This open-air mall consists of two buildings spread over a heritage area. The most recent renovation, accessible from Somerset Road, houses a Spar supermarket as well as boutiques selling everything from shoes to toys. There's also a lovely piazza area with alfresco restaurants. Over the road on Dixon and Waterkant streets sits the original Cape Quarter mall, with a handful of quality craft shops and restaurants. Strolling the cobbles between shops and cafés is very pleasant – a definite improvement on the usual mall experience.

Nap Living

Cape Quarter, 27 Somerset Road (021 421 6482, napliving.co.za). **Open** 9am-6pm Mon-Fri; 9am-4pm Sat; 10am-2pm Sun. **Map** p83 F6 ❿ **Homewares**

The kind of homeware shop that makes you want to start again and redecorate your entire house, Nap has some furniture but mainly stocks smaller interiors accessories. Muted greys, whites, glass and wood dominate, from vases and basketware to driftwood mirrors and creative lampshades. Accessories, jewellery, a small leisure clothing range and linens complete the stylish picture.

Pierre Cronje

Cape Quarter, 27 Somerset Road (021 421 1249, www.pierrecronje.co.za). **Open** 9.30am-5pm Mon-Fri; 9.30am-3pm Sat; 10am-2pm Sun. **Map** p83 F6 ⓫ **Homewares**

This established furniture business has built up a devoted clientele for its speciality: top-quality handcrafted furniture with pared town style. Here you will find no gimmicks, only durable, sturdy antiques of tomorrow and a no-holds-barred celebration of the timeless allure of wood.

V&A WATERFRONT

An inevitable stop for any visitor to Cape Town, the V&A Waterfront (021 408 7600, www.waterfront.co.za) on the Foreshore has something for pretty much everyone. The **Two Oceans Aquarium** and **Cape Wheel** appeal across generations; there are bars and restaurants aplenty; and the **Victoria Wharf** is a haven for shoppers.

Alternatively, you can simply stroll the dockside watching the working harbour. In 1860, Queen Victoria's second son, Alfred, tipped a ceremonial bucket load of stones into the sea, thus initiating the construction of Cape Town's

harbour. Today it's also the departure point for ferries to **Robben Island** and the museum that bears its name. The newly completed **Watershed** houses an inspiring array of arts, crafts, clothing and jewellery, If you're interested in learning more about the Waterfront's history, join a two-hour walking tour (book at the information kiosk).

Sights & Museums

Cape Town Diamond Museum

Level 1, the Clock Tower (021 421 2488, http:// capetowndiamondmuseum.org). **Open** 9am-9pm daily. **Admission** R50. **Map** p83 G3 ⓬

This glittering small museum is a homage to the diamond, and it's no surprise it's owned by Shimansky (*see p81* **It's a Bling Thing**), one of the top jewellery retailers in the country. A wander through teaches you about how diamonds are formed, the history of the diamond industry in South Africa since diamonds were first found in 1867; you can also see a replica of the world's largest diamond, the Cullinan. The tour neatly leads you to the shop's showroom where you can stock up on some bling of your own.

★ Cape Wheel

V&A Waterfront (021 418 2502, www.capewheel. co.za). **Open** noon-7pm Tue-Thur; 11am-10pm Fri; 10am-10pm Sat; 10am-8pm Sun. **Tickets** R100; R50 reductions; free under-4s. **Map** p83 F3 ⓭

See the city from a new vantage point as the Cape Wheel takes you on a sky-high 15-minute trip. Sunset rides are a favourite, as Table Mountain, Table Bay, Cape Town Stadium and Robben Island come into relief against the pink last rays of the sun.

Clock Tower Precinct

V&A Waterfront (021 405 4500). **Map** p83 G3 ⓮

Now a maritime mall-cum-heritage site, the brick-red octagonal clock tower was built in 1882 as the port captain's office, so that he could check the comings and goings in the harbour from the peace and comfort of his mirrored quarters. These days its precinct houses the ruins of the Chavonnes Battery,

---

IN THE KNOW CRUISES

See the Waterfront from a different angle from one of the many boat operators on Quay 5. There are a variety of cruise options available, from harbours to sundowners, and lunch or dinner cruises.

Operators include **Classic Cape Charters** (021 418 0782, capecharters. co.za), **Waterfront Adventures** (021 418 3234, waterfrontadv.co.za) and **Waterfront Charters** (021 418 3168, www.waterfrontcharters.co.za).

EXPLORE

Reuben's Restaurant. *See p88.*

one of the oldest European structures in the country (dating from 1714 to 1725), which was excavated nearby a couple of years ago.

★ Robben Island Museum

Ferries depart from Nelson Mandela Gateway, Clock Tower Precinct (021 413 4200, www.robben-island.org.za). **Open** *Museum* 7.30am-7pm daily. *Ferries* 9am, 11am daily, weather permitting; book in advance. **Admission** *Ferry & museum* R300. **Map** p83 G3 ⑮

A symbol both of centuries of cruel oppression and the triumph of hope, Robben Island has become synonymous with the former and first leader of the free and democratic South Africa, Nelson Rolihlahla

Mandela, who spent 18 years in its maximum security prison. For nearly 400 years the island served as a place of banishment – not just for supposed criminals but also for many other unwanted members of society, including lepers and the mentally ill. It was declared a World Heritage Site in 1999. The blinding-white limestone quarry, where political prisoners toiled away doing hard labour in the blazing heat, and Mandela's claustrophobic cell in the prison are but a few of the harrowing reminders of the injustices carried out during the apartheid era, and of the final defeat of the regime. Visits are weather-dependent as the sea can get quite choppy for the ferry ride to the island. The museum is closed on 1 May.

SA Maritime Museum

Union Castle Building (021 405 2880, www. iziko.org.za/museums/maritime-centre). **Open** 10am-5pm daily. **Admission** R20; R10 reductions; free under-5s. **Map** p83 G3 ⑯

This small museum, appropriately located at the V&A Waterfront, displays models of ships that have come and gone from this port city over the last hundred years or so. It boasts the largest collection of model ships in the country as well as some interesting information on the whaling industry, local wrecks and the history of Table Bay.

★ Springbok Experience

Portswood Road (021 418 4741, www.sarugby. co.za). **Open** 10am-6pm daily. **Admission** R65; R40 reductions. **Map** p83 E/F3 ⑰

IN THE KNOW
WHERE IT'S ART

Work is under way on the giant project that is in the process of transforming the historic grain silo at the V&A Waterfront into one of the most exciting art museums on the continent. The **Zeitz Museum of Contemporary Art Africa (Zeitz MOCAA)** is set to open at the end of 2016, with 6,000 square metres of exhibition space over nine floors. Until its opening, the Zeitz MOCAA Pavilion at North Wharf will showcase some items from the collection.

South Africans are mad about rugby, and this passion comes to life at this brand-new rugby museum. It boasts over 60 audio-visual displays as well as historic trophies and other memorabilia. Interactive areas where the kids and dads (and mums too) can kick and pass the ball add to the fun. Buy a Springbok jersey before you leave so you too can scream 'Go Bokke!' at the next game.

★ Two Oceans Aquarium

Dock Road (021 418 3823, www.aquarium.co.za). **Open** 9.30am-6pm daily. **Admission** R118; R57-R92 reductions; free under-4s. **Map** p83 F3 ⑱
This underwater wonderland offers some of the most bizarre sea life you might ever care to meet – schools of unicorn fish, lumo jellyfish and honeycombed moray eels all get their moment in the spotlight, and there's an abundance of cuter creatures too. Still capitalising on the popularity of the little clownfish from *Finding Nemo*, there's a tubular tank featuring about a zillion of the colourful critters swimming around where children can have their picture taken. Kids also love the touch tank where they can gently poke and prod seaweed and starfish. There's also a colony of penguins living in a rocky river-like environment, but the I&J Predator Tank is the undisputed *pièce de résistance*, with its mob of ocean predators, including ragged tooth sharks, blue stingrays and black mussel crackers, all drifting together in seeming harmony – until feeding time comes round, that is. While the children run around trying to keep up with all the action, take a seat and stare at the gently oscillating kelp forest – it provides instant calm for the weary parent.

Restaurants & Cafés

Balducci

Victoria Wharf (021 421 6002/3, www.balduccis. co.za). **Open** 9am-late daily. **Main courses** R140. **Map** p83 F2 ⑲ International
Plush, modern interiors, expansive alfresco seating and a standalone sushi bar are all part of the attraction at this popular spot. Italian fare is the standout, with pizza, pasta and grills. Sushi, Asian tapas and great burgers hit the spot with clean presentation and bags of flavour.

Belthazar

Victoria Wharf (021 421 3753/6, www.belthazar. co.za). **Open** noon-11pm daily. **Main courses** R165. **Map** p83 F2 ⑳ Steakhouse
This refined spot boasts classic decor and meaty fare. A vast bar dominates the space, and cases of wine are stacked to the ceiling, revealing a glimpse of the award-winning collection. There's even an on-site wine shop selling bottles from the 600-strong list. Choose from grain- or grass-fed beef as well as an array of seafood dishes. South African game meats are also on the menu if you're keen for a taste of something different – crocodile, anyone?

★ Grand Café & Beach

Granger Bay Road (off Beach Road), Granger Bay (021 425 0551, www.grandafrica.com). **Open** noon-late Tue-Sun. **Main courses** R120. **Map** p83 E2 ㉑ Mediterranean
Over-the-top, sand-in-your-toes beach-side luxury has come to town at the Grand. Recently reopened after an extensive revamp, this warehouse and beach space remains a fabulous place to lunch, have sundowners or feast the night away. The ambience is always celebratory in this see-and-be-seen spot where you can enjoy Mediterranean fare, cocktails and bucketloads of bubbly with the ocean glimmering at your feet.
Other location Grand Cafe & Society, 35 Victoria Road, Camps Bay (021 438 4253).

Melissa's The Food Shop

Victoria Wharf (021 418 0255, www.melissas. co.za). **Open** 9am-9pm daily. **Map** p83 G2 ㉒ Café
Putting home-style food on the map made Melissa's famous. Today there isn't as much of a novelty factor, but you can still enjoy breakfasts, bakery items and lunch from the freshly prepared harvest table – the likes of scotch eggs with bacon jam or smoked salmon, cream cheese and caper salsa on toasted sourdough, or stock up on treats to take home.
Other locations throughout the city.

Mondiall

Alfred Mall (021 418 3002, www.mondiall.co.za). **Open** 9am-10pm daily. **Main courses** R165. **Map** p83 G3 ㉓ Brasserie
One of the newest restaurants at the V&A, Mondiall looks sophisticated: think black leather, an open kitchen, warehouse styling and avant-garde lighting. The menu is a refreshing take on the classics. Hearty breakfasts and speciality coffees are followed by easy eats such a coq au vin, beer-braised beef short rib, salads and line-caught fish. The tapas menu encourages lingering on sunny afternoons, while the burger bar keeps things buzzing.

★ Nobu

One&Only Cape Town, Dock Road (021 431 5111, http://capetown.oneandonlyresorts.com/cuisine/ nobu.aspx). **Open** 6pm- midnight daily. **Main courses** R200. **Map** p83 F4 ㉔ Japanese fusion
Opulent interiors and impeccable service set this international restaurant brand apart. Known for combining Japanese and South American flavours, Nobu offers exquisite tastes. Start in the upstairs bar with a sake cocktail before moving downstairs to a loud Japanese greeting of 'Irashamase' from all the staff. Lobster and scallop tacos, ceviche, anticucho skewers and tempura are highlights, while the range of sushi is probably the best in town. Wagyu beef features in a variety of dishes, from flambé to tartare and tataki. Bento boxes are always a favourite, and the chef's menu is a great way of exploring what the restaurant has to offer. *Photos p88.*

EXPLORE

Reuben's Restaurant

*One&Only Cape Town, Dock Road (021 431 4511,
http://capetown.oneandonlyresorts.com/cuisine/
reubens.aspx).* **Open** 6.30am-10.30pm daily.
Main courses R165. **Map** p83 F4 **25** **Global**
For a contemporary take on local cuisine – with an
international touch – head to Reuben's at One&Only
Cape Town hotel. Sister restaurant to the epony-
mous spot in Franschhoek, Reuben's is run by well-
known South African chef Reuben Riffel. West Coast
mussels and oysters make for great starters, along
with generous sharing plates of pork belly, Karoo
lamb knuckle and crispy squid with garam masala.
Mains might be pasture-reared Chalmar beef fillet
or whole crayfish. Sommelier Luvo Ntezo is on hand
with excellent pairing recommendations, while regular wine dinners are a great way to sample some of
the excellent vintages in the cellar. *Photo p86.*

Sevruga

*Quay 5, Victoria Wharf (021 421 5134,
www.sevruga.co.za).* **Open** 11.30am-11pm daily.
Main courses R130. **Map** p83 G2 **26** **Global**
This swish harbour-front restaurant is famous for
its sushi and dim sum, yet there is so much more on to
try. Dishes have a South African, Mediterranean and
Asian focus with the likes of springbok carpaccio,
tiger prawn with ponzu dressing and smoked buf-
falo mozzarella with pesto to start. Mains of truffle
fillet, Asian prawn curry and slow-braised lamb are
hearty and flavourful.

Signal Restaurant

*Cape Grace Hotel, West Quay Road (021 410
7080, www.signalrestaurant.co.za).* **Open**
6am-10pm daily. **Main courses** R170. **Map**
p83 F4 **27** **South African**
Louis Ghost chairs, crystal chandeliers and discreet
nautical structural elements in wood add to Signal's
appeal as one of Cape Town's top hotel restaurants.
The heritage-inspired menu draws on the Cape's
history as a trading post for Europe, Africa and the
Far East. Pickled yellowtail with apricot chutney
and bobotie-spiced springbok are sophisticated
nods to traditional Cape Malay dishes. Wine-pairing
tasting menus showcase executive chef Malika van
Reenen's talents wonderfully.

Willoughby & Co

*Victoria Wharf (021 418 6116, www.
willoughbyandco.co.za).* **Open** noon-9.45pm daily.
Main courses R110. **Map** p83 G2 **28** **Seafood**
It's sushi all the way at this mall favourite and
always packed with punters enjoying California
rolls, sushi salads and an excellent array of Japanese
hot and cold dishes. You'd be forgiven for thinking it
only serves Asian fare but you can add line-caught
fish, calamari, fish cakes and seafood curry to the
list. A seat at the sushi bar is a good vantage point
from which to watch the chefs in action and the passing parade of shoppers.

Nobu. *See p87.*

Pubs & Bars

★ Bascule Bar

Cape Grace Hotel, West Quay (021 410 7100, www.capegrace.com). **Open** 10am-2am daily. **Map** p83 F4 ㉙

On the water's edge of the marina in the V&A Waterfront, Bascule is the perfect setting to take in the sights and sounds of the city. The generous tapas menu is complemented by the finest Cape wines, plus cocktails and a whisky collection – there are more than 500 from around the world. Learn about the history of whisky at daily tutored tastings. There's live music at weekends.

Mitchell's Scottish Ale House

Corner East Pier and Dock Road (021 419 5074, www.mitchells-ale-house.com). **Open** 11am-1.30am daily. **Map** p83 F3 ㉚

The V&A Waterfront is one of Cape Town's most popular tourist attractions, and it's not hard to understand why when you sit at the outdoor terrace at Mitchell's and marvel at the magnificent view of the mountain and the working harbour. The Ale House offers plenty of beers on tap; for a novelty, try one of the giant cocktails. Share it with a friend, or try to finish it on your own.

Vista Bar & Lounge

One&Only Cape Town, Dock Road (021 431 5888, http://oneandonlycapetown.com). **Open** 6am-2am daily. **Map** p83 F4 ㉛

With spectacular views of Table Mountain, this striking space houses a luxury bar and lounge providing a seamless flow of activity from morning to noon and then late on into the night. As the evening wears on, the ambience grows more sultry and seductive, with atmospheric live music and a fabulous collection of cocktails, from classic creations to new inventive blends.

Shops & Services

Ben Sherman

Victoria Wharf (021 425 8996, www.bensherman.com). **Open** 9am-9pm daily. **Map** p83 F2 ㉜ **Fashion**

This iconic British men's retailer continues to set style standards in the Cape. Not only do the signature shirts – whether relaxed or formal – manage to reflect the brand's image, but the accessories and other clothing retain the colourful mod look that Ben Sherman is famous for.

Cape Union Mart

Quay Four Adventure Centre (021 425 4559, www.capeunionmart.co.za). **Open** 9am-9pm daily. **Map** p83 F3 ㉝ **Outdoors**

Whatever your outdoorsy heart desires can be found at this retailer, whether you're an urban warrior or Bear Grylls wannabe. The gear here is good quality: all the clothing, shoes and tents, and every gadget and gizmo that you could possibly need to make your outdoor adventure a success.

Other locations throughout the city.

Carrol Boyes Shop

Victoria Wharf (021 418 0595, www.carrolboyes.com). **Open** 9am-9pm daily. **Map** p83 F2 ㉞ **Homewares**

The go-to shop for wedding gifts, Carrol Boyes offers a seemingly endless array of pewter and stainless steel kitchen accessories and home-decor items. Designs are distinctively chunky and unusual.

Cotton On

Victoria Wharf (021 418 1057, www.cottonon.co.za). **Open** 9am-9pm daily. **Map** p83 G2 ㉟ **Fashion**

One of the most recent additions of big-name high street retailers to reach South Africa's shores, Australian brand Cotton On offers a fast fashion fix for trendy young things, with good jeans, bright separates and easy-to-wear jackets. Regular sales and specials keep shoppers hungry for more.

Country Road

Victoria Wharf (021 405 4300, www.woolworths.co.za/store/country-road). **Open** 9am-9pm daily. **Map** p83 G2 ㊱ **Fashion**

This Australian fashion brand is available at Woolworths stores in South Africa but the Waterfront boasts a large standalone shop. Stylish separates that are classically cut are a hallmark, with signature blues always on the rails. There's also a small kids and homewares section.

★ Everard Read Gallery

3 Portswood Road, V&A Waterfront (021 418 4527, www.everard-read-capetown.co.za). **Open** 9am-6pm Mon-Fri; 9am-1pm Sat. **Map** p83 F3 ㊲ **Gallery**

South Africa's oldest commercial gallery, Everard Read was founded in Johannesburg in 1913. South African artists are the core focus in the plush space, with group as well as solo exhibitions well worth viewing. Illustrious contemporary artists such as Beezy Bailey, Ricky Dyaloki, Vusi Khamalo and Deborah Bell, and sculptors Dylan Lewis and Percy Konqobe are on the books, as well as local masters like Cecil Skotnes and Lucy Sibiya.

Exclusive Books

Victoria Wharf (021 419 0905, www.exclusivebooks.com). **Open** 9am-9pm daily. **Map** p83 G2 ㊳ **Books**

The big daddy of bookstores with a catalogue to match. You will find not only the newest and biggest selection of current books and magazines, but also slick stationery and a damn fine cup of coffee too (in this and other larger branches).

Other locations throughout the city.

EXPLORE

EXPLORE

Fabiani

Victoria Wharf (021 425 1810). **Open** 9am-9pm daily. **Map** p83 F2 ❸ **Fashion**

A long-time staple among style-seekers, Fabiani is the go-to institution for high-end wardrobe construction. The shop is heavy on labels and it's the place to go for that investment suit.

Jo Malone

Victoria Wharf (021 425 2258, www.jomalone. co.za). **Open** 9am-9pm daily. **Map** p83 F2 ❹
Perfumerie

Perfumier of choice for those in the know, Jo Malone offers an array of pure scents for body and home. Head here for a luxurious in-house treatment of scrub, body wash, massage, lotion and cologne while sipping on bubbly before deciding on your favourites. Seasonal perfumes are creative: think blackberry and bay or peony and blush suede. Round off the experience by taking home some scented candles.

Louis Vuitton

Victoria Wharf (021 407 9500, www.louis vuitton.com). **Open** 9am-9pm daily. **Map** p83 G2 ❹ **Fashion**

International big-hitting fashion and accessories brands have found their way to South Africa's shores, and few are more coveted than those with an LV monogram. The window display at this exclusive spot prevents the plebs from peering inside, but once there you can expect professional service while you browse bags, shoes and more.

MAC Cosmetics

V&A Waterfront (021 421 4886, www. maccosmetics.com). **Open** 9am-9pm daily. **Map** p83 G2 ❹ **Health & beauty**

Don't be intimidated by the impeccably made up, all-in-black staff at this cult make-up brand's store; they're here to help you with all your make-up needs: from applying foundation the right way to perfecting your liquid eyeliner flip, they've got it sussed. Book a makeover to learn some new tricks or for a special-occasion look and offset it against your purchase.

Made in SA

Victoria Wharf (021 419 4246). **Open** 9am-9pm daily. **Map** p83 G2 ❹ **Crafts**

A far cry from kitschy souvenir shops, Made in SA offers original arts and crafts made by local crafters and designers. Grab a quirky T-shirt, brightly printed canvas bag or piece of jewellery; or decorate your home with a vase, ceramic bowl or funky light.

Mango

Victoria Wharf, V&A Waterfront (021 418 0916, shop.mango.com/ZA/women). **Open** 9am-9pm daily. **Map** p83 F2 ❹ **Fashion**

The cult Spanish brand remains the twentysomething party girl's fashion life-saver, and this sparkling store is filled with fashionable must-haves.

Nespresso

Victoria Wharf (021 419 8941, www.nespresso. com/za/en). **Open** 9am-9pm daily. **Map** p83 F/G2 ❹ **Food & drink**

If it's good enough for George Clooney, then it's good enough for us… Capetonians love their coffee, and this store is always buzzing (could it be too much caffeine?). Taste new arrivals and learn about their flavour profiles before stocking up on your favourites.

Out of this World

Victoria Wharf (021 419 3246, http://outofthis world.co.za). **Open** 9am-9pm daily. **Map** p83 G2 ❹ **Crafts**

One of the most original African souvenir shops, Out of this World stocks fascinating items from all over the continent. If a ceremonial mask or headdress is too much, opt for beads, rings, figurines and *kikois*. Printed textiles are also a good bet, as are carpets and tableware.

Vaughan Johnson's Wine & Cigar Shop

Dock Road (021 419 2121, www.vaughanjohnson. com). **Open** 9am-6pm Mon-Fri; 9am-5pm Sat; 10am-5pm Sun. **Map** p83 F3 ❹ **Food & drink**

Expertise and enthusiasm are the watchwords at this wine store. A passion for showcasing South African wines is paramount and Vaughan's Top 100 list is an excellent guide for making a wine selection.

★ Watershed

17 Dock Road (021 408 7840, www.waterfront. co.za/Shop/watershed). **Open** 10am-6pm daily. **Map** p83 F3 ❹ **Gallery/crafts**

A brand-new bright and airy warehouse space showcases the work of over 150 artists and artisans. Capetonians love spending a morning browsing through designer clothing, jewellery and homewares, while tourists head for the curios, which are a cut above the usual that is found elsewhere. All the tenants have been carefully curated to include a broad spectrum of merchandise.

YDE

Victoria Wharf (021 425 6232, www.yde.co.za). **Open** 9am-9pm daily. **Map** p83 G2 ❹ **Fashion**

Young Designers Emporium continues to pioneer the mass-marketing of edgy with its always fresh, hipper-than-hip apparel. The store hosts ranges from over 50 local designers, from fashion to accessories and footwear.

GREEN POINT & MOUILLE POINT

Heading out from the V&A Waterfront, you'll pass **Mouille Point**, named after the French term for an anchoring ground. The storm-ridden coast here caused ships to run aground and a project to build a breakwater for safe anchoring was begun in the 18th century (it was eventually abandoned). The **Green Point lighthouse** – often mistakenly referred to as the Mouille Point lighthouse – provides a bright red-and-white candy-striped beacon both for the neighbourhood and ships at sea. The **Blue Train Park** (*see p149*) is a lovely spot for the little ones, while the **Green Point Urban Park** is the finest park in Cape Town. The **Cape Town Stadium**, built for the 2010 Fifa World Cup, dominates the space next to the park.

The **Promenade** also starts in Mouille Point, snaking along the coastline all the way to the end of Sea Point, providing space for a scenic stroll. You'll often find art installations along the way as well as children's jungle gyms and an outdoor gym on the lawns.

Sights & Museums

Cape Town Stadium
Access from Fritz Sonnenberg Road & Granger Bay Boulevard, Green Point (Tours 021 417 0120). **Tours** 10am, noon, 2pm Tue-Sat. **Admission** R45; R17 reductions. **Map** p82 D2 ⑩
Built for the 2010 Fifa World Cup, this 55,000-seat stadium has become a beacon on the Cape Town landscape. It cost a whopping R4.4billion and took 33 months finish. Today it's the home ground of Ajax Cape Town football club, and it has also hosted big music names such as U2, Red Hot Chili Peppers and, ahem, Justin Bieber, as well as conferencing events and rugby matches.

★ FREE Green Point Urban Park
Entrances in Bay Road & Bill Peters Drive, Green Point (www.gprra.co.za/green-point-urban-park. html). **Open** 7am-7pm daily. **Map** p82 B3 ⑪
A magnificent addition to Cape Town's green spaces, the Green Point Urban Park offers respite from city stresses. Endemic plants, including fynbos, can be seen here, and information boards provide background to many points of interest. There's an enclosed play area for small children, and a massive open one for bigger kids. Park visitors can play and learn with the water wheel, medicine garden, Khoisan *kraal* (village), labyrinth, sundial and open-air gym equipment. Acres of lawn, spotless toilet facilities and winding pathways add to the delights.

Restaurants & Cafés

★ El Burro
81 Main Road, Green Point (021 433 2364, www.elburro.co.za). **Open** noon-11.30pm Mon-Sat. **Main courses** R95. **Map** p82 D4 ⑫ **Mexican**
Waitresses clad in colourful skirts and headscarves offer friendly service and are quick with recommendations at this bright and bustling eaterie. There's no Tex-Mex here, just fresh-as-can-be eats made with real-deal Mexican ingredients – tortillas are made by hand every day, for example. Ceviche and fish tacos are zesty favourites, while the pork *carnitas* are addictive. There is a range of tequilas and mezcals as well as a selection of tangy cocktails that use them as ingredients. Booking is essential.

EXPLORE

Promenade

EXPLORE

Butcher Shop and Grill

★ Butcher Shop and Grill

125 Beach Road, Mouille Point (021 434 0813, www.thebutchershop.co.za). **Open** noon-10.30pm daily. **Main courses** R150. **Map** p82 A2 ⊕ Steakhouse

This Joburg stalwart has recently opened in Cape Town and is proving as successful as its up-country sibling. It's all about the meat here, and punters can go up to the butcher's counter to choose their own cut to be grilled to perfection. There are many South African classics on the menu too, such as salted lamb ribs, oxtail and venison pie. The excellent wine list and stylish contemporary decor add to an upscale experience. A bonus is that the butcher's is open late.

Caffe Neo

South Seas Building, 129 Beach Road, Mouille Point (021 433 0849). **Open** 7am-7pm daily. **Main courses** R65. **Map** p82 A2 ⊕ Café

End your walk on the Promenade with a bite to eat at this breezy Greek eaterie. The deck looks out on to the lighthouse and ocean, while the long communal wooden table inside provides a home-from-home ambience. Meze and sandwiches are good lunchtime options, while yoghurt with pistachios and honey is a breakfast favourite. If you're up for it, end with the traditional sweet treat of baklava.

Izakaya Matsuri

The Rockwell, 32 Prestwich Street, Green Point (021 421 4520, www.izakayamatsuri.com). **Open** 11.30am-3pm, 5pm-10pm Mon-Sat. **Map** p83 F5 ⊕ Japanese

A hidden gem if there ever was one, this tiny Japanese tapas and sushi bar serves authentic fare made with love by chef and owner Arata Koga. The open kitchen faces on to a small dining area, and it's best to order as you go. Sushi is deliciously fresh with some original choices, including baked and tempura rolls. The highlight is the signature *aburi* sashimi: tuna or salmon seared with hot sesame oil. A good range of yakitori-style skewers and daily specials

round off the choices. End off with a trio of ice cream: deep fried, wasabi and green tea. The alfresco seating area is magical on a nice evening.

Il Leone Mastrantonio

22 Coburn Street, Green Point (021 421 0071, www.mastrantonio.com). **Open** noon-3pm, 6.30-10.30pm Tue-Sun. **Main courses** R100. **Map** p83 F5 ⊕ Italian

This refined Italian restaurant, split over two levels, is always packed with locals – especially Italian families – enjoying the authentic cooking. Along with pastas and risotto, the gnocchi here is fêted as some of the best in town. Meaty mains include a massive Florentine *bistecca* – a good choice if you're really ravenous. The home-style atmosphere is complemented by top-notch service.

Manos

39 Main Road, Green Point (021 434 1090, www.mano.co.za). **Open** noon-late Mon-Sat. **Main courses** R110. **Map** p83 E4 ⊕ Brasserie

This perennially popular eaterie serves classic brasserie favourites to regulars amid a buzzing vibe. Caesar salads, burgers, pastas and beef fillet are all popular. You can sit outside at a pavement table to watch the world go by or inside in the bright and airy interior. You can't book, so it's best to come early or be prepared to wait for a table.

Pepenero

Two Oceans House, Beach Road, Mouille Point (021 439 9027, www.pepenero. co.za). **Open** noon-late daily. **Main courses** R140. **Map** p82 C1 ⊕ Seafood/Italian

Whether you decide to sit on the expansive deck, or in a private booth, Pepenero serves up uninterrupted views of the Atlantic in a stylish setting – this is a spot to see and be seen – alongside a versatile Italianesque menu. Go all out with crayfish ravioli or a decadent seafood platter.

Pigalle

57 Somerset Road, Green Point (021 421 4848, http://pigallerestaurants.co.za/capetown). **Open** noon-3pm, 7pm-late Mon-Sat. **Main courses** R120. **Map** p83 E/F5 ⊕ International

Embrace the sheer sense of retro occasion in this plush velvety diner, with post-dinner dancing to big band standards from the jazz combo. The menu is classic: seafood is big here and the steaks are equally good. There's a Portuguese slant to the food, so try *trinchado* or peri-peri chicken livers to start. It's a grown-up kind of place, hence no under-14s.

Pubs & Bars

Cabrito

Ground Floor, Exhibition Building, 81 Main Road (021 433 2364, www.cabrito.co.za). **Open** 3pm-2am Mon-Fri; 2pm-2am Sat. **Map** p82 D4 ⊕

Situated below and owned by El Burro, Cabrito specialises in tequila. It has the widest selection in Cape Town, as well as a large selection of craft beers, a few cocktails and a full bar. It's a great after-work drinks spot, and a lively bar in the evenings. The barmen are informed and will teach you a bit about tequila and mezcal to add to your experience. Platters of Mexican food can be arranged through El Burro.

Zenith Sky Bar
Cape Royale Hotel, 47 Main Road, Green Point (021 430 0500, www.caperoyale.co.za). **Open** 8am-midnight daily. **Map** p82 D4 ⑤
A pool bar with 180-degree views of the Atlantic Seaboard to one side, and Signal Hill to the other, this is a super place from which to see the sights while sipping something decadent. It's luxurious and you'll feel like a celebrity as you enjoy a cocktail while lounging by the rooftop pool. The venue usually hosts a glamorous New Year's Eve event from which you'll be able to see the famous midnight fireworks display at the V&A Waterfront.

Shops

★ Giovanni's Deli World
103 Main Road, Green Point (021 434 6893). **Open** 7.30am-9pm daily. **Map** p82 D4 ② **Food & drink**
The best deli you'll find in Cape Town is a veritable institution. The owners travel overseas to source the best produce, from whole sides of prosciutto to dried pastas and an array of sweets. Locally produced items such as olive oil and wine also get a look in on the floor-to-ceiling shelves that are filled to bursting. The deli counter heaves with ready-made foods, cold meats and cheeses, while the espresso bar does a roaring trade in coffee and croissants. Buy some fresh flowers from the seller outside before leaving.

SEA POINT

The Promenade continues at Sea Point, which has many seafront apartment buildings. You'll see dog-walkers, families and retirees out for a stroll. The peace and quiet is far removed from the mayhem on the main road one block up, where it buzzes with cheap eateries, Asian supermarkets and bars. The large **Sea Point Swimming Pool** is a well-known landmark and a favourite place to cool down on a hot day.

Sights & Museums

Sea Point Swimming Pool
Lower Beach Road (021 434 3341). **Open** *Winter* 9am-5pm daily. *Summer* 7am-7pm daily. **Admission** *Pool* R21; R10.50 reductions. **Map** p95 B4 ⑥
Practise your strokes in this Olympic-sized retro swimming pool that is set right beside the sea. The

complex also has a children's pool, splash pool and diving pool as well as changing facilities and lawns to relax on. It can get overcrowded during summer and school holidays.

Restaurants & Cafés

La Boheme Wine Bar & Bistro
34 Main Road (021 434 8797, www.laboheme bistro.co.za). **Open** 8am-10.30pm Mon-Sat. **Main courses** R85. **Map** p95 C3 ⑥ **Bistro**
This tiny space is permanently packed with those in the know digging in to tasty Mediterranean tapas and well-priced specials. If you're keen on sharing, there are paellas (try the seafood or rabbit option). La Boheme offers a range of wines by the glass, making pairing with dishes a fun experience.

Harveys at the Mansions
Winchester Mansions, 221 Beach Road (021 434 2351, www.winchester.co.za). **Open** 7am-10.30pm daily. **Main courses** R200. **Map** p95 C2 ⑥ **Classic South African**
Winchester Mansions is a poster child for a bygone era – from the gabled façade and heavy wooden revolving doors to the crisp, clean interior. Traditional dishes such as springbok loin with rooibos and prune compote, grilled sole with saffron mash or rib-eye with truffled emulsion suit the refined setting to a tee. The Sunday jazz brunches in the leafy courtyard are popular.

Kleinsky's Delicatessen
95 Regent Road (021 433 2871, www.kleinskys. co.za). **Open** 8am-5pm Mon-Sat; 8am-3pm Sun. **Main courses** R60. **Map** p95 B4 ⑥ **Deli**
A tiny slice of New York awaits in the heart of Sea Point. Kleinsky's is a family-owned establishment that offers real-deal deli fare: potato latkes with smoked salmon or challah French toast for breakfast; blintzes, bagels (with shmears) and authentic hot pastrami on rye with pickle will have you salivating. And if you're feeling poorly, well there's nothing better than chicken soup with matzo balls.

La Mouette
78 Regent Road (021 433 0856, lamouette-restaurant.co.za). **Open** 6pm-late Mon-Sat; noon-late Sun. **Main courses** R170. **Tasting menu** R295. **Map** p95 B4 ⑥ **Haute cuisine**
Chef Henry Vigar can be thanked for breathing new life into a stunning Victorian building in the heart of Sea Point. His gourmet approach and accessibly-priced tasting menus have a loyal fan base. Various dining rooms and a shaded courtyard make for a cosy and intimate experience, where diners can enjoy seasonal menus with well-constructed dishes (the likes of kingklip with radicchio, shitake and saffron emulsion or Kudu loin with rhubarb gel, sweet potato, oatmeal tofu and smoked emulsion) created with modern French flair. *Photos p94.*

EXPLORE

La Mouette. See p93.

★ La Perla
Cnr Church & Beach Roads (021 434 2471,
www.laperla.co.za). **Open** 9am-11pm daily.
Main courses R120. **Map** p95 B4 ⑥⑧ Italian
This old-school venue has stood the test of time. The
art deco bar is perfect for late-night drinks, or head to
the sunny, recently renovated terrace for a meal with
a view. Classic pasta, veal and seafood dishes are pre-
sented with flair by long-serving waiters.

Posticino
Albany Mews, 323 Main Road (021 439 4014,
www.posticino.co.za). **Open** 11am-10.30pm daily.
Main courses R85. **Map** p95 C3 ⑥⑨ Italian
A warm 'ciao' greets locals and tourists at this welcoming Italian trattoria. Pizzas are the thin-based
real deal, with hearty toppings to match. Create your
own pasta sauce with your favourite ingredients or
try the lasagna – it's rib-stickingly good.
Other location 6 Main Road, Hout Bay
(021 791 1166).

Pubs & Bars

Harvey's Bar Terrace
Winchester Mansions, 221 Beach Road (021 434
2351, www.winchester.co.za). **Open** 7am-11pm
daily. **Map** p95 C2 ⑦⓪
The interior is spacious and comfortable, but for the
best view, head out on to the narrow terrace, where
you can have afternoon tea, cocktails, wine, beer or
bubbly while soaking up the glorious Promenade
view (paragliders who took off from Signal Hill land
here) and nibbling on a bar snack. We recommend
the *flammkuchen*, which is similar to pizza.

CLIFTON

Four divergent beaches rub shoulders along this
breathtaking shoreline. Coming from the Camps
Bay (south) side, you'll find **Fourth Beach**,
which is the biggest, most crowded beach of the
lot – a place where the likelihood of being struck
by a wayward Frisbee is quite high. The calm
waters near the boulders on the left-hand side is
the ideal swimming spot for kids, should they
care to brave the freezing water. **Third Beach**,
aka C3, is where the tank-topped and toned gay
crowd soak up the sun; while **Second Beach**
sees sun-kissed scenesters getting in a bit of
topless tanning. Last in the line and popularity is
the quieter **First Beach**. Whichever you favour,
you'll need to tackle plenty of steps to gain access.

Restaurants/Bars

Bungalow
3 Victoria Road, the Glen Country Club (021 438
2018, kovecollection.co.za). **Open** *Summer* noon-
late daily. *Winter* noon-late Wed-Sun. **Map** p97 A2
⑦① Seafood/international

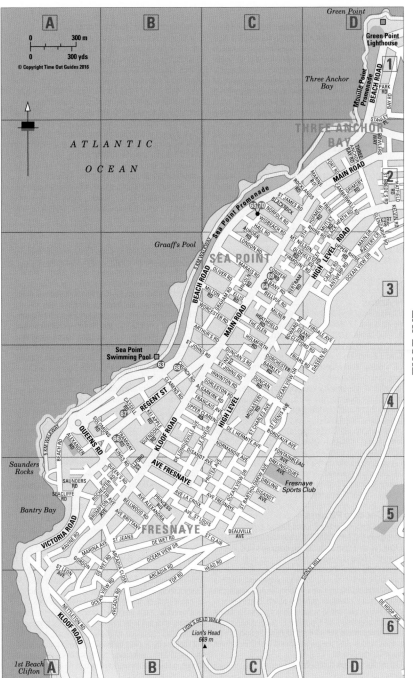

Watch the sun set over the sea from the dappled deck of the Bungalow; it has a prime position as the only venue in Clifton with nothing standing between you, sublime seafood, sushi and the vast big blue sea. Sip on classic cocktails or try one of the signature drinks, like a pomegranate mojito, banana and coconut daiquiri, or the perfect summer refresher, a watermelon martini. There is a full range of French champagne, as well as local cap classique sparklers, and an extensive wine list.

CAMPS BAY

The party spot on the Atlantic, Camps Bay's tree-lined beachfront has a profusion of bars and restaurants. On the beach, surfers wait for a few killer waves; at the southern end, you can practise your bobbing skills in the tidal pool. The current here is strong so it's not ideal for swimming, but the long stretch of beach makes for lovely morning walks. Massages on the beach and loungers and umbrellas for hire make it the most upmarket beach experience around.

Restaurants & Cafés

★ Azure

12 Apostles Hotel & Spa, Victoria Road (021 437 9029, www.12apostleshotel.com). **Open** 7-10.30am, 12.30-3.30pm, 6-9.30pm daily. **Main courses** R190. **Map** p97 A6 ⓑ **Haute cuisine**

Chef Christo Pretorius, newly appointed at the time of writing, has a flair for creating South African-inspired dishes with a contemporary twist. Expect the likes of sustainable seafood and Asian elements as well as local meats, with beautifully prepared dishes that could include springbok loin with sweet potato, guava gel and root vegetables, or grilled loin of lamb with lamb's liver, caramelised onion, cured lemon peel, dukkha spiced aubergine, baby gem and buttermilk curd. In addition, the menu features classics from hotel owner Bea Tollman, such as Cape Malay curry, seafood ceviche and rice pudding with salted caramel. There is a semi-formal dress code, so no flip-flops or shorts for men.

Col'Cacchio Pizzeria

Isaac's Corner, Corner Victoria Road & the Meadway (021 438 2171/0 www.colcacchio.co.za). **Open** noon-11pm daily. **Main courses** R90. **Map** p97 B3 ⓑ **Italian**

If you find it hard to make up your mind in restaurants, the multitude of pizza toppings on offer at this famous franchise will have you breaking into a slight sweat. If the pressure gets too much, however, you can always just build your own with a vast choice of fresh and delicious toppings. If pizza doesn't take your fancy there are also great pasta, gnocchi and salad choices. And the great news is that they deliver pizzas to the beach! **Other locations** throughout the city.

★ Roundhouse Restaurant

The Glen on Kloof Road (021 438 4347, www.theroundhouserestaurant.com). **Open** 11am-2.30pm, 6-9.30pm Tue-Sun. **Set menus** *4-course menu* R665; *tasting menu* R750. **Map** p97 C2 ⓑ **Haute cuisine**

What was once Lord Charles Somerset's 'shooting box' has been tastefully renovated into a refined restaurant. A setting on the slopes of the Lion's Head means that diners can take in the Camps Bay vista while enjoying an aperitif. Ingredients are locally sourced, even foraged, as can be seen in a winter dish of venison with Devil's Peak mushrooms. South African inspiration is evident in a dish of ostrich served with celeriac in a salt crust, served with fynbos elements. Diners can choose from set menus with choices or a special chef's tasting menu. Picnics and light meals on the Rumbullion lawn are a lovely way to spend a summer's afternoon. *Photo p98.*

Umi

201 The Promenade, Victoria Road (021 437 1802, www.umirestaurant.co.za). **Open** noon-midnight daily. **Main courses** R150. **Map** p97 B4 ⓑ **Asian fusion**

An utterly chic modern interior and unsurpassed view over Camps Bay beach are not the only draws to this elevated spot. Excellent sushi and imaginative platters go perfectly with killer cocktails (many featuring saké) and a big-hitting wine list. Tempura starters – from artichokes to crayfish – are excellent, and other Asian-inspired dishes include fusion favourites such as teriyaki-grilled beef fillet with truffle dip and calamari with yuzu dressing. Desserts lean toward fruity ingredients, with the likes of Fuji apple crumble with jasmine custard.

Pubs & Bars

Café Caprice

37 Victoria Road (021 438 8315, http://cafecaprice. co.za). **Open** 9am-2am daily. **Map** p97 B3 ⓑ This is the ultimate see-and-be-seen venue. Beautiful bronzed bodies float off the beach for their sundowners, hang out to wait for the DJs to start spinning their tunes, then roar off into the night in low-slung sports cars. It's recently been renovated.

Leopard Bar

The Twelve Apostles Hotel, Victoria Road (021 437 9029, www.12apostleshotel.com). **Open** 7am-2am daily (alcohol served from 11am). **Map** p97 A6 ⓑ This hotel is located on what is considered to be Cape Town's most scenic route, and the bar is *the* place to be come sunset. Jostle for space with visitors and locals on the bar's teeny terrace and sip on a Lazy Leopard cocktail (spiced rum, pineapple juice and method cap classique sparkling wine) while watching the sun disappear majestically into the Atlantic Ocean. Plush interiors with a colonial jungle theme, a full bar menu, live lounge music and long

EXPLORE

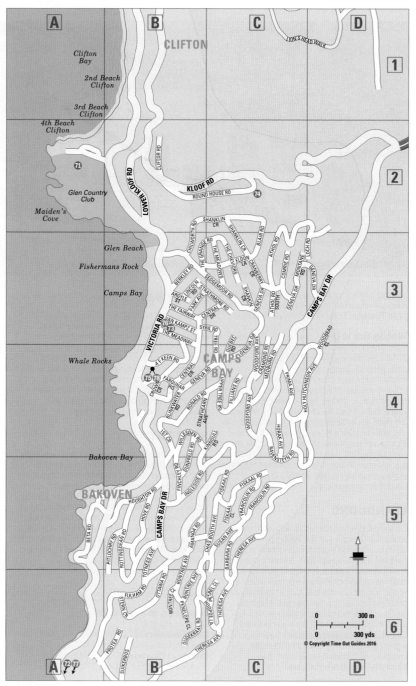

EXPLORE

Roundhouse Restaurant. See p96.

opening hours invite you to linger long after dark. Alternatively, visit by day for Tea by the Sea (*see p116* **Teatime Treats**), the hotel's afternoon tea.

Whisky Bar @ Umi

Umi, The Promenade, Victoria Road (021 438 2018, http://kovecollection.co.za). **Open** 6pm-late daily. **Map** p97 B4 ⓻
Stocked with more than 100 varieties of judiciously selected whiskies from around the world, this plush, refined spot is perfect for indulging in some rare single malts. Don't be intimidated if you're a novice; there are some recognisable brands on the list, and not everything is super-expensive. Located in an atmospheric alcove at the rear of Umi restaurant, on the first floor of the Promenade building, the 40-seater lounge offers an intimate night-time experience, a big contrast from the crazy party vibe downstairs at street level.

LLANDUDNO

On a wind-free day, this small, secluded cove wedged in the valley of the Twelve Apostles mountain range is worth the trek from the car park (which fills up quickly). A great hideaway for sundowners and an icy dip, Llandudno has it all – great surf conditions, a perfect swimming sea (if you can bear the cold, that is) and bulbous boulders for kids to scramble over. This is the last beach when heading south from which you can see the sun set in the water before mountains start obscuring the view, so it's a great place to enjoy a sundowner in the company of friends (bear in mind that alcohol is forbidden on beaches).

SANDY BAY

Naturists let it all hang out at this *au naturel* dune-shielded seaside spot, conveniently out of the way. It'll take you about 20 minutes' walk from Llandudno's parking lot before you find this hidden beach. Since it's so off the beaten track, make sure to bring ample refreshments. Its seclusion makes it very popular with gay men at weekends, but unfortunately has also made it a target for muggings, so don't go wandering around on your lonesome.

HOUT BAY

This harbour town has beach action, a boardwalk and bird-watching opportunities, while nearby **Seal Island** (or Duiker Island) is home to a large population of Cape fur seals. Spanning the area from the beginning of **Chapman's Peak Drive** to the harbour, Hout Bay's kilometre-long expanse of beach is great for kids and walkers. Hout Bay is also synonymous with horse-riding and you'll often spot riders along Valley Road. The **Bay Harbour Market** (*see p108* **Market Forces**), open from Friday to Sunday, has become a favourite meeting spot for food-lovers.

Sights & Museums

Boat Trips to Seal Island

Hout Bay Harbour.
Circe Launches *021 790 1040, www.circelaunches.co.za.* **Cost** *R60.*
Drumbeat Charters *021 791 4441, drumbeatcharters.co.za.* **Cost** R75.

Nauticat Charters *021 790 7278,*
www.nauticatcharters.co.za. **Cost** R80.
A variety of cruise operators offer trips to Seal
Island, also known as Duiker Island, which is where
around 60,000 Cape fur seals come to breed. Cruises
last about 40 minutes and you'll see a variety of
marine life on the trip. Operators also offer a variety
of other cruises seeing Cape Point or shipwrecks, in
addition to offering charter services.

★ Chapman's Peak Drive
*Toll road between Hout Bay & Noordhoek (021 790
9163, www.chapmanspeakdrive.co.za).* **Cost** R40
light motor vehicles.
Take your motion sickness meds before heading up
here: 114 curves snake over nine kilometres of sheer
cliffside. The road links Hout Bay and Noordhoek
and ranks at the top of the list of South Africa's most
scenic drives. If you can tear yourself away from the
view, marvel at the engineering feats of catch fences,
South Africa's first half-tunnel and bunker-like concrete impact protection canopies. Rockfalls are a danger and the drive is often closed after stormy weather.

World of Birds
*Valley Road (021 790 2730, www.worldofbirds.org.
za).* **Open** 9am-5pm daily. **Admission** R85; R40
reductions.
All squawk and plenty of action, this is the largest
bird park in Africa, with 100 pseudo-tropical walk-
through aviaries. Over 3,000 species flutter about the
place – you'll see everything from quails and cocka-
toos to owls, ostriches and flamingos, and can enjoy
feeding time for the penguins. Around 400 other
animal species also live here. The squirrel monkeys
are probably the most memorable: you can stroll
through their open-air cage and see them – if you're
not unnerved by monkeys jumping on your head,
that is. Tortoises, meerkats, snakes, guinea pigs and
marmosets will delight the very young.

Restaurants & Cafés

Chapman's Peak Hotel
*Chapman's Peak Drive (021 790 1036, www.
chapmanspeakhotel.co.za).* **Open** noon-11pm
Mon-Sat; noon-10pm Sun. **Main courses** R140.
Portuguese
Known for serving the best calamari in Cape Town,
Chapman's Peak Hotel offers other dishes too,
including Portuguese specialities. Dig in to prego
rolls, *espetada*, grilled sardines and line fish. The
expansive deck with ocean views get top marks for
location, while inside there's a more refined, old-
world charm. Start or finish your meal with a drink
at the bar or in the lounge around the fireplace.

Fish on the Rocks
*End of Harbour Road (021 790 0001, www.
fishontherocks.com).* **Open** 9.30am-8pm daily.
Fish & chip combo R60. Fish & chips

It doesn't get more basic than this: order and pay at
the counter, and wait for your number to be called
to collect your paper-wrapped feast. Grab a seat on
the benches outside or wander around next to the
dolosse (a South African invention of interlocking
blocks of concrete – their name roughly translates
as 'knuckle bones' – to protect sea walls and prevent
beach erosion) and watch seals at play. You'll have to
be fast or the seagulls will zoom in for a chip or two.
Calamari, hake, line fish, prawns and snoek come
accompanied with good old slap chips (soggy french
fries) doused in salt and vinegar.

Kitima Restaurant
*Kronendal Estate, 140 Main Road (021 790 8004,
www.kitima.co.za).* **Open** 5pm-late Tue-Sat; noon-
3pm Sun. **Main courses** R120. Asian
The top spot in Hout Bay for a sophisticated meal.
Set in an original Cape Dutch homestead dating
back to the late 1600s, Kitima is a refined restaurant
that serves delectable Asian cuisine. Curries are
excellent, or, if your tastebuds can't handle the heat,
opt for delicious dim sum or sushi. Sunday brunches
are a feast for the senses. Don't be spooked if you
see the ghost of a woman… apparently the house is
haunted by Elsa Cloete, who is said to have died here
of a broken heart in the 1800s.

Lookout Deck
*Quayside, Hout Bay Harbour (021 790 0900,
www.thelookoutdeck.co.za).* **Open** 10am-10pm
Mon-Fri; 9am-10pm Sat, Sun. **Main courses**
R105. Seafood
An unpretentious ambience and a superlative setting on the harbour edge are two attractions of the
Lookout Deck. Splashing seals and waterbirds will
delight the little ones, while adults can toast the
golden glow on Chapman's Peak in the distance
as the sun sets. Inside is more upmarket, while the
deck is filled with benches and umbrellas. The fare
is straighforward: pizzas, pints of prawns, calamari,
fresh line fish and sushi are the order of the day.
Those with meatier inclinations can enjoy burgers
and ribs. The rooftop deck, with its expansive view,
is the ideal place to while away a sunny day.

Massimo's
*Oakhurst Farm Park (021 790 5648, www.
pizzaclub.co.za).* **Open** 5pm-late Tue-Fri;
noon-late Sat, Sun. **Main courses** R85. Italian
A warm welcome awaits the diners at Massimo's,
which is very much a local institution, as popular with families who bring the kids to enjoy the
jungle gym as couples who coo in a corner by the
pizza oven. Start off with a selection of *spuntini*:
marinated baby artichokes, calamari with aïoli,
bruschetta with various toppings. For mains, pizza
and pasta are top of the list, with sauces including
pesto, parma ham and peas or fiery arrabiata. A vast
array of original pizza toppings and the personable
service keep the regulars happy.

EXPLORE

Woodstock

Gritty, cool, edgy, dodgy… that's Woodstock. Located on the eastern fringe of Cape Town's central area, historically this area was a mixture of industrial and residential buildings – with a mix of social classes and races living here during the apartheid era. Towards the end of the 20th century it became run-down, but thanks to the wave of urban gentrification that has taken hold in the city over the past ten years it has now emerged as a beacon of cool, with highlights – first among them the Old Biscuit Mill – being redeveloped. Meanwhile, Victorian houses have been snapped up by a stream of up-and-coming young professionals and creatives, and galleries now line Sir Lowry Road. But wherever you go, you'll also be sure to see other locals leaning out from their non-renovated balconies commenting on the passing show. While it's wise to park in well-lit areas and keep your wits about you, Woodstock is most definitely one of the city's most exciting places to eat and shop.

Test Kitchen.

Don't Miss

1 **Neighbourgoods Market** Get a taste of Cape Town's food culture on Saturday mornings (p109).

2 **The Kitchen** Dig into a 'Love Sandwich' (p102).

3 **Test Kitchen** One of the world's outstanding restaurants (p106).

4 **Tribe** Cool coffee roastery (p106).

5 **Goodman Gallery** Some of South Africa's best contemporary art (p102).

SIR LOWRY ROAD & SURROUNDS

This area still has an industrial feel, with mechanic shops next to flower suppliers, vintage furniture finds rubbing shoulders with old-school general dealers. But today it's also home to a number of excellent galleries, mostly thanks to the space available in revamped old warehouses.

Restaurants & Cafés

Dining Room
117 Sir Lowry Road, (021 4610463, www.dining-room.co.za). **Open** 7pm Tue, Thur. **Three-course menu** R290. **Map** p103 C2 ❶ **Global**
An elegant, refined space in which to indulge in Karen Dudley's fantastic food. Dudley takes her inspiration from around the globe, and highlights could include Korean glazed duck and fennel roasted lamb with chimichurri potatoes – all served on vintage tableware. The Dining Room is generally available for private functions, but on Tuesday and Thursday evenings it's open to all for three-course dinners.

★ Kitchen
111 Sir Lowry Road (021 462 2201, www.love thekitchen.co.za). **Open** 8am-3.30pm Mon-Fri. **Main courses** R65. **Map** p103 B2 ❷ **Café**
You may have to jostle for space in this tiny eatery, buzzing with happy punters and friendly staff. It's owned by caterer Karen Dudley and the space has a retro vibe with an open kitchen, walls crammed with spices and ingredients and vintage mirrors and prints on the walls. Order from the counter: the honey mustard sausages are ridiculously moreish, 'love sandwiches' are filled with everything that's delicious and the salads are fresh, packed with flavour, globally inspired and oh-so-good-for you.

Shops & Services

34 Fine Art
The Hills Building, Buchanan Square, 160 Sir Lowry Road (021 461 1863, www.34fineart.com). **Open** 10.34am-1.34pm Sat, or by appointment. **Map** p103 C2 ❸ **Gallery**
A space showcasing art that's modern and often avant-garde, 34 Fine Art is a good spot to stop if you're serious about collecting. The black-painted space allows art to pop out from the walls, and regular group and solo exhibitions are a good place to find inspiration or to be challenged by contemporary artists' work.

Blank Projects
113-115 Sir Lowry Road (021 462 4276, www. blankprojects.com). **Open** 10am-5pm Tue-Fri; 10am-1pm Sat or by appointment. **Map** p103 C2 ❹ **Gallery**
Artists Liza Grobler and Jonathan Garnham started Blank Projects with a gallery no bigger than a storage closet. They've now expanded into a bigger space, still showing work that's fresh and experimental. The gallery provides a space for established contemporary artists to let their hair down, while at the same time making room for exhibitions by emerging art stars.

★ Goodman Gallery
3rd Floor, Fairweather House, 176 Sir Lowry Road (021 462 7573/4, www.goodman-gallery.com). **Open** 9.30am-5.30pm Tue-Fri; 10am-4pm Sat. **Map** p103 C2 ❺ **Gallery**
The Goodman Gallery is a contemporary art stalwart. Its creator, Linda Givon, has made the careers of the biggest names in South African art today – including Willie Bester and William Kentridge. With a sister gallery in Johannesburg, this gallery is a big hitter when it comes to South African and African artists and should be at the top of the list of anyone who is serious about seeing, and investing, in art within an African context.

SMAC Gallery
The Palms, 145 Sir Lowry Road (021 422 5100, www.smacgallery.com). **Open** 9am-5pm Mon-Fri; 10am-3pm or by appointment Sat. **Map** p103 B2 ❻ **Gallery**
SMAC, which also has a gallery in Stellenbosch, is at the forefront of showcasing works by local and African contemporary artists. The Cape Town gallery opened in 2011 and moved to Woodstock in 2014. Its artists' residencies and exchanges promote artistic discourse and learning, and exhibitions have a strong focus on Cape Town as a contemporary art hub.

South African Print Gallery
109 Sir Lowry Road (021 462 6851, printgallery. co.za). **Open** 8.30am-4pm Tue-Fri; 8.30am-1pm Sat. **Map** p103 C2 ❼ **Gallery**
If you're after some original prints from both established and emerging South African artists, pop in here to browse the extensive collection. From Conrad Botes to Joshua Miles, Brett Murray to Cecil Skotnes, the variety of works on offer is excellent; you'll be able to find anything from a quirky decorative item to an investment piece.

★ Stevenson
Ground floor, Buchanan Building, 160 Sir Lowry Road (021 462 1500, www.stevenson.info). **Open** 9am-5pm Mon-Fri; 10am-1pm Sat. **Map** p103 C2 ❽ **Gallery**
A swanked-up vast old garage leads into one of Cape Town's most respected contemporary galleries. This swish, industrial-looking space boasts a variety of exhibition spaces, including a room packed with photographic prints, a side gallery for showcasing young artists and a ritzy courtyard. Modern local heavyweights in fields from conceptual art to photography such as Guy Tillim, Pieter Hugo, Nicholas Hlobo and Zanele Muholi are to be found here. Look out for exhibitions of international artists as well as emerging and established local talents.

EXPLORE

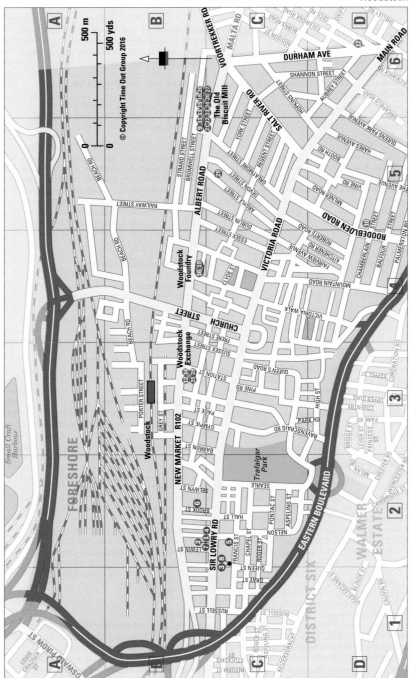

EXPLORE

ALBERT ROAD & SURROUNDS

What used to be a grungy (and not in a good sense) area of Woodstock has now become one of the hippest addresses in town, thanks to the complete renovation about ten years ago of the **Old Biscuit Mill** (373-375 Albert Road, www.theoldbiscuitmill.co.za), which went on to house the trend-setting **Neighbourgoods Market** (*see p108* **Market Forces**). It's here that all of Cape Town's hip young foodies congregate on Saturdays. A welcome spin-off from the market is that surrounding pockets of spaces have undergone similar redevelopment, with **Woodstock Exchange** (66-68 Albert Road, woodstockexchange.co.za) and **Woodstock Foundry** (160 Albert Road, woodstockfoundry.co.za) housing cool eateries, boutiques and studio spaces.

While it may be best to hop in a car or on a bus and stop at the various notable spots as Woodstock is not the safest place to wander around, you'll find this stretch provides a plethora of opportunities to spend your hard-earned cash on some unique buys.

Restaurants & Cafés

Burrata

Old Biscuit Mill, 373-375 Albert Road (021 447 6505, http://burrata.co.za). **Open** 6-10pm Mon; noon-10pm Tue-Fri; 10am-3pm, 6pm-10pm Sat. **Pizzas** R90. **Map** p103 B6 ❾ Italian

An industrial yet warm interior with wooden fittings and exposed brick walls juxtaposed with floor-to-ceiling glass doors makes Burrata a welcoming, modern space. The pizza oven from Naples is a focal point, and cooks them to perfection in seconds at 480°C. If you're not in a mood for pizza, opt for superior pasta dishes (think rigatoni with

---

IN THE KNOW
KEEP ON TRUCKIN'

Cape Town foodies have fallen in love with food trucks. So much so that a second annual street food festival (www.capetown streetfoodfestival.co.za) was held in July 2015, with vendors, food trucks and even talks by experts. There are a host of food trucks roaming the Mother City, many to be found at the Neighbourgoods Market in Woodstock's the Old Biscuit Mill on Saturdays, or Salt Circle Arcade (opposite the Old Biscuit Mill) on weekdays, offering everything from gourmet pizza to artisan coffee, authentic Mexican fare and burgers. Check the Facebook page 'Cape-Town-Food-Trucks' as well as Twitter@CTFoodTrucks for regular updates on where trucks are.

---

slow-cooked short rib) or beef sirloin with bone marrow. Co-owner Neil Grant is an experienced sommelier so you'll find some interesting wine choices to complement the Italian fare.

Chandani Indian & Vegetarian Restaurant

85 Roodebloem Road (021 447 7887, www.chandani.co.za). **Open** 11.30am-3pm, 6.30pm-late Mon-Sat. **Main courses** R120. **Map** p103 D5 ❿ Indian

Elaborately decorated with Indian furniture, this restaurant specialises in north Indian cuisine but also features a few Goan options. Vegetarians are very well catered for, with a range of lip-smacking dishes, the most notable of which is *paneer bhurjee*, a combination of mashed *paneer* (white cheese), onions, peas and spices. Lamb *rogan josh* is flavourful and hearty; those craving seafood will enjoy *machchi* Goan curry, kingklip in coconut with curry leaves and mustard seeds.

Espresso Lab Microroasters

Old Biscuit Mill, 373-375 Albert Road (021 447 0845, www.espressolabmicroroasters.com). **Open** 8am-4pm Mon-Fri; 8am-2pm Sat. **Map** p103 B6 ⓫ Café

Serious coffee-drinkers (let's face it, that's about all of Cape Town) head to this teeny tiny space for a perfectly roasted cup of coffee. The owners source coffee from small lots and showcase different coffees from around the world with tasting notes. Advice on best brewing methods means you can perfect your brew at home too.

Lady Bonin's Tea Parlour

Woodstock Exchange, 66 Albert Road (083 628 2504, www.ladyboninstea.com). **Open** 9am-5pm Mon-Fri; 9am-3pm Sat. **Map** p103 B3 ⓬ Café

A bright white space with wooden tables and chairs, hessian bags and bright red Persian carpets celebrates teas from around the world. Taste your way around the globe with black, green, white and herbal infusions before picking your favourite to brew at home. It also offers tea tastings, high teas and tea food pairings, which are fun and informative.

★ Pot Luck Club

Silo Top Floor, The Old Biscuit Mill, 375 Albert Road (021 447 0804, http://thepot luckclub.co.za). **Open** 12.30-2.30pm, 6-10.30pm Tue-Sat; 11.30am-3pm Sun. **Tapas** R80. **Map** p103 B6 ⓭ Global

See p105 **Masterchef**.

Superette

Woodstock Exchange, 66 Albert Road (021 802 5525, www.superette.co.za). **Open** 8am-3pm Mon-Fri; 8am-2pm Sat. **Map** p103 B3 ⓮ Café

This cool, modern and effortlessly funky spot with bright yellow chairs is the go-to place for breakfasts

MASTERCHEF

Luke Dale-Roberts is one of the city's – and the world's – favourite chefs.

Even though they can't get a booking for the next six months, Capetonians are still proud – smug even – that British-born chef Luke Dale-Roberts chose to settle in the Mother City after working in the Far East. It may have something to do with the fact that his clothing and interior designer wife, Sandalene, hails from Cape Town. But we like to think the fact that some of the world's top produce and hippest spots are to be found in Cape Town also played a part.

When Dale-Roberts opened the **Test Kitchen** (*see p106*) in gritty Woodstock at the end of 2010, not even he could have counted on his meteoric rise to foodie fame. Since its opening, it has steadily risen in the ranks of the World's 50 Best Restaurants, and in 2015 made the leap from 48th in the world to number 28.

A canvas for bold experimentation, exquisite flavours and adventurous techniques, the ten-course tasting menu, served at dinner, is like no other. Playfully echoing the restaurant's African location and making the most of the Cape's bountiful produce, with a touch of Asian inspiration, Dale-Roberts expertly crafts dishes that make the most of seasonality and are at the forefront of international trends. Lunches are more relaxed: the menu has à la carte options as well as a five-course tasting menu. With new art rotating on the walls, a completely open-plan kitchen and a masculine yet warm interior, the Test Kitchen should most definitely be on your list if you're serious about food.

Also at the Old Biscuit Mill, this time at the top of the converted silo, is **Pot Luck Club** (*see p104*), Dale-Roberts's fun and slightly tongue-in-cheek tapas-style restaurant. With its wraparound city views, New York loft feel and quick service, dinner here is playful yet by no means less tasty. Diners are encouraged to share small plates, divided on the menu into salty, sweet, bitter, umami and sour. Highlights include fish tacos, smoked beef fillet with black pepper and truffle café au lait and ash-baked celeriac. The pigs' tails have a cult following (and are not always available). Sunday brunches are a laid-back affair, with more small plate sharing and bottomless bubbly.

EXPLORE

Pot Luck Club.

EXPLORE

Test Kitchen.

and lunches that are fresh and simple – making the most of local produce. The Woodstock Bakery's delicious breads are used for sandwiches featuring the likes of spicy barbecued pulled pork, roast beef with caramelised onions and old favourite cheese on toast.

★ Test Kitchen

Old Biscuit Mill, 375 Albert Road (021 447 2337, www.thetestkitchen.co.za). **Open** 12.30pm-3.30pm, 7pm-8.30pm Tue-Sat. **Main courses** R175 (lunch). **Five-course menu** R525 (lunch); R590 (dinner). **Ten-course tasting menu** R975 (dinner). **Map** p103 B6 ⑮ **Contemporary South African**
See p105 **Masterchef**.

★ Tribe Coffee Roasting

Woodstock Foundry, 160 Albert Road (021 448 3362, www.tribecoffee.co.za). **Open** 7am-4pm Mon-Fri; 9am-1pm Sat. **Map** p103 B3 ⑯ **Café**
There are people who are passionate about coffee – and then there are the folks from Tribe… Up to nine different single-origin coffee beans from around the world make up Tribe's house espresso blend. They source green (unroasted) beans, and on any day you can taste your way from Indonesia to Malawi. Grab a seat in the courtyard or at the window and breathe in the intoxicating aroma of coffee beans being

roasted. If you feel like something substantial, the waffle with bacon should do nicely.

Pubs & Bars

★ Taproom

95 Durham Avenue (entrance in Cecil Road), Salt River (021 200 5818, www.devilspeakbrewing. co.za). **Open** 11am-4pm Mon; noon-10pm Tue-Sat. **Map** p103 A6 ⑰
Situated at the foot of Devil's Peak, the Taproom is an inviting pub and restaurant that showcases the latest creations from Devil's Peak Brewing Company. Enjoy a craft beer and food pairing board or simply relax with a pint and soak up the beautiful mountain views. A menu of pub fare features the likes of mini lamb burgers and shrimp and sweetcorn fritters to snack on, plus more substantial dishes such as Philly cheese steak roll or chicken and waffles. Tours of the on-site brewery can be arranged by appointment.

Shops & Services

Abode

Old Biscuit Mill, 373-375 Albert Road (072 261 3540, www.facebook.com/abodewoodstock). **Open** 9am-4pm Mon-Fri; 9am-2pm Sat. **Map** p103 B6 ⑱ **Homewares**

Abode stocks quirky, fresh and original designs for your home. There's a wide variety squeezed into a small shop, from delicate ceramicware to funky wooden lamps, and prints to bunnies – yes bunnies – in every shape and size. Larger furniture pieces have a retro vibe and a smattering of jewellery completes the picture.

Bronze Age Art Sculpture House

Woodstock Foundry, 160 Albert Road (021 447 3914, http://bronzeage.co.za). **Open** 8am-4.30pm Mon-Thur; 8am-3pm Fri; by appointment Sat, Sun. **Map** p103 B3 ⑲ **Homewares**
Combining a foundry, design studio and gallery space, the store focuses on bronze casting to create everything from bowls to vast commissioned sculptures. The foundry specialises in mould-making, patination, casting and mounting.

Clementina Ceramics

The Old Biscuit Mill, 373-375 Albert Road (021 447 1398, www.clementina.co.za). **Open** 9am-5pm Mon-Fri; 9am-3pm Sat. **Map** p103 B6 ⑳ **Homewares**
Clementina van der Walt's ceramics are beautiful, functional and one-off art pieces that enhance an ethnically accented home without dominating. Some items are quirky and bold, others more muted and restrained – yet all carry her signature style. The shop also sells works by other ceramicists as well as locally made crafts.

Cocoafair

Old Biscuit Mill, 373-375 Albert Road (021 447 7355, www.cocoafair.com). **Open** 8am-5pm Mon-Fri; 8am-2pm Sat. **Map** p103 B6 ㉑ **Food & drink**
Chocoholics will have to be dragged from this haven of the cocoa bean, where you can see chocolate being created from bean to bar. Organically grown beans are sourced directly from Fairtrade sources. Join a tour in the factory or simply watch from behind glass are beans are roasted, conched (a mixing process) and prepared to form delectable edibles. Cocoafair also offers chocolatier courses; or you can simply stock up on an array of top-quality white, milk and dark chocolates with a variety of flavours.

★ Heartworks

Old Biscuit Mill, 373-375 Albert Road (021 447 7183, www.heartworks.co.za). **Open** 10am-4pm Mon-Fri; 9am-2pm Sat. **Map** p103 B6 ㉒ **Crafts**
A colourful array of handmade crafts invites shoppers into Heartworks. Crafters from around southern Africa work in a vast variety of materials, from

EXPLORE

MARKET FORCES
Our favourite foodie markets around the peninsula.

Cape Town today is market obsessed. Big Daddy of them all, and the one that started the craze, is most definitely the **Neighbourgoods Market** (*see p109*) at the Old Biscuit Mill on Albert Road in Woodstock. Hipsters, tourists and families congregate here on Saturdays for quality produce and incredible eats. Start off your visit with potato rösti with smoked salmon and hollandaise, say, perhaps accompanied by a craft beer, before stocking up on breads, cheeses and cured meats. Or stick with enjoying your food in situ, the main focus of the market, with curries, gourmet sandwiches and dim sum constant favourites, not to mention giant crêpes filled with Nutella. It's not all about the food here, however: there's also original clothing and jewellery, and you can grab a bunch of proteas (South African flowers) on your way out.

With a rather more laid-back vibe, **Bay Harbour Market** in Hout Bay (31 Harbour Road, Hout Bay, www.bayharbour.co.za, open 5-9pm Fri, 9.30am-4pm Sat, Sun) also has great food – everything from sushi to curries, paella, soups, omelettes and moreish burgers – as well as live music on Friday evenings. You can browse arts, crafts, clothing and jewellery stalls while soaking up the market atmosphere. The fact that it's in an enclosed former fish factory space adds to the local appeal – especially when Cape Town's weather isn't playing along.

Staying along the coast, a popular spot for the yummy mummies of Noordhoek is the **Cape Point Vineyards Community Market** on Cape Point Vineyards Estate (Silvermine Road, http://cpv.co.za, open Thur evenings in summer, noon-3pm Sun in winter; *pictured*). It has a perfect location next to a dam with lawns and expansive ocean views, and there's an abundance of foods to enjoy on the spot.

Staying on the south peninsula, **Blue Bird Garage Urban Village Market** (39 Albertyn Road, Muizenberg, www.bluebirdmarket. co.za, open 4-10pm Fri) is a warm and atmospheric place to spend a Friday night. It's a bustling meeting place filled with speciality food producers. Its tag line – 'We bring you the Butcher, the Baker, the T-shirt Maker' – is an indication of the fun vibe you'll find here.

In the bustling V&A Waterfront, the **V&A Food Market** (www.waterfrontfoodmarket. com, open 10am-6pm daily) is a fairly recent addition, but a very successful one thanks to its extensive opening times. Set in the Pumphouse building off Nobel Square, near the Victoria Wharf Shopping Centre, the relatively compact market is home to artisan food retailers and street food stalls: enjoy an ice-cream or bubble tea while browsing stalls selling meat, dried fruits, pastries and more.

The **Bo-Kaap Market** community food and craft market (Bo-Kaap Civic Centre, Wale Street, open 10am-2pm 1st Sat of mth) takes place in the heart of this colourful area. You'll find Cape Malay specialities like koesisters, rotis, samoosas and curries. The market's Facebook page has more information.

Lovers of organic food will enjoy **Oranjezicht City Farm Market Day** (www.ozcf.co.za/market-day). Currently taking place in Granger Bay at the V&A Waterfront on Saturdays (9am-3pm), this market is where you can buy the harvest of the urban Oranjezicht City Farm, as well as delicious produce to enjoy on site. During summer it's set to return to its location on the manicured lawns of the official home of the Premier of the Western Cape, Leeuwenhof, in Hof Street, Gardens. Keep an eye on the website for the latest location information. And, at the **City Bowl Market** (14 Hope Street, Gardens, www.citybowlmarket.co.za, open 4.30-8.30pm Thur, 8am-1pm Sat), locals congregate on Thursday evenings for a wide range of global foods, while Saturday mornings are ideal for shopping from the producers selling everything from pestos to coffee, cheese and spices.

Many markets now offer credit card facilities or SnapScan (*see p72* **In the Know**), but it's a good idea to come armed with some cash.

wood to clay, beads, felt, and even plastic and scrap metal. The results are unique mementos and home decor items. Stock up on African-inspired Christmas tree ornaments.

Imiso Ceramics

Old Biscuit Mill, 373-375 Albert Road (021 447 7668, www.imisoceramics.co.za). **Open** 9am-4pm Mon-Fri; 9am-3pm Sat. **Map** p103 B6 ㉓ Homewares
Ceramics whiz kid Andile Dyalvane is rapidly amassing a cult following. Start collecting while you still can, as these exquisitely hand-crafted vessels – some functional and others unashamedly decorative – are as red-hot as the kilns in which they are fired. With pieces ranging from tiny teacups to tall, tubular, hand-built urns and vases, the hardest task is picking which one to give a home to.

Kat van Duinen

Old Biscuit Mill, 373-375 Albert Road (021 447 6582, www.katvanduinen.com). **Open** 9am-5pm Mon-Fri; 9am-3pm Sat. **Map** p103 B6 ㉔ Fashion
Gorgeous flowing tailoring, rich fabrics and feminine design are the hallmarks of Kat van Duinen's fashion. There's a city chic about all her pieces, many of which feature ethically sourced leather, raw silks and wool.

Kingdom

Woodstock Exchange, 66 Albert Road (060 430 4415, www.kingdomshop.co.za). **Open** 10am-5pm Mon-Fri; 10am-3pm Sat. **Map** p103 B3 ㉕ Fashion/ homewares
A treasure trove from travels near and far: this collection of clothing, accessories, furniture, art and decor items celebrates eclecticism in all its colourful glory. Local designers and artisans are showcased here as well as vintage collectibles sourced by the owners.

Mü&Me

Old Biscuit Mill, 373-375 Albert Road (021 447 1413, muandme.net). **Open** 9am-5pm Mon-Fri; 9am-3pm Sat. **Map** p103 B6 ㉖ Stationery
Welcome to the cute and colourful world of Mü&Me. Gift cards, stationery, bags and journals share the stories and lives of a host of characters: from Tau, the friendly lion who's the king of playing hide and seek, to Hugo, the elephant who admits that he does forget… Best to buy two of everything as you won't want to give away these collectible items.

★ Neighbourgoods Market

Old Biscuit Mill, 373-375 Albert Road (021 462 6361, www. neighbourgoodsmarket.co.za). **Open** 9am-2pm Sat. **Map** p103 B6 ㉗ Market
See p108 **Market Forces**.

Urban Africa Atelier

Woodstock Exchange, 66 Albert Road (021 447 6007, www.urbanafrica.co.za). **Open** 9am-5pm Mon-Fri; 10.30am-2.30pm Sat. **No credit cards**. **Map** p103 B3 ㉘Accessories

A striking array of locally made leather accessories: muted shades of grey, blue and brown add style to bags, books and wallets designed with functional, minimalist appeal. Nothing is wasted here; leather cut-offs are turned into items such as keyrings. Urban Africa also can also make bespoke items and customise leather products.

What If the World Gallery

1 Argyle Street (021 447 2376, www.whatiftheworld.com). **Open** 10am- 5pm Tue-Fri; 10am-2pm Sat; by appointment Mon, Sun. **Map** p103 C5 ㉙ Gallery
New Yorker Justin Rhodes and his South African partner Cameron Munro started What If the World with a tiny gallery in the East City Precinct. The idea was to create a community-conscious platform for emerging young artists, while also playing host to workshops, art events and collaborative initiatives. With the move to Woodstock a number of years ago, the space and concept has grown: the original artists have become established names, while the gallery continues to nurture new and upcoming talent from around the continent.

What If the World Gallery.

Southern Suburbs

Heading out of town, the landscape changes once you reach the M3 highway: it's cooler, greener and wetter behind Table Mountain, and it's this weather pattern that sees wineries in the Constantia Valley reaping rewards. Top of the list of must-sees in the Southern Suburbs is Kirstenbosch National Botanical Gardens, with its Boomslang Tree Canopy Walkway offering a bird's-eye view over the gardens below. Other major sights include the Groote Schuur Hospital, where the world's first heart transplant took place, and the renowned University of Cape Town, which dominates the lower slopes of Devil's Peak. Below this are the districts of Mowbray and Observatory. Rugby fans will love a tour and a live game at Newlands Rugby Stadium, while shopping haven Cavendish Square is nearby. Hikers and mountain-bikers, meanwhile, will enjoy the cool expanses of Tokai Forest.

Kirstenbosch National Botanical Gardens.

Don't Miss

1 Constantia Winelands For Cape heritage and heady wines (p119).

2 Newlands Rugby Stadium Watch the Springboks in action (p115).

3 Kirstenbosch National Botanical Gardens Floral beauty set against a mountain backdrop (p115).

4 South African Breweries Tour and a tasting (p115).

5 The Creamery Tuck into the best ice-cream in Cape Town (p117).

OBSERVATORY & MOWBRAY

Obz is a rough-around-the-edges area that's popular with students, artists and bohemians; while Mowbray's main drag is lined with reasonably priced restaurants popular with locals. The area is also home to Groote Schuur Hospital, scene of the world's first heart transplant in 1967.

Sights & Museums

Cape Town Science Centre

370B Main Road, Observatory (021 300 3200, www.ctsc.org.za). **Open** 9am-4.30pm Mon-Sat; 10am-4.30pm Sun. **Admission** R45; free under-3s.
For review, *see p149*.

Transplant Museum

Block E, Groote Schuur Hospital, Old Main Building, Hospital Road, Observatory (021 404 1967, www.heartofcapetown.co.za). **Tours** 9am, 11am, 1pm, 3pm daily. **Admission** R100 (R200 foreign visitors); R50 reductions.

On 3 December 1967, Dr Christiaan Barnard made medical history when he transplanted the world's first human heart. The attention to detail in this museum is astounding – from the carbon copy of Denise Darvall's (the first heart donor's) bedroom, to reams of correspondence, including a reluctant congratulatory letter from Barnard's American counterpart, Dr Norman Shumway. Step through the painstakingly recreated operating theatres where eerily realistic wax sculptures of Dr Barnard and his team are displayed, shown giving first heart recipient Louis Washkansky a new lease of life, complete with a soundtrack of clinking scalpels.

Restaurants & Cafés

Chai-Yo

95 Durban Road, Little Mowbray (021 689 6157, www.chaiyomowbray.co.za). **Open** noon-2.30pm, 6-10.30pm daily. **Main courses** R75. Thai
This unassuming spot serves authentic Thai fare – be prepared for some seriously hot curries if you dare. Starters include piquant tom yum soup or crispy prawn spring rolls. The green and yellow curries are made with a choice of chicken, beef, pork, seafood or vegetables, and there's also a range of tofu and sprout stir-fries.

Fat Cactus

47 Durban Road, Little Mowbray (021 685 1920, www.fatcactus.co.za). **Open** 11am-11pm daily.
Main courses R90. Mexican
South-of-the-border fun and food await at this wallet-friendly Mexican. Chilli poppers and margaritas are a great way to start the evening. Follow up with classic tacos, burritos, enchiladas, quesadillas and fajitas – fillings range from pulled pork to grilled vegetables. Big burgers are also on the menu, as is a healthy portion of tongue-in-cheek cheese.
Other locations 5 Park Road, Gardens, City Bowl (021 422 5022); Woodstock Foundry, 160 Albert Road, Woodstock (021 447 1713).

Magica Roma

8 Central Square, Pinelands (021 531 1489).
Open noon-2pm, 6-10pm Mon-Fri; 6-10pm Sat.
Main courses R95. Italian
Set deep in the heart of suburbia, Magica Roma is a long-time favourite with in-the-know locals, who lap up the delicious, authentic Italian fare and warm

EXPLORE

welcome. Whet your appetite with a selection of zesty antipasti before tucking into pasta, seafood or melt-in-the-mouth veal dishes.

Queen of Tarts
213 Lower Main Road, Observatory (021 448 2420, www.queenoftarts.co.za). **Open** 8.30am-4.30pm Mon-Fri; 8.30am-2.30pm Sat. **Main courses** R55. Café
The name says it all – this magical bakery serves everything from gorgeous cakes to delicious quiches, pies and salads in a bright space. If you're in the area for breakfast, savoury French toast and muesli with poached apricots are a great way to start the day.

RONDEBOSCH

Rondebosch is at the heart of student life in the city – it's home to the University of Cape Town, which dominates the back slopes of Devil's Peak. The area is also home to the historic Groote Schuur Estate, where Cecil Rhodes once lived.

Sights & Museums

Irma Stern Museum
Cecil Road, Rosebank (021 685 5686, www. irmastern.co.za). **Open** 10am-5pm Tue-Fri; 10am-2pm Sat. **Admission** R20; R10 reductions.
Set behind a rather unattractive wall in Rosebank, a neighbouring suburb of Rondebosch, is the house where one of South Africa's most revered artists lived, painted and entertained for nearly four decades. Stepping into the colourful main house, you'll get a sense of the intriguing, eccentric character Stern must have been. The collection of artefacts

from her travels through Africa and Europe includes a Congolese Buli stool that features prominently in her paintings, as well as masks from around the world. The sitting room is decked out with ornate, handcrafted furniture and features a green accent wall studded with portraits. The most personal element is the recreation of Stern's studio, complete with easel, muddied tubes of paint and colour-caked easel. The museum regularly hosts exhibitions of contemporary artists.

Mostert's Mill
Rhodes Avenue, Mowbray (088 129 7168, 021 782 1305, www.mostertsmill.co.za). **Open** varies.
This working windmill was built in 1796. Gysbert van Reenen used to own the surrounding wheat fields and built the mill to grind his own flour, naming it after his son-in-law, Sybrand Mostert. It was later acquired by the intrepid Cecil John Rhodes. It's open to Friends of Mostert's Mill who operate the mill on a volunteer basis. Get in touch with miller Paul Jaques (paul@jaques.co.za) if you'd like to see the mill in action.

Rhodes Memorial
Groote Schuur Estate, above UCT (www.rhodes memorial.co.za). **Admission** free.
This grandiose shrine, dedicated to imperialist Cecil John Rhodes, was built on his favourite lookout point in 1912, two years after his death. The monument features a steep set of stairs flanked by eight bronze lions leading up to a pillared faux Greek chamber. The chamber houses a bronze bust in his image, featuring an inscription by his friend Rudyard Kipling. The Rhodes Memorial Restaurant & Tea Garden (open 9am-5pm daily, 021 687 0000) has undergone a

Irma Stern Museum.

revamp in recent years, with a lovely kids' play area. Light meals and cakes can be enjoyed under the trees and it's a lovely spot to spend a relaxing afternoon, high above the buzz of the city.

★ University of Cape Town

Off M3, Rondebosch (021 650 3121,
www.uct.ac.za).
This is South Africa's oldest university and its ivy-covered buildings have seen their fair share of bright minds since its inception in 1829, including Nobel laureate JM Coetzee. The views over the city from Jameson Steps are enough to inspire anyone to higher learning. The university was internationally recognised for its continued opposition to apartheid, and recent student protests have seen a statue of Cecil John Rhodes removed from campus. UCT's arts and drama faculties are located at Hiddingh Campus, which has two theatres and a gallery.

NEWLANDS & CLAREMONT

South Africans are sports mad and Newlands is home to the city's cricket and rugby stadiums – cricket fans can watch the Cape Cobras or the Proteas national team in action, while rugby fans can cheer on the Stormers or Springboks – both with the majestic Table Mountain as a backdrop. The suburb of Newlands also has one of the highest rainfalls in the country, which explains the leafy lanes around here. This area and Rondebosch are home to some of the country's top schools, while Cavendish Square is the place to go for retail therapy.

Sights & Museums

DHL Newlands Cricket Ground

146 Camp Ground Road, Newlands
(www.capecobras.co.za).
Newlands Cricket Ground is just a drop-kick away from the rugby stadium and is also conveniently located next to South African Breweries. With Table Mountain keeping an ever-watchful eye over proceedings, this is definitely one of the country's more scenic stadiums – it was chosen to host the opening ceremony of the 2003 Cricket World Cup. During the guided tours (10am Tue or by appt, 021 657 2050, www.newlandstours.co.za, R25-R85) visitors can get a thrilling behind-the-scenes glimpse of the President's Suite, well-to-do South Club, scoreboard control room and third umpire's booth.

Josephine Mill

Boundary Road, Newlands (021 686 4939, www.
josephinemill.co.za). **Open** 10am-7pm Mon-Fri (4pm in winter); 10am-2pm Sat. **Admission** *Self-guided tour* R10. **Milling demonstration** R20.
In 1818, Johannes Dreyer built a watermill on the banks of the Liesbeeck River. Upon his death, his widow Maria employed a young lad by the name of Jacob Letterstedt (who had immigrated from Sweden to escape bad debt) to run the mill, and ended up marrying him a few years later. More than 20 years younger than Maria (a photo of her scowling face is displayed in the museum), Jacob is said to have fallen in love with the Crown Princess of Sweden, Josephine, and built a second watermill as

EXPLORE

Kirstenbosch National
Botanical Gardens.

a testament of his love for her. The on-site museum houses a few relics from the mill's heyday, and there are guided tours including a peek inside the gigantic engine room, where you can see cogs working to produce the stone-ground flour sold in the shop. Incidentally, Letterstedt went on to own the Mariendal Brewery, which still stands across the road at the SAB brewery.

★ Kirstenbosch National Botanical Gardens

Rhodes Drive, Newlands (021 799 8783, www. sanbi.org). Open Apr-Aug 8am-6pm daily. Sept-Mar 8am-7pm daily. Admission R50; R10-R25 reductions; free under-6s.

In 1913, Professor Pearson, then Chair of Botany at the South African College, set about developing this vast botanical gardens into what it is today – one of the country's most popular visitor attractions. Neatly tended lawns tumble down the eastern slopes of Table Mountain, punctuated by flowering gardens, ponds and indigenous trees all knitted together by paved pathways. First up for any visitor has to be the Tree Canopy Walkway that was opened in 2014. It's called the Boomslang (named after a local tree-dwelling venomous snake) because of its sinuous curves that allow you to meander through the treetops. The 130m walkway is sturdy and wheelchair-accessible, and gives stunning views from 12m up in the canopy.

As you walk through the gardens, you'll see sculptures dotting the grounds, from African stone pieces to magnificent bronzes by Dylan Lewis. There's also a new exhibition of life-sized tin dinosaurs in the Cycad

amphitheatre that will wow the kids. The grounds have a tangle of walking trails leading visitors to spots such as the Bath in the Dell, a wild almond hedge planted by Jan van Riebeeck back in the 1600s, and a lane of gigantic yellowwoods. Heading towards the fynbos-covered foot of Table Mountain, you'll find the beginnings of the Skeleton Gorge and Nursery Ravine hiking trails. The weekly Sunday summer sundowner concerts feature well-known rock and blues bands.

Newlands Rugby Stadium

11 Boundary Road, Newlands (www.wprugby.com).
At 119 years, Newlands is the second oldest rugby stadium in the world. On the guided tour (10am Tue or by appt, 021 686 2151, www.newlandstours. co.za, R25-R85) fans can retrace their heroes' steps via the players' entrance and locker rooms, before heading down the players' tunnel and out on to the chalky field where all the bone-crunching action takes place. The museum has a section dedicated to the evolution of the rugby ball, plus paraphernalia such as the country's first rugby caps, a replica of the 1995 World Cup trophy and the magic boot that made it all possible. Enjoy a blast from the past with radio commentaries from the 1950s, '60s and '70s covering legendary tries and kicks, or sit down on the old Newlands rugby benches and watch a medley of memorable rugby moments.

South African Breweries – Newlands Brewery

3 Main Road, Newlands (021 658 7440, www. newlandsbrewery.co.za). Tours 10am, noon, 2pm

EXPLORE

TEATIME TREATS

Capture the Cape's colonial heritage with a decadent afternoon tea.

A great way to experience the grandeur of some of Cape Town's top hotels is to have afternoon tea. Top of the list is the **Belmond Mount Nelson Hotel** (*see p222*). Sit inside on plush sofas or in the airy conservatory, with the mellifluous sounds of a piano in the background. Tuck into the tiered tray of savouries and a vast table groaning with cakes, pastries and all manner of delicate treats, along with an excellent selection of teas. Unsurprisingly, the whole thing doesn't come cheap and you'll need to book in advance. A slightly cheaper and less busy option is the pared-down morning tea, served at the table.

For utter refinement and exclusivity, the **Cape Grace** (*see p227*) has long been a favourite. Tea is served in the library, and while it's not on the same epic scale as some of the others, there's something wonderfully civilised about savouring

delectable cakes while watching the yachts glide by from the comfort of your armchair.

For serious glitz and glamour, few places can beat **One&Only Cape Town** (*see p227*), where you'll be treated to stunning views of Table Mountain from the newly refurbished Vista Lounge, plus sweet and savoury treats aplenty.

It's all old-world opulence and refinement in the airy lounge at the **Table Bay** (*see p228*), where tea comes on tiered trays laden with delicacies; the Leopard Lounge at the **Twelve Apostles Hotel & Spa** (*see p228*) matches sea views and sweet treats on offer; while the **Vineyard** (*see p229*) provides space to walk off the calories in its expansive riverside garden.

For slightly less opulent and more affordable teas, **Rhodes Memorial** (*see p113*) is a fine choice with its mountainside setting, while the **Kirstenbosch Tea Room** (*see p117*) provides good-value treats in a botanic garden setting.

Belmond Mount Nelson Hotel.

Mon, Thur; 10am, noon, 2pm, 6pm Tue, Wed; 10am, noon, 2pm, 4pm Fri; 10am, noon Sat. **Admission** R80 (no under-18s).

Book well in advance for one of these guided tours, where you can see how the guys at SAB transform humble hops and malted barley into golden elixir. Once you've worked up a sufficient thirst, head down to the Letterstedt Pub and taste all that fermentation and filtration come to fruition. Those interested in the history of South Africa's beer industry can check out relics from SAB's heyday in the museum, such as the old-school Lion Beer locomotive that was used to offload barley at the Mariendal Brewery. The tour includes a tasting and two drinks. There's a beer-and-food pairing every last Thursday of the month.

Restaurants & Cafés

Creamery

Newlands Quarter, Dean Street, Newlands (021 686 3975, www.thecreamery.co.za). **Open** 10am-11pm Tue-Sun. **Ice-cream** R28/scoop. **Café**

Creamery ice-creams are the finest in Cape Town and this bright little café is the best place to taste them. Seasonal fruits sourced from organic local farms form the basis of flavours such as raspberry choc chip, coconut lime swirl or apple crumble, and there'd almost certainly be a riot if they ever stopped making the salted caramel or sweet cream. There are also milkshakes, sundaes and waffles – topped with ice-cream, of course.

Kirstenbosch Tea Room Restaurant

Gate 2, Kirstenbosch Botanical Gardens, Rhodes Drive, Newlands (021 797 4883, www.ktr.co.za). **Open** 8.30am-5pm daily. **Main courses** R90. **Café**

After a lengthy stroll through the gardens, reward yourself with high tea – think scones, sandwiches, cakes and quiches – at this refreshingly unpretentious spot. Other options include sandwiches and salads, as well as more filling dishes such as burgers and Cape pickled fish. You can also order a picnic basket to enjoy in a shady spot while the children enjoy a runaround.

Myoga

Vineyard Hotel & Spa, Colinton Road (off Protea Road), Newlands (021 657 4545, www.myoga. co.za). **Open** 11.30am-3pm, 7-10.30pm Mon-Sat. **Main courses** R200. **Global**

An open kitchen and splashes of bright orange on the walls and oversized armchairs greet diners at Myoga. Expect global fusion fare with dishes such as tuna chipotle taco, hoisin *kabeljou* or biltong-spiced ostrich for lunch. The curries are excellent too. There's a private dining room in the basement wine cellar and a terrace for sunny days. Screens in the toilets project a live feed from the kitchen, so you don't have to miss a moment.

IN THE KNOW ON THE BRAAI

Nothing is more South African than lighting up a braai. The word can be used as a noun or a verb and pertains to a type of barbecue, where a wood fire is left to burn down and the meat is then cooked over the charcoal. It's as much a social ritual as a cooking method, and the country is so enamoured that Heritage Day on 24 September is now informally known as National Braai Day.

Square Restaurant & Sushi Bar

Vineyard Hotel, Colinton Road, Newlands (021 657 4500, www.vineyard.co.za). **Open** 7-10.30am, 12.30-3pm, 6-10pm daily. **Set menu** R195/3 courses. **Asian/South African**

There are few things more relaxing than a languid lunch on the terrace overlooking the Vineyard Hotel's perfectly manicured gardens and the mountains beyond. Lunchtime sees a laid-back menu of burgers, fish and chips, and salads, plus there's a kids' menu – which they'll enjoy if you can stop them running off looking for the giant resident tortoises. For dinner, head inside to the refined atrium space for South African beef and seafood or go Asian with some sushi. The wine list is top-notch and regular winemakers' dinners are a favourite on the calendar.

Pubs & Bars

Banana Jam

157 2nd Avenue, Kenilworth (021 647 0186, www.bananajamcafe.co.za). **Open** 11am-11pm Mon-Sat; 5-10pm Sun.

If it's craft beer you're after, this place is an absolute must: it has one of the biggest selections on tap in Cape Town, and almost three times as many brands in bottles. Find the ones you love best with tasting boards – sample six beers of your choice or go for the daily offering. If you get hungry, there are great pizzas and a Caribbean-themed menu with dishes such as jerk chicken or goat curry. There's also a daily cocktail happy hour (5-6pm).

★ Forresters Arms

52 Newlands Avenue, Newlands (021 689 5949, www.forries.co.za). **Open** 11am-11pm Mon-Thur; 11am-midnight Fri; 9am-11pm Sat; 9am-9pm Sun.

Forries (as it's affectionately known) is one of the oldest pubs in Cape Town and its proximity to Newlands rugby and cricket grounds means it's the destination of choice for pre- and post-match drinks. If you don't have tickets to the game, there are big screens. There's a cosy bar, as well as a large outdoor beer garden with a small jungle gym for the kids. The carvery is a favourite or tuck into classic pub fare.

EXPLORE

Home Bar

53 2nd Avenue, Harfield Village, Claremont (021 683 6066). **Open** 5-11pm Mon-Fri; 6pm-1am Sat.
Adjoining a restaurant serving down-to-earth food at reasonable prices, this place truly lives up to its name – it's a popular local hangout where regulars have 'their' bar stools. It's tiny and cosy, and there are a couple of couches with low tables, as well as an enclosed outside front patio. Parking is an issue on this narrow suburban road, so explore other options for getting there.

Oblivion

22 Chichester Road, Claremont (021 671 8522, www.oblivion.co.za). **Open** 11am-12.30am Mon-Thur; 8.30am-2am Fri, Sat; 9.30am-12.30am Sun.
This wine bar in the heart of the Southern Suburbs is the go-to place for eating, drinking and kicking back – the addition of a rooftop deck a couple of years ago has added to its allure. Oblivion is also a favourite with sports fans, with two big screens downstairs and two smaller screens upstairs.

Shops & Services

Body Shop

Ground Level, Cavendish Square, Dreyer Street, Claremont (021 671 1082, www.thebodyshop. co.za). **Open** 9am-7pm Mon-Sat; 10am-5pm Sun. **Health & beauty**

This global brand sells all manner of scrubs, soaps and body butters for some well-earned pampering.

Cavendish Square

1 Dreyer Street, Claremont (021 657 5600, www.cavendish.co.za). **Open** 9am-7pm Mon-Sat; 10am-5pm Sun. **Mall**

A weekly visit to this glam mall is an essential fixture for many style-savvy residents of the Southern Suburbs. Browse hip fashion and accessories boutiques, gift and decor stores galore, and shoe displays that'll make you drool. A large Woolworths and the recent addition of a Pick n Pay supermarket has given the mall a more all-round appeal.

Habits

1 Cavendish Close, Cavendish Street, Claremont (021 671 7330, www.habits.co.za). **Open** 9am-5pm Mon-Fri; 9am-1.30pm Sat. **Fashion**

Local designer Jenny le Roux is the doyenne of the Southern Suburbs fashion set. Stylish, easy-to-wear separates and statement jewellery are her hallmarks, all made in her factory employing local seamstresses. Habits offers a bespoke couture service as well as fashion consultations.

In Good Company

Shop 4B, Cavendish Street, Claremont (021 671 4852, www.ingoodcompany.co.za). **Open** 9am-5pm Mon-Fri; 9am-2pm Sat. **Stationery**

In Good Company's Cape Town store sells an inspiring array of stationery and party accessories – it's the go-to spot for party decor. Brides-to-be will also love the selection of favours, invites and tableware.

Johans Borman Fine Art Gallery
16 Kildare Road, Newlands (021 683 6863, www.johansborman.co.za). **Open** 9.30am-5.30pm Mon-Fri; 10am-1pm Sat. Gallery
This stately gallery displays South African old masters such as Gregoire Boonzaier, Ruth Prowse and Gerard Sekoto. More contemporary names are also on the books, such as Sanell Aggenbach, Marlene von Dürckheim and Joshua Miles.

★ Montebello Design Centre
31 Newlands Avenue, Newlands (021 685 6445, www.montebello.co.za). **Open** 9am-5pm Mon-Fri; 9am-4pm Sat; 9am-3pm Sun. Arts & crafts
This historic centre is home to various creative studios, from jewellers and ceramicists to township crafters. Browse at the Montebello Craft Shop for original items recycled from glass, paper and metal, before heading to the Gardener's Cottage (021 689 3158) for tea and cakes or a light meal under the trees.

Nicci Boutique
Cavendish Square, Dreyer Street, Claremont (021 683 9458, www.nicci.co.za). **Open** 9am-7pm Mon-Sat; 10am-5pm Sun. Fashion

Montebello Design Centre.

What do Southern Suburbs socialites, yummy mummies and razor-sharp businesswomen have in common? They all frequent this Claremont shop for well-cut, sexy clothing. You'll find a selection of imported and own-label items – from party tops to gala frocks.

Riga
8 Cavendish Street, Claremont (021 674 4394, www.rigaboutique.co.za). **Open** 9am-5pm Mon-Sat. Fashion
Fresh-off-the-plane fashions ensure you'll always be one step ahead of your friends at this elegant boutique. It's run by enthusiastic, knowledgeable staff who know how to put together a look just for you. Riga stocks plenty of Max Mara – from catwalk must-haves to streetwear.

Storm in a G Cup
4 Cavendish Street, Claremont (021 674 6629, www.storminagcup.co.za). **Open** 9.30am-5.30pm Mon-Fri; 9am-2pm Sat. Fashion
Despite the name, Storm in a G Cup is an elegant lingerie shop with a professional fitting service. The swimwear service is outstanding – staff will happily alter different sized tops and bottoms to fit your shape, as well as take in full-piece swimsuits to fit, and it's all part of the price. The boutique also stocks bras for special occasion outfits.

CONSTANTIA

Towering mountains, old Cape Dutch houses and, above all, vineyards characterise Constantia. Next to historic wine farms, some exciting new boutique estates have opened in the last few years. It's also worth heading to **Constantia Glen** (Constantia Main Road, Constantia, 021 795 6100, www.constantiaglen.com) for its Bordeaux-style red blends, and **Eagle's Nest** (Constantia Main Road, Constantia, 021 794 4095, www.eaglesnestwines.com) for picnics. While Tokai is a residential suburb, Tokai Forest is a favourite with families, hikers and mountain bikers.

Sights & Museums

Beau Constantia
Constantia Main Road, Constantia (021 794 8632, www.beauconstantia.com). **Open** *Tasting room* 10am-4.30pm daily. *Wine bar* noon-4.30pm Mon, Sun; noon-8pm Tue-Sat. **Tasting** R45.
Cutting-edge modern architecture makes a bold statement on the steep hillside at Beau Constantia. Enjoy the views from the balconies dotted with sofas upstairs in the tasting room. Floor-to-ceiling windows and water features add to the appeal of the space, and wines are paired with a variety of canapés. Alternatively, head down to the wine bar with its open verandahs and sushi counter. The Cecily Viognier is particularly good and has won a host of accolades.

EXPLORE

Buitenverwachting

Klein Constantia Road, Constantia (021 794 5190,
www.buitenverwachting.com). **Open** 9am-5pm
Mon-Fri; 9am-1pm Sat. **Tasting** R40.

A stroll around the tree-lined grounds of this historic manor house helps to work up a thirst. Head
to the tasting room to sample the award-winning
wines: a fruity, easy-drinking blanc de noirs, perhaps, or the flagship Christine. Feeling peckish?
Grab a bottle of the estate's Brut Cap Classique for
a bubbly picnic under the oak trees, try Coffee BloC
for delectable cakes and light meals or head for the
swanky restaurant serving global fare in an original
Cape Dutch building. If you're feeling flush, you can
even invest in some diamond baubles from Maack
and Martin jewellers while you're here.

★ Groot Constantia

Groot Constantia Road, Constantia (021 794 5128,
www.grootconstantia.co.za). **Open** 9am-6pm daily.
Admission *Museum* R30. *Tasting* R45. *Cellar tour*
R60 (incl tasting).

Founded in 1685, Groot Constantia Estate
was South Africa's first vineyard and was the
grape-stomping ground of Simon van der Stel, first
governor of the Cape. Over the years, the estate's
wines have tickled the palates of kings and con-
querors, and had poets and authors waxing lyrical.
The orientation centre, imposing old manor house
and Cloete Cellar wine museum cover the history

of winemaking and the estate. Or make straight for
the cellar for a guided tour and a chance to taste it
all, before heading off to one of the two restaurants.
Jonkershuis serves up Cape-inspired dishes, while
Simon's (*see p123*) offers bistro fare.

Klein Constantia

Klein Constantia Road, Constantia (021 794 5188,
www.kleinconstantia.com). **Open** 9am-5pm Mon-
Fri; 10am-5pm Sat (4pm in winter); 10am-4pm Sun
(closed in winter). **Tasting** R30.

Writers from Baudelaire to Jane Austen have praised
Klein Constantia's revered Vin de Constance mus-
cadel for 300 years. Today, winemaker Matthew Day

IN THE KNOW MEATY MZOLI'S

The most talked about place in the
townships is **Mzoli's** (NY 115, Gugulethu,
021 638 1355, 078 040 9821, no credit
cards), a butcher's where you choose your
meat from the counter, grab a plastic chair,
open your BYOB and wait for your chops,
sausage or chicken to come off the *chisa
nyama* (braai). The guys manning the coals
are deft and your food will be charred to
perfection. This is a no-frills place that's
full of great vibes and good food.

Steenberg Vineyards.

EXPLORE

works with the fruits of this historic estate's top terroir to create a beguiling range of wine that's served in some of the world's top restaurants.

★ Steenberg Vineyards
Steenberg Road, Tokai (021 713 2211, www. steenbergfarm.com). **Open** 10am-6pm daily. **Tasting** R20-R80. **Food pairing** R200.

It's said that Catharina Ras, the tough-as-nails first owner of Steenberg, originally named her farm Swaaneweide ('feeding place of the swans') in a bout of nostalgia when she mistook a few splashing spur-winged geese for the swans of her German home town of Lübeck. Unlucky in love (she married five times and was generally referred to as Widow Ras), Catharina focused her energy on toiling away on the piece of land that was granted to her by Simon van der Stel. The tasting room is a seriously sexy space with a spectacular installation of glass apples suspended above the circular tasting bar. For a relaxed tasting, head to the sofas and sample a cheese and wine pairing. The bubbly is top notch and this is also one of the few wineries to produce Nebbiolo in South Africa.

Tokai Forest
Tokai Road (021 712 7471). **Open** *Picnic area* 8am-6pm (last admission 5pm) daily. **Admission** R5 per person; R5 vehicles; R20 cyclists; R30 horse-riding day pass.

This huge pine forest, popular with everyone from foragers to families, is snaked with well-marked hiking routes. The hardest route is the two-and-a-half-hour trek to Elephant's Eye Cave, which offers breathtaking views of the surrounding area. The arboretum houses more than 247 tree species from across the globe, which were first introduced in 1885 by Cape Colony forest conservationist Joseph Lister. Despite the trees' alien vegetation status, the arboretum was declared a National Heritage Site and the trees thus escaped destruction by the Parks Board.

Restaurants & Cafés

5 Rooms
Alphen Boutique Hotel, Alphen Drive, Constantia (021 795 6313, www.alphen.co.za/5rooms). **Open** 6pm-late Mon-Sat; noon-3pm Sun. **Main courses** R150. **Global**

Old-world grandeur gets a hit of contemporary swank at 5 Rooms with cutting-edge lights sharing space with leather banquettes and old portraits on the walls. On the menu is a retro revival with a twist: crayfish cocktail, steak tartare, sirloin steak with parsley butter, east coast sole or duck-leg shepherd's pie.

★ La Belle Bistro & Bakery
Alphen Boutique Hotel, Alphen Drive, Constantia (021 795 6336, www.alphen.co.za/laBelle). **Open** 7am-10pm daily. **Main courses** R105. **Café**

This bustling space in a historic building is home to a large wooden table and bar with bespoke wooden shelving showcasing the delicious bakes of the day. It's a great spot for breakfast, or linger over a long lunch (salads, pies, burgers, charcuterie platters) on the verandah under the oak trees. At dinner, tuck into classic bistro fare such as caesar salad, seared tuna, steak or linefish.

Bistro Sixteen82

Steenberg Estate, Steenberg Road, Tokai (021 713 2211, www.steenbergfarm.com/bistro1682). **Open** 9-11am, noon-4pm, 4.30-8pm (tapas) daily. **Main courses** R150. Bistro

This modern bistro leading on from Steenberg's wine tasting room is a stylish spot for a weekend meal. Breakfast favourites include rösti with creamy truffled mushrooms or smoked trout and poached eggs. At lunchtime, start off with some oysters in shallot vinaigrette before moving on to seared beef carpaccio, risotto of the day or linefish with chickpea and tomato râgout. Or simply nibble on a plate of antipasti while enjoying the estate's wonderful wines – the outside terrace next to the water features is the prime spot.

Bistro Sixteen82.

Catharina's at Steenberg

Steenberg Estate, Steenberg Road, Tokai (021 713 2222, www.steenbergfarm.com/catharinas). **Open** 7-10am, noon-11pm daily. **Main courses** R125. South African

A light-filled interior with a flock of origami swans suspended from the ceiling and views over the vineyards and mountains sets the scene for a memorable meal. Chef Garth Almazan mixes heritage food and contemporary style. There's a daily-changing lunchtime chalkboard menu, while dinner offerings might include the signature seafood plate or venison on beetroot purée with root vegetables. The wine list has more than 100 South African wines and the Sunday roast is a local family favourite.

Chardonnay Deli

87 Constantia Main Road, Constantia (021 795 0606, www.chardonnaydeli.co.za). **Open** 7am-6pm daily. **Main courses** R75. Café

This new deli-café is a boon for lovers of organic produce, serving up delicious salads, pies and quiches on the verandah. Smoothies and superjuices are excellent too. Afterwards stock up on fresh fruit and vegetables, bakes (many gluten-free) and a variety of organic cupboard essentials, from oils to preserves.

★ La Colombe

Silvermist Wine Estate, Main Road, Constantia Nek (021 795 0125, www.lacolombe.co.za). **Open** noon-8.30pm daily. **Main courses** R200. **Set menus** *Lunch* R695. *Dinner* R495, R790. Haute cuisine

La Colombe moved to new premises in late 2014 and is now situated high up the mountain on Constantia Nek, in a misty, tree-filled eyrie. The modern decor features deep greys and crisp whites offset by modern

Open Door.

EXPLORE

art, black wooden beams and pops of colour from orchid flowers. It's an utterly refined experience with service to match. Chef Scot Kirton showcases his skill and classical training with the likes of beef cheeks with onion confit or duck breast with beetroot and liquorice. The wine list is an exciting compilation of local vintages and original choices from further afield.

Four & twenty

23 Wolfe Street, Chelsea Village, Wynberg (021 762 0975, www.fourandtwentycafe.co.za). **Open** 8am-5pm Tue-Sat; 10am-4pm Sun. **Main courses** R95. Café

This charming café is all about pretty things and delicious eats. The beautiful cakes look (almost) too good to eat, but do save space for them after a lunch of homemade chicken pie, cauliflower and truffle soup, or salad with chicken, saffron-poached pears and almonds. Sandwiches are hearty and globally inspired. Breakfasts, meanwhile, are a delight with the likes of roasted white chocolate, strawberry and nut granola or apple and bacon flapjacks. On your way out, grab some preserves or sweet treats from the shelves to take home.

★ Greenhouse at the Cellars

Cellars-Hohenort, 93 Brommersvlei Road, Constantia (021 794 2137, www.collection mcgrath.com). **Open** 7-9.30pm Tue-Sat. **Set menus** R590, R820. Haute cuisine

Refined food in a rarefied setting is on the cards at this exclusive dining destination. Executive chef Peter Tempelhoff's modern dishes are pared down, exquisitely plated and bursting with flavour. Set menus include vegetarian, tasting or African Origin, which focuses on local seasonal produce such as gamefish, pork and beef, winter melon, jerusalem artichokes and garden pine mushrooms. Expect gels, emulsions, powders and sponges aplenty.

Open Door

Constantia Uitsig, Spaanschemat River Road, Constantia (021 794 3010, www.opendoor restaurant.co.za). **Open** noon-9.30pm Mon-Sat; noon-3pm Sun. **Main courses** R120. Contemporary

The main dining space at newly launched Open Door has a distinctly formal feel with royal blues, dark wtood and a fireplace, while the various terraces are packed during summer. Dishes are pleasantly uncomplicated. Starters include the likes of pork rillettes or beef tartare, while mains might feature delicate linefish or braised lamb. There's also a café menu at lunchtime with burgers and the like.

▶ *If you bring the kids, load their bikes and helmets as the Bike Park (see p147) is next door.*

Peddlars & Co

13 Spaanschemat River Road, Constantia (021 794 7747, www.peddlars.co.za).
Volaré Ristorante Open noon-4pm, 6-10pm Tue-Sun. **Main courses** R100. Italian
Graciales Open 3-11pm Mon-Thur; noon-11pm Fri-Sun. **Main courses** R75. Tapas
Oak Terrace Open 11am-11pm daily.
Main courses R100. Classic

Old-school pub Peddlars has had a new lease of life. The pub is now the Local Peddlers *(see p123)*, and three restaurants share the space on this Constantia corner. Chef Brad Ball is at the helm and there's a strong emphasis on free-range, organic and sustainable produce. Volaré Ristorante serves authentic antipasti, pastas and mains, all making the most of local meats.

Bags packed, milk cancelled, house raised on stilts.

You've packed the suntan lotion, the snorkel set, the stay-pressed shirts. Just one more thing left to do – your bit for climate change. In some of the world's poorest countries, changing weather patterns are destroying lives.

You can help people to deal with the extreme effects of climate change. Raising houses in flood-prone regions is just one life-saving solution.

**Climate change costs lives.
Give £5 and let's sort it *Here & Now***

www.oxfam.org.uk/climate-change

Oxfam is a registered charity in England and Wales (No.202918) and Scotland (SCO039042). Oxfam GB is a member of Oxfam International.

Be Humankind ⊗ Oxfam

Bright, funky Graciales is all about sharing plates with global inspiration – from sticky Vietnamese ribs to beef sliders and lamb flatbreads. Family-friendly outdoor seating and easy eats are the name of the game at the Oak Terrace, with the likes of spaghetti and meatballs, fish and chips, and lamb shanks, plus salads and cheese and charcuterie platters.

Simon's at Groot Constantia
Groot Constantia Estate, Groot Constantia Road, Constantia (021 794 1143, www.simons.co.za). **Open** 9am-late daily. **Main courses** R80. **Bistro**
Far from the stuffy establishment you might expect at an award-winning wine estate, the mood here is family-friendly, the food is accessible and the surroundings are stunning. The menu changes seasonally, but expect dishes such as caramelised onion and goat's cheese tart, slow-braised pork belly, great burgers and salads.

Tasha's
Constantia Village, Constantia Main Road & Spaanschemat River Road, Constantia (021 794 5449, www.tashascafe.com). **Open** 9am-6pm Mon-Fri; 9am-5pm Sat; 9am-2pm Sun. **Main courses** R85. **Café**
This impeccably styled café has expanded from its Joburg home and Capetonians are lapping up the contemporary rustic styling and delicious eats. Grab a seat on a sofa or pull a chair up to a wooden bench and feast on fabulous breakfasts, exotic salads and moreish sandwiches. Fresh juices, smoothies and decent coffee round things off perfectly.

Pubs & Bars

Local Peddlars
Spaanschemat River Road, Constantia (021 794 7747, www.peddlars.co.za). **Open** 3-11pm Mon-Thur; noon-11pm Fri-Sun.
Suburban stalwart Peddlars has undergone a major revamp: the interior is funky and bright, and this inviting space spills out on to a terrace beneath the oak trees. Try a classic cocktail or something more innovative: maybe an Amarena Old Fashioned (Fabbri amarena cherries, fresh orange, bitters and bourbon) or a Basil-Melon Daisy (gin, basil, raspberry jam, melon, lemon juice and soda). The impressive wine list focuses on the Constantia Valley estates and there's also a selection of craft beers. To accompany drinks, try one of the delicious sharing plates, including chef Brad Ball's famous beef tataki, sticky pork belly and Vietnamese ribs.

Rose Bar
Alphen Boutique Hotel, Alphen Drive, Constantia (021 795 6300, www.alphen.co.za//the_rose_bar). **Open** 4pm-late Mon-Thur; 3pm-late Sat; noon-late Sun.
This outdoor bar and terrace with cushioned loungers and comfy sofas combines old colonial living with modern styling. It overlooks the expansive grounds of the Alphen Boutique Hotel, with its cascading pools, water features and lush manicured gardens. It's the ideal setting for lazy weekend get-togethers and special celebrations.

Shops & Services

Caroline's Fine Wine Cellar
Forest Glade House, Tokai Road, Tokai (021 712 2258, www.carolineswine.com). **Open** 9.30am-5.30pm Mon-Fri; 9.30am-1.30pm Sat. **Wine**
This Tokai branch opened fairly recently and offers the same fantastic array of wines from South Africa and all over the world as the City Centre original. You'll get expert advice on new world and European wines, as well as brandy and bubblies. Keep an eye on the website for tastings and events.
Other location Matador Centre, 62 Strand Street, City Centre (021 419 8984).

Constantia Village
Constantia Main Road & Spaanschemat River Road, Constantia (www.constantiavillage.co.za). **Open** 9am-6pm Mon-Fri; 9am-5pm Sat; 9am-2pm Sun. **Mall**
This small, single-level mall includes a massive Pick n Pay supermarket and Woolworths. Boutiques and beauty stores do a good trade and there are some good spots to grab a light meal or cup of tea.

Tsonga Shoes
Constantia Village, Constantia Main Road & Spaanschemat River Road, Constantia (021 794 8827, www.tsonga.com). **Open** 9am-6pm Mon-Fri; 9am-5pm Sat; 9am-1pm Sun. **Shoes**
This South African success story specialises in suede and leather hand-tooled footwear in a kaleidoscope of colours: from loafers to elegant Ugg-style boots and the comfiest slip-ons.

IN THE KNOW TOWNSHIP TOURS

These tour operators offer an insightful, informative glimpse into township living in Cape Town today. **Camissa Tours** (021 510 2646, www.gocamissa.co.za) provides specialised tours in addition to its standard ones – try one with a gospel, soccer or food theme. **Inkululeko Freedom Tours** (021 511 5642, 021 511 8215, www.inkululeko tours.co.za) starts off in District Six before heading to Langa and Khayelitsha. **Awol Tours** (021 418 3803, www.awoltours. co.za) offers biking tours. **Cape Capers** (021 448 3117, www.tourcapers.co.za) and **Cape Town Township Tours** (084 945 0739, www.townshiptourscapetown.co.za) take visitors to Langa, Cape Town's oldest township.

EXPLORE

South Peninsula

If it's scenic splendour and ocean vistas you're after, the South Peninsula is the place to be. A looping tour around to Cape Point can be done in a day, but there's so much to explore that you could spend a week on this finger of coastline. First stop is Muizenberg: known for its great surfing (and warmer waters), this stretch of coast is also home to great white sharks. Kalk Bay is a charming harbour town with seafood restaurants, boutiques and antiques shops. Simon's Town hosts an active naval base as well as a colony of African penguins: you can even swim with them off Boulders Beach. A scenic drive takes you to Cape Point with the lovely Cape of Good Hope Nature Reserve. Back towards the city, you'll find Noordhoek with its horsey set and vast beach before Chapman's Peak's twists and turns deliver you to Hout Bay.

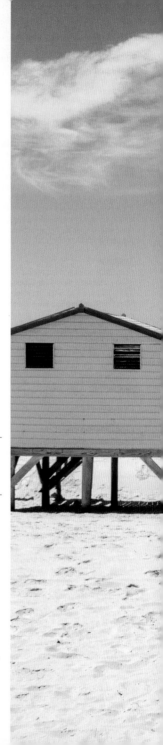

Muizenberg Beach.

Don't Miss

1 Cape Point Splendid scenery and a dash of wildlife (p135).

2 Boulders Beach African penguins call this beach home (p133).

3 Kalk Bay Boutiques, antiques and great eats in this harbour town (p130).

4 Silvermine Nature Reserve A glorious spot to hike, bike or braai (p137).

5 Muizenberg Beach Catch that perfect wave, dude (p128).

MUIZENBERG

Steeped in history, Muizenberg is a seaside resort popular with surfer dudes, beach babes and fun-seeking families. Synonymous with big breaks, Muizenberg's Surfer's Corner draws scores of boarders looking to catch that perfect swell. Recently, hip restaurants and cafés have opened up along the beachfront, giving a much-needed injection of development to the area. If you're after a relaxing, unpretentious day at the beach, this is an ideal spot to let down your hair and soak up the sun.

To reach the beach, turn into Atlantic Road from Main Road, pass under the bridge and take the second right to park at the mountain end, or continue straight to the parking area. The Catwalk is a level path between the sea and railway line along the shore between Muizenberg and St James. The walk takes around 40 minutes, but since there's so much to see and explore along the way (it's a great whale-watching hangout in season and the rock pools are lined with anemones) it might take longer.

Snaking between Muizenberg and Kalk Bay, Boyes Drive offers an impressive view of False Bay, and a convenient alternative route if you're seeking to avoid the occasionally bumper-to-bumper seaside road that seems to be undergoing perennial roadworks. The drive is dotted with lookout points from which to take in the expansive vistas, as well as starting points for various hiking routes.

Sights & Museums

FREE Het Posthuys
180 Main Road (021 788 7972, 021 788 5951). **Open** varies; phone in advance. **Admission** free; donations appreciated.
Formerly known as Stegmansrust, this inconspicuous, thatched Lego-block of a house is believed to be the oldest building in the False Bay area. Built by the VOC in 1673, it was used as a lookout point by the Dutch during their occupation of the Cape, and later became a toll-house for passing farmers who wanted to sell their produce to ships in Simon's Town (then Simon's Bay). Today, it houses a small museum featuring a few interesting displays about the Battle of Muizenberg (when the house came under fire) and historic photos of a Muizenberg long forgotten. As the museum is run by volunteers, it's best to phone ahead and make an appointment.

Tiger's Milk Restaurant & Bar.

Rhodes Cottage
242 Main Road (021 788 1816, 072 482 6131, 082 425 3092). **Open** 10am-2pm Mon-Sat. **Admission** R10. **No credit cards**.
This seaside chalet is where Cecil John Rhodes breathed his last, leaving behind a vast legacy at the relatively young age of 49. A mine magnate, politician and firm believer in the superiority of the white, Anglo-Saxon race, he did his utmost to expand the British Empire during his short life, colonising Rhodesia (now Zimbabwe) during his time as Prime Minister of the Cape Colony (1890-95). He built this house in 1899, dying here three years later from tuberculosis. You'll see photos, clippings and caricatures revealing the man behind the un-PC speeches (a treasure trove of which can be found in the well-thumbed copy of his last will and testament). The museum is manned by volunteer curators, so it's worth checking if the museum is actually open before you visit.

Surfing

Muizenberg is one of Cape Town's top surf spots, with consistently good waves and slightly warmer water than on the Atlantic Seaboard. If you're a novice, there are some excellent places to learn the ropes.

Gary's Surf School
34 Beach Road (021 788 9839, www.garysurf.com). **Lesson** R380/2hrs.

Learn2Surf
Beach Road (083 414 0567, www.learn2surf.co.za). **Lesson** R350/90mins.

Surfshack
13 York Road (021 788 9286, www.surfshack.co.za). **Lesson** R360/90mins.

Restaurants & Cafés

Empire Café
11 York Road (021 788 1250, www.empirecafeco.za). **Open** 7am-4pm Mon, Tue; 7am-9pm Wed-Fri; 8am-4pm Sun. **Main courses** R120. **Mediterranean**
If laid-back surfer chic is your thing, you'll love this unpretentious café, which dishes up saucy pastas, steaks, fresh line-caught fish and wraps. Wednesday burger nights are a local favourite.

Knead
82 Beach Road, Surfer's Corner (021 788 2909, www.kneadbakery.co.za). **Open** 8am-5.30pm Mon, Sun; 8am-7pm Tue-Thur; 8am-8pm Fri, Sat. **Main courses** R65. **Bakery**
Join the throngs of Muizenberg surfers for artisan breads, pastries, pies and pizzas – all fresh from the oven. You can make up your own platter with a choice of nine breads and toppings, or go the easy route and order ready-made rolls with fillings such as roast chicken, roast tomato and red onion.

★ Tiger's Milk Restaurant & Bar
Corner of Beach Road & Sidmouth Road (021 788 1860, www.tigersmilk.co.za). **Open** 11am-2am daily. **Main courses** R120. **Grill**
Proudly offering 'dude food', this new first-floor warehouse space ticks a lot of boxes: there's an open kitchen so you can watch the chefs at work, vast picture windows for expansive sea views, and craft beers on tap. Food is fast and filling – sticky ribs, calamari with aïoli, man-sized burgers and top-notch dry-aged steaks. It's a cool, masculine space, brightened with yellow furniture. To top it all off, there's a motorbike mounted on the wall.

FISH HOEK

Fish Hoek itself isn't much of a looker, but its lovely sandy beaches make it well worth the drive. Fish Hoek and Clovelly beaches are very family-oriented, with a playground for children to enjoy in between ice-creams. It's a great spot for snorkelling too. Jaeger Walk is named after Fish Hoek's first mayor. The short, wheelchair-friendly walkway hugs the False Bay coast from Fish Hoek Beach to Sunny Cove. There are benches along the way to sit down and take in the serene surroundings.

EXPLORE

KALK BAY

This quaint, laid-back harbour town is the ideal place to stop off for a lazy lunch. Around 1pm every day, fleets of local fishing boats return to the busy harbour with everything from snoek and chokka to red romans and yellowtail, all freshly plucked from the surrounding choppy waters. A seafood lunch is on the cards, but be sure to spend some time exploring the various boutiques (some hip, some hippy) and antiques shops lining the main road. A water taxi service between Kalk Bay and Simon's Town makes for a fun addition to your sightseeing trip (www.watertaxi.co.za).

Sights & Museums

Save Our Seas Shark Education Centre
28 Main Road (021 788 6694, www.sharkcentre. com). **Open** 10am-4pm Mon-Fri.
The immersive, multi-sensory exhibits at this centre aim to educate both young and old on the vital role sharks play in the ocean's ecosystem. The centre organises school outings to see marine life and champions awareness and environmental responsibility. A great place to take budding eco warriors.

Restaurants & Cafés

Cape to Cuba
165 Main Road (021 788 1566, http://cape tocuba.co.za). **Open** 9am-10pm daily. **Main courses** R100. **Cuban**
Step into old Havana at Cape to Cuba, a heady mix of heavy wooden furniture, palm trees, cigar paraphernalia, chandeliers, candles and Panama hats. It's a laid-back spot where you can sample a plethora of cocktails and tuck into Cuban and Cajun fare.

★ Harbour House
Kalk Bay Harbour, off Main Road (021 788 4133, www.harbourhouse.co.za). **Open** noon-4pm, 6-10pm daily. **Main courses** R165. **Seafood**
With a spectacular setting on the rocks, it's no wonder this is such a popular spot. Whitewashed walls and vast windows lend a beachy feel to the space. It's seafood all the way: start with signature masala-dusted calamari, oysters or seafood ceviche before getting stuck into seafood platters, linefish and crayfish. There are excellent grills and a sushi menu too.
Other location Quay Four, Ground Floor, V&A Waterfront (021 418 4744).

Kalky's
Kalk Bay Harbour (021 788 1726). **Open** 10am-8pm daily. **Main courses** R65.
No credit cards. **Seafood**
There are few things as satisfying as tucking into fish and chips with your fingers. It's as fresh as you can get at this tiny spot, which serves hake, snoek and linefish. Eat in or get a takeaway and scoff it sitting on the harbour wall – just mind the seagulls.

Live Bait
Kalk Bay Harbour (021 788 5755). **Open** noon-10pm daily. **Main courses** R100. **Seafood**
Step into a corner of the Med in this chilled-out, whitewashed space. For those with luxury tastes,

---

IN THE KNOW WHALE WATCH

Every winter and spring, southern right whales head to the Cape's south coast to give birth to their calves. Although the seaside town of Hermanus (see p184) is undoubtedly the whale-watching capital of the country, you may spot them from the following vantage points between August and November. Try the Catwalk (along the shoreline between Muizenberg and St James), Jaeger Walk (between Fish Hoek Beach and Sunny Cove) or simply park up on the Kalk Bay Harbour wall. Other top spots include the coast road between Fish Hoek and Cape Point, Chapman's Peak Drive (a toll road between Hout Bay and Noordhoek), Boyes Drive between Muizenberg and Kalk Bay (turn into Boyes Drive from Main Road in Muizenberg), or further afield off the R27 West Coast Road between Bloubergstrand and Melkbosstrand.

EXPLORE

Harbour House.

there's fresh sashimi, pan-fried spice-dusted calamari, and seafood platters that'll have the table groaning. For everyone else, there's scrumptious battered fish and chips.

Lucky Fish & Chips

157 Main Road (021 788 4133, www.luckyfish andchips.co.za). **Open** 10am-9pm Mon-Sat. **Fish & chips** R39. Seafood
This spot ticks the budget list and provides wonderfully fresh fish and chips in a bright, spotless setting. Choose from tender calamari, prawns, hake, linefish or snoek to eat in or take away. And don't forget to pick up one of the delicious rolls.
Other locations throughout the city.

★ Olympia Café & Deli

134 Main Road (021 788 6396). **Open** 7am-9pm Mon-Sat. **Main courses** R90. Mediterranean
Olympia is a Kalk Bay legend among laid-back locals and hip things from town. The breakfast at this informal deli is an institution – fluffy scrambled eggs, flaky croissants, mushrooms on toast. The daily-changing blackboard lunch menu is short and features the likes of tuna, linefish, creamy mussels or seafood linguine. It's a busy spot, so you'll probably have to queue to get in. Once inside, service is warm and welcoming.

Polana

Kalk Bay Harbour (021 788 7162). **Open** noon-4pm, 6-10pm daily. **Main courses** R140. Mozambican

Turn up the spice factor a notch with some Mozambican fare at this laid-back eaterie. Favourites include calamari stuffed with chorizo, peri-peri prawns, and a selection of grills. Those wanting a snack can choose from the tapas menu, which features a tempting seafood platter. The lounge space overlooking the crashing waves is a great spot to chill.

Pubs & Bars

Brass Bell

Kalk Bay Station, Main Road (021 788 5455, www.brassbell.co.za). **Open** 8am-2am daily.
Take the train to Kalk Bay and you can hop off at the water's edge. The ever-popular Brass Bell has several options – indoor and outdoor – and it's next to a tidal pool that kids will love. Upstairs is a traditional bar with nautical knick-knacks, while the decks downstairs have a more laid-back vibe. Service is bright and friendly, and there's live music some afternoons and evenings.

Shops & Services

Artvark

48 Main Road (021 788 5584, www.artvark.org). **Open** 9am-6pm daily (5pm in winter). Gallery
At this wonderful artists' showcase you can browse captivating paintings, ceramics, jewellery, crafts and textiles. The mixed media creates an eclectic feel, and it's definitely high up the list for original souvenirs and homewares.

Big Blue
82 Main Road (021 788 2399, http://bigblue.co.za). **Open** 9am-5pm daily. **Fashion**
Zany T-shirts, bright printed fabric dresses and crazy toys and gifts are all par for the course at this popular fashion stop. Locally branded onesies make fun gifts, while guys can grab a Madiba shirt. **Other locations** throughout the city.

Kalk Bay Books
124 Main Road (021 788 2266, www.kalkbaybooks. co.za). **Open** 9am-6pm daily (5pm in winter). **Books**
This quaint shop stocks classics and a quality selection of newer titles. There are also notable cookery and kids' sections, plus book launches and readings.

Kalk Bay Modern
1st Floor, Olympia Building, 136 Main Road (021 788 6571, www.kalkbaymodern.co.za). **Open** 9.30am-5pm daily. **Gallery**
Sculpture, photography and paintings share space with jewellery, textiles and ceramics at this gallery, all framed by lovely ocean views. There's an emphasis on nurturing new local talent, but there are also some more established names on the books, such as Beezy Bailey, Conrad Botes and Jurgen Schadeberg. A must-see is the contemporary southern African San art.

Quagga Art & Books
84 Main Road (021 788 2752, www.quagga books.co.za). **Open** 9.30am-5pm Mon-Sat; 10am-5pm Sun. **Antiques**

This is Cape Town's most authentic antiquarian bookshop, with a strong focus on Africana, art and history. Maps, pictures and objets d'art create a unique atmosphere.

Railway House Décor & Collectables
23 Main Road (021 788 4761). **Open** 9am-5pm Mon-Sat; 10am-5pm Sun. **Antiques**
This bargain-hunter's paradise consistently yields treasures for collectors of ephemera, curiosities and 20th-century antiques. The stock is suffused with overtones of the colonial, nautical and generally quaint – and prices are affordable.

ST JAMES

Images of the red, blue, green and yellow-coloured beach huts at St James Pool can be found splashed across tourist guides and postcards, but you still won't be able to resist the temptation to snap away. The calm waters of the saltwater pool are great for a leisurely bob and a lovely place to bring the kids for a splash if they're weary of being pounded by waves. To reach the pool, park near St James Station, then head through the tunnel running under the railway line.

Sights & Museums

FREE Casa Labia
192 Main Road (021 788 6068, http://casalabia. co.za). **Open** 10am-4pm Tue-Sun. **Admission** free.

Big Blue.

Casa Labia, built in 1929 as the residence of the Count and Countess Natale Labia, has undergone a massive renovation. Today it's a magnificent, opulent cultural centre and function venue that houses a gallery of modern South African art and the CasBah Design Boutique, selling beautiful crafts, clothing and jewellery from the African continent. The charming café spreads out from the drawing room and sunroom into the courtyard. Enjoy breakfast, light lunch or heavenly cakes and then stroll through the terraced gardens.

SIMON'S TOWN

Named for Cape governor Simon van der Stel, Simon's Town's sheltered harbour became a viable alternative to the often stormy Table Bay during Cape Town's early days. In 1806, a Royal Navy base was established here and the maritime tradition continues to this day – Simon's Town is still home to an active South African Navy base. A walk along St George's Street showcases some lovely examples of Victorian architecture with its signature use of *broekie* lace railings.

Sights & Museums

★ Boulders African Penguin Colony

Kleintuin Road, parking area in Seaforth Road (021 786 2329, www.tmnp.co.za). **Open** *Jan, Dec* 7am-7.30pm daily. *Feb, Mar, Oct, Nov* 8am-6.30pm daily. *Apr-Sept* 8am-5pm daily. **Admission** R60; R30 reductions; free under-2s.

The dunes here, reached via a boardwalk, shelter the endangered African penguins that call Boulders Beach home. The colony was established in 1983, and in 2011 there were an estimated 2,100 penguins here. Also known as jackass penguins, their braying call is ear-splitting. Prepare to be transfixed as they waddle around before heading into the water and surfing the waves like pros.

Heritage Museum

King George Way (021 786 2302). **Open** 11am-4pm Tue-Fri; 11am-1pm Sat; by appt Sun. **Admission** R5. **No credit cards**.
In 1965, Simon's Town was declared a 'whites only' area under the Group Areas Act and saw the forced removal of close to 7,000 'coloured' people from their homes. The Amlay family were the last residents to be evicted, in 1975, and the first to return in 1995. Today, the Amlay house has become the Heritage Museum, curated by Zainab Davidson (née Amlay) who tells the story of this turbulent time. The rooms are filled with photos, press clippings and historical artefacts such as handwritten *kitaabs* (books), bridal and haj attire and cooking utensils, all casting light on the culturally rich heritage of the town's erstwhile Muslim community.

Just Nuisance's Grave

By car: Naval Signal School, Klawer Valley Nature Reserve, off Redhill Drive (look for a sign just past Pine Haven). On foot: Historic Steps, Barnard Street (start of Runciman Drive).
Standing atop a steep set of stone steps, this bronze statue overlooking Simon's Town immortalises the spirit of probably the coolest seafarer ever to set foot (paw, in this case) on deck. During World War II, this beer-guzzling Great Dane was enlisted as an able seaman in the Royal Navy under the occupation 'Bone Crusher', which entitled him to his own railway pass, free access to all the ships in the harbour and his own bunk. Just Nuisance was a local at all the pubs in Cape Town, and accompanied many of his inebriated shipmates safely back to their quarters.

Kayak Cape Town

Wharf Street (082 501 8930, www.kayak capetown.co.za). **Trips** daily, weather permitting. **Cost** from R300/person for a two-hour trip.

EXPLORE

Paddle a two-person stable kayak from the harbour to Boulders Beach to admire the penguins, and even indulge in a spot of whale-watching in season. No experience is necessary. Experienced kayakers will enjoy the more extreme trip to Cape Point.

Mineral World & Scratch Patch

Dido Valley Road (021 786 2020, www.scratch patch.co.za). **Open** 8.30am-4.45pm Mon-Fri; 9am-5.30pm Sat, Sun. **Admission** free. *Scratch Patch R14 for a small bag.*

This multicoloured pebble paradise teeming with kids has been around since 1970. Buy a bag and delve through the Scratch Patch: mounds of tumble-polished tiger's eyes, amethysts and crystals. With enough patience, you might even manage to snatch a few of those elusive lapis lazuli from in front of your pint-sized neighbours' little noses. After you've filled your bag, head over to the Mineral World factory shop and see where the stones get their shine.
Other location Dock Road, V&A Waterfront (021 419 9429).

Simon's Town Boat Company

Wharf Street (083 257 7760, http://boatcompany. co.za). **Trips** daily. **Cost** *Seal Island cruise* R400. *Whale-watching cruise* R850.

A range of vessels offer visitors the chance to get up close to whales, seals, dolphins, penguins, sharks and marine birdlife along the False Bay coast. Local experts skipper and provide information during the cruises.

Simon's Town Museum

The Residency, Court Road (021 786 3046, www. simonstown.com/museum). **Open** 9am-4pm Mon-Fri; 10am-1pm Sat; 11am-3pm Sun. **Admission** R5; R1-R2 reductions. **No credit cards.**

Built in 1777, the Residency has been home to many of the town's colourful inhabitants, from postmasters to constables, crooks and ladies of ill repute. Today, it's home to a museum about Simon's Town's fascinating past: exhibits cover the late Stone Age until the forced removals of the 1960s. Some of them could do with a bit of sprucing up, but most visitors will find something to interest them – be it the Early History Room

Cape Point.

with its hunter-gatherer dioramas; the Military Room displaying artefacts from both World Wars; or the more light-hearted Just Nuisance Room, featuring the Great Dane's collar and newspaper clippings covering his antics. For the fear factor, head down to the cells and stare into the abyss of the black hole.

South African Naval Museum

Naval Dockyard, St George's Street (021 787 4686, www.simonstown.com/navalmuseum). **Open** 9.30am-3.30pm daily. **Admission** free.

Kids will love the ship and submarine models, life-size control room, torpedoes, anti-sub mortar, diving equipment and sea mines. Brave the menacingly steep flight of stairs for a look at the inner workings of the old clock tower. Naval uniforms and portraiture lend a poignant air to the display.

Warrior Toy Museum & Collectors' Shop

St George's Street (021 786 1395). **Open** 10am-3.45pm Mon-Thur, Sat. **Admission** R5.

IN THE KNOW LOCAL VOICES

For a different kind of tour guide, download some of the **VoiceMap** apps (www.voice map.me, prices vary) to take you on a walking tour of more than 20 areas around the Cape Town peninsula. Created by a local Capetonian, these audio walking tours are downloaded on to your phone and can then be used offline during your walk, aided by interactive maps and tips on the area. Passionate locals, journalists, novelists and tour guides share their favourite spots.

The tongue-in-cheek warning next to the chugging toy train warns: 'No smoking unless you're a train'. Shelves of 'celebrity' toy cars such as a flying Chitty Chitty Bang Bang and Mr Bean's yellow Mini stand side by side with older, more valuable examples. Other exhibits include a battalion of toy soldiers warding off an attack by spear-wielding Zulu warriors, and there's also a collection of glassy-eyed porcelain dolls.

Restaurants & Cafés

Bertha's
Wharf Street (021 786 2138, www.berthas.co.za). **Open** 7.30am-10pm daily. **Main courses** R100. Seafood/grill
Set right on the water's edge, this bright, airy restaurant lends itself to sun-drenched lunches overlooking the pier. While the vast space does cater to tour groups, the setting more than makes up for the distraction. There's a good choice of seafood on the menu, along with pastas, burgers and grilled meat.

Black Marlin
Main Road, Miller's Point (021 786 1621, www.blackmarlin.co.za). **Open** 9am-9pm daily. **Main courses** R150. Seafood
It may look like tourist central on a sunny day, but Black Marlin is a top choice for fish and seafood. Cape Malay seafood curry, kingklip skewer or seared tuna steak are popular choices. Or go the whole hog and share a seafood platter heaving with the ocean's bounty. On a clear day, the garden and verandah are the best spots – whales can be spotted in season.

CAPE POINT

At the tip of the South Peninsula lies verdant Cape Point. The Atlantic Ocean and Indian Ocean don't meet here, though, much as the marketing brochures try to persuade you otherwise (that's further down the coast at L'Agulhas). The surrounding areas have a few good stops next to the road to stock up on every conceivable African animal carved out of wood.

SHARK SAFETY
Staying safe in Cape Town's waters.

South Africa has an incredibly diverse shark population. A quarter of the world's shark species (98 to be precise) dwell in its waters and around 40 of these call the seas around Cape Town home. A scary thought, perhaps, but on average there's only one fatal attack per year.

The **Shark Spotters** (www.shark spotters.org.za or follow @SharkSpotters) organisation places spotters at strategic lookout points, mostly along the False Bay coastline, to advise on shark activity and promote beach safety. Beaches under surveillance include Surfers' Corner at Muizenberg, Danger Beach at St James, Fish Hoek Beach, and the Hoek, Noordhoek. Spotters communicate by walkie-talkie and use flags to signal to beachgoers. So, if you're planning a swim, learn the signals:

Green flag Spotting conditions good
Black flag Spotting conditions poor
Red flag High shark alert
White flag with a black shark Shark spotted!

Some tips before you hit the waves: familiarise yourself with the area before hitting the water; swim at a beach that has Shark Spotters; don't swim alone or far out (most bites take place beyond the surf break); and don't swim when there's fishing activity in the vicinit

Sights & Museums

★ Cape of Good Hope Nature Reserve
Cape Point (021 780 9010, www.capepoint. co.za). **Open** *Apr-Sept* 7am-5pm daily. *Oct-Mar* 6am-6pm daily. **Admission** R110; R55 reductions.

The vast, beautiful Cape of Good Hope Nature Reserve was declared part of the Cape World Heritage Site in 2004. Trails within the 7,750-hectare park lead to shipwrecks, tidal pools, lighthouses and Antonie's Gat, the hiding place of a slave turned Muslim saint. There's an abundance of wildlife – kids will have fun spotting Cape mountain zebra, eland and whales in season, while twitchers will delight in the 250 bird species found here. If you don't feel like walking to the pinnacle, climb aboard the Flying Dutchman funicular that will take you all the way from Cape Point to the upper lighthouse. For a meal with a spectacular view, head to the Two Oceans Restaurant.

FREE Cape Point Ostrich Farm
Plateau Road, off M65, opposite entrance to Cape Point (021 780 9294, www.capepointostrichfarm. com). **Open** 9.30am-5.30pm daily. **Admission** free. *Guided tours* R55; R25 reductions.

Forty pairs of birds live at this family-owned ostrich-breeding farm. Each pair has its own private outdoor suite to keep the romance alive (and also to keep a steady supply of eggs coming). The guided tour takes you through the incubators and breeding rooms, and features interesting facts on the history of the once-lucrative ostrich-feather trade. There's a coffee shop and a shop selling ostrich leather paraphernalia on site.

KOMMETJIE

This tiny village has a child-friendly beach that's also a haven for surfers. Slangkop Lighthouse is the tallest cast-iron lighthouse in the country, and it also has one of the brightest lights, with a range of 33 nautical miles (around 61km). It was first lit in 1919 and is still operational today.

Sights & Museums

★ Imhoff Farm
Kommetjie Road (021 783 4545, www.imhoff farm.co.za). **Open** 9am-5pm daily. **Admission** free, activities vary.

Upon ordering the construction of the Simon's Town refreshment centre in 1743, VOC commissioner Baron von Imhoff heard of a very special woman, widow Christina Diemer, who had been supplying sailors with produce from her farm, Swaaneweide. Suitably impressed with her initiative, he gave her a piece of land near Slangkop, which later became known as Imhoff's Gift. These days the farm is a commercial enterprise, with a variety of animal experiences: there's a snake park, camel and horse rides, and the chance for kids to feed the goats, pigs, rabbits, ducks and chickens. There are shops selling clothes, kids' toys, crafts, art, plants, chocolate and wine, plus a 4x4 trail. Relax over a meal while the kids run riot in the treehouse at Blue Water Café and stock up on home-made delights at the Farm Shop before you leave.

NOORDHOEK

The magnificent 8km-long Noordhoek beach is perfect for hiking and horse riding, and the adjoining wetlands ensure it remains an unspoilt area. It lies between Kommetjie and the end of Chapman's Peak Drive, which takes you to Hout Bay and the Atlantic Seaboard. Noordhoek is a haven for families and provides a bucolic escape from city life.

Sights & Museums

Silvermine Nature Reserve
Ou Kaapse Weg (021 780 9002, www.tmnp.co.za). **Open** 7am-7pm daily. **Admission** R30; R15 reductions. **No credit cards**.

Stretching all the way from the Tokai side of Table Mountain to the Noordhoek and Sun Valley area overlooking the sea, the Silvermine Nature Reserve was ravaged by a brutal fire in early 2015 that saw the South Peninsula ablaze for almost a week. What followed was an eerie moonscape scene of devastation, but the endemic fynbos (which requires fire to regenerate) has quickly sprung up again and the area is returning to its former glory. The reserve has trails ranging from easy-peasy to brutal, plus mountain-biking routes and bird-watching opportunities at every turn. Adrenaline addicts can get their kicks at the rock climbing area near the Silvermine reservoir or by exploring the sandstone caves. The picnic and braai areas offer panoramic views without the need for all that wearisome exercise.

Restaurants & Cafés

Café Roux
270 Chapman's Peak Drive, Noordhoek Farm Village (021 789 2538, www.caferoux.co.za). **Open** 8.30am-5pm daily. **Main courses** R100. Bistro

This child-friendly venue boasts a massive play area with jungle gyms and playhouses, where the kids can jump about while parents relax under umbrellas at the outdoor benches. Fare is simple, straightforward and satisfying: think burgers, salads, hearty breakfasts and great bakes. Gigs have become a local drawcard with the likes of Prime Circle and Kahn Morbee from the Parlotones gracing the bandstand.

★ Cape Point Vineyards
Silvermine Road (021 789 0900, http://cpv.co.za). **Open** *Tastings & picnics* 10am-5pm Mon-Sat. *Market* noon-3pm Sun (4-8pm in summer). **Cheese platter** R250; **Picnic basket** R395/2pers. Wine estate

This top winery with stunning mountain and sea views is popular with locals and visitors alike. Go for a wine tasting and linger over a cheese or charcuterie platter on the wooden deck, order a picnic to enjoy on the benches scattered all over the lawns, or enjoy fresh fare at the weekly community market. The function venue is set to be transformed into a 160-seater restaurant in late 2015 and, frankly, we can't wait.

★ Foodbarn
Noordhoek Farm Village, Village Lane (021 789 1390, www.thefoodbarn.co.za). **Open** noon-2.30pm Mon, Tue, Sun; noon-2.30pm, 6.30-9.30pm Wed-Sat. **Main courses** R150. South African/French

Refined fare in a rustic setting is the hallmark of the Foodbarn, where chef Franck Dangereux holds sway. Seasonal produce gets transformed into delicious eats: think Karoo lamb, kidney and pinotage pot pie or sustainable fish with crushed, caramelised butternut. More traditional French-inspired dishes could include a bouillabaisse of local seafood or goat's cheese fritters with roasted celeriac. Demo dinners as well as chef's tables paired with wine estates are proving popular with the local set. The Foodbarn Deli on the other side of Noordhoek Farm Village is perfect for coffee, breakfast or delicious pies, quiches and sweet treats to take away during the day. At night, enjoy a glass of wine with tapas.

Pubs & Bars

Beach Road Bar
Red Herring Restaurant, Corner of Beach Road & Pine Road (021 789 1783, www.theredherring.co.za). **Open** 10am-10pm Mon-Sat; noon-10pm Sun.

The newly revamped Beach Road Bar, located above the Red Herring Restaurant, is a Noordhoek favourite. With endless beach views from the expansive deck, a roaring fire in winter, great pizzas and a decent selection of beers on tap, this spot fits the bill for a laid-back afternoon. Live music adds to the appeal.

EXPLORE

Northern Suburbs

EXPLORE

Cape Town's Northern Suburbs are very residential, but while these areas aren't high on the sightseeing list they offer gorgeous views of Table Mountain. Head north from Cape Town up the west coast and top of the list for those views are the towns of Table View and Bloubergstrand. They might be windy, but they're a haven for kite-surfers and cocktail-drinkers come sunset. Heading inland, shoppers congregate at the massive Canal Walk mall, with 400 shops vying for their hard-earned cash. And, along the N1 highway, the Durbanville area is renowned for its award-winning wineries, with the sauvignon blanc cultivar doing especially well thanks to the cool Atlantic breezes from the ocean nearby. Here weekends are filled with outings to wine farms, many of them family-friendly, and long, lazy lunches of rustic eats with more great wines – and those views.

Don't Miss

De Grendel Restaurant.

1 **Bloubergstrand** For picture-perfect views (p140).

2 **Durbanville Wine Valley** Find top sauvignon blancs (p143).

3 **Canal Walk** For serious shopping (p141).

4 **De Grendel Restaurant** Haute cuisine in a historical setting (p144).

5 **Blue Peter** An ideal spot to hang out with the locals over a sundowner (p141).

Blue Peter Lower Deck.

WEST COAST: MILNERTON TO BLOUBERGSTRAND

The R27, off the N1, takes you all the way up the Cape West Coast. First up, though, is the industrial area of Paarden Eiland, which makes way for suburb-by-the-sea **Milnerton** – its beach by the lagoon is a lovely spot for walkers. The town of **Table View** comes next, with **Dolphin Beach** (Marine Drive): it's hardly the spot for a picnic as the wind here is almost as certain as death and taxes. But that wind makes for great kitesurfing; indeed, the beach is internationally renowned for it. What's more, the views of Table Mountain from here are picture-perfect.

The office parks and residential areas of **Century City** are dwarfed by **Canal Walk** shopping mall. You'll find pretty much anything you need here, but be warned, it's heaving on end-of-month weekends.

The small coastal town of **Bloubergstrand** is an outpost for both adrenaline junkies and cocktail drinkers. Its beach (Otto du Plessis Drive) is the perfect vantage point from which to trace the complete, iconic outline of Table Mountain ('Blouberg' translates as 'Blue Mountain'). It also gets its fair share of gale-force winds, which makes it as popular with kitesurfers as neighbouring Table View. If you're lucky enough to visit on a wind-free day, slather on the suncream and find a quiet spot on the sand before braving the icy waves.

Sights & Museums

Cape Town Ostrich Ranch

Van Schoorsdrif Road Philadelphia, off N7 (021 972 1955, www.ostrichranch.co.za). **Open** 9am-5pm daily. **Tours** R80; R31-R65 reductions.

There's more than just ostriches at this ostrich farm, where you'll see emus and rheas too, including chicks hatching in an incubator. The leather factory showcases a variety of products made with the sought-after skin, and there are plenty of eggshell mementos too. You can also sample lean ostrich meat at the on-site restaurant and your children will enjoy the playground. The highlight of a visit is posing on an ostrich with Table Mountain in the background.

EXPLORE

Restaurants & Cafés

Blowfish

*Dolphin Beach Hotel, 1 Marine Drive,
Bloubergstrand (021 556 5464, www.blowfish
restaurant.co.za).* **Open** 6.30-10.30am, 12.30-
10pm daily. **Main courses** R130. Seafood
A location right on Dolphin Beach provides this
upmarket seafood joint with a view of the Table
Mountain in all its postcard splendour. It's known
for its first-rate fish and sushi (which you can pick
off the conveyor belt). Diners also choose their fish
from the counter, which is then grilled and given a
feisty kick with some Cajun spices or flavoured with
milder garlic and lemon.

On the Rocks

*45 Stadler Road, Bloubergstrand (021 554 1988,
http://ontherocks.co.za).* **Open** 9am-10pm daily.
Main courses R150. Global
A local stalwart, On the Rocks enjoys a perfect setting right next to the ocean and a seat on the deck
under an umbrella is the perfect place to be on a
warm, windless day. The menu has global influences
– like Thai red chicken curry – as well as local dishes
and ingredients. You might start with springbok

carpaccio or bouillabaisse with mussels, before
moving on to pan-seared kingklip or beef fillet ross-
ini. Seafood platters with linefish (line-caught fish),
calamari and prawns are also popular .

Pubs & Bars

★ Blue Peter Lower Deck

*Blue Peter Hotel, 7 Popham Road, Bloubergstrand
(021 554 1956, www.bluepeter.co.za).* **Open**
10am-10pm daily.
Sipping sundowners at the Blue Peter has been a
Cape Town ritual for decades, and you'll see why
when you arrive during the twilight hours. The
sloping lawn outside the downstairs bistro and
bar is the perfect place to be on a warm afternoon,
with a few ice-cold beers from the tap. Casual eats
include crowd-pleasing pizzas from a wood-burn-
ing oven,while live music at weekends adds to the
relaxed vibe.

Shops & Services

Canal Walk

*Century Boulevard, Century City (021 555 4444,
www.canalwalk.co.za).* **Open** 9am-9pm daily. Mall

EXPLORE

TAKING IT TO EXTREMES
Climb every mountain, surf every wave.

With mountains to climb up, trails to run down, and waves to splash through, Cape Town has everything an adventure sportsperson could ask for.

Adrenaline junkies, thrill seekers, extreme-sports enthusiasts: whatever they want to call themselves (and it's probably none of the above), they'll find a place for their *Point Break* re-enactments in Cape Town. While most cities would settle for a mountain to climb up, a beach to surf at, or maybe just some waterways to explore, Cape Town gets its blood pumping with all of the above. And, if you don't mind a short drive up the coast, it even has a big sky to dive out of.

Naturally, much of the focus is on the mountain. **Abseil Africa** (021 424 4760, www.abseilafrica.co.za) uses a spectacular (and we don't use that word lightly) 112-metre abseil/rap jump site near Table Mountain's Upper Cableway Station, while the **Mountain Club of South Africa** (021 465 3412, www.mcsacapetown.co.za) can help you out with information on various local climbs and hikes. And on the days when Table Mountain's cold and cloudy 'tablecloth' makes climbing dangerous, the walls at **CityROCK Indoor Climbing Centre** (021 447 1326, www.cityrock.co.za) provide an indoor alternative.

Trail running is an increasingly popular activity for runners who are tired of pounding pavement – and again, the mountains around Cape Town (especially some of the lower Table Mountain trails) offer excellent routes and races. You can find information on organised events at www.trailrunning.co.za (072 924 2371).

If you'd prefer to wheel your way down the mountain, **Tokai Forest** has mountain-biking trails which – much to the relief of both bikers and hikers – are kept separate from the hiking trails. **Deer Park**, on the front slopes of Table Mountain, is another popular choice for mountain bikers, as are **Silvermine** (on the South Peninsula – you'll need to get a Wild Card from the Table Mountain National Park office at the foot of Ou Kaapse Weg) and **Majik Forest** (in the Northern Suburbs near Durbanville). **Downhill Adventures** (021 422 0388, www.downhilladventures.com) can help with routes and information.

Down below, meanwhile, the oceans and small lakes around Cape Town are great for paddling, canoeing, rafting, kayaking and surf skiing, with the relatively sheltered **Three Anchor Bay** and **Mouille Point** popular spots for sea kayaking. Surf kayakers, meanwhile, might prefer **Muizenburg, Hout Bay** or **Witsand** (near Misty Cliffs on the South Peninsula), while beginners – surf skiers especially – will want to try **Simon's Town** on the False Bay coast. (Just watch out for sharks, especially around the Fish Hoek side.)

There are many watersports shops and service providers in the city. Try the **African Paddling Association** (www.facebook.com/AfricanPaddlingAssociation) for information, **Brian's Kayaks & Sports** (Unit 8, Northgate Estate, Highway Park, Gold Street, Paarden Eiland, 021 511 9695, www.kayaks.co.za) and **Paddlers Online Kayak Shop** (021 786 2626, www.paddlers.co.za) for equipment, **Real Cape Adventures** (082 556 2520, www.seakayak.co.za) for trips and tours, and **Mocke Paddling** (084 251 5555, www.mockepaddling.com) for equipment, trips and lessons.

There are around 50 surf spots within an hour's drive of Cape Town – but pack a wetsuit, because about half of these are on the icy western side of the coast. **Muizenberg**'s Surfers Corner is always a popular spot for surfers, bodyboarders and stand-up paddlers (the water is warmer here), and there are plenty of good spots up the West Coast and to the south.

Consult Wavescape (www.wavescape.co.za) or *ZigZag* magazine's website (www.zigzag.co.za) for updates on the best swells. Or, if you're a beginner and you want to learn to surf, try **Roxy Surf School** (021 788 8687, 082 562 8687, www.surfemporium.co.za).

Kite surfing (yeah, that's also a thing here) tends to happen along the windy West Coast, centred specifically around **Bloubergstrand**. Learn the art and hire the gear at **High Five** (072 902 7899, www.high-five.co.za).

Sandboarding (it's like snowboarding or tobogganing – except, you've guessed it, on sand) is another fun option, if you can find a steep enough sand dune. **Sunscene Outdoor Adventures** (084 352 4925, 021 783 0203, www.sunscene.co.za) will help there.

Finally, about that big sky… Skydiving is a great way to enjoy some views over the Fairest Cape, with drop zones located 45 minutes out of town up the West Coast, or four hours out of town in Ceres. Options range from full courses to quickie tandem jumps with a qualified expert. Speak to **Skydive Cape Town** (082 800 6290, www.skydivecapetown.za.net) for more information.

Paragliding, meanwhile, gets you flying right over the city itself, with departure points on Lion's Head taking you over the Atlantic Seaboard to Camps Bay. Ask **Birdmen Paragliding** (082 658 6710, 021 557 8144, www.birdmen.co.za) or **Wallend-Air School of Paragliding** (083 300 1755, 021 762 2441 www.wallendair.com) about possibilities for getting airborne.

One of the most extensive shopping centres in the city, this mock Italianate complex delivers on two levels – big and bigger. Some 400 shops cater for every fashion, shoe, accessory, electronics, grocery, book and furniture whim you could have, while the arena-sized food court provides fuel for your shopping expeditions. Canal Walk Kids World Fun Zone keeps the little ones occupied with activities and events.

Milnerton Market
Otto du Plessis Drive, Paarden Eiland, Milnerton (www.milnertonfleamarket.co.za). **Open** 7am-5pm Sat, Sun. **Market**
Milnerton Market is more of a bazaar than a touristy flea market, and the rows upon rows of cars lined next to this dusty stretch should tip you off that this caravan of bakkies (pick-up trucks), boots and tents has a few aces up its sleeve. You can find everything from saws, mobile phones and face creams to beautiful crystal spirit decanters and vintage jewellery. Be prepared to rootle around to try and search out something special.

DURBANVILLE & SURROUNDS

In recent years the number of wine farms around the largely residential area of Durbanville has blossomed. With rolling hills, great views and family-friendly eateries, this area remains a popular inland suburb. The **Durbanville Wine Valley** (www.durbanvillewine.co.za) features 12 wine estates, and since the valley's fertile terroir makes for award-winning sauvignon blanc, it's a good idea to stock up on the good stuff as you make your way through them. Some are boutique, some are big; many are also home to good restaurants. There are some wonderful examples of Cape Dutch architecture on the estates, with some farms dating from the 1700s. It is worth noting that some estates are closed on Sundays, so Saturdays or weekdays are the best bet for wine-tastings.

This small area has some lively activities throughout the year. Making the most of the region's favourite cultivar, the Durbanville Wine Valley's Season of Sauvignon festival, which takes place towards the end of October, is great fun: wine farms have their best tipples on offer, in addition to food stalls and live music. There's also a harvest festival as well as a winter Soup, Sip & Bread fest.

Sights & Museums

Art.b Gallery
Library Centre, Carel van Aswegen Street, Bellville (021 917 1197, www.artb.co.za). **Open** 10am-5pm Tue-Fri; 10am-1pm Sat. **No credit cards**. **Gallery**
Cape Town's biggest public library is also home to a top-notch gallery. Run by the Arts Association of Bellville on a pro bono basis, it aims to generate public awareness of art and provide a platform for both

EXPLORE

established and emerging local artists. Exhibitions rotate almost monthly and the gallery showcases contemporary work in a wide range of disciplines.

Restaurants

Café Ruby

Klein Roosboom, Tygerberg Valley Road (021 975 7965, www.kleinroosboom.co.za). **Open** 8.30am-3.30pm Tue-Sun. **Main courses** R85. **Café** A charming and eclectic spot on boutique winery Klein Roosboom, Café Ruby serves delicious platters and seasonal fare – the likes of filled pitas, grills and salads – listed on a blackboard menu in a bright and airy setting. The place is a hit with parents as it has a lovely play area with a sandpit for the little ones, as well as a children's breakfast menu.

Cassia

Nitida Wine Farm, Tygerberg Valley Road (021 976 0640, www.cassiarestaurant.co.za). **Open** 9.30am-11pm Mon-Sat; 9.30am-3pm Sun. **Main courses** R140. **Contemporary South African** The restaurant's interior is all high-ceilinged, pared-down minimalism, and serves as the perfect backdrop for colourful contemporary dishes. The menu is small but varied, with dishes such as guinea fowl pot and Asian beef salad to start, before moving on to sous vide rack of lamb or springbok and cacao stew. The view over the dam is spectacular, and this is a deservedly popular spot.

De Grendel Restaurant

De Grendel Wine Estate, Plattekloof Road, Panorama (021 558 7035, http://degrendel.co.za).

Open noon-2.30pm, 7-9.30pm Tue-Sat; noon-2.30pm Sun. **Main courses** R160 (lunch). **Set dinner menus** R285 (2 courses); R315 (3 courses). **Contemporary South African** Set on the historic De Grendel farm, De Grendel restaurant is a culinary big hitter. With magnificent views all the way to Table Mountain, the space is elegance personified, with bespoke crockery, a glassed-in kitchen and historical photographs of the farm on the walls. Dishes make the most of seasonal availability, but diners can expect the likes of pasture-fed beef fillet, perfectly cooked linefish (line-caught fish) and excellent pork belly. Plating is refined and desserts are heavenly.

Diemersdal Farm Eatery

Diemersdal Wine Estate, Koeberg Road (021 976 3361, http://diemersdal.co.za). **Open** noon-3pm Tue-Sun; 6-9pm Thur-Sat. **Main courses** R130. **Sunday lunch** R195. **Bistro** One of the area's larger estates, covering 340 hectares, Diemersdal has been farmed since 1689. The rustic farm bistro is ideal for a casual lazy lunch or a relaxed dinner, with dishes like sweet potato and chorizo soup, sweetbreads with onion risotto and pork belly. The traditional Sunday lunch is always popular, with meats, veg and all the trimmings – but you'd be advised to book as this is a local favourite.

★ Durbanville Hills Restaurant

Durbanville Hills, M13 (021 558 1337, www. durbanvillehills.co.za). **Open** *Summer* 8.30am-3pm Tue, Wed, Sun; 8.30am-3pm, 6-10pm Thur-Sat. *Winter* 8.30am-3pm Tue-Thur, Sun; 8.30am-3pm,

Rust-en-Vrede Gallery.

6pm-10pm Fri, Sat. **Main courses** R120. **Tasting menu** R350. **Contemporary South African**
The wine estate's modern tasting room is like a beacon on a hill overlooking Table Mountain and the surrounding vineyards. After drinking in the views (and the wines), head to the restaurant, with more views. The food makes the most of South African produce, and there's a simple sophistication about dishes such as braised pork belly, butternut soufflé, grilled venison skewers and chicken pie. Summer picnics, catered for from April to October, are a relaxed way to enjoy the beautiful surroundings.

Eat@Altydgedacht
Altydgedacht Wine Estate, Tygerberg Valley Road (021 975 7815, www.eatataltydgedacht.co.za). **Open** 9am-3.30pm Mon-Sat; 11am-3pm Sun.
Main courses R75. **Café**
Grab a seat on the lawn, shaded by trees and umbrellas, at this historic wine farm, which was established in 1698. Food is simple and rustic: homemade pies and quiches, man-sized breakfasts and burgers. The platters are perfect for sharing, filled with cheeses, breads, salads and dips. On cold days, the barrel room is a special space for a cosy lunch.

Kitchen at Weylandts
22 Bella Rosa Street, Rosenpark (021 914 1440, www.weylandts.co.za). **Open** 9am-4pm Mon, Wed-Sat; 10am-5pm Tue; 10am-2pm 1st Sun of month.
Main courses R80. **Global**
Not only does Weylandts showcase stunning contemporary furniture, but this warehouse-style, multi-levelled shop houses a local secret: a small restaurant serving exquisite fare. Those in the know come for

cakes and teatime treats, while lunchtime sees the Kitchen producing fare such as 'Cape Malay snoek bunny chow', a fishy version of the traditional local dish of rabbit curry served in bread – in this case the rabbit is substituted by snoek in a fragrant Cape Malay spice blend – and Turkish lamb and quince pie.

Shops & Services

Rust-en-Vrede Gallery
10 Wellington Road, Durbanville (021 976 4691, www.rust-en-vrede.com). **Open** 9am-5pm Mon-Fri; 9am-1pm Sat. **No credit cards. Gallery**
While the Rust-en-Vrede Gallery has been around since the early 1980s and is very well-respected among the area's art enthusiasts, its Cape Dutch façade dates back to 1840, when the building housed a prison and police headquarters. These days the space hosts group and solo exhibitions by both emerging and established artists. There are also art studios and a clay museum where mostly contemporary clayware – representing various construction techniques – is displayed.

Willowbridge
39 Carl Cronje Drive, Tyger Valley (www.willowbridge.co.za). **Open** 9am-6pm Mon-Sat; 9am-5pm Sun. **Mall**
Quality decor and interiors shops are a highlight at this high-end outdoor lifestyle mall near Rosenpark. There is also a host of restaurants to choose from, making it a popular local spot for weekday suppers and weekend brunches. Saturdays sees the Willowbridge Slow Market (www.slowmarket.co.za), with stalls selling a variety of artisan foods and products.

EXPLORE

Arts & Entertainment

Children

Cape Town is the perfect playground for youngsters. With its wealth of natural beauty from oceans to mountains, animal encounters aplenty, and a vast array of venues encouraging little minds to explore, there really is no reason for anyone to be bored. Simple pursuits such as packing a picnic and spending a day on the beach splashing in rock pools, or taking a gentle hike through endemic fynbos, are low-impact and hassle-free. Or turn things up a notch by getting up close to wildlife, dangling from a rock face or performing science experiments. Whatever you choose, the city and its environs are rich in rewarding family experiences, and you're (almost) assured never to hear the cry 'I'm bored!' again.

INFORMATION

Child Magazine (www.childmag.co.za) is a free publication focusing on parenting advice and kids' resources in and around Cape Town and South Africa's other major cities. Its website provides good links to entertainment and events. Other online resources include www.capetownkids.co.za, and the kids' sections of www.capetownmagazine.com and www.capetownetc.com.

Most hotels and guest houses can arrange babysitting services. Many sights offer special packages for families, or, if you're planning a longer stay, it may be worth investigating annual memberships.

ANIMAL ENCOUNTERS

There's also a variety of animal attractions outside Cape Town, in Paarl (*see p176*) in the Winelands.

★ Boulders African Penguin Colony

Kleintuin Road, parking area in Seaforth Road, Simon's Town, South Peninsula (021 786 2329, www.tmnp.co.za). **Open** *Jan, Dec* 7am-7.30pm daily. *Feb, Mar* 8am-6.30pm daily. *Apr-Sept* 8am-5pm daily. *Oct, Nov* 8am-6.30pm daily. **Admission** R60; R30 under-12s; free under-2s.

There's nothing like seeing a wild animal up close, and this experience will last a lifetime. The boardwalks surrounding the breeding colony of African penguins (aka jackass penguins) at Boulders Beach give ample opportunity to spot these delightful creatures waddling about. You can also access the beach further along and spend the day swimming and sunbathing near the penguins. *See also p133.*

Imhoff Farm

Kommetjie Road, Kommetjie, South Peninsula (021 783 4545, www.imhofffarm.co.za). **Open** 9am-5pm daily. **Admission** free; activities vary.

Animals big and small, slithery and cuddly, are to be found at this collection of venues. Little ones will love feeding the pigs, goats, chickens and rabbits at the petting farm; the snake park will have youngsters (and some adults) screeching with delight (or dread), and the camel-rides will give you a whole new perspective on the world. Along with a family-friendly café and craft shops, this makes for a great outing. *See also p137.*

★ Two Oceans Aquarium

Dock Road, V&A Waterfront, Atlantic Seaboard (021 418 3823, www.aquarium.co.za). **Open** 9.30am-6pm daily. **Admission** R118; R92 14-17s; R57 4-13s; free under-4s. **Map** p252 G2.

It's official: Nemo has been found... kids will delight in posing inside the tubular tank at the entrance to the aquarium where hundreds of clown fish swim about. After that, there's a vast array of aquatic animals to ogle. Watch penguins being fed, turtles and sharks cruising around lazily, and jellyfish glowing in the dark. There's a sensory pool where children can grope starfish and seaweed, and the frog puppet show is fun and informative. *See also p87*.

World of Birds

Valley Road, Hout Bay, Atlantic Seaboard (021 790 2730, www.worldofbirds.org.za). **Open** 9am-5pm daily. **Admission** R95; R45-R55 reductions.

Walk through the interlinked aviaries to see more than 3,000 birds at this sanctuary. Flamingoes, owls and penguins vie for attention with spoonbills, peacocks, parrots and turacos. There are also spider monkeys, guinea pigs, tortoises and meerkats to be gawked at if the flurry of feathers gets too much. *See also p99*.

ARTS & CRAFTS

Artjamming

Breakwater Boulevard, V&A Waterfront, Atlantic Seaboard (021 425 5050, www.artjamming.co.za). **Open** 9am-9pm daily. **Rates** R95-R255. **Map** p252 G1.

Let the creativity flow at this entertaining painting venue. While funky music plays in the background, children and adults can paint and create to their hearts' content. Messy Play sessions for babies and toddlers are a wonderful way to allow them to experiment with paint, and play at the same time.

Mineral World & Scratch Patch

Dido Valley Road, Simon's Town, South Peninsula (021 786 2020, www.scratchpatch.co.za). **Open** 8.30am-4.45pm Mon-Fri; 9am-5.30pm Sat, Sun. **Admission** free.

Crawl around the Scratch Patch, covered in thousands of polished stones, and collect bright and shiny gemstones – tiger's eye, agate, amethyst and more. What you put in your container is up to you (a small bag costs R14), but you'll probably want to stick to the brighter semi-precious ones, and avoid the duller quartz pebbles. Good for tweens on a winter's day. Adults can browse the jewellery and other stone souvenirs in the gift shop.

Other location Dock Road, V&A Waterfront, Atlantic Seaboard (021 419 9429).

Rainbow Puppet Theatre

Constantia Waldorf School, Spaanschemat River Road, Constantia, Southern Suburbs (021 783 2063, www.facebook.com/TheRainbowPuppet Theatre). **Shows** 10am, 11.15am Sat. **Tickets** R20. **No credit cards**.

See a magical fairytale – *Hansel and Gretel*, perhaps or *Snow White* – told in this classic puppet theatre, which has been going since 1992 and has a loyal local following. Shows are recommended for ages four and up.

FUN & GAMES

Action Paint Ball

Imhoff Farm, Kommetjie Road, Kommetjie, South Peninsula (021 790 7603, www.actionpaintball.co.za). **Open** 9.30am-1pm, 1.30-5pm daily. **Rates** R140 per player per session.

Gung-ho children (and often their dads) love a good paintball session: dashing around a forest, creeping up to your opponent and ambushing the enemy. It's all good fun, and you'll work up a serious sweat doing it. Paintball is only for kids aged 11 and older, but you only have to be six to enjoy a game of LaserTag.

Bike Park

Constantia Uitsig, Spaanschemat River Road, Constantia, Southern Suburbs (081 833 4488, www.uitsig.co.za/the-bike-park). **Open** 8am-sunset daily. **Admission** R30.

Kids love this new outdoor bike track with its hills and turns. It's overseen by a pro and has been built to excellent specifications, with the aim of extending it to a 3.5km cross-country track. It's the ideal place for older kids to have fun, while parents enjoy food and wine at neighbouring Open Door restaurant (*see p122*), also on the estate.

Blue Train Park

Beach Road, Mouille Point, Atlantic Seaboard (084 314 9200, www.thebluetrainpark.com). **Open** *Summer* 9.30am-6pm Tue-Thur; 9.30am-6.30pm Fri-Sun. *Winter* noon-6pm Tue-Thur; 9.30am-6pm Fri-Sun. **Admission** R15. **Map** p252 E1.

This enclosed park next to the Green Point lighthouse may have the best location in Cape Town, as it overlooks the Atlantic Ocean. The miniature train ride (included in the entry fee) is always a hit, but the park offers so much more – the bouncy castles, jungle gyms, bike track and zipline will keep everyone entertained.

Bugz Family Playpark

56 Tarentaal Road, Joostenbergvlakte, Kraaifontein, Northern Suburbs (021 988 8836, www.bugz playpark.co.za). **Open** 9am-5pm daily. **Rates** R35; R45 children; free under-2s.

A vast range of activities awaits busy little bodies at this outdoor playpark. Pony rides, quad biking, train rides, a bouncy castle, rowboats, toddler tractors, a

ARTS & ENTERTAINMENT

IN THE KNOW PARK LIFE

There are few things nicer than spending time outside with the kids on a lovely day – and Cape Town has plenty of those. If the beaches are too crowded, pack a picnic, head for a leafy park and find a shady spot where the kids can play.

Kirstenbosch National Botanical Gardens (see p115) hasn't got any jungle gyms, but the acres of green space ensures that children will burn off lots of energy playing hide and seek, or simply running about. **De Waal Park** (Oranjezicht, City Bowl – with entrances on Camp, Upper Orange and Molteno Streets) is a suburban walled park, especially popular with dog walkers. The play area has loads to do, as well as a very, very high slide. The **Company's Garden** (see p48) is great for some respite from the city buzz – buy a packet of peanuts to feed the squirrels as you wander down Government Avenue.

If you want to be near the ocean, the **Sea Point Promenade** has a lovely lawn running alongside, with jungle gyms and monkey bars dotted about. **Camps Bay beach** also boasts a large jungle gym on the lawns at its southern end, for when the kids aren't keen on the beach anymore. The jewel in the crown, however, is the **Green Point Urban Park** (see p91), with its expanses of lawn, gurgling shallow streams and two play areas – one for tiny tots and one for bigger kids.

CityROCK.

waterslide and more will keep them entertained for hours. And on rainy days, the indoor area has a host of options too. It's specifically geared for two- to ten-year-olds, so best leave the teenagers at home.

CityROCK

21 Anson Street, Observatory, Southern Suburbs (021 447 1326, http://cityrock.co.za). **Open** 9am-9pm Mon, Wed; 9am-10pm Tue, Thur; 9am-6pm Fri-Sun. **Rates** Day pass R140; R80-R100 reductions; gear extra.

Come to the place where the phrase 'climbing the walls' is actually a positive experience. Children (over-5s only) will love the bouldering area at this indoor climbing gym, as well as the higher walls for more adventurous, rope-assisted climbing. If your little climber is keen, a course is a great idea – they'll learn about climbing techniques, rope skills, belay and general safety. All in preparation for when they tackle Table Mountain one day.

Cool Runnings

Carl Cronje Drive, Tyger Valley, Northern Suburbs (021 949 4439, www.coolrunnings.capetown).

Open 9am-6pm daily. **Rates** 1 ride R35-R40; weekend day pass R250.

The only toboggan track in Africa will take you around 17 corners of stainless-steel track, at up to 40km per hour. While young children need an adult to accompany them, tweens and older children can go it alone. A steel cable pulls the toboggan up a steep hill, and then you're let loose to hurtle down as fast as you want to. The café provides kid-friendly eats and there's plenty of shaded seating. It's great family fun, but be prepared to queue over weekends.

Ice Station

GrandWest Casino & Entertainment World, 1 Vanguard Drive, Goodwood, Northern Suburbs (021 535 2260, www.icerink.co.za). **Open** 10am-midnight Mon-Fri; 9am-midnight Sat; noon-8.30pm Sun. **Rates** R35-R50.

Practise your axels and spirals at this ice rink, or start with lessons in the basics. This popular spot boasts an Olympic-sized skating surface, so there's plenty of room to manoeuvre. You can also watch ice hockey and figure-skating training.

ARTS & ENTERTAINMENT

★ Jolly Roger Pirate Boat

5 West Quay Road, V&A Waterfront, Atlantic Seaboard (021 421 0909, www.pirateboat.co.za). **Open** 9am-5pm daily. **Rates** 1hr cruise R130; R60 children. **Map** p252 G2.

Ahoy, mateys! Come and pretend you're a pirate on this party boat and have some swashbuckling adventures. Little buccaneers will delight in the pirate show on this authentically kitted out vessel with its crew of costumed seadogs, while parents can enjoy the stunning scenery from Table Bay harbour. It's a popular venue for parties for kids – and adults too.

Jump Around

Unit 3, Table Bay Industrial Business Park, Milner Street, off Marine Drive, Paarden Eiland, Northern Suburbs (021 510 1997, www.jumparound.co.za). **Open** 9am-9pm Mon-Thur; 9am-10pm Fri; 8am-10pm Sat; 8am-8pm Sun. **Rates** R120 per hr.

With 50 interconnected trampolines, this warehouse venue is sure to have your kids expend every last drop of their energy. There's also a foam pit, dodgeball, soccer and basketball. All in all, it's a ridiculous amount of bouncy fun.

Kenilworth Karting

Cnr Warrington & Myhof Roads, Kenilworth, Southern Suburbs (021 683 2670, www.karting. co.za/kkarting). **Open** 1-11pm Mon-Fri; 9am-11pm Sat, Sun. **Rates** 10-lap race R110; R100 under-16s.

One for the bigger kids, this. A hard-to-find indoor go-karting circuit, Kenilworth Karting has a 310m track with ten-, 15-, 20- or 30-lap races – depending on what you book and how busy the circuit is when you visit. It's relatively safe too: the marshals keep a close eye on dangerous driving (and on cheats). Drivers must be at least 1.5m tall, and helmets and hair nets are provided.

Planet Kids

3 Wherry Road, Muizenberg, South Peninsula (021 788 3070, www.planetkids.co.za). **Open** 10am-6pm Wed-Sun. **Rates** 1hr R35, 2hrs R60 2-13s; free under-2s, adults. **No credit cards**.

A great spot whatever the weather, Planet Kids provides indoor and outdoor activities. Swings, a foefie slide, bouncy castles, a ball wall and slide – all with a galactic theme – make this a great place for families.

Ratanga Junction

Canal Walk, Century City, Northern Suburbs (086 120 0300, 021 550 8504, www.ratanga.co.za). **Open** Western Cape school holidays 10am-5pm daily. **Admission** R95-R181; R70 fun pass.

Cape Town's only theme park is a hit during the school holidays (weather permitting). There are over 30 rides and attractions here, including the Slingshot cable flight (R55 extra) and Monkey Falls log flume. The Cobra is only for the brave (or mad): travelling at speeds of up to 100kmh over nearly

800m of track, you're suspended from above on this twisting maniac of a rollercoaster.

MUSEUMS

★ Cape Town Science Centre

370B Main Road, Observatory, Southern Suburbs (021 300 3200, www.ctsc.org.za). **Open** 9am-4.30pm Mon-Sat; 10am-4.30pm Sun. **Admission** R45; free under-3s.

A must-visit for enquiring little minds, this museum will entertain young and old for hours. The Lego playpit and building blocks are fun, but the real hit is the large simulated building site, where kids don hard hats, yellow safety vests, and trundle foam bricks in wheelbarrows and along conveyor belts. They are all stackable, so the foundations in the play area can be completely built up by industrious kids. Numerous physical puzzles, interactive experiments and live demonstrations will turn them into budding scientists (and mom and dad may also learn a thing or two in the process).

Planetarium

25 Queen Victoria Street, City Bowl (021 481 3900, www.iziko.org.za/museums/planetarium). **Shows** times vary; check website. **Admission** R40; R20 reductions. **Map** p254 G4.

Here's a rare chance, in our light-polluted modern times, to see all the stars in the night sky. The Planetarium (part of the South African Museum) offers a range of shows, with many designed specifically for children. The reclining seats, state-of-the-art projector and stellar presentation will hush even the liveliest children.

Iziko South African Museum

25 Queen Victoria Street, City Bowl (021 481 3800, www.iziko.org.za/museums/south-african-museum). **Open** 10am-5pm daily. **Admission** R30; R15 reductions. **Map** p254 G4.

Founded in 1825, the South African Museum moved to its present building in the historic Company's Garden in 1897. While children will probably run (or yawn) their way through the social history exhibits, they'll enjoy the natural history displays, especially the Whale Well and Shark World. The hall full of stuffed animals is rather eerie, but a great way to show kids what the animals in their storybooks look like in (almost) real life.

Warrior Toy Museum & Collectors' Shop

St George's Street, Simon's Town, South Peninsula (021 786 1395). **Open** 10am-3.45pm Mon-Thur, Sat. **Admission** R5.

This museum is packed with about 4,000 model cars, 500 dolls and teddy bears, plus miniature dolls' houses, toy soldiers and pretty much any other plaything you can think of, including two fully operating railroads. If your kids don't love it, the kid in you certainly will.

WATER BABIES
If in doubt, head to the beach.

There are few things that delight children as much as water. And, despite the Atlantic Ocean being icy, Cape Town has plenty of beaches that are perfect for little ones.

Bakoven beach, near Camps Bay, may be tiny, but its rocks are great for scrambling on and locals love it for early morning swims. The South Peninsula is probably the most family-friendly beach destination with its warmer waters: **Fish Hoek** has lovely gentle waves for swimming and splashing; at **Muizenberg**, children can learn to surf or have fun on the water slides at the Muizenberg Pavilion; **St James** has a tidal pool and a multitude of rock pools, ideal for very small kids; and then there's **Boulders Beach** – where else can you splash about with penguins waddling past?

And if you can't face sand between your toes, **Slide the City** (http://slidethecitysa.co.za) is coming to Cape Town for the 2015-16 summer season. While not much information was available at time of writing, we do know that the 304-metre long, three-laned water slide is going to be a massive hit when it finally arrives.

It's crucial to remember that the African sun is extremely harsh. Stay inside between 11am and 3pm, slather on high SPF sunscreen, make sure everyone wears a hat and stays hydrated.

ARTS & ENTERTAINMENT

RESTAURANTS

Café Roux
270 Chapman's Peak Drive, Noordhoek Farm Village, Noordhoek, South Peninsula (021 789 2538, www.caferoux.co.za). **Open** 8.30am-5pm daily. **Main courses** R70-R130.
The playground with its expansive jungle gym, old tractor and Wendy house will keep the children happy in between stopping by the table for child-friendly eats. Meanwhile, the adults can tuck into one of the killer brekkies or hearty lunches at this popular bistro.

Deer Park Café
2 Deer Park Avenue, Vredehoek, City Bowl (021 462 6311, www.deerparkcafe.co.za). **Open** 8am-8pm daily. **Main courses** R70-R90.
A City Bowl eatery that opens on to a safe public park (Rocklands Park), the Deer Park Café wins purely on location. You can sit out on its terrace while your brood tears around the hilly, grassy enclosed park with its variety of swings, jungle gyms and slides.

Dunes
1 Beach Crescent, Hout Bay, Atlantic Seaboard (021 790 1876, www.dunesrestaurant.co.za). **Open** noon-midnight Mon-Sat; noon-6pm Sun. **Main courses** R80-R200.
At Dunes, you can literally feel the sand between your toes. A stone's throw from the beach, the out-door seating area is family central, with its sand floor and large jungle gym. Kids can enjoy a range of meals, from pizzas to fish and chips. Parents can enjoy the view, a much-needed glass of wine, and dishes such as steamed mussels, burgers, steak or lamb curry.

Franky's Diner
303A Main Road, Sea Point, Atlantic Seaboard (021 433 0445, www.frankysdiner.co.za). **Open** 24hrs daily. **Main courses** R55. **Map** p251 C2.
This old-school diner hits the fun notes, with curly fries, burgers and hot dogs keeping both adults and children happy. Slide into a booth, send the kids to the enclosed play area, and try not to steal your offspring's delicious mega milkshake.

Millstone at Oude Molen

Oude Molen Eco Village, Alexandra Road, Pinelands, Southern Suburbs (021 447 8226, www.oudemolenecovillage.co.za/village-millstone-farmstall-cafe). **Open** 9am-5pm Tue-Sun. **Main courses** R45.

The set-up might be a bit hippy for some, with make-shift chairs and tables, and a laid-back vibe, but the kids love it. The tree house is straight out of Enid Blyton's *The Magic Faraway Tree*, and pony rides add to the kiddy-friendly appeal. The light meals and bakes are delicious, and you can stop at the farm shop to purchase some goodies before you leave.

Primi Piatti

Cavendish Square, Dreyer Street, Claremont, Southern Suburbs (021 671 9781, www.primi-world.co.za). **Open** 7am-6pm Mon-Fri; 8am-6pm Sat; 8am-3pm Sun. **Main courses** R100.

With a supervised play area, kitchen counter for pizza and biscuit making as well as a dedicated kids' menu, Primi Piatti's Primi Pods are a hit with families who are keen on a meal out, but very aware that little people simply don't want to sit still for over an hour. **Other locations** throughout the city (not all have Primi Pods).

SHOPS

Earthchild

Victoria Wharf, V&A Waterfront, Atlantic Seaboard (021 421 5033, www.earthchild.co.za). **Open** 9am-9pm Mon-Sat; 10am-9pm Sun. **Map** p253 H1.

If you're loath to clothe your precious bundle in artificial textiles and garish chain store numbers, head for this shop, which specialises in 100% cotton gear for little girls and guys. Lots of room to move and fashionable cuts too, making them a great bet for stylish wardrobe basics.

Hamleys

Victoria Wharf, V&A Waterfront, Atlantic Seaboard (021 418 2927, www.hamleys.com, www.facebook.com/HamleysSouthAfrica). **Open** 9am-9pm daily. **Map** p253 H1.

The iconic British toy store has landed in South Africa with a bang. Opened to great fanfare at the end of August 2015, this massive retail space promises a vast array of toys, games and experiences for children – and it delivers. Little princes and princesses can get glitter tattoos, pose for a selfie with Barbie and hug Hamley bear. Interactive displays make a visit here a visual feast. Once you're done abusing the credit card, pop the children on the Hamleys train that chugs around the V&A Waterfront.

Kiddiwinks

Blue Route Mall, Tokai Road, Tokai, Southern Suburbs (021 712 5202, www.kiddiwinks.co.za). **Open** 9am-7pm Mon-Sat; 9am-5pm Sun.

It's Lego all the way at this shop dedicated to the ever-popular building blocks. In addition to having every model a child (or parent) can dream of, they also offer party activities in the Claremont outlet or at your home, as well as training and competitions in Lego robotics. If your kids weren't obsessed to start with, they soon will be.

Other locations Palmyra Junction, Claremont, Southern Suburbs (021 671 4525); Willowbridge Mall, Tygervalley, Northern Suburbs (073 312 0250).

Merry Pop Ins

201 Bree Street, City Bowl (021 422 4911, www.merrypopins.co.za). **Open** 10am-5pm Mon-Fri; 10am-2pm Sat. **Map** p254 G4.

This is where moms-in-the-know go to find quality second-hand items, from prams and strollers to clothing, toys and cribs. You'll often find designer gear for both boys and girls, and there's also a donation section for items you don't want anymore to be sent to local charities.

Naartjie

Victoria Wharf, V&A Waterfront, Atlantic Seaboard (021 421 5819, www.naartjie.co.za). **Open** 9am-9pm Mon-Sat; 10am-9pm Sun. **Map** p253 H1.

This South African kids' clothing success story adds colour and charm to any wardrobe, thanks to their trademark prints, worn-in cottons and comfy cuts for boys and girls. The baby gear is too cute for words, the girls' dresses and stretch cotton leggings with tutu frills are loved by all ages, and the boys' printed sweaters and heavy-duty cargoes are right on the money. The Hout Bay factory shop is great for discounted end-of-season ranges.

Other locations throughout the city.

Polly Potter's Toy Store

Gardens Shopping Centre, cnr Mill & Buitenkant Streets, Gardens, City Bowl (021 461 0579, www.pollypotterstoystore.co.za). **Open** 9am-7pm Mon-Fri; 9am-5pm Sat; 9am-2pm Sun. **Map** p253 H5.

While the toys at this charming store don't come cheap, there is a lovely selection to choose from. Puzzles, wooden toys, cuter-than-cute stuffed bunnies and collectible figurines can all be found here.

Toy Kingdom

Breakwater Boulevard, V&A Waterfront, Atlantic Seaboard (021 421 1192, www.toykingdom.co.za). **Open** 9am-9pm Mon-Sat; 10am-9pm Sun. **Map** p252 G1.

Parents beware, there's simply no way you'll leave this massive toy emporium without a couple of bags filled to the brim. Toy Kingdom sells pretty much everything, from Disney characters in all shapes and sizes to fancy-dress costumes, Lego, wooden toys and electronics.

ARTS & ENTERTAINMENT

Film

South Africans love a blockbuster, and if it's in 3D, all the better. Most of the cinemas in town cater to the masses with surround sound and popcorn by the bucketload. There are, however, a handful of arthouse venues showing lesser-known films and foreign movies. The big guys, the main cinema chains Ster-Kinekor and Nu Metro, offer online booking facilities, which makes for less queueing once you're at the cinema. Cape Town has also burgeoned as a location in the past decade, so you may just spot a famous actor around town.

CINEMAS
Multiplexes

Nu Metro
Canal Walk Shopping Centre, Century Boulevard, Century City, Northern Suburbs (www.numetro. co.za). **Tickets** R40-R80. **Screens** 17.
Although mainstream fare is the name of the game here, the country's second largest cinema chain also has a few surprises up its sleeve. The Canal Walk branch is definitely the biggest star of the show, with a staggering 17 screens to choose from and a regular selection of Bollywood romps to spice up the schedule, alongside the usual mainstream Hollywood blockbusters.
Other location GrandWest, V&A Waterfront.

Ster-Kinekor
Cavendish Cineplex, Cavendish Square, 1 Dreyer Street, Claremont, Southern Suburbs (www.sterkinekor.com). **Tickets** R68-R120. **Screens** 8.
To make up for its higher prices, Ster-Kinekors offers a wider selection of snacks and drinks to enjoy with your film, such as nachos and coffee. Half-price Tuesdays for movie club members helps to lessen the financial blow too. This cinema has 3D screens as well as two new Cinema Prestige screens, where spectators pay a premium for in-movie service and large individual reclining seats.
Other locations Bayside, Blue Route Mall, Tygervalley Mall, and other suburbs throughout the city.

Ster-Kinekor Cinema Nouveau
Victoria Wharf, V&A Waterfront, Atlantic Seaboard (www.sterkinekor.com). **Tickets** R70-R135. **Screens** 6. **Map** p253 H1.
Ster-Kinekor's arthouse cinema is a film buff's dream. It even brings out its own magazine, profiling the latest releases. Now the only Cinema Nouveau in the Cape, it showcases new releases in a high-tech setting.

Independents

Cine 12
Twelve Apostles Hotel & Spa, Victoria Road, Camps Bay, Atlantic Seaboard (021 437 9000, www.12apostleshotel.com). **Dinner & film** R475.
This is as decadent as it gets. Enjoy a four-course meal at spectacular seaside hotel Twelve Apostles' super-swanky restaurant Azure. Then sit back with some gourmet snacks – including proper movie treats like ice-cream, popcorn and hot chocolate – and watch a film in its state-of-the-art 16-seater cinema. The schedule changes weekly, but if you book the venue for a private screening you have a selection of about 300 films to pick from.

Galileo Open Air Cinema
Various locations (www.thegalileo.co.za). **Tickets** R80.
Summer sees an array of classic films screened at various outdoor locations around the Peninsula, such as Kirstenbosch, Hillcrest Quarry in Durbanville and the V&A Waterfront. Pack a picnic, grab a blanket and get set for a night with the stars, under the stars.

Labia Theatre

68 Orange Street, Gardens, City Bowl (021 424 5927, www.labia.co.za). **Tickets** R45. **Screens** 4. **Map** p254 G2.

A much-loved Cape Town institution, this cinema recently managed to stay afloat and acquire much-needed new digital projectors thanks to a massive crowdfunding endeavour. This means locals can continue to enjoy its old-world charms including an art deco box office and licensed concession stand. A good range of new and classic arthouse movies, along with regular curated film festivals and dinner specials with nearby restaurants, keep this a buzzing venue.

Pink Flamingo Rooftop Cinema

Grand Daddy, 38 Long Street, City Centre, City Bowl (021 424 7247, www.granddaddy.co.za) **Tickets** R100. **Screens** 1. **Map** p254 H3.

Much-loved classics of all sorts (drama, action, comedy, romance) are shown outside on the roof of the Grand Daddy boutique hotel, next to their signature Airstream trailers. A welcome drink is included in the price, seats are comfortable couches and there are plenty of nibbles and a full bar to round off the experience.

IN THE KNOW FILM FESTS

An annual highlight for film fans and documentary aficionados, **Encounters South African International Documentary Festival** (www.encounters.co.za) presents an array of local and international productions by emerging and established filmmakers. In 2015, a total of 42 films were showcased in Cape Town and Johannesburg during the ten-day June event. The festival has done much to raise the bar for South Africa's documentary-making industry, and also features workshops and talks. Much-lauded online magazine Design Indaba has added the ten-day **Design Indaba Film Fest** (www.designindaba.com/film) to its creative offerings. In February 2015, the Labia Theatre (*see left*) was the venue for local and international documentary premières focusing on design, be it fashion, comics, music or creative individuals.

ARTS & ENTERTAINMENT

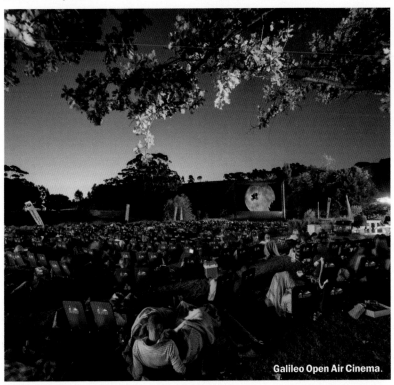

Galileo Open Air Cinema.

ARTS & ENTERTAINMENT

ESSENTIAL SOUTH AFRICAN FILM

The big screen brings the country to life.

Mandela: Long Walk to Freedom

MANDELA: LONG WALK TO FREEDOM
JUSTIN CHADWICK (2013)

Idris Elba cuts an impressive figure portraying Nelson Mandela, father of the nation. The film chronicles his life from his childhood in a rural village in the Eastern Cape, to his political activist years and eventual imprisonment on Robben Island. After his release in 1990, he became the first democratically elected president in South Africa in 1994.

DISTRICT 9
NEILL BLOMKAMP (2009)

Nominated for four Oscars, this dystopian sci-fi film was set in Joburg, but tackled some very real issues throughout South Africa concerning xenophobia in townships, especially towards immigrants from other African countries. Sharlto Copley plays Wikus van de Merwe, a lowly bureaucrat who becomes infected with an alien chemical, turning him into one of the alien beings being kept in refugee slums.

INVICTUS
CLINT EASTWOOD (2009)

A feel-good film if there ever was one. Morgan Freeman is President Nelson Mandela in 1995, when South Africa is hosting the Rugby World Cup. Based on real events – with a good dash of poetic licence – the film depicts the relationship between Mandela and Springbok captain François Pienaar (played by Matt Damon) and how by winning the Cup that year, the Bokke and Mandela used rugby to unify a scarred nation.

BLOOD DIAMOND
EDWARD ZWICK (2006)

While not entirely shot in Cape Town, there are definite glimpses of the Mother City and Winelands. Leonardo DiCaprio stars as Danny Archer, a Rhodesian-born dealer in conflict diamonds in Sierra Leone. The V&A Waterfront can be clearly seen as the backdrop to his and Maddy's (Jennifer Connelly) reunion in Cape Town, and he meets a private gun for hire on a wine farm.

TSOTSI
GAVIN HOOD (2005)

Bringing home the Academy Award for Best Foreign Language Film in 2006 was an incredible accolade, not only for *Tsotsi*, but also for South African filmmaking. This story about a violent, slum-living teenager, who has left home to escape an abusive father and hijacks a car with a baby in it, may be set in Joburg, but it resonated with the entire country through its portrayal of township gang life.

U-CARMEN EKHAYELITSHA
MARK DORNFORD-MAY (2005)

This operatic film is based on Georges Bizet's 19th-century opera *Carmen*, but was set and filmed (in Xhosa) in the Cape Town township of Khayelitsha. The original setting of a poor area in Seville translates perfectly to modern township life, with its energy, passion and gangs.

Gay & Lesbian

Cape Town is most definitely the gay capital of southern Africa, and its pink heart lies in De Waterkant: a historic area squeezed between the City Bowl and Atlantic Seaboard. Among quaint cobbled streets and brightly painted houses are bars, clubs and restaurants galore. You're sure to have a ball here during the summer, thanks to the proximity of some of the most pristine beaches in the world, while, in winter, the social scene is busier than ever. You'll also be pleasantly surprised by the sense of camaraderie and open-minded spirit. But, as with any place, there are still some locals who frown upon the queer community, so refrain from extreme behaviour in the more public spots and always keep an eye on your own safety. Also, AIDS and STDs are a reality, with South Africa topping the stats tables for HIV-infection rates, so be savvy and keep those condoms handy.

THE SCENE

The 'Pink Strip' in De Waterkant is filled with chic and trendy shops, restaurants and bars, so you're sure to find places to keep you entertained during your stay. One of the best ways to experience the sights and sounds of Cape Town is with a gay-friendly tour operator. **Friends of Dorothy** (021 465 1871, www.friendsofdorothytours.co.za) are the go-to people for exploring the city and the Winelands, with their fun, vivacious and camp guides. For adventures further afield, **Out 2 Africa** (www.out2africa.com) specialises in luxury tours to more than 100 destinations across southern Africa.

One of the greatest advocators for the LGBT community, the **Triangle Project** (021 448 3812, helpline 021 712 6699, www.triangle. org.za), has made great strides in ensuring that the rights of all gay, lesbian, bisexual and transgender people are protected. Contact them if you have any troubles during your stay in Cape Town, need advice or just want some holiday tips.

To brush up on any information, stats and facts about Cape Town, visit www.capetown.tv, www.capetown.gaycities.com or www.gay capetown4u.com. And if you're looking for new friends or a casual fling during your stay, you can also hop on to www.mambaonline.com, www.gaydar.co.za, www.manhunt.com, www.mambagirl.com or www.lushcapetown.co.za.

BARS & CLUBS

Amsterdam Action Bar

10-14 Cobern Street, De Waterkant, Atlantic Seaboard (no phone, www.amsterdambar. co.za). **Open** 4pm-2am daily. **Admission** free. **Map** p254 G2.

The father of the Gay Village, award-winning Amsterdam Action Bar is deemed the top watering hole for gay men. It's a hit with both locals and international visitors, so you'll be sure to bump into someone here from a different corner of the globe. Downstairs has a bar, non-smoking and smoking areas, comfortable seating and a pool table, while upstairs is for more risqué patrons. With vibey tunes playing in the background, it's the perfect hangout for a quick nightcap or an intimate setting in which to get to know your date a bit better.

Bar Code

18 Cobern Street, De Waterkant, Atlantic Seaboard (no phone, www.leatherbar.co.za). **Open** 10pm-late

Piano Bar.

Wed-Sun. **Admission** R80 including 1 free local beer. **Map** p254 G2.

If kink is what you're looking for, then Bar Code is the place to be. This men-only leather, rubber, uniform and jeans bar nestled in the heart of the gay district is strictly for the more adventurous, with theme nights such as Wednesday's Underwear and Friday's Jeans & Leather. Give *Fifty Shades* a nod with the BDSM-inspired rooms, or try the outdoor deck for a more subtle approach. Like them on Facebook at 'BarCode' for instant replies.

Beulah

28 Somerset Road, De Waterkant, Atlantic Seaboard (021 418 5244, www.facebook. com/beulahbar). **Open** 9pm-4am Fri, Sat. **Admission** R30. **Map** p254 G2.

You can paint the town pink at Beulah bar. Dance the night and your troubles away in this spacious club with its funky DJs playing a mix of modern

---

IN THE KNOW TALK THE TALK

Brush up on your 'Gayle', gay alliterative slang using women's names.

Beaulah beautiful
Cilla cigarette
Dora drink (noun or verb)
Hilda hideous

---

pop, rock, dubstep and hip hop. The combination of friendly bar staff and fun-loving patrons means it's easy to have a ball and make a new friend or two. It's aimed predominantly at lesbian and bi-curious girls, but gay men and straight women also enjoy themselves here.

Café Manhattan

74 Waterkant Street, De Waterkant (021 421 6666, www.manhattan.co.za). **Open** 10am-midnight daily. **Admission** free. **Map** p254 G3.

This Wild West-themed bar in the heart of the De Waterkant village has the best vibes if you want to wind down after a long day, meet up with someone for a couple of drinks, or have a late-night naughty rendezvous. The terrace is perfect for romantic alfresco dining. Signature cocktails include the Cucumber Smash and Manhattan Mojito, while the US-inspired menu majors on burgers, steaks and the likes of southern fried chicken.

Crew

30 Napier Street, De Waterkant, Atlantic Seaboard (073 204 3706, www.facebook.com/ CrewBarCapeTown). **Open** 7pm-4am daily. **Admission** R30-R40. **Map** p254 G2.

Gorgeous bartenders, hunky go-go boys in risqué underwear, contemporary rave, pop and dubstep music jamming over the speakers and a great group of partygoers is what Crew Bar has to offer. Two dancefloors and multiple bars are spread across the two-storey building. There are no entry restrictions, so whether you're a girl or a boy looking to dance the night away, you're always more than welcome.

GAT Party

Theo Marais Park, Koeberg Road, Milnerton, Northern Suburbs (no phone). **Open** 1st, 2nd & last Sat of mth. **Admission** R40. **No credit cards.**

In the depths of the northern suburbs, you'll find the GAT Party, which brings a *kiki* (gathering) like no other to the LGBT-community of Cape Town. With a vibrant mix of Afrikaans *sokkie* music, modern-day pop hits and American line dancing, you'll find yourself exercising muscles you knew you never had. It might remind you of a senior prom at times, but the eclectic mix of people having fun creates an infectious party spirit. If you're brave enough, ask one of the boys or girls to teach you how to *sokkie*. Check them out on Facebook.

Piano Bar

Cnr of Jarvis & Napier streets, De Waterkant, Atlantic Seaboard (021 418 1096, www. thepianobar.co.za). **Open** noon-late daily. **Admission** free. **Map** p254 G3.

This New York-styled music revue bar is a winner, offering a great atmosphere, value for money and a plethora of local talent – pianists, singer-songwriters and more. There's a menu of tapas and burgers, decent cocktails and craft beer and a wraparound terrace with views over the harbour. Check the website for updates on events.

Stargayzer

16 Caxton Street, Parow, Northern Suburbs (no phone). **Open** 8pm-1am Thur; 9pm-4am Fri, Sat. **Admission** R30.

If the hustle and bustle of the city is getting you down, this unpretentious gay club in the northern suburbs is just what the doctor ordered. Everyone is allowed in, and the order of the day is to have fun at all times. The music policy is wonderfully eclectic, taking in showtunes, pop, rock and a bit of dubstep, so you won't be stuck in the corner all night long. Alternatively, hustle a game of pool or have a few drinks at the bar. Look for 'Stargayzer Caxon Street' on Facebook.

RESTAURANTS & CAFÉS

Beefcakes

Sovereign Quay, 34 Somerset Road, De Waterkant, Atlantic Seaboard (021 425 9019, www.beefcakes. co.za). **Open** 6pm-midnight Mon-Sat. **Map** p254 G3.

This trendy and popular burger joint-cum-revue bar in the heart of the gay district serves some of the best burgers in town. The choice of toppings includes Gourmet (cranberry jelly and camembert) and Hawaiian Hunk (guacamole, crispy bacon and a pineapple ring). The friendly, hunky staff aren't ashamed to flash their abs or pose for a selfie, and

live entertainment and themed nights add to the fun; the top-notch drag shows will have you dancing in the aisles.

Beluga

Foundry, Prestwich Street, De Waterkant, Atlantic Seaboard (021 418 2948, www.beluga.co.za). **Open** noon-10pm daily. **Map** p254 G2.

This globe-trotting restaurant serves some of the best sushi and dim sum in town, at the best prices. Also on offer are pasta, bistro classics and lots of seafood, but the sushi specials are what draws the crowds. With a beautiful outdoor courtyard and a bold industrial look inside, it's a stylish spot to see and be seen. They also stock an excellent range of local wines – ask your waiter for recommendations.

KOS

Village Lodge, 49 Napier Street, De Waterkant, Atlantic Seaboard (021 421 1106). **Open** 7.30am-10.30pm daily. **Map** p254 G3.

KOS (the word means 'food' in Afrikaans) serves traditional South African dishes in very generous portions. For great local flavours, try the ostrich bobotie and boerewors stir-fry. The simple decor (white tablecloths, local photos) and scenic alfresco seating area add to the relaxed vibe.

Richard's Supper Stage & Bistro

229A Main Road, Sea Point, Altantic Seaboard (021 434 6738, www.richardscapetown.co.za). **Open** 8am-11pm daily. **Map** p251 C2.

Dinner theatre is still a relatively new concept in Cape Town, but co-owner Richard Loring knows his stuff as a theatre producer of many years' standing. During the day, the ground floor is a bustling bistro, serving everything from breakfast pastries to burgers, salads and pasta. Come the evening, the first floor is transformed into a theatre where the entertainment is mostly African performers showing off their talents.

SPAS & SAUNAS

Amani Man Spa Waterfront

Radisson Blu Hotel, Beachfront Road, Granger Bay (021 441 3321/2/3, www.amanispas.co.za). **Open** 8am-8pm daily.

Overlooking the breathtakingly beautiful Table Bay, Amani Man Spa Waterfront is the best medicine for a tired soul. Whether you're looking to unwind in the sauna, or to rest those tired muscles in the steam room or with one of their renowned massages, this spa offers perfect pampering options. Choose between a full day, half-day, corporate wellness or customised package to suit your needs and your pocket. The Vitality Pool is also a must in the summer, while their signature Amani Hydro Journey is talked about by guests from far and wide. Be sure to try the Jewel of Africa Massage, which uses various African oils to help you ease all that pent-up tension.

ARTS & ENTERTAINMENT

Pink Rose Guest House.

ARTS & ENTERTAINMENT

Glasshouse
Foundry, Prestwich Street, De Waterkant, Atlantic Seaboard (021 419 9599, www.glasshousemen. com). **Open** 9am-7pm Mon-Fri; 9am-5pm Sat. **Map** p254 G2.
Treat yourself at one of Cape Town's top spots, frequented by celebrities and models. Glasshouse boasts a vast product range, from Instantly Ageless to Dermalogica, and caters to a wide range of men's skincare and grooming needs. You'll be able to dazzle up your hair, manicure those nails, manscape a bit to keep your situation under control and have a pedicure that will set you up perfectly for your next trip to the beach.

Hot House
18 Jarvis Street, De Waterkant, Atlantic Seaboard (021 418 3888, www.hothouse.co.za). **Open** noon-midnight Mon-Wed; noon-2am Thur; 24hours Fri-midnight Sun. **Rates** R75-R150. **Map** p254 G3.
Hot House is just the place to unwind after a long night's partying. It's got all the facilities to relieve tired muscles, including a steam room, spacious sauna and hot tubs, plus a sun deck if you wish to catch up on your tanning. Downstairs is a fully stocked bar. There are also private cabins, TV and video lounges, and an adult store.

IN THE KNOW BEAULAH BEACHES

Cape Town's unofficial gay beach is **Clifton 3rd** (Victoria Road, Clifton, just north of Camps Bay). It's perfect for sunbathing as it's protected from the south-easterly winds and offers great eye-candy. Just remember the water is icy.

WHERE TO STAY

De Waterkant Lodge
35 Dixon Street, De Waterkant, Atlantic Seaboard (021 419 2476, www.dewaterkantplace.com). **Rates** from R750. **Map** p254 G3.
De Waterkant Lodge is a handy, centrally located place to stay. It's within walking distance of the gay district and its myriad attractions, so you're sure to save a dime or two on taxis. The beautifully renovated three-storey building has a homely, colonial design; all rooms have fantastic views over the Mother City, and the large rooftop terrace is ideal for enjoying the sunset with a sundowner. Most of the rooms are standard B&B, but there are also apartments that can sleep up to six adults.

Glen Boutique Hotel
3 The Glen, Sea Point, Atlantic Seaboard (021 439 0086, www.glenhotel.co.za). **Rates** from R990. **Map** p251 C3.
Chic, urban, with a dash of modern styling: welcome to this centrally located Sea Point hotel, with its sea and mountain views. There are 24 individually styled ensuite rooms, most featuring their own private garden, terrace or balcony, plus double-volume showers and Italian designer features. For the ultimate in comfort, book the penthouse with its 360° views and own private lift. The Rain Forest Spa, equipped with a sauna, steam room and indoor Jacuzzi, adds to the sense of indulgence.

Pink Rose Guest House
15 Lantana Street, Helderview, Somerset West (021 855 5189, www.pinkroseguesthouse.com). **Rates** from R795.
This gay-men-only guesthouse and spa is set in the heart of Somerset West, 40 minutes' drive from Cape Town and near Stellenbosch. Each of the four stylish rooms has king-sized beds, a small kitchenette, satellite TV and internet access, and is serviced daily. The breakfast lounge boasts breathtaking views, and there's a sauna and massage room as well as a clothing-optional swimming pool. Breakfast is provided, but lunch and dinner can be arranged too.

Rockwell All Suite Hotel & Apartments
Cnr Prestwich & Alfred streets, De Waterkant, Atlantic Seaboard (021 421 0015, www.rockwell hotel.co.za). **Rates** from R2,250. **Map** p254 H3.
Within strolling distance of the Pink District, the V&A Waterfront and the City Bowl, the Rockwell is a New York-styled apartment building. It offers 18 one-bedroom, 29 two-bedroom and five amazing penthouse apartments; smart and modern in design, all come with a designer kitchenette, spacious lounge area and a generous balcony. All apartments are serviced daily and Wi-Fi is available. For a great night out without leaving the premises, enjoy dinner theatre (Michael Jackson tribute acts, top-notch comedy, drag shows) at the Rockwell's very own theatre.

JOIN THE PARTY

Cape Town's LGBT community knows how to celebrate.

The city's biggest pink event, **Cape Town Pride** (www.capetownpride.co.za) has increased rapidly in success and size in the past few years. Held in mid to late February, the ten-day celebration culminates in a fantastic parade through the streets of the Pink District. All the gay clubs host special events, and there are street parties lasting through the night.

Along the Garden Route, in the charming town of Knysna, the five-day **Pink Loerie Mardi Gras & Arts Festival** (www.pinkloerie. co.za) usually happens over the last weekend of April. The town is painted a brighter shade of pink with floats, performers, DJs, assorted cultural events, and loads of parties thrown by various sponsors.

Gay Day, a brand-new event organised by Cape Town Pride, showcases local musical talent and DJs. It's held in early October, so some people see it as the kick-off party for the summer. Streets in De Waterkant are closed off for the event.

For one night, and one night only, the **Mother City Queer Project** (www.mcqp. co.za) is the place to be. Launched in 1994, it's grown to become 'Africa's biggest queer bash', attracting thousands of visitors, gay and straight, to the city. This over-the-top fancy-dress extravaganza in December is held at a different major landmark each year. Past themes have included Royal Navy and Space Cowboys.

Nightlife

Cape Town has a lively and varied nightlife scene to suit most tastes and budgets, ranging from intimate speciality bars to weekend-long outdoor parties and music festivals – and pretty much everything in between. The festivities usually begin before dark: sundowners along the Atlantic Seaboard, enjoying the stunning coastline with gorgeous views, are a popular way to ease into the night. From there, your choice could be a dive bar in Harrington Street followed by a night of dancing at a club within walking distance, or you could dip into some top-shelf spirits somewhere more upmarket before discovering gems of musical talent at a live show.

CLUBS

Cape Town's city centre is where you'll find most of the nightclubs devoted to the hedonistic pleasures of the dancefloor. Although some clubs are located near one another, if you're planning on serious club-hopping it's highly recommended that you use a reputable metered taxi company or Uber – the streets are not safe for walking, and neither are random unmarked cabs.

When it comes to dancing the night away, you can take your pick of musical genres: deep house beats, commercial radio hits, R&B, hip hop, jungle, dubstep and classic 1980s rock. At **Decodance** in Sea Point, for example, you'll know the words to all the songs even if you weren't born when they were hits. In a notoriously fickle city where the in-crowd moves from the latest hotspot to the next within a week, clubs can come and go in the blink of an eye. But there are some mainstays that have stood the test of time, such as **Fiction**, **Galaxy** and **Tiger Tiger**.

Hitting a nightclub is the perfect excuse to dress up in your best party clothes, pile on the bling, and break out those dance moves. Weekends are the hottest and busiest times to see and be seen, but for a more mellow night out, look for the places also open during the week.

Club 31

31st Floor, Absa Building, 2 Riebeek Street, City Centre, City Bowl (021 421 0580, *www.thirtyone.co.za).* **Open** 10pm-4am Fri, Sat. **Admission** R50. No under-21s women; no under-23s men. **Map** p254 H3.

In true Cape Town style, this is a late bloomer – in other words, don't think of arriving too early. It's stylish and sophisticated and, as far as nightclubs go, has the best view of the city. The dress code is smart casual, so make an effort, and note the age restrictions. The 31st floor setting makes for stunning views of the city – you'll feel, literally, on top of the world.

★ Decodance

120 Main Road, Sea Point, Atlantic Seaboard (084 330 1962, 021 433 2912). **Open** 8.30pm-4am Wed, Fri, Sat. **Admission** after 10pm R40. No under-22s. **Map** p251 C2.

Relocated from Woodstock's Old Biscuit Mill a few years ago, Decodance remains one of the best all-round rocking party nights in Cape Town. The music is old-school – hits of the 1960s-80s, maybe even a few songs from the 1990s at a push. You can sing along, you can let loose, you can be a party animal. The club and its patrons are big fans of themed dress-up nights. Follow them on Facebook for updates.

Dragon Room

84 Harrington Street, East City, City Bowl (021 461 4920). **Open** 10pm-4am Fri, Sat. **Admission** R70-R100. **Map** p254 H4.

A fabulous venue with several interlinking rooms, dancefloors and multiple bars, and great decor, Dragon Room hosts regular big – and we mean big

– events such as Trash Cabaret (a feast for the senses with music and performance art), and massive DJ line-ups to keep you going all night long. Follow on Facebook for regular updates, as the club is sometimes closed for private functions.

ERA

71 Loop Street, City Centre, City Bowl (021 422 0202, www.eracapetown.com). **Open** 10pm-4am Fri, Sat. **Admission** free before 11pm. No under-21s women; no under-23s men. **Map** p254 H3.

This newcomer celebrates electronic music in all its forms (house, deep house, techno and so on), with some pretty fancy technological trickery, including walls and ceiling covered in LED lights, a motion-active wall and a killer sound system. Upstairs, a café serves tapas to a soundtrack of lounge beats. Downstairs, take to the dancefloor for the full-blown audio/visual experience.

Fiction DJ Bar & Lounge

226 Long Street, City Centre, City Bowl (021 424 5709, www.fictionbar.com). **Open** 10pm-4am Tue-Sat. **Admission** R40-R50. **Map** p254 G4.

A favourite place for many clubbers – as borne out by the fact it's been around for years, delivering a mix of alternative music that keeps punters coming back for more. There are regular club nights such as Peroxide (1980s synth) and Untamed Youth (indie, disco and electro), but expect different genres whenever you visit. Head to the rooftop bar for a breath of 'fresh' city air. Alternatively, there's a wraparound balcony looking down on the manic buzz of Long Street.

Galaxy/West End

400 College Road, Rylands, Southern Suburbs (021 637 9132, 021 637 9027). **Open** *Galaxy* 9pm-4am Thur-Sat. *West End* (no under-21s) 5pm-4am Fri, Sat. **Admission** R50.

Generations of Capetonians have partied here; the place has been open for decades and is a popular Cape Flats destination. Local DJs take to the decks to keep the crowd going until the early hours of the morning. Thursday nights are particularly off the wall.

Gonzo's

Gabriel House, 203 Main Road, Plumstead, Southern Suburbs (021 797 2393). **Open** 11am-4am daily. **Admission** R20 after 9pm Fri, Sat.

Ask a local about partying in this southern suburb and they'll probably look at you as if you're mad. Most of the venues in the area can be a bit dodgy, but Gonzo's hosts some of the top names on the DJ circuit, such as Dean Fuel and Euphonik – and for a much lower cover charge than fancier places in the City Bowl. It's much less pretentious too. There's the added advantage of pool tables when you need a break from dancing.

Le Roi

Promenade, Camps Bay, Atlantic Seaboard (021 437 1791). **Open** *Summer* 4pm-2am Mon-Thur; 2pm-2am Fri, Sat. *Winter* 4pm-2am Tue-Sun. **Map** p250 A8.

It's posh and regal – the name means 'king' in French – so you can expect to party the night away in an

Shimmy Beach Club. See p165.

ARTS & ENTERTAINMENT

TRANCE NATION
Get ready to party.

If you've arrived in Cape Town during the summer months, congratulations! You've got here just in time for the trance season, an epic part of the city's entertainment and lifestyle scene. The outdoor festival calendar – rain or shine – traditionally opens with **Earthdance** (www.earthdancecapetown.co.za), close to the spring equinox in late September, although in 2015 that was pre-empted by the **Sunflower Festival** at the end of August, headlined by Skazi from Israel.

What follows are open-air parties almost every weekend, with dozens of DJs pumping out non-stop tunes. SA's home-grown guys and gals are legendary, and big international names often turn up, keen to play to appreciative crowds in some of the most spectacular settings on the planet. Lighting and decor outdoes itself year on year, providing pretty, colourful shade during the day, which turns into a magical UV-lit playground at night. Costumes, make-up, toys and an adventurous spirit provide eye-candy.

Venues are chosen for their natural outdoor beauty, which is not difficult within the two- or three hour-drive radius from Cape Town's city centre. The best ones will be alongside a river, or near a dam, where you can cool off during the day or skinny-dip at night. Whether you camp in your car, or build an elaborate home from home in the bush, event organisers go all out to provide all the amenities you'll need, from showers and portable toilets (OK, those are never going to be great after the first day), to food vendors, clothes stalls and fully stocked bars. There are the big guys such as **Vortex** (www.intothevortex.co.za) and **Alien Safari** (www.facebook.com/aliensafari), but you only have to be active on social media to get the lowdown on the smaller but no less enjoyable weekly events.

For more information, check out places in Long Street such as Ska Clothing (no.161) and internet café Computeria (no.206), as well as backpacker lodges, which are dropping-off points for flyers and tend to have clued-up staff too.

During the rainy months there are often big indoor events, at venues such as the **Dragon Room** (*see p162*). On Facebook, Cape Town Trance Parties and Cape Town PsyTrance Parties are good resources – both post regular updates.

Armed with the right attitude, you can spend every weekend stomping up a storm, but New Year's Eve is always the biggest party of all; depending on the day it falls it can turn into an up to five-day extravaganza. If you're a veteran you'll know how to handle yourself, but if it's your first time in Cape Town, remember to pack tons of sunblock and stay hydrated with lots of water.

opulent setting. It's Camps Bay, so prices are high, but at least there's no admission charge. We recommend you arrive early for the sundowner hour, then dance the night away to sexy, sultry beats.

Shimmy Beach Club

12 South Arm Road, V&A Waterfront, Atlantic Seaboard (021 200 7778, www.shimmybeachclub. com). **Open** 11am-4am daily. **Admission** (weekends) R50 women, R100 men. **Map** p253 I1.
The ultimate glamour destination, Shimmy is a restaurant by day where yummy mummies and hot young things congregate: at night, it's a bar and club. The decor is gorgeous, and the place epitomises Cape Town's world-class status as tourist hotspot. It's smack bang in the middle of a working harbour, with its own beach and splash pool. *Photo p163.*

Tiger Tiger

Stadium on Main, 103 Main Road, Claremont, Southern Suburbs (021 683 2220, www.tigertiger. co.za). **Open** 8pm-4am Thur; 9pm-4am Fri, Sat. **Admission** R40 members, R50 non-members.
With a reputation for drawing a very young and irresponsible crowd, this venue has received a lot of negative publicity for the actions of its clientele. And yet it remains one of the most popular nightclubs in the southern suburbs, year after year. It has eight bars (which might account for some of what happens after patrons leave the premises), and two dancefloors. The music is house and commercial.

★ Vice City

4 Buiten Street, City Centre, City Bowl (073 747 2033, www.vicecity.co.za). **Open** 10pm-4am Thur-Sun. **Admission** R50. No under-21s. **Map** p254 G4.
Psy trance, house, techno, bass – every night a different genre is showcased at one of the city's newest nightclubs, which opened in April 2015. It's just off Long Street, so it's party central. Locals are loving it, raving about the vibe, the people and the superb, state-of-the-art sound and lighting system. There's nothing new about the formula, but a cool interactive approach by management is putting this place on the map.

MUSIC

Venues dedicated solely to live music have declined drastically over the past few years, but there is a core of supporters in the city who do their best to keep the scene alive. One of Cape Town's oldest live gig venues, **Mercury**, very nearly disappeared into history recently but has been revived, much to the joy of music lovers and musicians alike. While not necessarily their pure focus, there are many bars and restaurants that provide live music and/or DJs for their patrons' aural pleasure, which can be enjoyed before or after a meal without the hassle of rushing from one place to the next.

There's a growing number of outdoor weekend music festivals, including Up the Creek, Rocking the Daisies and Dusty Rebels & The Bombshells (which celebrates rockabilly culture). There are also regular events throughout the year at **Hillcrest Quarry** – adjoining a wine farm, for the best of both worlds – such as the Table Mountain Blues Summit and the Blues Meets Rock festival. Events are undercover in winter and open-air in summer, and new things are being added to the calendar every year. The sundowner concerts (*see p115*) at **Kirstenbosch Botanical Gardens** every Sunday from November to April are a huge crowd-pleaser, and have become a Cape Town institution.

Jazz

★ Crypt

St George's Cathedral, 1 Wale Street, City Centre, City Bowl (079 683 4658, www.thecryptjazz.com). **Open** 6.30pm-late Tue-Sat. **Admission** R75 Tue-Sat; R100 special nights. **Map** p254 G4.
Based in the stone crypt below historic St George's Cathedral, this swanky city-centre jazz club and eaterie is arguably one of the Mother City's most distinct spots in which to experience the sweet sounds of jazz. Though the melodies take centre stage, the venue, with plush furnishings and low-key lighting, also serves tasty tapas and other dishes, and a range of top-notch wines. The jazz line-up changes nightly, and the carefully curated variety of acts is what sets this upmarket joint apart from the pack.

Marco's African Place

15 Rose Street, Bo-Kaap, City Bowl (021 423 | 5412, www.marcosafricanplace.co.za). **Open** 3-11pm Mon, Sat, Sun; noon-11pm Tue-Fri. **Admission** R20 diners; R40 non-diners. **Map** p254 G3.
Get a taste of Africa with a meal influenced by the magnificent continent, and enjoy eclectic beats most nights of the week. Regular artists include the band Young Bakumba and local singer Fancy Galada. Many jazz greats have played here over the years, among them Jimmy Dludlu, Hugh Masekela, Sibongile Khumalo and Sylvia Mdunyelwa.

Marimba Restaurant

CTICC, cnr Walter Sisulu Avenue & Heerengracht Boulevard, City Centre, City Bowl (021 418 3366, www.marimbasa.com). **Open** 8am-late Mon-Fri; 6pm-late Sat. **Map** p254 H3.
Musicians and DJs provide the tunes for diners at this venue in the Cape Town International Convention Centre, which also happens to be the location for the annual Cape Town International Jazz Festival (*see p33*). If you're in town, and a jazz lover, this is the perfect place to hang out because you never know who might pop in to jam.

ARTS & ENTERTAINMENT

ARTS & ENTERTAINMENT

Piano Bar

47 Napier Street, De Waterkant, Atlantic Seaboard (079 028 4628, www.thepianobar. co.za). **Open** 3pm-midnight Mon-Thur; 3pm-late Fri; 4.30pm-late Sat; 4.30-11pm Sun. **Map** p252 G3.

This trendy, New York-inspired revue bar is the perfect spot in which to relax, delicious cocktail in hand, while listening to some jazz, blues, folk, or nu world music. A variety of artists perform on regular rotation, with frequent new additions. It's an elegant venue where you can have dinner while enjoying the show, or simply explore the large and varied wine menu or the commercial and craft beers on tap.

Straight No Chaser

79 Buitenkant Street, East City, City Bowl (076 679 2697, www.facebook.com/straightnochaserclub). **Open** *Shows* 8.30pm, 10pm Wed-Sat. **Admission** R60-R140. **Map** p254 H5.

Straight No Chaser is a jazz and music venue which hosts some of the best talent to come out of South Africa. It's a concert set-up with rows of chairs in front of a stage, where you sit down, shut up and listen. The bar is open on concert nights from 7pm. It's a small, intimate venue, so booking ahead is essential; call or check Facebook for the latest updates.

Swingers

1 Wetwyn Road, Ottery, Southern Suburbs (021 762 2443). **Open** 10am-3am Mon-Thur, Sun; 10am-7am Fri, Sat. **Admission** *Fri, Sat* R20 karaoke, R30 club.

If Cape Town is the home of jazz, then this is the comfy lounge where family and friends hang out for contemporary African and jazz tunes. Delight at the sounds of Melanie Scholtz and Erika Lundi at this timeless venue. Monday nights are the best, when musicians visiting the city tend to drop by.

Rock/pop/alternative

Aandklas

43A Bird Street, Stellenbosch, Winelands (021 883 3545). **Open** 11am-2am Mon-Sat.

Stellenbosch is famous for its wine farms – and for its university. Which is why this is a cool student hangout with pub quizzes, beer pong and sport on the big screens. But the main reason for heading to this out-of-town spot is its top-class live music, which focuses strongly on local talent and specifically Afrikaans musicians such as Fokofpolisiekar and Koos Kombuis. Follow the venue on Twitter and Facebook for event updates.

Aces 'n' Spades

62 Hout Street, City Bowl (081 895 3555, 076 207 4698, www.acesnspades.com). **Open** 5pm-2am Mon-Sat. **Admission** free. **Map** p254 H3.

Super cool, super trendy, super busy. With fabulous black and white photography on the walls and leather upholstery, this is one of the hottest tickets in town. The Robfather DJs some nights, bands such as Taxi Violence play intimate gigs, and every Wednesday you can humiliate yourself with rock 'n' roll karaoke. What more do you need?

★ Assembly

61 Harrington Street, East City, City Bowl (021 465 7286, www.theassembly.co.za). **Open** 9pm-2am Wed-Sat. **Admission** varies. **Map** p254 H4.

Besides Mercury, Assembly is one of the stalwarts of the live music scene in Cape Town. Converted from a warehouse, it retains some of the industrial feel typical of the East City. It has hosted most of the big names in the industry, consistently showcasing the best and brightest musicians and DJs in all genres, be they local or international, rising stars or household names. The venue also has an online radio station.

Hillcrest Quarry

Tygerberg Valley Road, Durbanville, Northern Suburbs (021 976 4959, www.thequarry.co.za). **Open & admission** varies.

This stunning venue is, as the name suggests, located in a quarry – with a large dam. It hosts regular outdoor concerts and festivals at weekends. In the winter months, or when it rains, there is a huge marquee to use, so there's no damper on the fun. The quarry adjoins Hillcrest wine and olive farm, so do pop in for a tasting while you're in the area.

Mercury

43 de Villiers Street, Zonnebloem, East City, City Bowl (021 465 2106, www.mercurylive.co.za). **Open** 4.30pm-2am daily. **Admission** varies. **Map** p254 H5.

This is the longest-standing mainstream live music venue in the city, where every local band (and some big international names) has played a gig at one time or another – and it has a very special place in Capetonians' hearts. After some ups and downs, it very nearly closed in 2015, causing music fans and bands to cry into their beers, but it was rescued by Cape Audio College, revamped and reopened with better sound, lighting and recording capabilities. It is the best, and is true to the spirit and love of live music.

Obviouzly Armchair

135 Lower Main Road, Observatory, Southern Suburbs (021 460 0458, www.obviouzly armchairbackpackers.hostel.com). **Open** 10am-2am daily. **Admission** varies.

In the heart of Obs, this backpacker venue has a bar, a live music stage run by Cape Audio College, and an outside courtyard. As such, there are gigs every Friday and Saturday, and open mic nights on Tuesday when you may make some amazing discoveries. The bag gets shaken up with comedy

ESSENTIAL CAPE TOWN MUSIC

Listen to the sounds of the city.

AUTOBIOGRAPHY
ABDULLAH IBRAHIM
(1978)

Cape Town's greatest jazz pianist is the living embodiment of the city's diverse cultures. Ibrahim writes and plays music ranging from gospel and jazz to traditional African songs. This live recording has him telling his story.

ANOTHER UNIVERSE
ARNO CARSTENS
(2003)

Carstens was (and is again) front man for democratic South Africa's first truly great rock act, the Springbok Nude Girls. His solo debut won a South African Music Award, while its anthemic title track provided the soundtrack to a Volkswagen TV ad.

PERCEPTIONS OF
PACHA
GOLDFISH (2008)

Chilled. Laid-back. Soulful. The sophomore album from Cape Town's scruffy-surfer jazz-house duo – featuring the catchy lead single 'Cruising Through' – is exactly what a sweaty summer night at a Mother City beach bar should sound like.

KAROO KITAAR BLUES
DAVID KRAMER
(2001)

Singer, songwriter and playwright Kramer, known for his raucous musicals about the Cape Coloured community, goes into the remote Karoo semi-desert, discovering 'a harsh Southern African sound that reflects how the sun has affected our voices'.

NOMVULA
FRESHLYGROUND
(2004)

This is Afro-fusion at its most upbeat and accessible, blending blues, jazz, indie rock, African folk and kwela. 'Doo Be Doo' is made for singing along to, while 'Mowbray Kaap' is probably the most Cape Town song you'll ever hear.

TEN$ION
DIE ANTWOORD
(2012)

Hidden beneath Capetonian duo Die Antwoord's hilariously overplayed 'def' image and shock-rap-rave stylings are some incredibly catchy tunes. You – like David Letterman – will catch yourself singing 'I fink you freeky and I like you a lot' for weeks on end.

ARTS & ENTERTAINMENT

COME OUT AND PLAY
Festive musical fun awaits all year round.

With stunning outdoor venues a reasonably short drive from Cape Town, it's no wonder there are so many open-air music festivals during the year. Pack the tent, sunblock, some rehydration tabs, a sleeping bag and good vibes before heading out to the following.

You'll also need a lilo in order to languish in the Breede river near Swellendam while listening to rock music at **Up the Creek** (www. upthecreek.co.za; *pictured*). It usually takes place around the end of January, so the river is the perfect place to chill. For die-hard rock fans, **Rocking the Daisies** (http://rocking thedaisies.com), which usually happens on the West Coast, is a must. It's held in October, so pack warm clothes and closed shoes. It's young, fun and most definitely raucous.

The third annual **Cape Town Nu World Festival** (http://capetownnuworldfestival. com) took place in City Hall in July 2015, bringing together a vast array of local and international acts. The festival also included workshops and talks with a focus on the music industry.

If you're keen on an adventure, the South African version of Burning Man is **AfrikaBurn** (http://afrikaburn.com) in April/May: a heady event in the middle of the Tankwa Karoo (about 300 kilometres from Cape Town, but the gravel roads are arduous, so it'll take most of a day to drive there). You'll need to bring every single

thing you need, including food and water, as there is absolutely nothing near the site. Magnificent artistic creations, a strong sense of community and an anything-goes attitude are what you'll discover.

Girls, don your heels and petticoats and paint your lips red; guys, don leathers and get into gear – for the **Dusty Rebels & the Bombshells** 'rockabilly lifestyle' festival (www.dustyrebelsandthebombshells. co.za). It's toe-stomping fun and the vibe is extremely inclusive.

on Wednesday and Sunday, and a 'bring and braai' every sunny weekend from noon till 4.30pm.

Rabbit Hole
Scher Street, Durbanville, Northern Suburbs (074 077 4169, www.therabbitholebar.co.za). **Open** noon-2am Tue-Sun. **Admission** R10-R40.
The events are titled 'We're All Mad Here Down The Rabbit Hole', so that should give you an indication of what to expect. A great showcase venue for bands from Cape Town as well as those from other cities in South Africa, it hosts everything from metal to rockabilly, to quieter acoustic sessions. If that's not enough, there are trivia, pool competitions and open mic nights as well.

Roar/Gandalfs
299 Lower Main Road, Observatory, Southern Suburbs (083 330 0700). **Open** 9pm-4am Thur-Sat. **Admission** R10. **No credit cards**.

Let's not sugar-coat this – it's dark, dirty and grungy. Your feet will stick to the floor. But it's cheap, and it's where you'll get your fix of punk in Cape Town, and for that it's the right environment. The crowd is young, the bands are enthusiastic, and it does boast one of the best sound systems in the city.

★ Waiting Room
273 Long Street, City Centre, City Bowl (021 422 4536, www.facebook.com/WaitingRoomCT). **Open** 8pm-midnight Tue-Sat. **Admission** varies. **Map** p254 G4.
Originally opened as, quite literally, a waiting room for diners in the Royale Eatery & Kitchen burger joint on the two floors below, this has become a dedicated live music venue, hosting a range of bands and solo artists, as well as DJs. The vibe is laid-back, with lots of couches and armchairs, and theres a balcony lit by fairy lights overlooking Long Street, as well as a roof deck.

Performing Arts

South Africans are a creative bunch, especially with the universities of Cape Town and Stellenbosch's drama and music faculties honing young talents. Venues big and small, outdoor and seasonal, create platforms for expression in theatre and music, and dance stalwarts such as Jazzart and Cape Town City Ballet still produce excellent shows. Summer outdoor concerts are a perfect way to spend an evening, with many esteemed wine estates hosting assorted events. Recently, classic dinner theatre has seen a revival, with accessible musicals, comedy and live music shows on the boards. Comedy remains popular, and South Africans are really adept at having a laugh at themselves.

TICKETS

Online resources include **Computicket** (http://online.computicket.com/web) and **Webtickets** (www.webtickets.co.za). With Computicket, you sometimes need to go to a Checkers supermarket to pick up printed tickets, which can be a hassle. Tickets can also be purchased in advance from theatre box offices. Ticket prices vary massively, from R50 for children's pantomimes to around R400 for large operatic productions. As elsewhere in the world, costs vary according to where you're sitting, but compared to overseas prices, shows can often be a bargain for international visitors.

THEATRE & COMEDY

Eyelash-curling queer cabaret, contortion acts or monster puppets: the Mother City has them all, in addition to its fair share of Shakespeare and serious local drama. The range of cultural expression pretty much matches the diversity of the country. Playwrights and directors are unafraid to tackle topical issues of the day; and comedians love to get under the skin of local issues.

Venues

Artscape Theatre Centre
DF Malan Street, Foreshore, City Bowl (021 410 9838, www.artscape.co.za). **Map** p253 I3.

Artscape is the home base of such major players as the Cape Town City Ballet (*see p173*) and Cape Town Opera. The fully equipped opera house is the largest in the Western Cape, seating 1,187 people. The lighting, sound and production work is impressive, and even considered world class by most virtuosos. First-rate theatre productions are also to be seen here. There's plenty of parking, but it might take you a while to get to your seat, so try to arrive half an hour before curtain-up.

Baxter Theatre Complex
Main Road, Rondebosch, Southern Suburbs (0861 915 8000, www.baxter.co.za).
There's a certain retro appeal to the huge orange lampshades dangling from the ceiling of the Baxter. Set on the University of Cape Town's grounds, the complex presents performing arts from diverse cultures, including international classics as well as works by local composers. The three-venue complex has great acoustics and stages a wide range of productions, from cutting-edge and major drama from Africa and beyond, to comedy, dance and children's theatre.

Cape Town Comedy Club
Pumphouse, Dock Road, V&A Waterfront, Atlantic Seaboard (021 418 8800, 079 495 3989, www.capetowncomedy.com). **Map** p253 H1.
At Cape Town's dedicated comedy space, you can watch new and established names, both local and

from overseas, cracking jokes while you enjoy a meal and a drink. Wednesdays to Sundays see a handful of comedians sharing the stage, so you're sure to have a giggle or two.

★ Fugard Theatre

Caledon Street, East City, City Bowl (021 461 4554, www.thefugard.com). **Map** p253 H4.

This beautifully restored space is home to one of the most happening theatres in the city. Named for Athol Fugard, one of South Africa's most important playwrights, the theatre's ample bar area and exposed brick walls create an atmosphere that's both convivial and historic. Massive hits have included local productions of *The Rocky Horror Show* and *Cabaret*. It seats 335 people and also has safe parking.

Galloway Theatre

Waterfront Theatre School, Port Road, Green Point, Atlantic Seaboard (021 418 4600, www. waterfronttheatreschool.co.za). **Map** p253 H2.

Watch the great actors and performers of tomorrow tread the boards at this theatre-school venue. Musicals are a favourite, so you can tap your toes to the great showtunes from *Grease*, *Chicago* or *Hairspray*.

Grand Arena

Grand West Casino & Entertainment World, 1 Vanguard Drive, Goodwood, Northern Suburbs (021 505 7777, www.grandwest.co.za).

The city's biggest entertainment venue can seat a whopping 5,000 punters. It focuses mainly on international headline acts such as funny man Russell Brand, muso Rodriguez, 1980s band Roxette (who knew they'd stage a comeback!), as well as sports shows, magic acts and comedy fests. You have to

walk past the heaving casino and food courts, so it takes a while to get out once the show is finished.

Little Theatre Complex

Hiddingh Campus, 37 Orange Street, Gardens, City Bowl (021 480 7129, www.drama.uct.ac.za). **Map** p254 G5.

The Little Theatre Complex is home to the University of Cape Town's drama and fine arts departments. The Little Theatre is, despite its name, the biggest of the three auditoria here, with 240 seats. The Intimate Theatre and Arena offer space for 70 and 80 people respectively. Between them, the trio offer varied delights performed by students, from cutting-edge drama by critically acclaimed playwrights to work by emerging performers and students.

Masque Theatre

37 Main Road, Muizenberg, South Peninsula (021 788 6999, www.masquetheatre.co.za).

Think you can act? Now's your chance to prove it. This community seaside theatre, next to the Muizenberg train station, has been around since the 1950s. It's run by the Muizenberg Dramatical Society and everyone stands a chance to tread its boards (provided they've auditioned for a part, of course).

Theatre on the Bay

1 Link Street, Camps Bay, Atlantic Seaboard (021 438 3300, www.theatreonthebay.co.za). **Map** p250 A8.

Behind a concrete curtained façade – a stone's throw from Camps Bay's palm-fringed beachfront – you'll find Pieter Toerien's Theatre on the Bay. Toerien is a legend in South African theatrical circles, best known for importing big-budget international shows to Africa. Here, the focus is on adapting

Fugard Theatre.

SOUNDS OF SUMMER
Head outdoors for some memorable music.

Warm summer evenings combined with a host of talented musicians and singers means outdoor concerts and performances are high on the to-do list for both locals and visitors. Pack a picnic, some lovely Cape wine, a blanket and jacket for when the sun sets and get ready to groove to classical and contemporary sounds.

Kirstenbosch Summer Sunset Concerts (www.facebook.com/KirstenboschSummer SunsetConcerts) sees big-name artists and an electric vibe at Cape Town's gorgeous botanical gardens. In the Winelands, **Starlight Classics** under the magnificent camphor trees at historical Vergelegen (www. vergelegen.co.za) makes for a sophisticated night out, while the **Oude Libertas Summer Season Festival** (www.oudelibertas.co.za) invites patrons to enjoy a picnic on the lawns before heading to the amphitheatre for a variety of concerts, from rock to classical and jazz. The outdoor **Hope@Paul Cluver Amphitheatre** (www.cluver.com), located at the Cluver wine estate in the Elgin Valley, is set in a natural forested space; performers here have included hip musos Jeremy Loops, the Parlotones and Suzanne Vega.

Such musical delights aren't confined to summer, though. From June to December, the historic Nederburg wine estate (www. nederburg.com) in Paarl presents the **Nederburg Concert Series**, showcasing chamber music every last Sunday of the month. The final concert is on New Year's Eve.

Broadway and West End productions, such as *Little Shop of Horrors*, for the local stage, as well as one-man comedy shows and popoular theatre productions including *Morecambe and Pythonesque*.

Dinner & bar theatre

Alexander Bar Café Theatre
76 Strand Street, City Centre, City Bowl (021 300 1088, www.alexanderbar.co.za). **Map** p254 H3.
A tiny performance area above buzzy Alexander Bar provides an intimate space for quality productions, from live music to drama, comedy and readings. There are some one-off international pieces too.

Kalk Bay Theatre
52 Main Road, Kalk Bay, South Peninsula (021 788 7257, www.kalkbaytheatre.co.za).
A historic Dutch Reformed Church in Kalk Bay houses a charming independent theatre. The venue has room for only 78 people, and the resulting sense of intimacy is a great part of its appeal. Top theatre personalities have graced this tiny stage in productions ranging from one- and two-man plays to magic shows, comedy acts and children's theatre. Start with dinner on the first floor before enjoying the show downstairs.

Richard's Supper Stage & Bistro
229A Main Road, Sea Point, Atlantic Seaboard (076 144 4809, www.richardscapetown.co.za). **Map** p251 D2.
Co-owned by veteran theatre producer and showman Richard Loring, this dinner theatre venue (which also has an all-day bistro) focuses on crowd-pleasing musical tributes and comedy. A highlight is *Kaapse Stories*, where you're taken on a musical journey through the Cape.

Roxy Revue Bar
Grand West Casino & Entertainment World, 1 Vanguard Drive, Goodwood, Northern Suburbs (021 505 7777, www.grandwest.co.za).
As the name suggests, productions on offer are mostly thigh-slapping, booty-shaking musical-variety shows, where patrons get the opportunity to travel through time and swivel crotches with Elvis or clap hands in time with Queen.

Theatre@The Rockwell
Rockwell All Suite Hotel & Apartments, 32 Prestwich Street, De Waterkant, Atlantic Seaboard (021 421 0015, www.rockwellhotel.co.za/theatre). **Map** p254 G3.

This funky hotel has recently launched its own dinner theatre. Punters can enjoy comedians such as Barry Hilton treading the boards, or a drag show – perfectly at home here in Cape Town's pink district.

Outdoor

★ Maynardville Open-Air Theatre
Cnr Wolfe & Church streets, Wynberg, Southern Suburbs (021 421 7695, www.artscape.co.za/ maynardville-open-air-theatre).
The bard's legacy is celebrated every summer (January and February) when Shakespeare enthusiasts congregate to enjoy his plays under a blanket of stars. Well-known directors vie for a chance to interpret the plays, often lending them their own twist. Cape Town City Ballet also puts on a show here every year; think ethereally beautiful classic pieces to suit the sylvan setting, such as *The Firebird or Giselle*.

Oude Libertas Amphitheatre
Oude Libertas Centre, Adam Tas Road, Stellenbosch, Cape Winelands (021 809 7473/7380, www.udelibertas.co.za).
For years now, Capetonians have been packing a picnic and making the annual summer pilgrimage to the Oude Libertas Amphitheatre in Stellenbosch to indulge in a selection of top dance, drama, comedy and music under a star-studded sky. These days, the scales are tipping more towards live music, but theatre acts are still on the menu; past productions have included work by acclaimed local heavyweights.

OPERA & CLASSICAL MUSIC

If you're keen on classical music, you'll find an abundance of talent, with frequent performances by the reputable Cape Philharmonic Orchestra as well as large opera productions. Cape Town Opera is known for putting on classic productions with a uniquely African twist. The city is a musical melting pot of Western and African influences, and many classic operas are localised with stunning sets and costumes. For jazz and rock music, *see pp161-167* **Nightlife**.

Venues

Artscape Theatre Centre
See p169.

★ City Hall
Darling Street, Grand Parade, City Bowl.
Map p254 H4.
This impressive building, built out of honey-coloured limestone in 1905, is home to the famous and much-acclaimed Cape Philharmonic Orchestra (www.cpo.org.za). The CPO is robustly active, presenting a multitude of performances with local and international

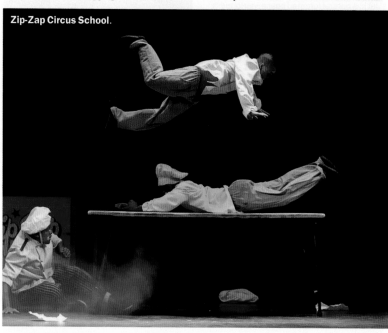

Zip-Zap Circus School.

guest musicians and operatic singers. The hall's organ, which was specially designed by UK pipe organ maker Norman & Beard, has 3,165 pipes and is probably the best in the country. The clarity of the acoustics is particularly impressive, and no amplification is used. The venue (no longer used for civic offices) also hosts concerts by other regulars.

Endler Hall

Cnr Neethling & Victoria streets, Stellenbosch, Cape Winelands (021 808 2358, www.sun.ac.za).
Endler Hall is where musical purists gather to enjoy a wide variety of classical music. The venue is also known for its world-class Marcussen organ. The University of Stellenbosch's Symphony Orchestra is in residence, but others ensembles, such as the CPO and the scholastic Hugo Lambrechts orchestra, can often be heard too. To find events, simply search for 'Endler' on the university website listed above.

St George's Cathedral

5 Wale Street, City Centre, City Bowl (021 424 7360, www.sgcathedral.co.za). **Map** p254 G4.
This beautiful, richly historic Anglican cathedral opened its doors in 1848 – and became known for keeping those doors open to people of all races during apartheid. It boasts a Hill organ that raises the roof at every ceremony, and whether it's a service or a choral concert, expect crisp, clear pitch.

DANCE

Outreach dance organisations are making a big impact on impoverished youth, while classic companies such as the Cape Town City Ballet have a loyal following.

Companies & classes

Cape Town City Ballet

Based at UCT School of Dance, Woolsack Drive, Rosebank, Southern Suburbs (www.capetown cityballet.org.za).
Founded in 1934, South Africa's leading ballet company is still going strong and consistently putting on productions of an international standard. The focus is on reinterpreting classics such as *Swan Lake* and *Carmen*, but from time to time contemporary pieces, including rock ballets and tributes to the tango, are stirred into the mix. It's also involved in various outreach programmes. The company performs at the Artscape Theatre Complex (*see p169*).

Dance for All Youth Company

10 Aden Avenue, Athlone, Southern Suburbs (021 697 5509, www.danceforall.co.za). **Classes** 2-5.30pm Mon-Sat. **Rates** R100 per mth (2-4 classes per wk).
In 1991, Philip Boyd, former principal dancer with CAPAB (now Cape Town City Ballet), started teaching ballet to historically disadvantaged children in the township of Gugulethu. In the years since, this non-profit social uplift organisation has blossomed into a highly esteemed dance school, producing top-notch professional dancers. The Dance for All Youth Company, boasting its own signature style with a neoclassical/Afro-contemporary repertoire, was launched in 2005.

Jazzart Dance Theatre

Artscape Theatre Centre, DF Malan Street, Foreshore, City Bowl (021 410 9848, www.jazzart. co.za). **Classes** Mon-Thur. **Rates** R50 per class. **Map** p275 I3.
The country's top contemporary dance company employs an amalgamation of Western and African dance styles in its productions. It's renowned for coming up with groundbreaking work and for its involvement in outreach initiatives. Their pieces are enthralling, original and a must-see.

CIRCUS

Circus performances are enchanting for young and old. They're often used as a method of uplifting local children from impoverished communities, and the physical skills and confidence children learn are invaluable.

Companies

South African National Circus School

2 Willow Road, Hartleyvale, Observatory, Southern Suburbs (083 496 3972, www.sancircus.co.za, www.facebook.com/thesouthafricannational circusschool). **Shows** 1pm Sat. **Tickets** R90; R60 children. **No credit cards.**
Aerial acrobatics, helicopter neck spins, human pyramids, unicyclists, stilt-walkers and a one-of-a-kind contortionist act. These are just some of the fantastical antics the performers of the South African National Circus School regularly get up to. Saturdays are open circus days, where you can try your own prowess with equipment (R10 per item), followed by a show. At time of writing, the school had been given notice to vacate their premises by the City of Cape Town, so check their Facebook page for venue updates.

★ Zip-Zap Circus School

Founders Garden, Jan Smuts Street, City Bowl (021 421 8622, www.zip-zap.co.za). **Map** p253 I3.
At Zip-Zap, children of all backgrounds, from those born in mansions to those living in township shacks, are taught the ways of the circus – for free. The troupe has wowed audiences around the world with its wonderful shows. Encouraging young people to learn impressive physical skills, and watching these come to fruition in performance, creates a wonderful sense of community support. As well as classes at its home base in Jan Smuts Street, the school holds regular outreach workshops in an attempt to bring the magic of the big top to disadvantaged communities.

ARTS & ENTERTAINMENT

Escapes & Excursions

Escapes & Excursions

The Western Cape is blessed with a vast diversity of landscapes. The closest excursion, and by far the most popular, is the Cape Winelands. Not only are the quaint towns of Stellenbosch, Paarl and Franschhoek filled with historical buildings and tree-lined streets dotted with cafés; there's also wine, and lots of it… If this is all too perfect, then head north, up the rugged West Coast, for windswept beaches and the towering crags of the Cederberg. Moving eastwards from Cape Town, the Whale Coast provides a mix of bucolic charm and seaside splendour. The many towns that line the coast are favourite local holiday spots, and top dog Hermanus is one of the best places in the world for land-based whale watching. Further east still is the Garden Route. And never was a name more fitting: lush greenery encroaches on the N2 highway; forests and vast nature reserves await exploration. The lagoon-side town of Knysna is a charming spot for boating and enjoying oysters, while Plettenberg Bay's warm waters, family-friendly beaches, animal encounters as well as gourmet hideaways make it the jewel in the Garden Route crown.

Winelands

The Cape Winelands conjures up images of blue mountains, rolling vineyards, gourmet restaurants and fine wines… and while all this is most certainly true, it's worth interspersing wine estate hopping with a stroll around the historic towns of Stellenbosch, Paarl and Franschhoek – each with its own charms and beauty. With plenty of artisan producers, wine farms with award-winning restaurants, world-class wine and ridiculous amounts of natural beauty, a visit to the Winelands – just an hour's drive from Cape Town – is a must for a day or longer.

PAARL

Dominating the skyline of Paarl is the **Afrikaans Language Monument** (Gabbema Doordrift Road, 021 863 4809, www.taalmonument.co.za, admission R25), which was completed in 1975 to commemorate 50 years of Afrikaans being an official language in South Africa. The granite Paarl Rock nearby resembles pearls when it shines in the rain, hence the name, derived from the Dutch *parel*. Main Street below stretches for 12 kilometres, and visitors will see charming examples of Victorian and Cape Dutch architecture.

The main attractions, however, are outside town, where there are some excellent animal encounters. You can see rescued big cats at **Drakenstein Lion Park** (R101, between Klapmuts and Paarl, 021 863 3290, www. lionrescue.org.za, admission R40); a magical display of colour at **Butterfly World** (R44, Klapmuts, 021 875 5628, www.butterflyworld. co.za, R65); and small mammals, reptiles and a giraffe at **Giraffe House** (intersection of R304 & R101, 021 884 4506, www.giraffehouse.co.za, admission R45). Or head to **Le Bonheur Crocodile Farm** (R45, 021 863 1142, www. lebonheurcrocfarm.co.za, admission R48) for a reptilian horror-fest as you view over 1,000 crocs from suspended walkways.

The goat tower at **Fairview Wine Estate** (Suid-Agter-Paarl Road, 021 863 2450, www. fairview.co.za) makes for a cute photo, before you head inside to taste wine and a fantastic array of cheeses made on the estate. The **Goatshed Restaurant** (021 863 36 09, www.goatshed.co.za) offers delicous breads and cheese boards as well as heartier eats.

Making the most of the current interest for all things local and artisan, **Spice Route** (Suid-Agter Paarl Road, 021 863 5200, www.spice route.co.za) is ideal for a day out as it showcases everything from chocolate-making to beer-brewing and grappa-distilling in buildings dotted about this historic estate. Visit artist galleries and a glass-blowing studio and taste your way through all the foodie offerings before settling down for a meal of pizza, tapas, bistro fare or deli items at the various restaurants.

Accommodation in Paarl is mostly in the form of B&Bs in town or cottages on nearby farms.

If you're keen on splashing out, head to the old-world grandeur of the **Grande Roche** (Plantasie Street, 021 863 5100, http://granderoche.com, rates from R3,900 per room per night).

Heading out towards Franschhoek on the R45, you'll come across one of the top destinations in the area: **Babylonstoren** (R45, Simondium, 084 275 1243, www.babylonstoren.com, admission R10). It's one of the oldest Cape Dutch farms in the vicinity and no expense has been spared to create a magical visitor experience. Start by strolling through the eight-acre garden, which is based on the design of the original Company's Garden in Cape Town. Rose bowers and rosemary hedges frame a seasonal bounty of fruit and vegetables, with a turkey, duck and chicken or two pecking around for good measure. Guided garden tours are highly recommended. Light meals such as salads, sandwiches and cakes can be enjoyed at the Greenhouse, while Babel Restaurant is renowned for its emphasis on seasonal ingredients simply prepared. At the shop, stock up on baked goods, wine, cheese and kitchenware. Add the luxurious **Farm Hotel** (from R3,700 per room) and spa to the list and you may never want to leave…

Across the way, **Cape Winelands Riding** (R45, 082 924 6728, www.capewinelandsriding. co.za) offers horse-riding tours for novices to seasoned riders – they are keen to accommodate visitors of all abilities. Choose from short outrides into the vineyards with tastings or multi-day tailor-made itineraries around the Winelands.

For a taste of something different, head to **Cosecha Restaurant** on Noble Hill Wine Estate (R45, 021 874 3844, www.cosecharestaurant.com).

Babylonstoren.

The open-air restaurant serves authentic Mexican food – ceviche, empanadas, tacos and zesty guacamole prepared at the table. For kids, they can make up a delightful food hamper and there's ample space to run around.

Tourist information

Paarl Tourism Association *216 Main Road (021 872 0860, www.paarlonline.com).*

Getting there

Paarl is 60km from Cape Town. Take the N1 north, then turn left on to the R45.

FRANSCHHOEK

There's no escaping Franschhoek's French heritage: the *tricolore* adorns the main drag and it's 'le' or 'la' in front of just about every venue. But fromaginess aside, Franschhoek (meaning 'French corner') town and its surrounding wine estates is deservedly known as the food and wine capital of the Cape.

Before you start quaffing and eating, there are some activities to enjoy: take a walk around the Huguenot Monument, then pop into the **Huguenot Memorial Museum** (021 876 2532, www.museum.co.za, admission R10) to learn more about the French Protestants who fled persecution and settled in the Cape in the late 1600s.

Petrolheads should head to the **Franschhoek Motor Museum** (L'Ormarins wine farm, R45, 021 874 9020, www.fmm.co.za, admission R60), with its collection of over 200 vehicles; around 80 are on display at a time.

A novel approach to visiting wineries is the **Franschhoek Wine Tram** (Franschhoek Square, 32 Huguenot Road, 021 300 0338, www.winetram.co.za, R200). Hop on and off while learning about the area's history and wines, with tastings and lunch at various farms.

You'd be advised to undo a notch in your belt in preparation for the gastronomic onslaught… In town, **Reuben's** (19 Huguenot Road, 021 876 3772, www.reubens.co.za) offers sophisticated, locally inspired bistro dishes from one of South Africa's hottest chefs, Reuben Riffel; while, across the road, chef Margot Janse's **The Tasting Room** at Le Quartier Français (16 Huguenot Road, 021 876 2151, www.lqf.co.za) regularly features on the World's 100 Best Restaurants list with her contemporary take on South African ingredients. Make an occasion of it and book into one of the bold, luxurious suites (from R4,300 per room, high season) – many overlook the lovingly tended garden. Next-door sister hotel **Delicious** (11 Wilhelmina Street, 021 876 2151, www.delicioushotels.com, from R1,200 per room) is bright, fun and excellent value.

New kid on the block is **Foliage** (11 Huguenot Road, 021 876 2328, www.foliage.co.za), chef Chris Erasmus's ode to seasonal, often foraged ingredients, with stellar harvest fare on the menu.

With over 50 wine farms to choose from in the area, there is no shortage of fascinating cellar tours, tastings and buying opportunities. Many wineries have excellent restaurants, encouraging visitors to linger longer. Big hitter **Haute Cabrière** (Cabrière Estate, Franschhoek Pass, 021 876 3688, www.cabriere.co.za; *photo p180*) offers entertaining tours on Saturdays that include sabrage of their famous MCC (Methode Cap Classique – *see left* **In the Know**). The mountainside restaurant serves refined fare with an emphasis on seasonal ingredients, and offers a special vegetarian menu. Sit outside with a bird's-eye view over the valley below or inside overlooking the cellar.

One of the most exclusive destinations is **Grande Provence** (Main Road, Franschhoek, 021 876 8600, www.grandeprovence.co.za). Chef Darren Badenhorst conjures up modern gourmet fare in a pristine setting at the Restaurant, while the Owner's Cottage and La Provençale provide refined accommodation options (from R2,500 per person per night, high season).

Fairly new to the fine-dining fray is **The Kitchen@Maison** (Maison Wine Estate, R45, 021 876 2116, www.maisonestate.co.za). It belongs to the owner of Weylandts interior stores, so the decor is cutting edge and contemporary. The food joins the party, with fresh, modern, unpretentious dishes. The verandah overlooking the vineyards is the choicest position – be sure to grab a moment in the vast daybed hanging from an oak tree.

Across the road, **La Motte** (R45 Main Road, 021 876 8000, www.la-motte.com) offers an array of experiences for the discerning visitor. Start at the museum with its collection of artworks by celebrated South African artist JH Peirneef, before heading out on the Historic Walk, taking in the buildings on the estate. Or for those with an interest in flora, the Sustainable Walk discovers fynbos, landscaped gardens and vegetable and herb gardens. Lunch at Pierneef à La Motte is wonderful; sit outside under the huge oak trees

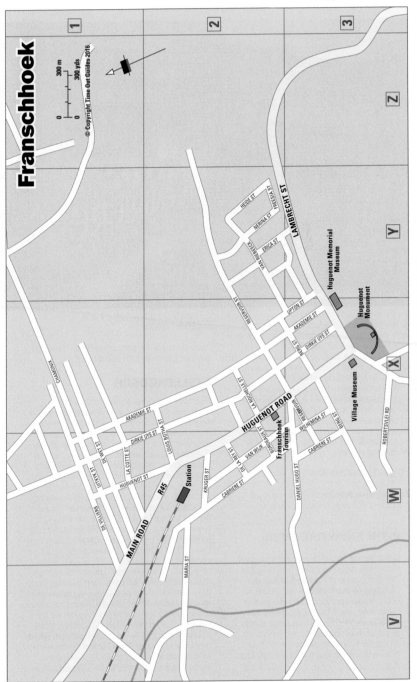

Franschhoek

300 m
300 yds

© Copyright Time Out Guides 2016

HEIDE ST
NERINA ST
FREESIA ST
LAMBRECHT ST
VAN RIEBEECK ST
ERICA ST

Huguenot Memorial Museum

Huguenot Monument

UPTON ST
AKADEMIE ST
BERG ST
DIRKIE UYS ST

BESHOFF ST

Village Museum

ROBERTSVLEI RD

CHAMONIX

AKADEMIE ST
DIRKIE UYS ST
LA ROCHELLE ST

HUGUENOT ROAD

Franschhoek Tourism

BURGANS ST
DE WET ST
VAN WIJK ST

WILHEMINA ST
RESERVOIR
BERG S

CABRIERE ST

DE WET ST
UITKYK ST
LA COTTE ST
LOUIS BOTHA ST
HUGUENOT ST

KRUGER ST
CABRIERE ST

DANIEL HUGO ST

DE VILLIERS

R45

Station

MAIN ROAD

MARIA ST

ESCAPES & EXCURSIONS

Haute Cabrière. *See p178.*

or inside in a refined space where old meets new with innovative design elements such as a chandelier made of broken VOC-inspired ceramics. Food is inspired by original Cape Dutch cuisine but with a distinctly modern approach. The farm shop sells lovely kitchenware.

An excellent place to lay your head after all the eating and drinking is **Le Franschhoek Hotel & Spa** (Excelsior Road, 021 876 8900, www.lefranschhoek.co.za, from R2,085 per room). Rooms are decorated in crisp whites with floral accents, while the Camelot Spa offers quality pampering sessions.

Tourist information

Franschhoek Tourism *62 Huguenot Road (021 876 2861, http://franschhoek.org.za).*

IN THE KNOW FIREWATER

Did you know South Africa makes some of the world's best brandies? You can get at tour and tasting at the **Klipdrift Brandy Distillery** (4 Voortrekker Road, 023 626 3027, www.klipdrift.co.za) in the town of Robertson, about two hours' drive from Cape Town. You'll leave a bit wiser about this multi-faceted drink… and possibly a bit tipsier. For more information on South African brandies, visit www.sabrandy.co.za.

Getting there

Franschhoek is 78km from Cape Town. Take the N1, then follow the R301 or R45 (via R101).

STELLENBOSCH

This university town is full of charm; from students cycling on oak-lined roads to historic wine estates, Stellenbosch is a stunner. The second-oldest town in South Africa, it was named in 1679 by Simon van der Stel, the Cape governor. If you thought Franschhoek had an extensive food and wine culture, Stellenbosch is the big daddy with over 200 wine estates (www.wineroute.co.za) and many restaurants on these estates constantly hitting top-ten status in local restaurant awards.

Bubbly lovers will enjoy **Cuvée** restaurant (Kromme Rhee Road, Koelenhof, 021 888 4932, www.simonsig.co.za/cuvee), with its modern setting, while **Delaire Graff Estate** (Helshoogte Pass, 021 885 8160, www.delaire.co.za) has an exclusive lodge, spa and the exotic Indochine restaurant. Across the way, **Tokara** (Helshoogte Pass, 021 808 5959, www.tokararestaurant.co.za) has a wonderfully relaxed deli eaterie, a stunning art collection and, the highlight, Tokara restaurant, where chef Richard Carstens serves innovative food in a newly revamped, contemporary setting.

Unassuming in its simple approach and pared-down decor, **Jordan Restaurant** (Stellenbosch Kloof Road, Vlottenburg, 021 881 3441, www.jordanwines.com) is where chef George Jardine holds sway. A bucolic setting with mountain views is the backdrop for a menu that features the best local ingredients, simply prepared with an emphasis on authentic flavours. The Bakery is a more laid-back spot for lazy brunches, while the kids can run riot on the lawn.

Towards Somerset West, off the R44, are three more big-hitters: **Overture** (Hidden Valley Wine Estate, Annandale Road, 021 880 2721, www.dineatoverture.co.za) provides a stellar setting with staggering views and seasonal, local ingredients, freshly prepared; **Rust en Vrede Restaurant** (Rust en Vrede Estate, Annandale Road, 021 881 3881, www.rustenvrede.com) is a refined choice, while **Terroir** (Kleine Zalze Estate, R44, 021 880 8167, www.kleinezalze.com) offers a classically inspired menu with deeply flavoursome sauces (chef Michael Broughton's signature) – a lunch under the trees can easily last until the early evening.

For active pursuits, the **Jonkershoek Nature Reserve** (Jonkershoek Valley, 021 866 1560, www.capenature.org.za, entrance R40 per person) provides a blissful escape for walks and bike rides; **Dirtopia Trail Centre** on Delvera Farm (R44, www.dirtopia.co.za) is ideal for serious mountain bikers and hikers.

Many exclusive boutiques, galleries and African craft shops line Church and Dorp streets, so it's worth taking a stroll through town. **Oom Samie se Winkel** (84 Dorp Street, 021 887 2372) sells old-fashioned sweets, traditional leather goods and collectibles, while **Schoon de Companjie** (7 Church Street, 021 883 2187, www.decompanje.co.za) is the place for award-winning baked goods, delicious eats and treats.

One of the top draws outside town is **Spier Estate** (Lynedoch Road/R310, 021 809 1100, www.spier.co.za): you can do a wine tasting, jump on a Segway for a tour (R250), see birds of prey up close at Eagle Encounters (R70), then enjoy a harvest meal at Eight restaurant or a picnic in the grounds. The hotel has 153 rooms built in a villa style as well as a Camelot Spa.

There's a vast choice of accommodation in and around Stellies, as the town is known. Having undergone a thorough renovation, **Oude Werf** (30 Church Street, 021 887 4608, www.oudewerf hotel.co.za, from R2,470 per room) is an excellent central choice, as is **Coopmanhuijs** (33 Church Street, 021 883 8207, www.coopmanhuijs.co.za, from R1,960 per unit) with its luxurious, Cape Dutch-inspired interiors. For old-world grandeur, **Lanzerac Hotel & Spa** (Lanzerac Street, 021 887 1132, www.lanzerac.co.za, from R1,090 per person sharing) will have you swooning. Modern **Majeka House** (26-32 Houtkapper Street, Paradyskloof, 021 880 1549, www.majekahouse. co.za, from R1,600 per person sharing) wins hands-down in the style stakes and has a sexy bar, spa and Makaron restaurant, which offers local produce served with international flair.

MARKET FORCES
Artisan trading places.

These days, faster than you can say 'artisan chocolate', it seems that yet another market pops up selling fresh, delicious and, yes, artisan everything. Food, craft beer and wine are the main focus, but you'll also find stalls selling art, decor items and clothing. Most markets happen at weekends, and make the perfect start to a day trip to the Winelands – but arrive early if you're not keen on crowds. Here's our pick of the crop of regular markets.

BLAAUWKLIPPEN FAMILY MARKET
Blaauwklippen Estate, Stellenbosch (www.blaauwklippen.com/attractions). **Open** 10am-3pm Sun.
Trestle tables under the trees invite visitors to browse while listening to live music. There's ample space for kids to play and the pony rides are a hit. It's also decidedly doggy-friendly and has a relaxed vibe.

LOURENSFORD HARVEST MARKET
Lourensford Estate, Somerset West (http://lfhm.co.za). **Open** 10am-3pm Sat, Sun.
Scour for handmade wares and snap up fresh organic produce at one of the oldest wine estates (www.lourensford.co.za) in the country. It's a charming spot to while away a morning, and there's special entertainment for children too. The estate itself is worth a visit for its historical significance as it was founded in 1700, as well as for its top wines and beautiful setting.

ROOT 44 MARKET
Audacia Wine Farm, Stellenbosch (www.root44.co.za). **Open** 10am-4pm Sat, Sun.
Protected from the elements by marquee tents, this market offers a vast array of tasty home-made food – either to eat on site with a glass of local wine or craft beer, or to take home. The kids will enjoy the play area and there are many other stalls selling clothing, homewares, crafts and more.

STELLENBOSCH SLOW MARKET
Oude Libertas, Stellenbosch (www.slowmarket.co.za). **Open** 9am-2pm Sat.
More than 100 stalls sell organic fruit and veg from local farmers, baked goodies, quality wines and craft beers. Stock up on olive oils, cheeses and preserves while sampling a variety of street food, from fiery curries to healthy salads and sweet treats.

FAR, FAR AWAY
Explore Vergelegen.

History buffs and garden enthusiasts alike should make a visit to **Vergelegen** (Lourensford Road, 021 847 1334, www.vergelegen.co.za, admission R10) a priority. The name means 'situated far away', and you can happily spend a couple of hours exploring the estate's sights. The homestead dates from the 18th century (the farm was established in 1700), and its rooms are authentically furnished with period furniture. The library houses a priceless collection of books amassed by Sir Lionel Phillips (estate owner 1917-41), and you can also visit the mill ruins and slave lodge. Vergelegen's magnificent gardens (17 in all) echo its heritage, and there are a number of significant trees, including an English oak and a white mulberry, both planted over 300 years ago. In addition to wine tasting, the estate offers picnics under the centuries-old camphor trees, fine dining in old-fashioned grandeur at Camphors at Vergelegen restaurant, and more casual eating at the modern, family-friendly Stables bistro.

Tourist information

Stellenbosch Tourism *36 Market Street (021 883 3584, www.stellenbosch.travel).*

Getting there

Stellenbosch is 45km from Cape Town. Take the N1 north, and turn off at the R304.

Whale Route

The southern Cape coast is a boon for local holidaymakers, with charming seaside towns such as Hermanus reaching bursting point during the summer. Heading towards L'Agulhas, the southernmost tip of the African continent, you'll find Gansbaai, home of shark-diving experiences, while, inland, there are lovely fynbos-filled hiking trails in the mountains and farm stalls aplenty.

ELGIN AREA

Traditionally farming country, as you'll realise from all the orchards lining the N2 highway, the Elgin area has recently become a weekend destination in its own right. It's only about an hour's drive from Cape Town and provides plenty of opportunity to get into the great outdoors, with mountain biking and trail running both popular pursuits. The adventurous should consider an adrenalin- and fun-filled day tubing or rafting down the Palmiet river with **Gravity Adventures** (021 683 3698, www.gravity.co.za, from R550 per person for tubing), or high-flying thrills with **Cape Canopy Tour** (021 300 0501, www.capecanopytour.co.za, R695) where you'll spend four giddy hours whizzing by zipwire to 13 platforms dotted about the valley. You'll get a bird's-eye view of the mountains and waterfalls, with professional guides on each trip.

A must-stop is **Peregrine Farm Stall** (021 848 9011, www.peregrinefarmstall.co.za) and its Red Tractor Café. Grab a seat in the newly revamped interior or sit outside on the shaded verandah and munch on salads and burgers. The farm produce is especially convenient if you're staying in a self-catering place; you'll find everything from fresh fruit and veg to heavenly home bakes and pies – the venison comes recommended. There's also a jungle gym on the side if the kids need to expend some energy before getting back into the car.

There are 16 excellent wineries to visit on the **Elgin Wine Route** (www.elginwine.co.za) with some providing lovely lunch stops too. The **Pool Room** at Oak Valley (021 859 4111, www.oakvalley.co.za) has charcuterie from its own acorn-fed pigs and grass-fed beef as well as succulent grills;

Cape Canopy Tour.

Fresh at Paul Cluver (071 563 6020, www.fresh atpaulcluver.co.za) offers uncomplicated, seasonal cooking; and **Gallery Restaurant** at South Hill (021 844 0033, www.southhill.co.za) serves bistro-style food in an art gallery.

One of the top places to stay in the area is **Old Mac Daddy** (021 844 0241, www.oldmacdaddy. co.za, from R895 per trailer during the week to R2,700 for the villa on weekends). Here, individually decorated Airstream trailers dot the hillside, each with a crazy bedroom theme (Mexican wrestling, anyone?), while the attached lounge and bathroom is all clean Scandi lines and minimalism. The views over the valley are fantastic, if you can pull yourself away from exploring the MTB trails (they hire out bikes), the pool, or, for children, the two jungle gyms and games rooms. Daddy's Villa is ideal for groups and families: it's a self-catering house with three bedrooms and an outdoor bath. Brinny Breezes restaurant serves local fare, wood-fired pizzas and locally produced beers and ciders on tap.

A bit further on, towards Botrivier, lies **Gabriëlskloof** winery (028 284 9865, www. gabrielskloof.co.za), where you can stock up on their wines and olive oils, and have a meal at the laid-back yet stylish restaurant. You'll need to book well in advance for **KolKol Mountain Lodge** (076 913 6014, www.kolkol.co.za, from R1,550 per cabin per night, high season), a highly prized accommodation spot with self-catering rustic wooden cabins (each with a hot tub on the outdoor deck) and all home comforts. You can hike, cool off in the dam, do some birdwatching or simply relax.

Tourist information

Peregrine Farm Stall *N2 (021 848 983, www.elginvalley.co.za).*

Getting there

Elgin is about 70km south-east of Cape Town on the N2.

HANGKLIP COAST

A detour via the Hangklip coastline is ideal for exploring the **Kogelberg Biosphere Reserve** (028 271 5138, www.capenature.co.za, R40 conservation fee). This pristine reserve covers

100,000 hectares, including coastline and mountains. Accommodation comes in the form of the Oudebosch Eco Cabins: these modern, glass-fronted wooden structues (R1,060 per night) sleep four and provide all the amenities you need, including braai (barbecue) areas.

The well-maintained **Clarence Drive** (R44) offers plenty of points at which to take in the stunning views, and leads to the seaside holiday towns of Rooi Els, Pringle Bay, Betty's Bay and larger Kleinmond. Pringle Bay has a good choice of restaurants, while a stop at **Stony Point Penguin Colony** (admission R10) at Betty's Bay is wonderful for all ages. It's best to arrive early in the morning or late afternoon, otherwise the African penguins will be out fishing. It is one of only two shore-based breeding colonies in South Africa.

Tourist information

Kleinmond Tourism *Protea Centre, Main Road, Kleinmond (028 271 5657, www.kleinmond tourism.co.za).*

Getting there

Take the N2 out of Cape Town, and before Sir Lowry's Pass turn off on to the R44. Kleinmond is about 110km from Cape Town.

HERMANUS

This coastal town is packed during the school holidays, and you can be assured you'll find a vast array of shops, restaurants and activities to keep you entertained, not to mention the beaches. The main appeal, though, is that it is one of the 12 best land-based **whale-watching** spots in the world. Between June and October, southern right whales (*Eubelaena australis*) come to the sheltered coves here to give birth and care for their calves. If you want a close look, join a whale-watching cruise, which are allowed to venture within 50 metres of these massive beasts. There are a variety of cruise operators at the New Harbour, with prices costing about R700 per adult.

The **Hermanus Cliff Path** is a lovely way to see the coast, whether you opt to walk its entire ten-kilometre length or simply take a short stroll. It winds from the New Harbour to the mouth of the Klein River, passing fynbos, tidal pools, fishing spots and lookout benches. The more energetic can head to **Fernkloof Nature Reserve** (Fir Avenue, 028 312 3011, www.fernkloof.com, free) which offers 60 kilometres of hiking trails on the Kleinrivier mountains, with a vast array of fynbos – 1,474 species have been identified in the 1,800-hectare reserve.

The quaint Old Harbour has colourful fishing boats on its concrete shores, and is home to the

Whale-watching.

Old Harbour Museum (028 312 1475, www. old-harbour-museum.co.za), which sheds light on the town's fishing and whaling history. **De Wet's Huis Photo Museum** (028 313 0418) in the market square depicts life in Hermanus way back in the day, while the **Whale House** (028 313 0418) next door is a new addition with stylishly designed touch-screen displays, as well as a southern right whale skeleton.

Up from the Old Harbour are assorted restaurants and cafés, most with outdoor seating to make the most of the expansive views over Walker Bay. At the **Fisherman's Village**

Craft Market, you can shop for all the souvenirs your heart desires, while the many outlets in the **Village Square** (028 312 2761, www.village-square.co.za) sell everything from kids' clothes to handmade jewellery, swimwear to art.

Bientang's Cave Restaurant & Wine Bar (below Marine Drive, between Old Harbour & Marine Hotel, 028 312 3454, www.bientangscave. com) is a quaint setting for lunch: inside a cave that was home to Koi Strandloper Bientang at the turn of the 19th century. The food is pretty standard, but the experience of watching whales in the water below is unsurpassed. In the New Harbour, clifftop restaurant **Harbour Rock** (028 312 2920, www.harbourrock.co.za) is the place for sushi, seafood platters and cocktails against a spectacular ocean backdrop.

For a gourmet treat, you can't beat the restaurants at the **Marine Hotel** (028 313 1000, www.collectionmcgrath.com). Head to the Sun Lounge for drinks, the laid-back SeaFood at the Marine for a bounty of fresh ocean delights and the Pavilion for exquisite tasting menus. The wine cellar is a triumph too. The hotel's rooms (from R5,400 for a room to R24,000 for a villa in peak season) are the epitome of crisp oceanside elegance, and the clifftop location is stunning. Add in five-star service and amenities such as a spa and swimming pool, and you're all set.

For more food and wine experiences, a drive up the scenic **Hemel-en-Aarde Valley** (meaning 'heaven and earth' in Afrikaans) is recommended. The Saturday morning Hermanuspietersfontein food and wine market (www.hpf1855.co.za) takes place in Hemel-en-Aarde Village, where you can stock up on produce and meet the locals. Further up the valley you'll find some major wine farms (www.hermanuswineroute.com) and some excellent restaurants. The **Restaurant at Newton Johnson** (Hemel-en-Aarde Road/R320, 021 200 2148, www.newtonjohnson.com) sees chef Eric Bulpitt showcasing unusual cuts of meat and seasonal ingredients in a small but perfectly formed menu. **Creation** (Hemel-en-Aarde Road/R320, 028 212 1107, www. creationwines.com) offers food and wine pairings, chocolate pairings and fun pairings for children as well as biodiversity tours of the estate.

Tourist information

Hermanus Tourism *Old Station Building, cnr Mitchell & Lord Roberts streets, Hermanus (028 312 2629, www.hermanustourism.info).*

Getting there

Hermanus is 125km from Cape Town. Take the Hermanus off-ramp off the N2 near Bot River and follow the R43 for 35km.

GANSBAAI AREA

The coastal area of Gansbaai has become synonymous with one thing: **shark-cage diving**. Don a wetsuit, hoist yourself into a cage and come face to face with an apex predator. There are many operators and tour packages, which depart from the harbour in Kleinbaai; expect to pay around R1,500 for a day trip. Contact Gansbaai Tourism Bureau for recommended operators.

While you're in the vicinity, enjoy the cliffs and caves at De Kelders (just keep an eye on the tide if you head to the beach). Danger Point lighthouse is the perfect vantage point from which to see the many shipwrecks dotting the coastline.

For a nature getaway of note, **Grootbos Private Nature Reserve** (R43, 028 384 8008, www.grootbos.com, from R2,230-R5,170 per person sharing) is set in 2,500 hectares of fynbos, afromontane and milkwood forests. Stay in the family-friendly Garden Lodge, in stone and timber cottages, or Forest Lodge, with its contemporary and elegant design. A Flower Safari in an open-top Land Rover reveals the secrets of local flora, and they can organise pretty much any adventure that you want, from helicopter flips to horse-riding. An excellent spa and delicious food round off the experience.

Tourist information

Gansbaai Tourism Bureau *Great White Junction, Kapokblom Street (028 384 1439, www.gansbaaiinfo.com).*

Getting there

Gansbaai is 175km from Cape Town. Take the Hermanus turn-off from the N2 near Bot River and follow the R43 for 85km through Hermanus, Stanford and De Kelders into Gansbaai.

AGULHAS AREA

Take a selfie at the southernmost tip of the African continent… to tick this off your bucket list, head to **L'Agulhas**, a wind-blown holiday town. Recently built walkways makes the wander to the cairn at the southern tip quite pleasant, with benches and information boards. Once there, a visit to the **lighthouse** (028 435 6078) is a fun way to pass half an hour, though the ladder climbs are a tad vertiginous. Supposedly modelled on one of the seven wonders of the world, the pharos of Alexandria (albeit a bit less grand at just 27 metres high), it was installed in 1849.

Agulhas National Park (028 435 6078, www.sanparks.org/parks/agulhas, admission R34-R136) has plenty for nature lovers, but there are also some lovely towns to discover. **Napier Brewery** (Monsanto Road, 072 109 8590) offers

ESCAPES & EXCURSIONS

DAYS AT DE HOOP

Get close to nature.

A spectacular destination for a few days is **De Hoop Nature Reserve** (028 542 1253, reservations 021 422 4522, www.dehoop collection.com, conservation fee R40 per person). This pristine spot is a Marine Protected Area and includes the De Hoop Vlei, a 19-kilometre stretch of water and land that is a Ramsar site of ecological importance, which means there's an incredible array of flora and fauna to be experienced. Whale sightings are common, and guided marine walks will uncover oceanside ecosystems – simply put, you'll be splashing about in rock pools tickling anemones and finding fishies.

Day visitors are welcome, but three days are ideal to make the most of the facilities and activities on offer. Mountain biking, birdwatching, eco-quad biking, guided fynbos walks and dune hikes are some of the highlights. Add to that the zebra and bontebok grazing around you, ostriches welcoming you at the reception area and the distant call of baboons and you'll certainly feel far from the city bustle.

There are bikes, a pool and a dedicated programme to keep the children busy, while the Fig Tree restaurant offers country fare and picnic baskets for the day. The range of accommodation is vast, from camping to cottages (from R1,325), rondavels, converted historical buildings and suites in the manor house (from R950 per person).

The reserve is three hours' drive from Cape Town: take the N2 to Caledon, turn on to the R316 to Bredasdorp. From there, follow the R319 towards Swellendam, and take the De Hoop turn-off. Note there is about 35 kilometres of gravel road to the reserve.

craft beer, while **Napier Farm Stall** (108 Sarel Cilliers Street, 028 423 3440, www.facebook.com/ NapierFarmStall) offers wonderful bakes and treats, and a great farm breakfast.

Bredasdorp is the economic hub of this farming and fishing area. **Bredasdorp Square** (Long & Clarendon streets, 028 425 1420, www. bredasdorpsquare.co.za) offers a lovely eatery, four Victorian-inspired suites and an interiors/ gift shop filled with covetable items. The **Elim** wine area (028 482 1618, www.elimwines.co.za) offers an array of excellent wineries. Do stop at **Black Oystercatcher** (Moddervlei Farm, R37, 028 482 1618, www.blackoystercatcher.co.za) to enjoy farm-to-table fare on the verandah overlooking the hills. If you want to explore the area further, there are rustic cottages on the farm.

Heading to the seaside, **Struisbaai** is a fishing village with a massive 14-kilometre white sand beach. For excellent fish and chips, as well as fish fresh off the boat and selected deli items, visit **Fish and More** (11 Cinneraria Street, 028 435 7096, www.fishandmore.co.za).

The jewel in this area is the tiny village of **Arniston** (also known as Waenhuiskrans). Head on to the beach for a dune hike to see the famous **Waenhuiskrans Cave** (accessible at low tide only). Slap-bang on the harbour, with a little beach on its doorstep, is the **Arniston Spa Hotel** (028 445 9000, www.arnistonhotel.com, R1,200-R4,000 per room). Rooms are tastefully decorated with seaside themes, and in summer you can enjoy eats and drinks on the vast deck while the children play on the enclosed front lawns. The newly built sushi bar at the pool is sure to be a hit too. The on-site **Ginkgo Spa** (028 445 9000, www.ginkgospa.com) offers excellent treatments and good-value monthly specials as well as a sauna and relaxation room.

Tourist information

Website www.xplorio.com has good information on the area and its towns.

Getting there

Arniston is about 220km from Cape Town. Take the N2 to Caledon, turn on to the R316 and follow the signs to Napier and Bredasdorp. From there, it's about 38km to Agulhas and Struisbaai via the R319.

Garden Route

Synonymous with endless beaches, pristine forests and scenic views that stretch as far as the eye can see, the Garden Route is a honeypot for holidaymakers, both local and international. This is especially true during the summer holidays in December and January, when the area is heaving:

Plettenberg Bay is where matrics come to celebrate the end of school; the hippies and adventure seekers head to the Tsitsikamma forest, and urbanites flock to genteel Knysna with its sheltered lagoon.

GEORGE TO SEDGEFIELD

The Garden Route starts with the city of **George**, which also has a small airport for local and charter flights. With the Outeniqua Mountains in the background, this bustling place is famous for **Fancourt Hotel & Country Club Golf Estate** (Montagu Street, Blanco, 044 804 0000, www. fancourt.co.za, from R2,899 per room, high season) with three Gary Player-designed courses; children can be entertained at the holiday club and pools, and parents can relax at the spa with its Roman heated bath-style pool, steam room, sauna, hot tub and tepidarium. Accommodation consists of 115 bedrooms and suites in the classically stylish hotel, and 18 suites in the luxurious Manor House. Once hunger pangs set in, there's **La Cantina** for authentic Italian fare, and **Henry White** for fine dining in a rarified setting.

Once you head out of George, the real beauty of the Garden Route begins to reveal itself. **Wilderness** beach stretching in front of you is a visual reminder that you're in one of the most scenic parts of the country.

Past Wilderness, stop in at **Timberlake Village** (www.timberlakeorganic.co.za) for healthy eats and interesting shops selling locally produced foodstuffs and crafts. Their motto of sustainability and eco-awareness is clearly visible. If you feel like swinging, zipping and climbing, head to **Acrobranch Wildwoods Tree Adventures** (044 050 0591, http://acrobranch. co.za, R80-R250 per person), which has routes for children and adults and for varying fitness levels.

At Sedgefield, don't miss the perennially popular **Wild Oats Community Farmers' Market** (www.wildoatsmarket.co.za) on Saturday morning. One of the first organic country markets, it helped kickstart South Africa's love for all things market-related.

Tourist information

George Tourism Office *124 York Street (044 801 9299, www.georgetourism.org.za).*
Sedgefield Tourism Info *Shop 2, Sedge Bus Centre, Main Road (044 343 2658, www.gardenroute.com).*
Wilderness Tourism *Leila's Lane (044 877 0045, www.wildernessinfo.org).*

Getting there

George is about 430km from Cape Town. Take the N2. Wilderness is 20km beyond George, and Sedgefield a further 20km.

IN THE KNOW
MONKEY BUSINESS

In addition to whales, the creatures you're sure to see plenty of in the mountainous coastal Overberg area are baboons. And while it can be amusing to watch their antics, there is a more serious side to their existence in this part of the world. When you see signs asking you to not feed them, pay attention (as is true for any wild animal, of course).

A documentary filmed by *National Geographic* in 2012 saw filmmakers deliberately enticing baboons to raid a house in Pringle Bay, much to the uproar of locals and conservationists. Such habituation can cause huge problems, with baboons losing their natural fear of humans and trying to get into houses; this in turn can cause potentially aggressive interactions with humans, which will inevitably result in the monkeys having to be put down. So, no, do not feed the animals!

KNYSNA

Stretching around a serene lagoon, Knysna caters happily for a mix of hippies and urbanites. The Knysna Heads that flank the mouth of the lagoon lead out to a tempestuous sea, and many ships have run ashore here. The town's roots as a forestry station that boomed in the 1800s is evident in a multitude of woodworking shops and well-restored Victorian buildings.

Thesen Island (www.thesenislands.co.za) is a Hamptons-style development of clapboard-clad buildings next to the water, where you'll find trendy boutiques and some restaurants.

For a glimpse into the heart of the forest, visit **Rheenendal**, 12 kilometres west of Knysna, a district that's popular with artists and crafters. You can visit the deserted **Old Millwood Mining Village** and tour the old gold mine. The **Red Barn** (Rheenendal Road, 082 739 0962, www.theredbarn. co.za, closed in winter) offers home-style cooking, including delicous wood-fired pizzas and Sunday roasts. It's a winner with kids too.

The surrounding forests and Outeniqua Mountains are perfect for keen hikers, but if you're short on time a short stroll in the **Garden of Eden** just past Knysna will provide a magical glimpse into a world filled with ferns, mossy trees and brooks. There are plenty of other outdoor activities to enjoy. Golfers have **Pezula Golf Club** (Lagoonview Drive, 044 302 5300, www.pezulagolf. com) and **Simola Golf & Country Estate** (1 Old Cape Road, 044 302 9600, www.simola.co.za).

Knysna.

The **Featherbed Company** (Remembrance Avenue, off Waterfront Drive, 044 382 1693/7, www.featherbed.co.za), offers a variety of lagoon trips and cruises to the Western Head and the **Featherbed Nature Reserve** where you can hike, swim and picnic. The lagoon offers a multitude of watersport options; contact Tourism Knysna for information on kayaking, sailing and fishing.

Restaurants make the most of the waterside setting, and Knysna is famous for its oysters, so do enjoy some while visiting. **Sirocco Restaurant** (Long Street, Thesen Island, 044 382 4874, www.sirocco.co.za) serves sushi and Mediterranean fare in stylish surrounds, while **Firefly Eating House** (152A Old Cape Road, 044 382 1490, www.fireflyeatinghouse.com) specialises in curries from around the globe. **Zachary's** at the **Conrad Pezula Resort**

& **Spa** (Lagoonview Drive, 044 302 3333, www. placeshilton.com/pezula) is a sophisticated spot offering seasonal, organic fare. This prestigious resort also has suites with a Balinese theme, an award-winning spa and varied activities from horse-riding on Noetzie beach to hiking and helicopter trips.

The **Turbine Boutique Hotel & Spa** (Sawtooth Lane, Thesen Islands, 044 302 5746, www.turbinehotel.co.za, from R1,570 per person sharing) offers urban living in a revamped power station, with the old machinery being repurposed as decorative elements.

If you're keen to stay among the trees, luxurious **Phantom Forest Lodge** (Phantom Pass Road, Westford Bridge, 044 386 0046, www. phantomforest.com, from R4,632 for two people sharing, B&B, high season) or frill-free **Teniqua Treetops** (5km after Sedgefield, N2 Karatara/Ruigtevlei turn-off, 044 356 2868, www.teniqua treetops.co.za, from R1,400 per night) should be on your list. Both are within the forest, filled with birds and monkey life.

Tourist information

Tourism Knysna *40 Main Street (044 382 5510, www.visitknysna.co.za).*

Getting there

Knysna is 500km from Cape Town on the N2.

IN THE KNOW BAKING BAD

Renowned Thesen Islands bakery and restaurant Île de Païn was destroyed by a fire in May 2015. A place of pilgrimage for its fresh bistro fare, heavenly breads and artisan pastries, many are mourning its loss. Keep an eye on its Facebook page (www.facebook.com/iledepain) to see what owner/baker Markus Farbinger has planned next.

PLETTENBERG BAY

Plett, as it's popularly known, has excellent beaches, plentiful restaurants and covetable boutiques, making it an appealing choice for city slickers. Every December, matriculants head here from across the country to celebrate leaving school, so avoid the start of the holidays if you're not keen on partying with teenagers till dawn. Luckily, there are plenty of other things to do, from retail therapy to animal encounters and hikes in the serene Tsitsikamma Forest.

Robberg Nature Reserve (www.cape nature.co.za, conservation fee R40), situated south of town, is a wonderful place to hike and spot birds, small mammals and whales (in season). If you feel like really getting away from it all, stay at the beachside **Fountain Shack** (from R875), only reached by hiking two hours (and not suitable for children). Sleeping eight in bunk beds, it's back to basics as it has no electricity, but the setting is unbeatable for lovers of rugged living.

You're assured of good food in this bustling town. You could start the day with a freshly roasted coffee at hip **Doubleshot** (Checkers Centre, Main Street, 044 533 0842, www. doubleshotplett.co.za); **Le Fournil de Plett Bakery** (Lookout Centre, Main Street, 044 533 1390, www.facebook.com/lefournildeplett) offers delicate French bakes and light meals in a charming courtyard, and the **Table Restaurant & Bar** (9 Main Street, 044 533 3024,

www.thetable.co.za) is the place to go for cocktails, great pizzas and pastas and a fun vibe – what's more they have an indoor play area for youngsters. The **Lookout Deck** (Hill Street, 044 533 1379, www.lookout.co.za) offers fuss-free dishes – baskets of prawns, calamari and fish – washed down with draught beers. The highlight is the view over Lookout Beach from the expansive terrace.

As far as accommodation goes, you're spoilt for choice. The **Plettenberg** (40 Church Street, Lookout Rocks, 044 533 2030, www.collection mcgrath.com, from R5,250 per room) has one of the best views in town, first-class service and luxurious surrounds. There are two pools to choose from, as well as a Fresh Wellness Spa around the corner. The Sandbar has an excellent list of martinis, while SeaFood at The Plettenberg specialises in fresh fish and local, seasonal produce.

For over-the-top, eclectic grandeur, the **Grand Café & Rooms** (27 Main Road, 044 533 3301, www.grandafrica.com, from R750 per person sharing) wins hands down. The seven Moorish-inspired rooms feature four-poster beds, open concrete showers, double baths and ocean views. The café serves tasty salads, grills, pizza and pasta on a charming verandah.

Another hotel with a view is **Emily Moon River Lodge** (Rietvlei Road, off N2, 044 533 2500, www.emilymoon.co.za, R1,610 per person sharing). African artefacts greet the visitor to

IN THE KNOW SNAP SHOT

While visiting the Garden Route's incredible game reserves, you're bound to be taking photos on your camera or smartphone. Do make sure, however, that no geolocation information is saved while you're snapping away and posting to your favourite social media sites. This information can easily be used by tech-savvy poachers to find out where rhino are located. In fact, many rangers these days do not share information about how many rhino may be on a reserve or where they are to be found. The lives of these animals, and the safety of the people who protect them, are simply too valuable.

at work, enjoy Portuguese fare at Sao Goncalo's Kitchen, buy lovely linens at Mungo, and shop for clothes, 'raw wood' furniture and crafts at the other shops.

A bit further on the N2 you'll encounter Keurboomstrand, a popular holiday beach. Enjoy lunch with a view at convivial **Ristorante Enrico** (044 535 9818/9585), right on the beach. Dishes include fresh line-caught fish, veal, pizzas and pasta, and it's popular so you'll need to book.

Further along is the **Crags** (www.cruisethe crags.co.za), a tourist destination with numerous shops, wildlife activities and restaurants scattered around the area. It's very well organised and you'll see brochures for it everywhere. Animal encounters are plentiful: head to **Tenikwa Wildlife Awareness Centre** (044 534 8170, http://tenikwa.com, from R185) to see wild cats up close, the highlight being a sunrise or sunset cheetah walk; at **Monkeyland** (044 534 8906, www.monkeyland.co.za, from R175), take a forest hike to see monkeys in their natural habitat – the lemurs are a favourite; while **Birds of Eden** (044 534 8906, www.birdsofeden.co.za, from R175) is the largest free-flight aviary in the world, home to more than 3,000 birds from 200 species, enough to make any twitcher deliriously excited. At the **Elephant Sanctuary** (044 534 8145, www.elephantsanctuary.co.za, from R500), you can walk trunk in hand with these giant

this romantic spot overlooking the Bitou river; the ten lodges all feature decks, underfloor heating and African-inspired decor. Emily's Restaurant offers a lavish balcony, roaring fireplace and a small menu of seasonal fare, and newly opened Simon's Bar serves pizzas and cocktails.

Outside town, **Old Nick Village** (N2, 044 533 1395, www.oldnickvillage.co.za) is a fun place to while away an hour or so. Stop in at the market (Wednesday) for fresh produce, watch weavers

pachyderms, help feed them and even have a bareback ride on an elephant.

Several arts and crafts shops in the Crags showcase local work, such as mohair clothing and interior products at the **Mill** (044 534 8997, www.mohairmillshop.com).

Once you've done with animal interactions and shopping, **Bramon Wine Estate** (044 534 8007, www.bramonwines.co.za) and its restaurant is the perfect place to unwind: grab a sofa among the vines, snack on delicious tapas-style fare and enjoy the wine.

Next up is **Nature's Valley**: a winding forested descent leads to a lovely lagoon and a beach hidden behind milkwood trees. This is also the finishing point for the famous **Otter Hiking Trail** (book up to a year in advance) – an arduous five-day hiking trail that stretches over 43 km, up cliffs, over rivers and across beaches. Walking boots are strung up on the shoe tree at **Nature's Valley Inn** (corner Forest & St Michaels, 044 531 6835) by hikers who have successfully finished the trail.

Although technically in the Eastern Cape, the Tsitsikamma section of the **Garden Route National Park** (www.sanparks.co.za) is a natural marvel. If you only have an hour, take a gentle stroll to the Big Tree – a yellowwood that towers over 36 metres high and is nine metres in circumference. Or if you have a few days, base yourself in **Stormsriver Village**, the adventure hub of

the area. **Stormsriver Adventures** (042 281 1836, www.stormsriver.com) offers canopy tours and forest drives. Serious adrenalin junkies should head to Bloukrans bridge to hurl themselves off the world's highest commercial bungee jump, 216 metres above the Bloukrans river (042 281 1458, www.faceadrenalin.com, R85).

Tourist information

Plettenberg Bay Tourism Centre *Melville's Corner, Main Street (044 533 4065, www.plett-tourism.co.za).*

Getting there

Plettenberg Bay is 550km from Cape Town. Take the N2.

OUDTSHOORN

An oasis in the arid Klein-Karoo (which is, strictly speaking, outside the Garden Route), Oudtshoorn has many claims to fame that make it a popular tourist destination. Ostrich farming was the key to its success, notably during two ostrich-feather booms in the 1860s and at the start of the 20th century.

If you want to get up close to these quirky feathered creatures, visit **Highgate Ostrich Show Farm** (R62, 044 272 7115, www.highgate.co.za, R14), **Cango Ostrich Show Farm** (R62, 044 272 4623, www.cangoostrich.co.za, R85) or **Safari Ostrich Show Farm** (R328, 44 272 7312, www.safariostrich.co.za, R100). You'll learn about the economic importance of these birds, and have the chance to feed them and even ride them if you're feeling adventurous. In a slightly macabre turn, the on-site restaurants often serve ostrich meat (delicious, slightly gamey and naturally low in fat) and there are plenty of ostrich leather, shell and feather souvenirs to stock up on.

The **Cango Caves** (off the R328, 30 kilometres from Oudtshoorn, 044 272 7410, www.cango-caves.co.za, from R80) is probably the most famous local attraction. Known to man since the early Stone Age,

Emily Moon River Lodge. *See p189.*

Bungee jumping at Bloukrans Bridge.
See p191.

these limestone caves have magnificent and vast dripstone caverns. Choose from the heritage tour, which takes you to the larger, airier chambers, such as Fairy Queen's Palace and the Drum Room; or the adventure tour, which goes deeper and further, through the narrow Devil's Chimney and Devil's Postbox, where wriggling through very narrow spaces on your belly is compulsory. Note, the latter is not for the large of girth or the claustrophobic and is a circular route that cannot be reversed.

Every year during the April school holidays, the **Klein-Karoo Nasionale Kunstefees** (www.kknk.co.za) draws Afrikaans-speakers from across South Africa for a week of performing arts, live music and general bonhomie.

IN THE KNOW CUPPA TEA?

Rooibos herbal tea is derived from the plant *Aspalathus linearis*, a fynbos species that only grows in the Cederberg region. The tea is packed with antioxidants, is caffeine-free and loved by South Africans – and increasingly the rest of the world too.

The surrounding Swartberg and Outeniqua mountains are great for hiking, cycling, quad-biking or kloofing (a sport involving descending into ravines and watercourses). **Minwater Eco Adventures** (Oudtshoorn Road, 044 279 1285, www.minwater.co.za) in the Gamka mountains offers floral hikes and 4x4 adventures and has well-equipped bush camp sites.

If you're after a bigger game experience, **Cango Wildlife Ranch** (R62, 044 272 7410, www.cango.co.za, R100) is an option for a half-day trip. You could see everything from snakes to big cats such as cheetah, serval, white lion and leopard, as well as cute lemurs. If you're feeling extra brave, head into the water for a crocodile cage dive. **Buffelsdrift Game Lodge** (R328, 044 272 0000, www.buffelsdrift.com, from R1,365 per person sharing) offers game drives in open-air safari vehicles to spot elephant, rhino, hippo and giraffe as well as over 200 bird species. Luxury tents overlooking the water hole add to the appeal.

To see the antics of meerkats in the wild – always an entertaining sight – try **Meerkat Adventure**s (R62, 084 772 9678, www.meerkat adventures.co.za, R200 birdwatching tour, R550 meerkat tour).

IN THE KNOW WILD THINGS

If you don't have the time to head up to the north of South Africa to see the spectacular wildlife of the Kruger National Park, the Garden Route is your best bet for some safari action. There are a good number of private game reserves where you'll be enticed by luxury accommodation, open-vehicle game drives and knowledgable rangers, sharing information not only about the variety of wildlife you'll encounter, but also about the flora of the area.

Good options are: **Garden Route Game Lodge** (028 735 1200, www.grgamelodge.co.za), **Gondwana Game Reserve** (021 555 0807, www.gondwanagr.co.za) and **Plettenberg Bay Game Reserve** (044 535 0001, www.plettenbergbaygamereserve.com). Each offers a different atmosphere, from colonial to modern eco to African. A bonus is that all are located in malaria-free areas.

There are plenty of eateries to choose from in Oudtshoorn: try **Bello Cibo** (79 St Saviour Street, 044 272 3245, www.bellocibo.co.za) for Italian grills, pizzas and pasta, or **Jemima's** (94 Baron van Reede Street, 044 272 0808, www.jemimas.com) for South African-inspired cooking.

The yellow Victorian façade of the **Queen's Hotel** (5 Baron van Reede Street, 044 272 2101, www.queenshotel.co.za, from R1,690 per room sharing) welcomes guests to its manicured garden and refreshing pool (essential in summer). It has 40 rooms decorated in crisp whites and creams, the Colony Restaurant for South African fare, and Café Brûlé for light meals and coffees.

Tourist information

Oudtshoorn Tourism Bureau *80 Voortrekker Street (044 279 2532, www.oudtshoorn.com).*

Getting there

Oudtshoorn is 420km from Cape Town. Take the N1, turn off at Worcester and follow the R60 and R62 to Oudtshoorn. Alternatively, take the N2 to George, and then the N12 to Oudtshoorn.

West Coast

The Cape West Coast is a place of extremes: icy Atlantic waters, windblown beaches, spectacular sunsets, carpets of colourful flowers in spring… and it is this rugged aspect interspersed with natural beauty that make it such a favoured destination. It's the perfect place for long walks through veld covered with flowers, fresh seafood and getting away from it all. The seaside towns of Langebaan and Paternoster are key attractions, while, inland, the dramatic Cederberg mountain range lures keen hikers and campers.

LANGEBAAN

The town of Langebaan is a well-known holiday destination, much loved for its lagoon. This warm body of water is a life-giver to some 70,000 birds that migrate here for the summer each year. In similar vein, sun-seekers from far and wide descend upon the lagoon during the summer holidays, transforming the otherwise quiet town into a rather rowdy mix of fishermen, watersports fanatics and sunbathers.

The **Cape Sports Center** (98 Main Street, 022 772 1114, www.capesport.co.za) offers lessons and gear hire for all sorts of watersports, including kiteboarding, kayaking and windsurfing. Expertly trained staff are on hand if help is required.

For a more relaxing time, seafood specialist **Die Strandloper Restaurant** (off the road to Club Mykonos, 022 772 2490, 083 227 7195, www.strandloper.com) is a toes-in-the-sand kind of place, bang on the beach, where you'll feast on fresh fish grilled on an open fire. **Friday Island** (92 Main Street, 022 772 2506, 082 640 9319, www.fridayisland.co.za, R370-R550 per person sharing, high season) offers laid-back accommodation in the form of whitewashed rooms right on the water and casual eats – think meze and seafood – at its **Robinsoncruisethru** restaurant (022 772 2634).

The newly opened **Windtown Lagoon Hotel** (9 Bree Street, 022 772 1064, www.windtown-sa.com, R1,200-R1,500 per room including breakfast, peak season) has a boutique vibe. Plop on an oversized bean bag next to the pool or walk 150 metres to the beach. For something a tad more elegant, the **Farmhouse Hotel** (5 Egret Street, 022 772 2062, www.thefarmhousehotel.com, R2,500-R5,000 per room, peak season) offers genteel living in a Cape Dutch-style homestead.

If you can't bear to be off the water, **Kraalbaai Houseboats** (Langebaan Lagoon, 021 526 0432, www.kraalbaaihouseboats.co.za) has two floating palaces with everything you need. Larus (R2,100) accommodates six guests while Nirvana (R10,125) can take up to 24. Braai on the deck, anyone?

You'll need a day to explore the charming **West Coast National Park** (www.sanparks.co.za, entrance R42-R128, depending on country of residence and season), located about 100 kilometres from Cape Town off the R27. The Postberg section is wonderful in season with its spread of flowers, or pack a picnic and head to the Preekstoel and splash around with the kids in the lagoon at Kraalbaai.

Tourist information

Langebaan Tourism Bureau *022 772 1515,*
www.capewestcoastpeninsula.co.za.

Getting there

Langebaan is 124km from Cape Town. Take the
R27 north.

PATERNOSTER

This quaint fishing village of whitewashed houses
is the place to enjoy excellent fresh fish at a variety
of quality establishments, including, in season,
crayfish galore. Star of the show is **Oep ve Koep**
(Die Winkel op Paternoster, St Augustine Road,
022 752 2105, www.facebook.com/oepvekoep),
where young chef Kobus van der Merwe wows
diners in an unpretentious garden setting with
foraged produce and a light touch with seafood
and local meats. The attached shop sells leather
shoes, preserves and baked goods.

Situated right on the beach, **Gaatjie Salt
Water Restaurant** (off Sampson Street, 022
752 2242, www.saltcoast.co.za) has stellar views.
Order a bottle of chilled white wine, tuck in to
excellent local fare and watch the beach goings-
on from the verandah.

Abalone House & Spa (022 752 2044,
www.abalonehouse.co.za, R750-R3,500 self-
catering, R3,150-R4,700 room, peak season)
offers pretty much everything. It has eclectically
designed, luxurious boutique accommodation,
a Healing Earth Spa specialising in treatments
that use African ingredients, and Reuben's
restaurant, which showcases South African
dishes in a cosy interior and expansive deck.

If you're a fan of camping head to **Tietiesbaai
Campsite** (022 752 2718, R15 day visitor, R130
camping for six people), five kilometres from
Paternoster in the Cape Columbine Nature Reserve.
Set on a secluded rocky beach, it's pretty heavenly.
The reserve is great for meandering walks between
coastal fynbos and succulents, with a 1930s
lighthouse nearby.

Tourist information

Paternoster Tourism www.paternoster.info.

Getting there

Paternoster is 145 kilometres from Cape Town.
Take the R27 north to the junction with the R45;
turn left and follow the signs to Vredenburg and
then Paternoster.

CEDERBERG

A wilderness area of 83,000 hectares, one of the
most pristine in the Western Cape, the Cederberg
lies about 200 kilometres from Cape Town off the
N7 highway. Set between Citrusdal town, famous
for its lush orchards of citrus fruits and dotted
with farm stalls, and past Clanwilliam, where the
dam provides watersport fun, the Cederberg is
rugged and harsh in its mountainous beauty. As
well as hiking and bouldering activities, the area
is known for its striking rock formations such as

IN THE KNOW LIVING HISTORY

For a unique glimpse into the culture of one
of South Africa's most ancient peoples,
head up the West Coast. At the **!Khwa ttu
project** (022 492 2998, www.khwattu.org),
San Bushmen share their nomadic culture
with visitors. On the guided tour you will
learn about animal tracking and plant
identification, as well as the history of the
San. Aside from a community benefit craft
shop, there's an on-site restaurant where
San Bushmen kitchen and restaurant
trainees serve locally grown and produced
fare, including home-made breads and
mouthwatering cakes. What's more,
you can stay the night, with a variety of
accommodation options, such as the Bush
House or Tented Bush Camp. The project
is on the R27, four kilometres before the
Yzerfontein/Darling turn-off. Entry is free,
while the guided tours, at 10am and 2pm
daily, cost R150 per person.

**Bushmans Kloof Wilderness
Reserve & Wellness Retreat**.

the Maltese Cross, Stadsaal Caves and Wolfberg Cracks in the south. Excellent examples of San rock paintings are to be found in the area.

En route to the Cederberg, take a step back in time at the **Baths** (off the N7, just before Citrusdal, 022 921 8026/7, www.thebaths.co.za, R90 weekend day visitors). They offer a variety of accommodation from rooms in the Victorian homestead (R690-R1,060 double) to camping (R110). Spend your time between the pools and naturally heated rock pools while the kids enjoy the trampoline, pool table and tennis court.

To reach the southernmost area of the **Cederberg Wilderness Reserve** (021 483 0190, www.capenature.co.za, R60 conservation fee), turn off the N7 at the sign to Algeria and drive 17 kilometres. It's centred around **Algeria campsite** (027 482 2403, R315 camping for six people), which has long been a favourite for hikers in the area with its clean facilities and inviting rock pools. You can get your permits and maps here, and they're currently adding six self-catering chalets.

Continue past Algeria to **Cederberg Private Cellar** (Dwarsrivier Farm, 027 482 2827, www.cederbergwine.com) to swirl and sip top wines in an unsurpassed setting. Deep in the Rocklands area of the Cederberg lies **Alpha Excelsior Guest Farm** (027 482 2700, www.alphaexcelsior.co.za, R200-R400 per person, peak season), an ideal spot if you're a keen rock climber or need some serious solitude. You can stay in country cottages, the original farmhouse or even a retro caravan. In addition, you can taste their hand-made wines and olive oils.

Red Cederberg (027 482 2815, www.red cederberg.co.za, R190-R890) is an incredible find, with guest cottages in a variety of styles in completely private settings – you can hike, climb and relax in utter privacy. It's great for groups and if you don't have a 4x4, the owners will provide transport to the more remote cottages.

For top-notch pampering, try a stay at **Bushmans Kloof Wilderness Reserve & Wellness Retreat** (021 437 9278, www.bushmans kloof.co.za, R4,410-R7,715 per person, peak season). Luxurious rooms look out on to the river and rock formations, and game drives, rock art walks, spa treatments and gourmet cooking are on the to-do list. It's 40 kilometres from Clanwilliam.

The town of **Wupperthal** (information office 027 492 3410) is worth a detour: this tiny spot has been a Moravian mission station since 1865 and has some excellent finds such as original *velskoens* (leather shoes) and a rooibos tea factory.

Tourist information

Cederberg information *www.cederberg.com.*
Citrusdal Tourism *022 921 3210, www.citrus dal.info.*
Clanwilliam Tourism *027 482 2024, www.clanwilliam.info.*

Getting there

From Cape Town, head north on the N7. It's about 170km to Citrusdal, and 240km to Clanwilliam. It takes about three hours to reach the Cederberg, depending on where you are going.

In Context

History

_Settlers and struggle: the making of
a cultural crossroads._

TEXT: MAX DU PREEZ

To say that the African continent is steeped in
history is an understatement. It is, in fact, the
seat of humanity. The area around present-day
Cape Town was inhabited by early man long before
those first peoples began to migrate out of Africa.
Europeans returned to their African roots in the
16th century, when the Dutch East India Company
established a presence on the Cape, with a
refreshment station for sailors working the Far
East route. Within decades a colony had been
established. Other settlers arrived: Calvinist
Protestants who would later call themselves
Afrikaners; Muslims from Indonesia and around,
who would come to be known as Cape Malays;
indentured servants from India; slaves from
elsewhere in Africa; the British. European
commercial agriculture threatened the way of life of
the Cape's indigenous Khoikhoi people, and many
resorted to life as labourers on settler farms. The
basis for the complicated racial, ethnic and social
jigsaw that still characterises the Cape was formed.

Bartolomeu Dias

IN CONTEXT

DISTANT PAST
South Africa is an ancient land. Its rocks and plains date from the time when Africa was still part of Gondwanaland, a composite continent made up of South America, Africa, Antarctica, India and Australia that existed until more than 100 million years ago. Human beings walked these plains and rocks hundreds of thousands of years ago, when the species developed along the east side of Africa. Some of the oldest fossilised remains of our pre-human ancestors were found in South Africa, in places such as the Cradle of Humankind outside Johannesburg.

The area around present-day Cape Town and along the coastlines to the west and east was inhabited by Homo Sapiens long before other continents were discovered. The human remains excavated in caves at Klasies River Mouth on the southern Cape coast were between 75,000 and 120,000 years old – the oldest examples of Homo Sapiens to date. In 1993, it was proved that the people who occupied the Blombos Cave in the same area, at least 77,000 years ago, had a well-developed culture.

It was around this time that some started to leave Africa, gradually moving through the Middle East, southern Europe, and southern and south-east Asia. Climate, culture, diet and genetic isolation meant that those settling in Europe, Asia and the Americas developed different physical features over time. Only 500-odd years ago did those pale-skinned humans return to 'discover' the southern part of the continent of their origin.

ORIGINAL LOCALS
At the time of colonisation, the indigenous people of the area were known collectively as the Khoikhoi ('men among men', or 'real people', as *khoi* means 'person'). The first Europeans to meet them named them the Hottentots, apparently after a word used in the Khoikhoi welcoming dance. Historians now believe the Khoikhoi derived from aboriginal hunters who lived in northern Botswana, and that they moved down the Atlantic Coast to the western Cape about 2,000 years ago, after they had switched from hunting to herding. At first they only kept fat-tailed sheep, but by the time the Europeans encountered them, they had acquired cattle, most likely from the Bantu-speaking farmers in the eastern Cape.

The Khoikhoi were closely related to a hunter-gatherer people whose ancestors probably never left the subcontinent. The first Dutch settlers called these hunters Bosjesmannen (men of the bush, later Boesmans or Bushmen) and the Khoikhoi called them Sonqua or San. They spoke a variety of languages characterised by the use of clicks or implosive consonants, very similar to the sounds of the Khoikhoi.

While the San lived mainly in caves and overhangs in small, mobile groups with a weak hierarchical system, the Khoikhoi lived in round reed huts in larger settlements. Each clan had a headman, a hereditary position, and the villages of a particular tribe fell under a chief. The chief ruled by the consent of a council of elders. They acted as a court to settle disputes and hear criminal cases. The Khoikhoi had a complex system of customs such as initiation rituals, weddings and funerals, and livestock were central to much of their culture. Biogeneticists recently found that the San and Khoikhoi have genetic threads linking them to the first ever human beings.

EUROPEAN INTEREST
In February 1488, the Portuguese seafarer Bartolomeu Dias rounded the Cape and landed at Mossel Bay, east of Cape Town.

He was met by the Khoikhoi, and when they tried to defend their precious watering hole, Dias's men killed one of their group with a crossbow. This incident could be regarded as the first act of resistance by the indigenous people of southern Africa against European colonialism, and the beginning of the struggle for land. Others point to an incident 11 years later when Dias's colleague, Vasco Da Gama, planted a cross and a *padrao* (commemorative pillar) on the Mossel Bay dunes. As they sailed away, they saw the Khoikhoi men defiantly push the cross and the *padrao* over.

If Dias and Da Gama had travelled a little further along the east coast, they would have come across another group of indigenous people, the amaXhosa. They were part of a large family of farmers, together called the Bantu-speakers, who had migrated in stages from Africa's Great Lakes District to the south around 2,000 years ago.

The early European settlers, and to some extent even the Bantu-speakers, regarded the San hunter-gatherers as primitive beings not worth much more than animals. Many were killed in unequal battles with settlers. Only small groups of San survive today in Namibia and Botswana, but their ancestors left an astonishing legacy in the form of rock paintings and engravings all over southern Africa, the oldest surviving examples being 20,000 years old. The paintings reflect a very complex spiritual relationship with the environment. Thousands of examples have, remarkably, survived across South Africa. Many San were assimilated into Bantu-speaking societies – the clicks in the Xhosa language are a result of this.

SETTLING IN THE CAPE

After Bartolomeu Dias's 1488 visit, many European ships on their way to the East stopped at the Cape to replenish water and food supplies. Without exception, the seafarers' diaries reflect the astonishment they experienced when Table Mountain, the peaks of the Peninsula and the bay came into view. Dias himself named it Cabo de Boa Esperanca, Cape of Good Hope, although neither he nor Da Gama actually went into Table Bay. Antonio de Saldanha was probably the first European to land there, in 1503. He climbed the mountain and named it 'The Table of the Cape of Good Hope'.

San art

It was not until 1652 that Europeans settled at the Cape. The Dutch East India Company, or VOC, had decided that the mortality rate among sailors of their fleet trading with the East was too high, especially due to scurvy, and ordered Jan Van Riebeeck to establish a halfway refreshment station with vegetable gardens and a hospital at the Cape. On 6 April 1652, Van Riebeeck arrived with three ships in Table Bay. He was met by Autshomato, also called Herrie die Strandloper, a Khoikhoi chief who had spent a year with the English on a trip to the East between 1631 and 1632. Fluent in English, he was enlisted as Van Riebeeck's interpreter. Later he fell out of favour and was jailed at first in Van Riebeeck's fort and then on Robben Island (see p209 **The Long Walk to Freedom**), from where he escaped in a leaky boat.

Initially, the VOC had no intention of creating a colony on the Cape. But within five years it allowed a number of its employees to set up private farms around Cape Town. The presence of 'free burghers' increased quickly over the next few decades.

The new colony needed more people, and before the end of the 17th century groups of French Huguenots and German immigrants joined the Dutch settlers at the Cape. Most of them were Calvinist Protestants. The descendants of these settlers would later call themselves the Afrikaners. Most of the Huguenots were given farms in the Franschhoek ('French corner') and Paarl areas and contributed greatly to South Africa's wine-making culture. Almost from the beginning the free burghers were in conflict with the authorities, and distrusted the government. Their sense of vulnerability as frontiers people would inform their behaviour for three centuries.

IN CONTEXT

'A slave woman who married a white man was integrated into white society, together with her children. It was a female slave's easiest way to get her freedom.'

The development of commercial agriculture soon threatened the Khoikhoi's way of life. As early as 1659, a group of Khoikhoi attacked the settler farms, driving off much of the livestock. Van Riebeeck tried to keep settlers and Khoikhoi apart by planting a hedge of bitter-almond on the outskirts of Cape Town. Khoikhoi society quickly disintegrated under settler pressure. Many resorted to lives as labourers on settler farms, others moved inland, only to be displaced later by settler farmers. Many Khoikhoi died during the smallpox epidemic of 1713.

SLAVE TRADE

The VOC did not want to encourage more European labourers to come to the Cape, because they proved to be troublesome. Still, they did need more workers on the farms, so in 1658, the first ships carrying slaves arrived at the Cape. The slaves came from Dahomey, Angola and Mozambique in Africa and from India, the East Indies and Madagascar. Between the arrival of the first slave ships and the end of the slave trade in 1807, about 60,000 slaves were brought to the Cape.

Slavery changed the basic political and social character of the Cape of Good Hope. By 1795, two-thirds of the burghers around Cape Town and three-quarters of the farmers in the districts of Stellenbosch and Drakenstein owned slaves. The burghers' European tradition dictated that the sanctity of property rights was central to their own freedom. Slave owners included their slaves on inventories of property together with their cattle and sheep. All slaves were black, and this instilled a distorted image of black people in many white minds. Add to this the perpetual fear of slave uprisings on isolated farms and it becomes easier to understand white attitudes in the following centuries, which ultimately resulted in formalised apartheid.

DARK DAYS

Apartheid, the ideology of racial separation formally adopted by the National Party government in 1948, theoretically presupposed that pure races existed in South Africa. Yet there had been thousands of 'mixed' marriages during the first century of colonialism on the Cape, the majority between settler men and slave women. Virtually all old Afrikaner families can trace a slave mother somewhere in their past.

A slave woman who married a white man was integrated into white society, together with her children. It was a female slave's easiest way to get her freedom. There were more white men than women in the colony and almost twice as many male slaves as females. On the farms outside Cape Town, the best chance male slaves had to find a wife was among the Khoikhoi. A child between a slave and a Khoikhoi would be born free, but forced to work on the farm for a period. These offspring were later called Baster Hottentotte, and they occupied a very low position on the social ladder. Descendants of white and Khoikhoi relationships outside of marriage and without formal acceptance by the church were called Basters, and they enjoyed much more freedom than the Baster Hottentotte. The Basters later formed the nucleus of the Reheboth Basters of Namibia and the Griqua, mostly of the northern Cape.

Between the two main cultural-economic groups, those being the Christian European group and the Muslim or 'Cape Malay' group, another group existed at the Cape – some were slaves, some were freed slaves, some were Baster Hottentotte, some were the offspring of white and black liaisons but were not claimed by their white fathers. This group was later called the Cape Coloureds.

The VOC had discouraged the use of French and German among the first settlers, with Dutch being the dominant language. But the slaves, the Basters, the Cape Malays and the Baster Hottentotte who worked on the farms and in the kitchens developed a creolised version of Dutch to communicate with their masters and one another. This developed into a fully fledged indigenous language later called Afrikaans – the language white Afrikaner nationalism later claimed as its own property and tribal symbol.

In 1795, Britain conquered the Cape, then returned the colony to the Dutch eight years later – only to reclaim it in 1806. It would remain a British colony for more than a century. Under pressure from British missionaries working in the Cape and humanitarians in Britain, the British government scrapped the regulations limiting the rights of the Khoisan and freed slaves in 1828. In 1834, all slaves

were liberated, although they had to serve four years of 'apprenticeship' before they were completely free. By this time, the settler farmers had expanded their operations in the interior and along the coast to what became known as the Eastern Cape, where they started to compete with another indigenous group, the amaXhosa. This conflict had the same root as the conflict with the Khoikhoi: land.

UPHEAVAL

Around 3,000 years ago, black farming peoples who lived in the region of the Great Lakes of Africa developed a common language that was later called Bantu. During the next 1,000 years, many of them migrated south. These farmers kept cattle, sheep and goats and grew sorghum and millet. They had an advanced social culture and mostly lived in large permanent settlements. A thousand years ago one of the main centres of power of the Bantu-speakers of southern Africa was at Mapungubwe Hill on the border between South Africa and Zimbabwe,

Jan Van Riebeeck. See p201.

IN CONTEXT

now best known for the finely crafted gold artefacts that were found there.

The migrators split into four language groups as they moved into South Africa: the Nguni-speakers moved down the east coast, the Venda and Tsonga stayed in the north, and the Sotho-Tswana-speakers migrated down the centre. The Xhosa were the Nguni-speakers who moved all the way down to the Eastern Cape, while those who spoke the Zulu dialect of Nguni settled in present-day KwaZulu-Natal.

At the end of the 18th century, these black farmers (the term 'Bantu' that was used to depict them became a derogatory word during the apartheid years) were living in a number of small chiefdoms. The early years of the 19th century brought a great social upheaval. It was a period of serious suffering, but also nation-building. By the end of it Shaka had forged the Zulu nation from several chiefdoms and Mzilikazi established the Ndebele and Matabele under his leadership. Moshoeshoe, an extraordinary diplomat and statesman for his time, had collected a number of chiefdoms and thousands of refugees – Nguni-speakers as well as Sotho-Setswana-speakers – at his mountain stronghold in Lesotho and formed the Basotho. The Tsonga and Venda remained in their mountainous territory in the north; Sekwati built up the Pedi; Sobhuza the Swazi. In the Eastern Cape, the Xhosa developed a form of unity with smaller groups such as the Thembu, the Mfengu and the Mpondo.

A small community, the Lemba, whose individuals have great artistic skill, believe that they are descendants of black Jews from the Middle East, and they still live among the Venda. Their claim was recently proved to be correct after extensive DNA testing. Many Lemba still live strictly as Orthodox Jews.

WAR TIME

The trekboers, as the burghers who had moved well away from the Cape were called, waged war against the Xhosa, but while the trekboers had firearms, the Xhosa had greater numbers. When the British Army was deployed against the Xhosa after 1811, the balance of power was tipped. During the brutal war of 1834-35 the Xhosa king, Hintsa, was decapitated. The Eighth Frontier War of 1850-52 was the most savage war against the Xhosa. Some 16,000 Xhosa were killed,

and large numbers of settlements burned and cattle captured.

A great tragedy that befell the Xhosa can partly be explained by the trauma of these wars. In 1856, a young woman called Nongqawuse had a vision in which two men who were long dead told her that a great resurrection of her people was about to occur. To ensure that it happened, the people had to kill all their cattle and not plant any more crops. She convinced her uncle, a well-known seer named Mhlakaza, of the authenticity of the vision and he convinced paramount chief Sarili. The killing took place over the next year. By the end of December 1857, tens of thousands, perhaps as many as 50,000, Xhosa had died of starvation. More than 25,000 left for the Cape Colony to seek work.

THE BRITISH

In 1820, the British settled some 4,000 British subjects, mostly farmers and tradesmen, in the Eastern Cape. The colonial government started promoting the use of English at the expense of Dutch-Afrikaans and elevated the new British settlers into public positions. This caused deep bitterness among the Cape burghers.

Around the middle of the 19th century, developments in South Africa started to move away from the Mother City. But events in the central and northern interior would have a direct and lasting impact on Cape life.

After the 1835 war against the Xhosa, the Afrikaner trekboers in the Eastern Cape started to plan to move north into the interior of South Africa. They were unhappy about Britain's abolition of slavery, felt insecure so close to the frontier with the Xhosa, and needed more land for their cattle. Between 1835 and 1845, 15,000 Afrikaners, accompanied by 5,000 servants, left the colony in convoys of oxwagons and on horseback. They were called Voortrekkers. Their migration, which was later known as the Great Trek, would change South Africa fundamentally and ultimately lead to the formation of a formal nation-state. The Voortrekkers took with them the European convictions and traditions of white dominance and used these in structuring their relations with the black peoples of the interior.

The Voortrekkers staked out farms in what are today the provinces of KwaZulu-Natal,

Nongqawuse.

Gauteng, the Free State and Mpumalanga. The black societies in most of these regions were still suffering the after-effects of the great upheavals of the beginning of the century. Some of these areas were therefore not actively occupied at the time of the Voortrekker settlement, but others were and this led to violent clashes with the black tribes.

The Voortrekkers declared the Republic of Natalia in Natal, but Britain annexed it as a colony in 1843. Most of the Voortrekkers trekked further west and declared the South African Republic with Pretoria as its capital in 1843 and the Republic of the Orange

Free State with Bloemfontein as its capital in 1854. With the Cape and Natal under British colonial rule, the whole country was now occupied by whites.

From 1860 onwards, another population group was added to South Africa's ethnic diversity. Shiploads of indentured labourers from India were taken to Natal to work in the new sugar plantations. Later, Indian traders came to South Africa under their own initiative, mainly to set up shops in the towns of Natal, the Free State and the Transvaal. In 1893, an Indian lawyer arrived on a legal assignment to Indian traders in Pretoria. He decided to stay on when he suffered racial discrimination by whites and realised that Indians' rights were threatened. His name was Mohandas Gandhi, and he later became one of the most powerful moral influences in the world.

DIAMONDS CHANGE THE WORLD

Britain's two South African colonies were not regarded as prize possessions back in London, but this changed dramatically when diamonds were discovered near the confluence of the Gariep and Vaal Rivers in 1867 and gold outside Pretoria in 1886. But the Boers of the Free State, as well as the Griqua of Griqualand, claimed ownership of the diamond area and the gold reef fell inside the South African Republic. The diamond fields were extraordinarily rich and attracted fortune-seekers from all over the world.

The town of Kimberley developed rapidly amid the abundant diamond pipes. The British declared that the Orange Free State border ran about a mile east of the richest mines, and annexed the area into the Cape Colony, together with the whole of Griqualand West.

In 1888, Cecil John Rhodes, an entrepreneur and ardent believer in British imperialism, acquired the monopoly over the four Kimberley diamond pipes. His company was called De Beers Consolidated Mines. Rhodes later became the prime minister of the Cape Colony. Tens of thousands of black people from all over South Africa rushed to Kimberley in the hope of finding jobs. It was De Beers who first started the practice of employing rural black men and putting them up in closed barracks. Thus a system that lasted in some form to the end of the 20th century was established. Men from the rural areas were employed in the cities and put up in single-sex accommodation, only seeing their families once or twice a year. It was called the migrant labour system.

In 1886, a reef of gold, the richest deposit in the world, was discovered in the South African Republic. Once more there was a rush of fortune-seekers, but again big mining houses stepped in and within a few years eight conglomerates controlled all the mining on what became known as the Witwatersrand. Virtually overnight a city sprang up, named Johannesburg. Black workers from across the subcontinent rushed to the mines and were employed under similar conditions to those at the diamond mines.

SCORCHED EARTH

The discovery of diamonds and gold gave a new urgency to British plans for a confederation of the four political units in South Africa. It put such pressure on the South African Republic that its president, Paul Kruger, declared war with Britain in 1899. The Republic was joined by the Republic of the Orange Free State.

It was the fiercest war ever fought on the African subcontinent. More than 300,000 British soldiers took on the two republics with a total white population of around 300,000 and fewer than 70,000 soldiers. It was an uneven war, but the Boer commandos were highly mobile, sometimes using tactics that would later be called guerrilla warfare. By 1902, most Boer women and children were in diseased concentration camps and the captured men and boys in prisoner-of-war camps in Ceylon (Sri Lanka), St Helena and Burma. These practices did much to destroy the Boers' spirit, as did the British 'scorched earth' policy toward the end of the war, burning farmsteads and crops and killing cattle. In May 1902 the two republics surrendered and signed the Peace of Vereeniging.

The war, which was for a long time called the Anglo-Boer War but is now called the South African War, did not only affect the Boers and the British soldiers. Thousands of black and Coloured South Africans fought on both sides, although most fought with the British. Tens of thousands of blacks, mostly farm workers, were also put in concentration camps and 30,000 died there. Some 110,000 white women and children were put in concentration camps; 27,000 of them died. And 30,000 farms were destroyed. The war created deep bitterness and anti-British sentiment among Afrikaners for generations.

WHITE MIGHT

In May 1908, delegates from the Cape, Natal and the two former republics met at a National Convention to negotiate the establishment of a united South African state. Only white delegates were invited. Despite the fact that there were four times as many black people as whites in the four regions, black people were only given a very limited franchise in the Cape alone. The South African Act was approved by the British Parliament. On 31 May 1910, the Union of South Africa came into being, with

IN CONTEXT

four provinces. Parliament was to be seated in Cape Town. The exclusion of the majority black population from political power in South Africa was now formalised.

Black intellectuals and community leaders protested against the new constitution, but when their protest fell on deaf ears in Cape Town and London, they formed the South African Native National Congress in January 1912. It was the first national body of indigenous people in South Africa and the first co-ordinated movement to resist white domination. The executive of 11 were all highly educated, five of them having studied in the US or Britain. The movement later changed its name to the African National Congress. The ANC stepped up their protest in 1913, after the Native Land Act was adopted, limiting black land ownership to about eight per cent of the land surface. The figure was increased to 13 per cent in 1936.

Two years after the ANC's birth, white Afrikaners also formed their first national political party, the National Party. In 1918, a secret males-only body, the Afrikaner Broederbond, was formed to further the cause of Afrikaner nationalism in business, education and culture. It became very powerful in later years. In 1938, Afrikaner nationalism experienced a massive upsurge with a national re-enactment of the Great Trek a century earlier. Ten years later the National Party defeated the United Party of General Jan Smuts in the general election. The party ruled South Africa until 1994.

SPLITTING A NATION

Racial separation and a denial of black South Africans' political and human rights began in 1652 and continued under British rule until 1948. But the National Party turned these practices and attitudes into a formal ideology they called apartheid, literally meaning 'separateness'. The new government spent considerable energy during its first years in power to write numerous apartheid laws. The population was classified according to race; sex between mixed couples and marriages across the colour bar were criminalised; separate residential areas and public amenities were enforced; separate education was instituted; and the movement of black South Africans was regulated by the carrying of pass books.

'One of the cruellest aspects of apartheid was that over three million blacks were forcibly removed over four decades because the areas where they lived were declared 'white'.'

The National Party later called their policies 'separate development', protesting that they did not discriminate, but that for the sake of peace and fairness black Africans should exercise their political rights in ten tribal states, or homelands. The theory was that South Africa proper was white man's land where blacks would enjoy limited rights, but that their homelands would eventually become independent, sovereign states where they would enjoy full rights. Some of those Bantustans, like Transkei, Ciskei and Bophuthatswana, did later become 'independent', but South Africa was the only country that recognised them. The man who championed the homelands policy and under whose leadership South Africa left the Commonwealth and became a republic in 1961 was Dr Hendrik Verwoerd, the National Party's third prime minister.

The ANC slowly grew as a movement and organised a successful 'Defiance Campaign' in 1952 to protest against unjust laws. In 1955, delegates from all over the country gathered in Kliptown outside Johannesburg to adopt the Freedom Charter. This document, which was headed 'The people shall govern!', remained the ANC's ideological compass for four decades. But a group of Africanists in the ANC did not like the fact that the Charter acknowledged whites as full citizens with equal rights, and in 1957 they broke away to form the Pan Africanist Congress (PAC) with Robert Sobukwe as their first leader.

In 1960, the PAC organised protests against the pass laws, forming large demonstrations. It was at one of these,

IN CONTEXT

in Sharpeville south of Johannesburg, that the police panicked and killed 69 people. Later the same day a crowd of 6,000 from Langa and Nyanga just outside Cape Town marched to the city, led by a young PAC activist, Philip Kgosana. The police opened fire, killing three and injuring 47.

These two events were turning points in South African history. The government banned the ANC and PAC, and both organisations went underground and formed military wings: the ANC formed Umkhonto we Sizwe (Spear of the Nation) and the PAC formed Poqo (Pure). Most of the first Umkhonto we Sizwe leaders, including the young lawyer Nelson Mandela, were arrested in 1963 and jailed on Robben Island. Some ANC leaders went into exile. It was also during this time that many African colonies gained their independence.

In March 1960, Verwoerd declared: 'A psychotic preoccupation with the rights, the liberties and the privileges of non-white peoples is sweeping the world – at the expense of due consideration of the rights and merits of white people. The fundamental reality being disregarded is that without white civilisation, non-whites may never have known the meaning of idealism or ambition, liberty or opportunity.'

Verwoerd was stabbed to death in his seat in Parliament, Cape Town, in September 1966. A court declared that his killer, a parliamentary messenger named Demitrio Tsafendas, was mentally disturbed.

SWEPT AWAY

One of the cruellest aspects of apartheid was that over three million blacks were forcibly removed over four decades because the areas where they lived were declared 'white'. In Cape Town, this was a particularly painful experience.

District Six was a vibrant, colourful suburb situated right next to the Cape Town City Centre at the foot of Devil's Peak. The majority of the residents were Coloured – their ancestors had been living there since the emancipation of the slaves in the 1830s – but whites, blacks, Indians and Chinese also lived in the area. Between 1965 and 1967, it was declared a 'white' area under the Group Areas Act. The same fate befell Coloured residents living in Kalk Bay and Simonstown.

The residents were moved to new Coloured townships miles away on the Cape Flats and

Mitchell's Plain behind Strandfontein. District Six was then razed to the ground, saving only the churches and mosques. The new townships were situated far from shops and places of work; parts of them soon developed into slums. Gangsterism and crime increased progressively.

PUTTING UP A FIGHT

The arrests of ANC leaders in the early 1960s forced the ANC into a period of near dormancy, but internally the resistance simmered. During the early 1970s a charismatic young intellectual, Steve Biko, gained a strong following with his Black Consciousness views. Early 1973 saw a series of strikes and industrial unrest. In June 1976, Soweto schoolchildren protested against the Bantu Education system and the use of Afrikaans in schools. Some were shot dead by police. Many youngsters left to join the ANC in exile, injecting the movement with new energy. Steve Biko was detained in the Eastern Cape in August 1977. He was first assaulted in the police cells, then thrown naked into a police van for the trip to Pretoria. He died on the way.

That same year a scandal broke over the way funds for the Department of Information were misused, and a year later Prime Minister John Vorster resigned and was replaced by his minister of defence, PW Botha. Botha appointed General Magnus Malan as minister of defence. In response to internal and international opposition to apartheid, they militarised South Africa. Important decision making shifted to the State Security Council, and security forces believed they had a licence to kill anti-apartheid activists. Hundreds of young white men were conscripted into the Defence Force, which was engaged in destabilising operations in neighbour states and a full-scale war in Angola.

But Botha also tried to reform apartheid and instituted a programme of 'power sharing' with Coloured and Indian South Africans getting their own chambers of Parliament. But the exclusion of blacks provoked deep anger and was one of the motivating factors for the birth of a new national resistance movement, the United Democratic Front, which was formed in Cape Town in 1984. The United Democratic Front was ideologically aligned with the ANC, as was the new trade union movement, the Congress of South African Trade Unions (Cosatu).

THE LONG WALK TO FREEDOM
The story of Robben Island.

Robben Island is rather innocently called Seal Island ('rob' is the Dutch word for seal), but the story of this place is mostly a sad, and often brutal, one.

The island was known for thousands of years to the indigenous San and Khoikhoi people, but it is unlikely that they ever went there before the first European ships arrived in the 15th century. And when they did go to the island, it was more often than not as prisoners. During the 16th and early 17th century many Khoikhoi who displeased the Dutch, English or Portuguese seafarers were left on the island as punishment. But it was also used as a post office during this period, because many of the seafarers were afraid of the Khoikhoi on the mainland and preferred to pick up their post, fresh water and seal or penguin meat here.

In 1610, ten English criminals who had escaped the gallows and been taken to work in the Cape instead, fled from the mainland and lived on the island for more than a year. The 'Newgate Men', as they were called, were eventually taken back to England and hanged.

After Jan van Riebeeck of the Dutch East India Company established a permanent refreshment station at Cape Town, many 'troublesome' Khoikhoi were banished to Robben Island, the first being a man called Autshomato, who spoke English and was used as an interpreter by the Dutch.

When the European settlers clashed with the Xhosa in the Eastern Cape in the early 19th century, rebellious Xhosa leaders and chiefs were regularly imprisoned on the island. Later that century it was also used as a colony for lepers and those suffering from mental illness.

During World War II the South African Navy took control of the island. It built houses and roads and installed heavy cannon to defend Cape Town from possible enemy ships. In 1961, the Prisons Department took over the island and built a new jail. From the early 1960s onwards many political prisoners were sent to the jail, but kept apart from the sentenced criminals.

Among the most famous political prisoners were Nelson Mandela, Walter Sisulu and Govan Mbeki. Robben Island became 'the University' where hundreds of young activists were taught by Mandela and his older friends – and where some prisoners obtained university degrees through correspondence study. In 1986 Mandela was transferred from Robben Island to Pollsmoor prison, but some prisoners remained until 1990.

Robben Island was transformed into a museum after 1994 (*see p86*).

IN CONTEXT

VIOLENT TIMES

The period between 1984 and 1990 was a turbulent one. There were regular violent protests, often put down by overwhelming force. Month after month the streets of Cape Town's townships, even the inner city, reverberated with the stomping feet of marchers and the crackle of gunfire, while tear gas often lingered in the air. At one stage the police sprayed protestors in the city with purple-dyed water so they could be identified later. The purple stains remained on city walls for days, and then a famous graffito appeared: 'The Purple shall govern!'

On 15 October 1985, a truck travelled through a crowd of protesting youths in Athlone on the Cape Flats. It turned round and drove past them again. This time they hurled stones and bricks at it. Suddenly armed men hidden in empty crates at the back of the truck leapt up and started firing with shotguns. Three youngsters were killed and 20 wounded. The incident, called the Trojan Horse shootings, caused great anger in Cape Town. The period was also marked by strikes and mass action by trade unions that destabilised the economy, already crippled by international sanctions and financial restrictions by international banks.

ROAD TO RECONCILIATION

It was in the late 1980s that the government and the ANC came to realise that neither side could win the battle and that a settlement was the only way to stop South Africa from being completely ruined. Nelson Mandela started secret talks with the government from his jail cell, and government agents had several meetings with ANC leaders in exile.

In January 1989, PW Botha suffered a stroke and in August that year FW de Klerk became president. UDF leaders in the Cape called his bluff after his first reconciliatory speech and staged a mass march through the streets of Cape Town, led by Anglican Archbishop Desmond Tutu. It led to a nationwide demonstration of 'People's Power', with marches in most cities and many towns. In October, at the request of Mandela, the first group of political prisoners, all old stalwarts of the ANC like Walter Sisulu, were released from jail after more than 25 years behind bars.

In November 1989, the Berlin Wall fell and the Soviet Union started to disintegrate. This meant the old National Party argument, that

the ANC had to be suppressed because they were tools of communist imperialism, fell away. A month later Nelson Mandela and FW de Klerk had their first face-to-face meeting in the president's Cape Town office. The Old South Africa was fast unravelling.

De Klerk opened the 1990 session of Parliament on 2 February with announcements that stunned the world. He unbanned the ANC, PAC and Communist Party; lifted large sections of the emergency regulations; and announced the release of many political prisoners. And, he declared, Nelson Mandela would be released unconditionally within a few days.

De Klerk ended his speech: 'The season of violence is over. The time for reconstruction and reconciliation has begun… I pray that the Almighty Lord will guide and sustain us on our course through uncharted waters.'

BIRTH OF DEMOCRACY

In the late afternoon of 11 February 1990, Nelson Mandela walked out of prison after 27 years of incarceration. South Africans and the world were stunned to witness his lack of bitterness and huge capacity for reconciliation.

By April most senior ANC leaders in exile had returned to South Africa, and on 3 May, the first formal meeting between the government and the ANC took place at the official state residence, Groote Schuur in Cape Town. Senior ANC delegate Thabo Mbeki remarked after the first day that the delegates 'quickly understood that there was nobody there with horns'. After three days the meeting issued the Groote Schuur minute that contained a commitment to negotiations and a review of security legislation and of the armed struggle.

After 18 months of intense negotiations, the Convention for a Democratic South Africa, comprising most of the country's political parties, met on 20 December 1991 at Kempton Park to begin the task of preparing an interim constitution for a democratic South Africa.

Election, 1994

The next two years were complicated by politically inspired violence, especially between supporters of the Inkatha Freedom Party and the ANC, and dramatic events such as the assassination of the popular Communist Party leader Chris Hani, a right-wing attack on the Codesa building and an abortive invasion of the Bophuthatswana homeland by the Afrikaner Weerstands-beweging. But each time the two main sides, led by Nelson Mandela and FW de Klerk, brought the negotiators back to the table.

In the early hours of 18 November 1993 the parties agreed to the final text of the Interim Constitution, and two months later a parallel government, the Transitional Executive Council, was established.

NEW BEGINNING

On 17 April 1994, millions of South Africans of all races and classes queued together at polling stations for the first election in a united South Africa. The ANC won by a large majority and formed a Government of National Unity with cabinet seats for the National Party and the Inkatha Freedom Party.

On 10 May 1994, Thabo Mbeki and FW de Klerk were sworn in as deputy presidents in Pretoria. Then Nelson Mandela took the oath as the first president of a democratic South Africa. Six fighter planes, which had only a few years earlier dropped bombs on ANC camps in neighbouring states, flew past in a salute. Mandela ended his inauguration speech with the words: 'Let freedom reign. God bless Africa.'

The elected members of Parliament formed a Constitutional Assembly to define a final Constitution. It was adopted on 18 November 1996 and signed into law by President Nelson Mandela on 10 December in Sharpeville. That same year the Truth and Reconciliation Commission, which was part of the negotiated settlement, started to hear evidence that came from victims of past human rights violations. It was chaired by Nobel Peace Laureate Archbishop Desmond Tutu. The Commission also had the power to grant amnesty to the perpetrators, most of them security policemen. In the years that have passed since the first elections of 1994, South Africa has become a stable, progressive democracy with a vibrant economy and a strong leadership role in Africa. District Six was given back to its original owners; large numbers of other displaced communities were given their land back or were compensated for their loss; more than a million new homes were built for the homeless within the first ten years and millions of people had clean water on their doorstep for the first time.

Now in the third decade of democracy, South Africa is not a land without problems. Violent crime remains unacceptably high, and the wave of xenophobic violence against immigrants in 2008 shocked many. The HIV/AIDS figures make for grim reading. The economic disparity between the wealthy minority and the vast majority has only worsened these social problems. As the tough realities of change replace the doe-eyed hopes for a post-apartheid panacea, huge numbers of skilled white professionals are now emigrating.

But despite the complex challenges of crime, HIV/AIDS and the 'brain drain', South Africans can draw on many positives. The country is a continental leader: the African Union was launched in Durban in July 2002, with South Africa's then premier, Thabo Mbeki, serving as its first president; Mbeki was also one of the key figures behind the African economic development programme NEPAD (New Partnership for Africa's Development). He was replaced as president by Jacob Zuma in April 2009.

Thanks to the 2010 FIFA World Cup, long-overdue upgrades of everything from sports stadiums and transport systems to safety and security were implemented, bringing with it billions of rands in investment.

But in the last few years, general discontent with the ruling party has become more apparent. Julius Malema's Economic Freedom Fighters party contests the ANC's decisions loudly and constantly, while service delivery in municipalities around the country has become massively problematic. Add to that the Nkandla report about upgrades to the presidential compound tallying up to over R240 million of taxpayers' money, and the mismanagement and lack of maintenance that has resulted in national electricity provider Eskom's inability to provide sufficient electricity, making 'load shedding', or blackout sessions, a daily occurrence.

Yet, despite these stumbling blocks, South Africans remain fiercely patriotic and there is a sense of determination coupled with innovative thinking that provides hope for the future.

IN CONTEXT

KEY EVENTS

1488 Portuguese explorer Bartolomeu Dias rounds lands at Mossel Bay, where he is met by the indigenous people, Khoikhoi.

1652 Jan Van Riebeeck arrives. Cape Town becomes the Dutch East India Company's mainland base of operations.

1795 British occupation of the Cape Colony.

1816-28 Shaka emerges as one of Africa's greatest military leaders, his Zulu army becoming one of the most powerful in southern Africa.

1836-38 Afrikaners (white farmers of mainly Dutch descent) leave the Cape and British rule. These 'Voortrekkers' embark on the Great Trek north.

1867 Fortune-seekers descend after diamonds are discovered in Kimberley. The British seize control of the area in 1871.

1888 Cecil Rhodes's De Beers conglomerate takes over diamond operations in Kimberley.

1899-1902 Thousands of British soldiers and Boer guerrillas are killed in the Boer War, and thousands more women and children die in concentration camps. The war ultimately results in the formation of the British-ruled Union of South Africa in 1904.

1910 Britain grants independence, but the government of the Union of South Africa continues to recognise only the whites' rights.

1912 The South African Native National Congress (later the ANC) is founded.

1948 The National Party begins its domination of South African politics with election victory. Laws turn apartheid practices into official policy: ethnic groups are officially defined, separate institutions are created and intermarriage is outlawed.

1960 ANC President Albert Luthuli is awarded the Nobel Peace Prize. The ruling National Party Government officially leaves the Commonwealth and later becomes the Republic of South Africa. Many are killed during anti-pass law protests in Sharpeville. The ANC is then outlawed; the government declares the first State of Emergency.

1961-62 The ANC abandons non-violent protest and takes up arms against the government. Nelson Mandela undergoes training in Algeria, and on his return is arrested and sentenced to five years in prison.

1963-64 The leaders of the ANC's military wing are arrested and tried. Mandela sentenced to life imprisonment.

1976-77 A student revolt in Soweto ignites protests throughout the country, and tensions escalate when black-consciousness activist Steve Biko dies while in police custody.

1984 Cabinet minister Piet Koornhof announces that 'apartheid is dead'.

1985 Township leaders launch a civil disobedience campaign to protest against apartheid (which appears to be still alive), prompting the National Party to establish South Africa's third State of Emergency.

1990 President FW de Klerk announces the end of the ban on the ANC and authorises the release of political prisoners. Mandela released from prison and elected president of the ANC.

1993 Mandela and de Klerk share the Nobel Peace Prize.

1994 South Africa holds first free elections. The ANC wins with over 60 per cent of the vote, and on 10 May Nelson Mandela is inaugurated as President of the Republic of South Africa.

1995 Truth and Reconciliation Commission, chaired by Archbishop Desmond Tutu, is established to expose apartheid crimes.

1999 Thabo Mbeki is elected State President.

2004 South Africa wins the bid to host the 2010 FIFA World Cup.

2006 South Africa named a non-permanent member of the UN Security Council.

2009 Jacob Zuma elected president.

2010 South Africa hosts FIFA World Cup.

2013 A new political party, the Economic Freedom Fighters (EFF), is formed by Julius Malema, garnering the support of young black South Africans.

2013 On 5 December Nelson Mandela dies at age 95, after a prolonged respiratory infection.

2014 ANC wins majority in elections. Jacob Zuma assumes second term as president.

2014 Public protector Thuli Madonsela releases full Nkandla Report on spending on upgrades at the president's compound in KwaZulu-Natal.

2015 The Democratic Alliance, the official opposition, elects its first black leader, Mmusi Maimane.

IN CONTEXT

Architecture

Cape Town's mix of old and new buildings creates an edectic urban landscape.

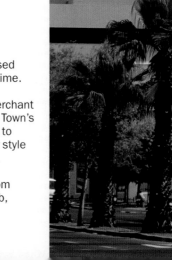

Early Cape Dutch buildings can be found dotted throughout the city, their style based on contemporary Dutch architecture of the time. Later arrivals, the British, brought Victorian architecture with them; rows of Victorian merchant warehouses still line Long Street. And Cape Town's many examples of art deco were an attempt to move away from the British idiom with a new style drawing on the ancient world for inspiration.

A leisurely morning's walk can reveal the interesting tale of the city's development from small Dutch settlement to cosmopolitan hub, told through its buildings.

Tuynhuys.

EARLY DAYS

In the mid 1600s, the city was little more than a trading post, set up by the Dutch East India Company (VOC) to provide food and water for its ships en route to Asia and the spice lands, and inhabited by VOC officials and settlers hoping to make a new life for themselves in this exotic, bountiful land. Over time, as merchants and the more well-off citizens came into their own, the architecture of the settlement began to take on the look and feel of a Dutch town, with typical steep pitched roofs. The architectural style morphed with the arrival of German sculptor Anton Anreith and Parisian architect Louis Thibault, who relished the opportunity to realise their creativity on the many buildings being constructed at the time. They brought new ideas and energy and the result is the Cape Dutch vernacular, typified by single-storey thatched and gabled homes, as well as flat-roofed, pedimented double-storey houses of the same period, many with the trademark 'T', 'U' and 'H' interior layout plans.

Koopmans de Wet Huis (see p50) has one of the most beautiful and well- preserved Cape Dutch vernacular façades in the city, thought to be the work of Louis Thibault and much

lauded for its symmetry and beautiful interior displays of antique Cape Dutch furniture.

Other fine examples of the style include **Martin Melck House** (96 Strand Street, City Centre), which was built in the style of a typical Dutch townhouse and has Cape Town's last surviving *dak kamer* or roof room. **Tuynhuys** in the Company Gardens was home to Dutch and English governors of the Cape for over 200 years. Its façade features a semicircular pediment with the Dutch East India Company logo. **Rust-en-Vreugd** (*see p51*) was built in 1777 and is characterised by its striking teak veranda and rococo-style upper-storey window by Anton Anreith. It is a typical 18th-century Cape Town upper-class house design – it's one of the city's finest examples of the style, and is also said to be one of its most haunted houses.

BRIGHT BUILDS

The **Bo-Kaap** (*see p65*) came into being as local artisans and families of freed slaves established their first homes in an area above – '*bo*' in Afrikaans – the city. The legacy of the predominantly Muslim population still remains, with the sounds of the muezzin calling the faithful to prayer a feature of the area's daily soundtrack. Rose and Wale streets are the main thoroughfares here, but wander the steep and narrow roads that branch off them and you'll get a little closer to the heart of the suburb. The **terraces** of Cape Dutch meets Edwardian-style cottages are painted in a spectrum of bright colours.

The building that now houses the **Bo-Kaap Museum** (see p65) was built in 1768. Today it is furnished as a typical Muslim home of the 19th century. Another important building for the area's history, **Auwal Mosque** (see p65), was built in 1798 as the first mosque in the Bo-Kaap. It is still very much in use. Today the building looks very different than it did at its inception, with only two of the original walls having remained intact after it collapsed back in the 1930s.

VICTORIAN RULE

British rule came to the Cape in 1814 and, in just a few years, merchants, tradesmen and missionaries were flocking to this imperial outpost to make their fortunes – or convert the locals. As they prospered, so their desire increased to transform the city from a rural Dutch settlement with open sewerage systems to a more sophisticated and 'civilised' town. Modern shops appeared and many Georgian-influenced red-brick homes were built. They stood in direct contrast to the typically whitewashed Cape Dutch buildings. Excellent examples of Cape Victorian architecture can be seen throughout the city, especially on **Long Street** (see p44), where tradesmen and wholesalers struck business deals in the warehouses that lined the streets.

Long Street still has its original street-level shop fronts, for premises that are now hip boutiques and restaurants. Many of these original buildings have been restored and their intricate styles enhanced with colourful coats of paint. 'Broekie lace' ironwork is typical of this vernacular and gives Cape Victorian architecture its 'prettied' look. Many of the upstairs balconies feature great examples of this Victorian ironwork.

Adderley Street in the City Centre also has many beautiful examples of Victorian architecture and was once full of smart shop fronts, while hip hangout **Origin Coffee** (28 Hudson Street, de Waterkant) is housed in a well-preserved Victorian warehouse on the outskirts of the original city.

The **Belmond Mount Nelson Hotel** (see p222) is a beautiful example of Victorian architecture, complete with interiors furnished to reflect this. Built in 1899, it is one of the city's most well-loved grand dames.

DECO DARLINGS

In among the quaint Victorian architecture and the Cape Dutch buildings so prevalent in the city are a series of buildings that stand out from the crowd. Much of the detailing so typical of the art deco era that began to take shape in the early 1900s takes its reference from ancient civilisations, despite the fact that deco emerged as a conscious move away from the styles of the past. Having been bruised in the Anglo-Boer war, South African architects of the period embraced the style that was so atypical of the British vernacular that had previously been so celebrated in this country.

IN CONTEXT

Adderley Street.

Cape Town has numerous examples of art deco architecture. The area of **Vredehoek** has the largest concentration of such buildings in one suburb in South Africa (visit Wexford, Bellair and Davenport roads for a taste).

Mutual Heights (14 Darling Street, City Centre) is the most noted art deco building in Africa, thanks to the fact that it was once the tallest building on the continent, as well as its immense deco detailing. Look out for a façade that incorporates carved figurines and triangular windows and stick your head in the door (it's now a swish apartment block) for a peek at the impressive marble banking hall.

Another superb example of art deco architecture is the **African Banking Corporation (ABC) Building** (130 Adderley Street, City Centre). Occupying an entire city block, it's a listed heritage building and is now occupied by the upmarket Riboville restaurant (complete with private dining in the bank vault). **Market House** (Greenmarket Square, City Centre), is an ornate example from the deco era, complete with detailed figurative and relief work on the exterior, while **Mullers Optometrists** (corner Parliament & Longmarket streets, City Centre), is a beautifully preserved building complete with original lead glass windows and chrome inlays in the façade.

MODERN LIVING

Though the various vernaculars of Cape Town architecture give an outstanding sense of the city's history, there's no denying the impact that some of the city's newer buildings have had on the urban landscape.

The FIFA 2010 World Cup not only brought about a massively updated public transport system – **Cape Town Station** (Strand Street, City Centre) underwent a major overhaul, with a new concourse and underground track system – but also a brand new stadium of immense proportions. Seating 55,000, **Cape Town Stadium** cost R4.4 billion and boasts high-tech design elements like the skin that covers the stadium to limit the force of the wind on it and the undulating roof. Designed to mimic the lines of Signal Hill behind it, it has a sculptural beauty. These days it hosts big international rock gigs as well as football games.

Cape Town International Convention Centre (1 Lower Long Street, Foreshore), meanwhile, is an exercise in clean lines and a contemporary approach to public building design. The CTICC resembles a large ship from the side situated closest to the V&A Waterfront, a reference to its proximity to the city's port.

The modernist structure of **Cape Town Jewish Museum** (88 Hatfield Street, City Centre) is clad in Jerusalem stone and acts as a bridge between old and new, joining the city's oldest synagogues and the Albow Centre, housing the Cape Town Holocaust Centre.

Cape Town's newest and tallest building is **Portside** (5 Buitengracht, Foreshore) completed in 2014 at a height of 139 metres. It may not be able to compete with buildings in New York or Dubai, but it has nevertheless impacted on the city's skyline.

Cape Town Stadium.

SCULPTING THE CITY

Old and new sculptures create heated debate.

IN CONTEXT

Mesmerising artworks are all around you in Cape Town. Here's our guide to the city's weird and wonderful sculpture.

The Knot (1981) by Eduardo Villa, perched behind the Civic Centre (12 Hertzog Boulevard), resembles an over-sized jungle gym, while **Mythological Landscape** (1992) by John Skotnes in Thibault Square (Hans Strijdom Avenue) is an intricate mishmash of animals and birds.

The sculpture set at **Pier Place** (Heerengracht Avenue) by Egon Tania (2007) is an uncanny depiction of the people that live and work in the city: a man on a bench, another walking while talking on his phone, a woman playing with her child and one carrying shopping. Life-sized and incredibly life-like too.

Africa (1999) by Brett Murray is St George's Mall's famously idiosyncratic sight: a totem-like sculpture covered in… Could it be Bart Simpson? Erupting from the smooth bronze African limbs and head are stylised heads of the American cartoon anti-hero in bright yellow plastic – it's the ultimate in mixed messages.

The Company's Gardens hosts older sculptures that recall the Cape's earlier history. Look out for the 1908 bronze cast of **Cecil John Rhodes** and a stone sculpture of **Jan Smuts**. In early 2015 a statue of Cecil John Rhodes was removed from the UCT campus after protests by students, sparking huge debate.

South Africa's four Nobel Peace laureates – **Albert Luthuli**, **Desmond Tutu**, **FW de Klerk** and **Nelson Mandela** – are honoured at the V&A Waterfront (*pictured*). The diminutive bronze statues here were created by Claudette Schreuders in 2006.

The **PharoX** is a five-storey-high star made from fencing reclaimed from Robben Island and unveiled at the end of 2014. It perches on the top of Signal Hill and is lit by LED lights at night. Created by Christopher Swift, it has raised some eyebrows in the public art and corporate funding debate as it is sponsored by Southern Sun hotel chain. The plan is to donate the lights to homes in Khayelitsha township after a year.

There's been huge controversy, too, over the **Perceiving Freedom** sculpture honouring Nelson Mandela – a giant pair of stainless steel Ray-Ban Wayfarer sunglasses on the Sea Point promenade looking out to sea and Robben Island. While artist Michael Elion defends his piece, it has been lambasted as thinly veiled commercial promotion.

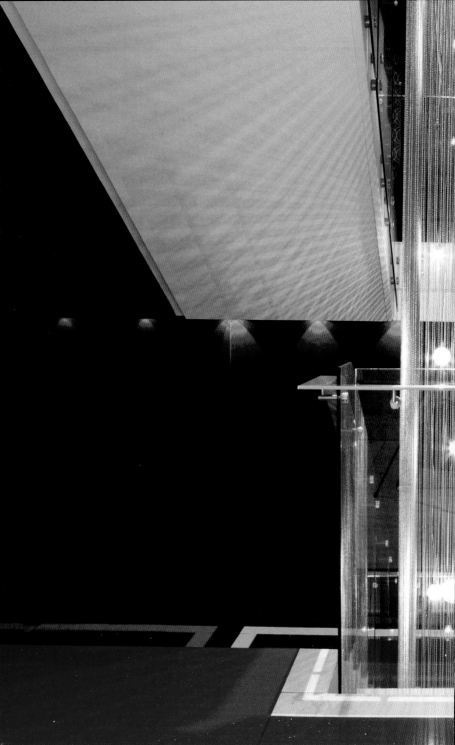

Essential Information

Hotels

Thanks to the 2010 Fifa World Cup, there isn't a shortage of beds in the Mother City. Luxury havens, boutique boltholes, self-catering apartments and good budget options are plentiful: the decision is more about where you want to be based, since there is a variety across the peninsula. Cape Town also makes the most of its eclectic and creative side with innovative sleeps (Airstream trailer, anyone?), as well as some seriously cool and fabulously funky options. While you're not necessarily going to get a bargain, despite the exchange rate, the winter months see many larger hotels offering decent special deals.

PRICES AND INFORMATION

Seasons see prices fluctuating dramatically, with high season from October until the end of April (or after the Easter holidays), with a peak during December and January, when local schools close for six weeks' holiday.

There are a variety of online booking resources available: try local sites www.safarinow.com and www.sa-venues.com as well as international ones such as www.booking.com.

If you prefer non-hotel accommodation, the Airbnb phenomenon means that you're likely to find an apartment or a house to suit pretty much any taste and price – an ideal option for longer stays. *See also p224* **Home from Home**.

CITY BOWL

Deluxe

★ Belmond Mount Nelson Hotel
76 Orange Street, Gardens (021 483 1000, www.mountnelson.co.za). **Rooms** 201. **Map** p254 G5.
The Nellie, as it's affectionately called, ticks all the boxes of old-world opulence. Rooms are awash in silks and velvets, the gardens perfectly manicured, the service is discreet and the amenities are spot-on. The spa and pool terrace are wonderful places to relax in during the day, or grab a seat on a ridiculously comfortable couch in the lounge and indulge in afternoon tea. Planet Bar offers delicious cocktails in a very sophisticated space, while chef Rudi Liebenberg plies his gastronomic magic at Planet restaurant. Disabled access.

Taj Cape Town
Cnr Wale Street & St George's Mall, City Centre (021 819 2000, www.tajcapetown.co.za). **Rooms** 176. **Map** p254 G4.
Opulence comes to town in the form of hallways glittering with marble and exquisite chandeliers. Set in the former reserve bank at the bottom of the Company's Garden, this five-star hotel boasts 176 rooms and suites decorated in a classic style, many with stunning mountain and Garden views. Expect all the bells and whistles, including walk-in closets and Molton Brown toiletries. The hotel restaurants add to the appeal, especially Bombay Brasserie with its authentic Indian cuisine, while Twankey Bar has a loyal local following. Head to Jiva Grande Spa for restorative Ayurvedic treatments. Disabled access.

Westin Cape Town
Convention Square, 1 Lower Long Street, City Centre (021 412 9999, www.westincapetown.com). **Rooms** 483. **Map** p254 H3.
A modern icon with expansive views over the harbour and V&A Waterfront, the Westin is preferred by business people and savvy travellers. Facilities at the glass-fronted hotel include a jazz bar, restaurants and gym. The spa, heated infinity pool and relaxation room on the 19th floor have the best views in the city. The hotel's location right next to the Cape Town International Convention Centre makes it an excellent choice. Disabled access.

Expensive

African Pride 15 on Orange Hotel

*Cnr Orange Street & Grey's Pass, Gardens
(021 469 8000, www.africanpridehotels.com).*
Rooms 129. **Map** p254 G4.

If you're a bit of an exhibitionist (or a voyeur), check in to one of the pod rooms that overlook the interior foyer and dining areas with a glass wall. All rooms are well equipped and spacious, with a modern edge. Quirky features such as a lift fitted with a golden armchair add to the vibe. The Murano Bar is perfect for a drink or two while admiring the mesmerising Murano glass chandelier. On the top floor is a pool as well as Suntra Spa. Disabled access.

Cape Cadogan

*5 Upper Union Street, Gardens (021 480 8080,
www.capecadogan.co.za).* **Rooms** 15. **Map** p252 F5.
Located just off lively Kloof Street, Cape Cadogan is a charming and elegant accommodation option set in a lovely Georgian/Victorian building. Choose from a hotel room, an apartment or the Owner's Villa. What sets the place apart is its sense of privacy in a quiet street, and the spacious rooms.

★ Cape Heritage Hotel

*90 Bree Street, City Centre (021 424 4646, http://
capeheritage.co.za).* **Rooms** 17. **Map** p254 G3.

With the city's oldest grape-bearing vine (dating from around 1781) in its courtyard, the Cape Heritage Hotel makes the most of its historical setting in an 18th-century building. The rooms and suites are exquisitely furnished, each in an individual style with original artworks, and also have all the contemporary features the modern traveller needs, such as luxurious bathrooms, air-conditioning, DVDs and a minibar. Original yellowwood floors, sash windows and teak beams dating back 200 years make this a remarkable place to stay.

Hilton Cape Town City Centre

*126 Buitengracht, Bo-Kaap (021 4813 700,
www3.hilton.com).* **Rooms** 137. **Map** p254 G3.
As you'd expect from the Hilton brand, this hotel caters well for both leisure and business travellers with its functional yet warmly decorated rooms and suites – many boasting wonderful views across the city and mountains. Numerous amenities for both work and play include an outdoor pool, a business centre, a north Indian restaurant, a relaxed bistro and a cool terrace overlooking Signal Hill. Disabled access.

Kensington Place

*38 Kensington Crescent, Higgovale (021 424 4744,
www.kensingtonplace.co.za).* **Rooms** 8.
One of the quintessential boutique hotels in Cape Town, Kensington Place is located in the leafy and sought-after suburb of Higgovale on the slopes of

ESSENTIAL INFORMATION

African Pride 15 on Orange Hotel.

HOME FROM HOME

Self-catering takes on a whole new meaning with these stylish spots.

Self-catering villas and apartments are still a good bet, especially if you're travelling with little ones or fancy a longer stay. Here is our pick of the best.

Top choice in the centre of the city is **Three Cities Mandela Rhodes Place Hotel & Spa** (021 481 400, www.mandelarhodesplace. co.za), where you can choose from studios to two-bed apartments. Glossy touches and a spa add to the appeal. **More Quarters** (021 487 556, www.morequarters.co.za) has set a new benchmark in self-catering accommodation. With exquisitely decorated apartments and even a house in its portfolio, it offers the privacy and comforts of self-catering, but also adds all the hotel amenities you can't live without, such as breakfast, Wi-Fi, concierge service, shuttles and babysitting.

Cape Royale Luxury Hotel (021 430 050, www.caperoyale.co.za) and the **Peninsula All-Suite Hotel** (021 430 777, www.peninsula. co.za) are perfectly situated for exploring the V&A Waterfront and are good family choices.

For something that's up there in the style stakes, why not book a private villa? **Cape Portfolios** (021 438 3416, www.cape portfolios.com), **Village & Life** (021 437 9700, www.villageandlife.com), **Icon Villas** (086 184 5527, www.iconvillas.travel) and **Cape Villa Rentals** (021 424 1777, www.capevilla rentals.com) have a phenomenal collection of buildings across the peninsula and further afield. Villas are ideal for larger groups too.

If you want to be in the centre of the action, head to **Daddy Long Legs** (*see p226*) in Long Street. Its eclectic and arty apartments are a well-priced option.

ESSENTIAL INFORMATION

Table Mountain. Contemporary luxury is the name of the game in the eight suites and the personal service is legendary – as is the breakfast. Relax by the pool, gaze at the view from your balcony or plan excursions with the concierge team.

Pepperclub Hotel & Spa

Cnr Loop & Pepper streets, City Centre (021 812 8888, www.pepperclub.co.za). **Rooms** 211. **Map** p254 G4.

A hot address in the city centre, Pepperclub is around the corner from buzzing Long Street and hip Bree Street. Rooms offer modern comfort and have fully equipped kitchens; many have outstanding views too. Facilities include a pool, gym and spa, as well as 24-hour concierge and a private cinema where you can feel like a movie star. They also offer shuttles to their private Beach Club in Camps Bay to add to the rock star vibe. Disabled access.

Southern Sun Cape Sun

Strand Street, City Centre (021 488 5100, www.tsogosunhotels.com). **Rooms** 368. **Map** p254 H4.

One of the grand dames of the Cape hotels, the Cape Sun is famous for its glass lifts, wonderfully illuminated at night and providing a bird's-eye view of the city skyline. All the usual facilities are provided, including a restaurant specialising in traditional Cape food, Camelot spa, an indoor pool and a gym. The lobby bar and lounge evoke a grand era. Disabled access.

Southern Sun the Cullinan

1 Cullinan Street, City Centre (021 415 4000, www.tsogosunhotels.com). **Rooms** 394. **Map** p254 H3.

Excellently located for both the V&A Waterfront and the city, the Cullinan offers everything you'd expect from a top-notch hotel chain. There's a large swimming pool, 24-hour room service and free Wi-Fi as well as a bar and restaurant. The rooms and suites are decorated in a luxe style with satins and velvets adorning beds and couches. Disabled access.

Moderate

Cape Milner

24 Milner Road, Tamboerskloof (021 426 1101, www.capemilner.com). **Rooms** 57. **Map** p252 F4.

Modern neutral tones with splashes of teal and mustard greet guests to this hotel. Rooms are stylishly comfortable and open bathrooms add to the contemporary feel. A vibey pool deck, gym and lounges add to the appeal. Disabled access.

Grand Daddy Boutique Hotel Cape Town

38 Long Street, City Centre (021 424 7247, www.granddaddy.co.za). **Rooms** 33. **Map** p254 H3.

Grand Daddy has an ideal location on Long Street. Rooms were designed by local style guru Tracy Lynch: expect vibrantly patterned wallpapers, soothing colours and interesting lighting, all echoing South

African themes in a subtle way. The Pink Flamingo Rooftop Cinema is a quirky spot for a movie, while the Daddy Cool bar brings bling to a new level and the Sky Bar offers fantastic views of the city and mountain. Disabled access. For Airstream trailer accommodation on the hotel's roof, *see p227* **In the Know**.

Ikhaya Lodge & Conference Centre

Dunkley Square, 8 Wandel Street, Gardens (021 461 8880, www.ikhayalodge.co.za). **Rooms** 11. **Map** p254 G5. With African-inspired decor, and decks and balconies overlooking greenery, you'd be forgiven for thinking you're in a more exotic tropical location. Rattan chairs, woven textiles and crafts adorn the rooms at Ikhaya, which means 'home' in Xhosa. Head to the restaurant for some authentic African fare.

★ Protea Hotel Fire & Ice! Cape Town

New Church Street & Bree Street, City Centre (021 488 2555, www.proteahotels.com). **Rooms** 213. **Map** p254 F4.

This is a fun spot to lay your head – if you can tear yourself away from the hotel facilities, that is. The first-floor swimming pool plays on a surfing theme, while the downstairs lobby bar is the place for live music and rockabilly nights, alcoholic milkshakes of the ginormous variety and a fun vibe all around. The light and airy restaurant is dotted with pots of herbs, and they make a mean hamburger too. Rooms are on the small side, but well designed to make the most of the space. Disabled access.

Southern Sun Waterfront Cape Town

1 Lower Buitengracht, City Centre (021 409 4000, www.tsogosunhotels.com). **Rooms** 534. **Map** p254 H3.

At the biggest hotel in the Mother City, you can expect a range of top amenities such as DStv, Wi-Fi and 24-hour room service, as well as a fitness centre and outdoor pool. Rooms are contemporary with splashes of bright colours in soft furnishings, and local landmarks showcased on the walls. Disabled access.

Urban Chic Boutique Hotel & Café

172 Long Street, City Centre (021 426 6119, www.urbanchic.co.za). **Rooms** 20. **Map** p254 F4.

The central location in Long Street and striking views of Table Mountain through the large windows make this hotel a popular choice, while its clean lines and contemporary feel are what set it apart from the rest. Pops of red and orange provide accents in the 20 suites. If you're keen for some pampering, why not get an in-room spa treatment? Disabled access.

Budget

Ashanti Lodge Backpackers

11 Hof Street, Gardens (021 423 8721, www.ashanti.co.za). **Rooms** 72 dorm beds, 18 private beds. **Map** p254 G5.

Twelve Apostles. *See p228.*

One of the best budget options in the city, this backpackers is set in a refurbished Victorian home and boasts a lovely pool and deck. Eat at the bar or cook at the communal kitchen. Accommodation ranges from camping and dorms to single or double rooms with shared bathrooms. Along the road you'll find two houses with rooms with their own ensuite bathrooms. There's also a travel centre on site. Ashanti has another hostel in Green Point, offering dorms and ensuite doubles.

Daddy Long Legs Art Hotel

134 Long Street, City Centre (021 422 3074, www. daddylonglegs.co.za). **Rooms** 13. **Map** p254 G4.
Daddy brought quirky to Long Street: the Daddy's World group offers self-catering apartments (*see p227* **Home from Home**) and the Art Hotel, as well as cool vintage trailers in the Overberg (*see p183* Old Mac Daddy in Elgin). For a riot of creativity, a night or two in the Art Hotel is a must. Each of the 13 rooms has been individually decorated by a local artist; opt for the endless Karoo views in Far From Home or access your inner diva in Please Do Not Disturb, which is done up like a sound studio and stage.

Glam

40 Burg Street, City Centre (021 424 1006, www.theglam.co.za). **Rooms** 10. **Map** p254 G4.
Just because it's budget doesn't mean it can't be glamorous. Stylish black and white decor celebrating movie

stars of yester year set the tone at this historic building in the centre of town. Some rooms offer shared ablution facilities, but some have their own bathrooms. The Glam provides a fashionable new benchmark in budget accommodation. Disabled access.

WOODSTOCK
Moderate

DoubleTree by Hilton Cape Town – Upper Eastside

31 Brickfield Road (021 404 0570, http:// doubletree3.hilton.com). **Rooms** 183.
The opening of this fashionable hotel is ample proof of Woodstock's gentrification. Decor in the public areas is opulent, bold and bright, while the guest rooms are pared-down contemporary in style. Loft suites have a kitchen and dining area. A fitness room, beauty salon, business centre and babysitting services are just some of the facilities on offer. Disabled access.

ATLANTIC SEABOARD
Deluxe

★ Cape Grace

West Quay Road, V&A Waterfront (021 410 7100, www.capegrace.com). **Rooms** 120. **Map** p252 H2.

One of the most discreetly exclusive hotels in Cape Town, the Cape Grace is frequented by the rich and famous who want to keep a low profile. With its location in the heart of the V&A and yacht marina, five-star service and variety of suites (from penthouse to three-bedroomed), this hotel oozes class. The classic decor, with historic artefacts, adds to the appeal, as do the in-house Signal restaurant (the Sunday brunch is legendary) and popular Bascule bar with its impressive whisky collection. Disabled access.

Ellerman House

180 Kloof Road, Bantry Bay (021 430 3200, www.ellerman.co.za). **Rooms** 13. **Map** p250 A4.
Expansive views of the Atlantic aren't the only reason to stay at this superior boutique hotel. An impressive art collection, library, spa, lap pool, gym, whisky bar, excellent cuisine and purpose-built gallery showcasing South African wine – all in a perfectly private setting – ensure this is at the top of the list for the discerning traveller. As well as rooms in the main house, there are two spectacular villas, ideal for groups.

★ One&Only Cape Town

Dock Road, V&A Waterfront (021 431 5800, http://capetown.oneandonlyresorts.com). **Rooms** 131. **Map** p252 G2.
Despite its size and status, or maybe because of it, you'll receive a very warm welcome at One&Only Cape Town. Choose from rooms and suites in Marina Rise or head to the Island Suites for a true resort feel, as these are reached via a bridge over the canal and hidden behind tropical foliage. Relax around the spacious infinity pool, head to Vista bar and lounge for cocktails or high tea, enjoy local fare at Reuben's restaurant or feast on sushi and Asian/South American fusion dishes at stylish Nobu. The spa is one of the best on the continent, with heated jet pools, steam rooms and quality treatments – you will leave blissed out. Your child may never want to leave either: the KidsOnly Club offers supervised games, activities and crafts, while the numerous baby amenities will keep any baby, and parent, happy. Disabled access.

IN THE KNOW
TRAILER-PARK DREAMS

One of the most original sleeps in the city is the rooftop trailer park on top of the **Grand Daddy Boutique Hotel** (see *p225*). The seven Airstream trailers have been whimsically decorated with road trip themes, so expect beach house, safari and, our favourite, gold rush, with blinged-out headboards and golden skulls dotted about. Each trailer comes with a fridge, TV, shower and air-con, so you can be quirky in comfort.

IN THE KNOW
BRAND-NEW BEDS

A massive hotel complex is currently under construction in the city centre, following a R680 million investment by the Tsogo Sun group. Set to open in September 2017, it will include a 200-bedroom SunSquare hotel and 300-bedroom StayEasy hotel, as well as conference venues, restaurants and parking.

Sun the Table Bay

Quay Six, V&A Waterfront (021 406 5000, www.suninternational.com). **Rooms** 329. **Map** p253 H1.

In the heart of the V&A Waterfront and with a walkway directly linked to the mall, the Table Bay offers classic luxury and supreme comfort. The classy Camissa Brasserie offers a quality dining experience, while afternoon tea enjoyed in the airy lounge is one of the highlights to look forward to at this five-star establishment. Disabled access.

★ Twelve Apostles

Victoria Road, Camps Bay (021 437 9255, www.12apostleshotel.com). **Rooms** 70.

Is this the best located hotel in town? It hangs on the edge of the fynbos-clad mountain overlooking the tempestuous Atlantic. Rooms and suites face either the mountain or the sea (both are equally stunning), and decor echoes the seaside location with a multitude of blue hues. Sundowners at the Leopard Bar are a must, while dinner at Azure makes the most of local ingredients showcased in classic dishes and modern versions of South African favourites. For proper pampering, head to the spa with plunge pools set in underground rock; or enjoy movie night at the 16-seat private cinema. Disabled access. *Photos pp226-227.*

Expensive

Bay Hotel

69 Victoria Road, Camps Bay (021 430 4444, www.thebay.co.za). **Rooms** 78. **Map** p251 A8.

Who needs the beach right across the road when there are four hotel pools to choose from? Situated on the Camps Bay strip, the Bay Hotel is ideally located for leisure seekers. Head to the beach (if you must), grab a drink at one of the many bars on the road or opt for a massage at the spa with its sauna and steam room. Rooms and suites have a bright and airy feel in keeping with the beachside location. Disabled access.

Hout Bay Manor

Baviaanskloof, off Main Road, Hout Bay (021 790 0116, www.houtbaymanor.com). **Rooms** 16.

This chic hotel in a historic building makes a funky nod to its African setting through clever decor touches that combine ethnic and opulent styles. The in-house restaurant, Pure, offers flavoursome food, sourced locally, while the Inzolo Wellness Suite is the place to go for restorative treatments using African ingredients.

Marly

201 The Promenade, Victoria Road, Camps Bay (021 437 1287, www.themarly.co.za). **Rooms** 11. **Map** p250 A8.

The Marly's seriously sexy rooms – all in crisp, cool whites, from the Barcelona chairs to the marbled bathrooms – are visions in contemporary opulence. Cleverly placed feature mirrors reflect the ocean views. Luxurious, indulgent touches include a bath butler service, your own Jacuzzi (in two of the suites) and the relaxing poolside terrace.

O on Kloof Boutique Hotel & Spa

92 Kloof Road, Bantry Bay (021 439 2081, www.oonkloof.co.za). **Rooms** 8. **Map** p251 B4.

O on Kloof offers modern boutique luxury at its best. There's a gym, library, sun deck with Jacuzzi, heated indoor pool, bar and alfresco dining. Rooms are sumptuous, bathrooms are marbled and there is an in-house spa – if you're in need of even more pampering. It is clear why this boutique hotel has been showered with accolades and awards.

Moderate

Chapmans Peak Beach Hotel

Chapman's Peak Drive, Hout Bay (021 790 1036, www.chapmanspeakhotel.com). **Rooms** 32.

Clean lines with splashes of blue echoing the sea views are the hallmark of the tidy bedrooms at this well located hotel. For the best views, book one of the penthouse suites. Head to the restaurant's sun terrace for a great meal of seafood (the calamari is delicious) or steak, or simply grab a drink at the sociable bar. Disabled access.

Protea Hotel Victoria Junction Waterfront

Somerset & Ebenezer Roads, Green Point (021 418 1234, www.proteahotels.com). **Rooms** 172. **Map** p254 G2.

The bold, modern rooms here have bare-brick walls for added urban appeal. There are also double-storey loft apartments, which are ideal if you are planning a longer stay. You can break a sweat in the gym and pool, then socialise in the on-site bar and restaurant. Disabled access.

Winchester Mansions

221 Beach Road, Sea Point (021 434 2351, www.winchester.co.za). **Rooms** 76. **Map** p250 C2.

Old-world elegance personified, Winchester Mansions is wonderfully located on the Sea Point

Promenade. Harvey's Bar verandah is packed during summer for sundowners, while the hotel's leafy inner courtyard is the place for Sunday jazz brunches. Choose between rooms with a classic or contemporary design. Disabled access.

SOUTHERN SUBURBS

Deluxe

★ Cellars-Hohenort

93 Brommersvlei Road, Constantia (021 794 2137, www.cellars-hohenort.com). **Rooms** 52.

Deep in the heart of leafy Constantia is this exquisite hotel surrounded by acres of beautiful gardens. Echoing the historic setting, the rooms and suites are lavishly furnished in soothing whites and creams. Money no object? Book the separate Madiba Villa with its three double bedrooms and private pool. There are also tennis courts, golf facilities and the tranquil Fresh Wellness Spa. This is also a gastronomic destination of note. The Martini Bar pops with colour, while the Fern Bar is a tranquil space in which to enjoy a drink before dinner at the elegant Greenhouse restaurant, which celebrates South African produce with international flair. For a more relaxed meal, there's the Conservatory, set around a 200-year-old oak tree surrounded by glass.

Expensive

Alphen Boutique Hotel

Alphen Drive, Constantia (021 795 6300, www.alphen.co.za). **Rooms** 19.

Over-the-top opulence awaits at this heritage hotel set amid 11 acres of perfectly manicured gardens. Suites combine modern amenities such as Wi-Fi, docking stations and espresso machines with upmarket glamour. Relax in daybeds next to the pool, or head to the Rose Bar for drinks, 5 Rooms for fine dining or La Belle Bistro & Bakery for homemade treats and great breakfasts.

Steenberg Hotel

Steenberg Estate, Tokai Road, Tokai (021 713 2222, www.steenbergfarm.com). **Rooms** 24.

Set on what's claimed to be the Cape's first farm, founded in 1682, Steenberg has much to offer visitors, including an 18-hole golf course. Rooms and suites are decorated in a Cape colonial style, filled with dark woods and interesting art pieces – especially the double-storey 'heritage suites'. Some rooms are more contemporary in design, but no less luxurious. Facilities include the excellent Ginkgo Spa and a host of eating options: you can enjoy tapas and Mediterranean-inspired dishes at chic Bistro Sixteen82, try wines at the adjoining tasting room, or head to Catharina's for a curated wine list and gourmet fare.

Vineyard Hotel

Colinton Road, Newlands (021 657 4500, www.vineyard.co.za). **Rooms** 207.

Magnificent gardens and walkways next to the bubbling Liesbeek River make this hotel a haven for both guests and day visitors. Once the home of Lady Anne Barnard, the hotel displays antiques and items of historical significance in the common areas. Suites ooze contemporary comfort and make the most of garden and mountain views. Spend the morning at the internationally renowned Angsana Spa, where Thai therapists will work your muscles into submission, before heading to the Square for a light lunch – salads, gourmet sandwiches, burgers and steak; come evening, the menu focuses on South African classics. There's also fusion cuisine at Myoga restaurant and a poolside café. Look out for the gigantic resident tortoises roaming around the gardens. Disabled access.

SOUTHERN PENINSULA

Expensive

Rodwell House

Rodwell Road, St James (021 787 9898, www.rodwellhouse.co.za). **Rooms** 8.

The St James tidal pool welcomes guests to this majestic five-star mansion. Each of the eight suites is individually decorated, with original art and antique furniture to the fore. On a sunny day, relax on the terraces or in the attractive poolside garden.

Moderate

Monkey Valley Resort

Mountain Road, Noordhoek (021 789 8000, www.monkeyvalleyresort.com). **Rooms** 38.

For rustic comfort overlooking the endless Noordhoek beach, come to Monkey Valley. Hidden in a milkwood forest, boardwalks link charming wooden cottages with decks, a restaurant and a pool. The cabins have thatched roofs and self-catering facilities, or you can book a room in the main building – many come with fireplaces and their own decks. The resort's direct access to the beach is a bonus. Disabled access.

Budget

Simon's Town Quayside Hotel

Jubilee Square, St Georges Street, Simon's Town (021 786 3838, www.quaysidehotel.co.za). **Rooms** 26.

Ships ahoy at this hotel overlooking the yacht basin in Simon's Town. The nautical theme extends into the rooms, which are basic but comfortable. The central location means most of Simon's Town's sights are within easy walking distance. Disabled access.

Getting Around

ARRIVING & LEAVING

By air

Cape Town International Airport
021 937 1200, www.acsa.co.za.
The airport is about 22km from
Cape Town's city centre and the
N2 highway is the fastest and
most direct route between the two.
Excluding any unexpected delays,
it should take you about 30 minutes
to drive into the centre outside
peak hours (7-9am and 4.30-6pm);
otherwise it can easily take up to an
hour. Reputable airport car rental
companies include **Avis** (www.avis.
co.za), **Hertz** (www.hertz.co.za),
Europcar (www.europcar.co.za)
and **Budget** (www.budget.co.za).

If you are not driving, you can
make your way to the city with one
of the airport's shuttle services such
as **Airport Shuttle Cape Town**
(www.airportshuttlecapetown.co.za)
or **Citi Hopper** (www.citihopper.
co.za). Alternatively, you can
organise a **Rikkis** shuttle (0861
745547, www.rikkis.co.za) or take
an **Uber** (www.uber.com) ride.
Depending on which company you
use, the journey to the centre should
cost R350.

There is a **MyCiti** (http://myciti.
org.za) bus stop at the airport; buses
run to the centre of Cape Town every
30 minutes (5.30am-9.30pm Mon-Fri;
6.30am-9.30pm Sat, Sun).

Major airlines

Besides the national carrier, **South
African Airways** (www.flysaa.
com), other international airlines
with direct flights to Cape Town
include **British Airways** (www.
britishairways.com), **KLM** (www.
klm.com), **Air Namibia** (www.air
namibia.com), **Emirates** (www.
emirates.com), **Singapore Airlines**
(www.singaporeair.com) and **Air
Mauritius** (www.airmauritius.com).
Domestic carriers are **SAA**
(www.flysaa.co.za), **Airlink**
(www.saairlink.co.za) and **British
Airways** (www.ba.co.za). There are
always flight specials on offer at the
various carriers, so it's a good idea to
keep checking their websites. There
are three budget domestic airlines,
namely **Kulula.com** (www.kulula.
com), **Mango** (www.flymango.com)
and newly launched **Fly Safair**
(www.flysafair.co.za) and **Skywise**

(www.skywise.co.za) which offer
good deals, although you'll be paying
in cash for snacks and drinks.

PUBLIC TRANSPORT

Plans are currently under way by
the City of Cape Town to roll out a
MyConnect system, whereby trips
on MyCiti buses, minibus taxis and
Metrorail trains can be undertaken
with a single card.

A useful contact is the City of
Cape Town's Transport Information
Centre (TIC) – 080 065 64 63.

Buses

Cape Town's public transport has
received a boost thanks to the
modern, efficient **MyCiti** bus
service. Buy a card at convenience
stores or major stops. It's easy to
navigate and links the city and
Atlantic Seaboard up to Hout Bay
with ease. Visit www.myciti.org.za
for more information.

The **City Sightseeing** bus
(www.citysightseeing.co.za) caters to
foreigners, touring the expanses of
the Southern Peninsula on the Blue
Route, exploring the City Bowl sights
on the Red Route, hopping around
downtown on the Yellow Route and
doing some wine-tasting on the
Purple Route. The first bus leaves
from the Aquarium at the V&A
Waterfront at around 9am (and every
20 minutes thereafter until 7pm and
later in summer). Day tickets (where
you can hop on and off to your heart's
content) will set you back about R170.

Minibus taxis

In South Africa the term 'taxi' can
refer either to a meter-running sedan
vehicle (*see below*) or to a gung-ho,
packed-to-the-rafters minibus. The
latter is one of the country's most
popular modes of transport because
they're cheap (about R10 for an inner-
city trip) and super-speedy. However
the driving is notoriously erratic and
many vehicles leave a lot to be desired
safety-wise.

Taxis

Sedan taxis are also an ever-present
fixture in the city, but are more
expensive, charging around R12
a kilometre. The Cape Town
Tourism Visitor Information

Centre (021 426 4260) will point you
in the right direction with a list of
their recommended taxi companies.

Call **Rikkis** taxis (086 174 5547,
www.rikkis.co.za) for free from one
of the many canary-yellow Rikki
phones scattered about the city. Fares
are fixed-rate rather than metered,
so it works out better value than
ordinary taxis if you are taking a
long journey or sharing the ride
with others. **Uber** (www.uber.com)
has taken Cape Town by storm and
provides a service that is reliable
and safe. Download the app for
your phone.

Trains

The Cape Town railway service,
Metrorail (www.capemetrorail.
co.za), is not reliable, with local
trains being bang on time one day
and hopelessly delayed the next –
so don't bank on this mode of
transport if you need to be punctual.
The **Cape Town Railway Station**
(080 065 6463) in Adderley Street is
the centre of all train networks in the
Western Cape and has recently had
a welcome facelift.

The safest time to travel is
between 7am and 9am and 4pm and
6pm. Minimise unnecessary risks
by travelling first class and keeping
all your valuables close at hand and
out of sight. Most long-distance
trains have dining cars and catering
trolleys, and it's definitely worth
opting for a first-class cabin. Ticket
prices and timetables are available
from **Shosholoza Meyl** (086 000
8888, www.shosholozameyl.co.za).

If you really want to splash out,
there's also the option of travelling
up-country with one of South Africa's
two luxury train services. The **Blue
Train** (www.bluetrain.co.za) or
Rovos Rail (www.rovos.co.za).

CYCLING

There are several options if you have
a penchant for getting about on two
wheels rather than four. You can hire
a bicycle from the adventure travel
experts, **Downhill Adventures**
(021 422 0388, www.downhill
adventures.com), **Cape Town
Cycle Hire** (www.capetowncycle
hire.co.za) and **Bike & Saddle**
(www.bikeandsaddle.com). **Cape
Bike Rentals** (www.capebike
rentals.com) offers bike and scooter

rentals, or you can rent a Harley from **Harley-Davidson Cape Town** (021 401 4260, www.harley-davidson-capetown.com).

DRIVING

Driving is on the left. Maybe it's the fresh mountain air or the sunshine and sea breezes, but Capetonians seem pretty casual in their approach to driving: they aren't particularly bothered about trivialities like indicating before changing lanes or checking their blind spots, and minibus taxis are no exception. Road safety statistics aren't much to shout about either – drink driving and speeding are the biggest culprits for accidents, especially at Christmas. Don't take unnecessary (and pricey) risks by speeding or driving under the influence; it's just not worth it.

Vehicle hire

If you're over 25 and have an international driver's licence, hiring a car in the Mother City is easy. There's a list of rental agencies as long as your arm, but the most reputable of these remain **Avis** (www.avis.co.za) and **Europcar** (www.europcar.co.za). The rates are generally worked out according to the amount of kilometres travelled. It's worth doing comparative price checks beforehand – some agencies offer specials like free mileage. 'No frills' rental companies include **Value Car Hire** (www.valuecarhire.com) and **Budget** (www.budget.co.za).

Petrol stations

There's no shortage of petrol (gas) stations in the city, particularly along main roads such as Buitengracht, Orange and Somerset Roads.

Most of these stations are open 24 hours, and most have convenience stores offering midnight snacks and essentials, but it's never advisable to drive around in the sticks if you are low on petrol. At the time of writing, petrol cost R12.46 per litre in coastal areas (it's more expensive inland). It's customary to tip your pump attendant or 'petrol jockey' R5-R10 after filling up, if you've had good service and a friendly smile.

Insurance

Make sure to establish whether or not your car insurance covers road damage to the car – driving around on gravel roads tends to be tricky, and even dangerous. When renting a car, check your agreement for all details pertaining to damage and liability insurance, as levels of cover vary. If you don't have a home policy that covers you for every eventuality, it's best to pre-book via a multinational car hire company while still in your home country.

Parking

Although Capetonians still moan about paying for parking in the city centre, there are plenty of parking lots dotted about. If you park on the street, pay the parking monitor in cash upfront – you'll be issued with a printed receipt.

When parking on the street during the day, don't under any circumstances leave your car on a yellow or red line, because your vehicle will be fined, clamped or towed, resulting in a painfully tedious and pricey recovery process. If your car has been towed, contact the traffic department's towing section (021 406 8861).

Make sure to park in a well-lit, populated area if you can't find an official parking lot when going out at night.

WALKING

Apart from the City Bowl, which is easily navigable on foot, the rest of Cape Town is really more of a driver's town, predominantly because of the distances involved, but also because it's the safest way to get around. The city centre, V&A Waterfront and beachside promenades lend themselves to leisurely strolling and are quite safe thanks to efforts made through local initiatives and authorities. Walking around the periphery of the City Bowl on your own isn't advisable if you're unfamiliar with the area though – tourists unfortunately make the softest targets. Here are some general safety tips worth bearing in mind:
● Avoid dark, isolated areas.
● Don't walk alone.
● When lost, try to find a police or traffic officer, or go to the nearest shop or petrol station to ask for directions.
● Wearing a flashy camera around your neck is tantamount to carrying a neon sign flashing, 'Tourist!'. If you're packing valuables, keep them in a backpack or shoulder bag and carry it close to your body.
● Never carry large sums of cash with you. Keep small change in your wallet or purse and bank notes and credit cards in an inside pocket.
● Steer clear of anyone claiming to have a stash of Calvin Klein perfume at a special discount or offering you the opportunity to get rich quickly. Sadly, there are also con artists who'll play on your sympathies to make a quick buck.
● When in doubt, call a cab. Always carry the number of a reliable company (*see p230*).

ESSENTIAL INFORMATION

Resources A-Z

AGE RESTRICTIONS

The legal age for both driving and buying (and drinking) alcohol is 18. The age of consent is 16. Smoking and purchasing tobacco is legal for people over 16.

ATTITUDE & ETIQUETTE

A generally friendly, informal atmosphere reigns in South Africa and people usually introduce themselves by their first name, even in the context of business relationships. As a rule of thumb, Capetonians are more relaxed and laid back than their Gauteng brethren – much to the disdain of many people from Gauteng. Most organised events start on time, but a true Capetonian will always manage to be at least half an hour late for informal gatherings.

BUSINESS

Business organisations

Cape Chamber House
19 Louis Gradner Street, City Bowl
(021 402 4300, www.capechamber. co.za).
The Cape Regional Chamber is the principal source for business information and services. Cape Town is regarded as the hub of South African commerce.

Wesgro
021 487 8600, www.wesgro.co.za.
Wesgro is the official Trade and Investment Promotion Agency for the Western Cape and is the first point of contact for local exporters, foreign importers and investors wishing to take advantage of investment opportunities in the Cape.

Conventions & conferences

Cape Town International Convention Centre
021 410 5000, www.cticc.co.za.
A strong array of facilities, including a dedicated exhibition space and generous facilities for both meetings and banquets.

Couriers

DHL Worldwide Express
086 034 5000, www.dhl.co.za.
Fedex *080 003 3339,*
www.fedex.com/za.
TNT *086 012 2441, www.tnt.com.*
XPS *086 000 0977, www.xps.co.za.*
UPS *021 555 2745, www.ups.com.*

Shipping

Britannia *021 556 9448,*
www.britannia.co.za.
Island View Shipping *021 425 2285, www.ivs.co.za.*

Translators & interpreters

Folio Online *021 426 2727,*
www.folio-online.co.za.
SATI – South African Translators' Institute *021 976 9563, 011 803 2681, www.translators.org.za.*

CONSUMER AFFAIRS

Call these organisations with any consumer-related problems, enquiries and complaints:

Consumer Affairs Office
021 483 5133.
Consumer Complaint Line
0800 007 081.

CUSTOMS

There is a huge list of prohibited goods. Visit www.sars.gov.za to view the list and follow the Customs link, or call 086 012 1218.

Used personal effects are duty free, as are new personal effects up to the value of R3,000. For additional goods up to the value of R12,000, a flat rate of 20% duty will be charged. Other allowances for visitors to South Africa are as follows (per adult):
1 litre of spirits
2 litres of wine
400 cigarettes
50 cigars
50ml perfume
250ml eau de toilette

People under 18 are not allowed to bring any tobacco or alcohol products into the country, and adults need a permit for firearms (available at entry points, valid for 180 days).

DISABLED

Since Cape Town is such a major international tourist destination, most of its hotels, attractions and malls have some form of disabled access and are usually graded according to how disabled-friendly they are. If you're disabled you can usually arrange with your airline for someone to come and meet you on arrival and they will also make the necessary arrangements for you while on board the plane. Most reputable car-hire companies provide vehicles with hand control. For any further enquiries phone the Association for the Physically Disabled (011 646 8331, www.apd. org.za), based in Johannesburg or, for the blind, the SA National Council for the Blind (012 452 3811, www. sancb.org.za), based in Pretoria.

DRUGS

Cannabis, or dagga as it's locally known, is available around some dodgy street corners in Cape Town, but it remains illegal, and its possession is a punishable offence. Harder drugs are also available, but once again, prohibited and could land you in prison if you are caught with them in your possession. Cape Town also has a huge problem with the drugs mandrax (or buttons), heroin, crack cocaine and especially crystal meth, locally know as tik.

ELECTRICITY

The power supply in South Africa is 220/230 volts AC. The standard plug in South Africa is the 15-amp round-pin, three-prong plug. Euro- and US-style two-pin plugs, and UK-style three-pin plugs, can be used with an adaptor, available at supermarkets; bring transformers along for larger appliances where necessary. Most hotels have 110-volt outlets for electric shavers.

Due to shortages by electricity provider, Eskom, there are frequent power outages, known as load shedding. There are now apps available that indicate when the next one will occur, and towns are divided into sections (central Cape Town and Atlantic Seaboard fall into zone 7), and various stages mean load shedding at different times. It gets complicated, so be sure that your phone is charged and keep a small torch handy.

EMBASSIES & CONSULATES

Check the local phone book or *Yellow Pages* for a complete list of foreign consulates and embassies in Cape Town, or call directory enquiries on 1023.

British Consulate General
Southern Life Centre, 8 Riebeek Street, City Centre (021 405 2400). **Map** p254 H3.

Canadian Consulate General
19th Floor, Reserve Bank Building, 60 St George's Mall, City Centre (021 423 5240). **Map** p254 H4.

French Consulate
78 Queen Victoria Street, Gardens (021 423 1575). **Map** p254 G4.

German Consulate General & Embassy
19th Floor, Safmarine House, 22 Riebeek Street, City Centre (021 405 3000). **Map** p254 H3.

Netherlands Consulate General
100 Strand Street, corner Buitengracht, City Centre (021 421 5660). **Map** p254 G3.

US Consulate
2 Reddam Avenue, Westlake, Tokai (021 702 7300).

EMERGENCIES

Ambulance *10177.*
ER24 (private EMS) *084 124.*
Fire *021 480 7700.*
General emergencies *107* from a landline, *021 480 7700* or *112* from a mobile phone.
Mountain Rescue Service *021 948 9900.*
Netcare (private EMS) *0860 638 2273.*
Poison Crisis Centre *021 689 5227.*
Poison Information *0800 333 444.*
Police *10111.*
Red Cross War Memorial Children's Hospital *021 658 5111.*
National Sea Rescue Institute *021 449 3500.*

GAY & LESBIAN

For more on gay and lesbian Cape Town, *see pp157-161.*

Triangle Project *021 686 1475, helpline 021 712 6699, www. triangle.org.za.*
Counselling, medical services, confidential HIV testing. For more on HIV/AIDS, *see right.*

HEALTH

Cape Town has a number of private and public hospitals. Tourists are recommended to use the private ones for treatment, as the doctor-to-patient ratio is much better, facilities are cleaner and there is less waiting time – and any costs should be paid by your travel and medical insurance cover. Cape Town's hospitals are considered to be world-class and have a high standard of both medical facilities and expertise.

Contraception & abortion

Government hospitals and clinics offer free services like family planning counselling, pregnancy tests and abortions to both South Africans and tourists. Free contraceptive pills are handed out at most family planning clinics, and condoms are readily available at clinics and most public toilets in Cape Town. Over-the-counter pregnancy tests are available from most Clicks (a health, beauty and pharmacy chain store) outlets and can be bought for around R30, while the morning-after pill can cost anywhere from R40 to R90.

Doctors & dentists

Both the Talking Yellow Pages (10118) and Cape Town Tourism Bureau (021 426 5639, www. tourismcapetown.co.za) should be able to supply you with a list of registered medical practitioners and dentists in or near the area where you are staying. However, if you're a tourist wanting to visit a doctor or dentist, you'll probably be expected to pay your bill up front.

Netcare Travel Clinic
Room 1107, 11th Floor, Picbel Parkade, 58 Strand Street (021 419 3172, www.travelclinic.co.za). **Map** 254 H3.
A national network of specialised mobile medical centres offering services to locals and tourists. Services include immunisations, pre- and post-travel examinations, malaria pills and first-aid travel kits.

Helplines

All helplines run 24 hours a day, seven days a week.

Alcoholics Anonymous
021 510 2288.
Childline
0800 055 555.
Gender Violence Helpline
0800 150 150, www.stopwomen abusehelpline.org.za.
LifeLine
021 461 1111, www.lifeline.co.za.
Narcotics Anonymous
083 900 69 62, www.na.org.za.
National AIDS Helpline
0800 012 322.
Rape Crisis Centre
021 447 9762, www.rapecrisis.org.za.

HIV & AIDS

South Africa's AIDS and HIV statistics are among the highest in the world, resulting in millions of rand having been invested in HIV/AIDS research and educational programmes, that are now of a first-world standard. If you suspect that you might have contracted the virus call the National AIDS Helpline (0800 012 322) immediately for assistance and anti-retroviral treatment.

Other clinics providing support and assistance to HIV/AIDS sufferers include the following:

Cape Town Reproductive Health Centre *Shop no P21 E, 1st floor, Adderley Street, Golden Acre (021 425 2004).* **Map** p254 H4.

Chapel Street Clinic *Corner Chapel & Balfour Streets, Woodstock (021 465 2793).*

Dorp Street Reproductive Health Clinic *3 Dorp Street, City Centre (021 483 4662).* **Map** *p254 G2.*

Marie Stopes *91 Bree Street, City Centre (080 011 7785).* **Map** *p254 G3.*

Hospitals

Cape Town MediClinic *21 Hof Street, Oranjezicht, City Bowl (021 464 5555, www.mediclinic.co.za).* **Map** *p252 G5.*

Groote Schuur Hospital *Main Road, Observatory (021 404 9111, www.gsh.co.za).*

Netcare Christiaan Barnard Memorial Hospital *181 Longmarket Street (021 480 6111); Accident and Emergency Room (021 480 6171/2).* **Map** *p254 G3.*

Pharmacies

These pharmacies are all open late:

Clicks Glengariff Pharmacy *2 Main Road, Sea Point (021 434 8622).* **Open** 8.30am-8pm Mon, Tue, Thur, Fri; 9am-8pm

Wed; 8.30am-7pm Sat; 9am-7pm Sun. **Map** p251 B3.

Lite-Kem Pharmacy *24 Darling Street, City Centre (021 461 8040).* **Open** 8.30am-11pm Mon-Fri; 9am-11pm Sat, Sun. **Map** p254 H4.

ID

Since it's the legal age for drinking alcohol, you have to be 18 years or older to get into a club. However, bouncers rarely ask for ID unless you look like a teenager. Don't carry your passport with you when sightseeing for the day. Instead, it's better to leave it in your hotel safe.

INSURANCE

As is the case in all countries, you are strongly advised to take out travel insurance that also covers repatriation to your home country in the event of serious medical problems or accidents.

INTERNET

Most hotels in Cape Town have Wi-Fi as do restaurants and cafés. Speed, though, does not compare to Europe or the States, so be prepared to be patient when waiting for downloads.

LANGUAGE

South Africa has no fewer than 11 official languages: Afrikaans, English, Ndebele, Sepedi, Sesotho, Setswana, siSwati, Tsonga, Venda, Xhosa and Zulu.

In the Western Cape, English, Afrikaans and Xhosa are the most commonly spoken. Since there is such a large international community based in Cape Town, staff at some establishments and attractions speak other languages, principally German, French or Italian.

LEFT LUGGAGE

Left Luggage *Cape Town Airport, Ground Floor, Parkade 2 (072 384 2954)*

LEGAL HELP

Cape Law Society *29th & 30th Floors, ABSA Centre, c, City Bowl (021 443 6700).* **Map** p254 H3.

Legal Resources Centre *54 Shortmarket Street, City Bowl (021 481 3000).* **Map** p254 H4.

Leza Legal Wise *Office 1, Thibault Square Pavillion, Thibault Square, City Bowl (021 419 6905).* **Map** p254 H3.

LIBRARIES

You can register as a temporary member at any Cape Town City Library branch (see the telephone directory under Municipality of Cape Town for local branch details). City Library Head Office (021 467 1500) can also help.

LOST PROPERTY

If you're missing luggage following a flight, phone Cape Town International Airport (021 937 1200), who'll put you in contact with the police.

If you've lost something in the city, report it to the police (see p236).

For lost and stolen credit card helplines, see right.

MEDIA

Magazines

The magazine stands are positively groaning under the weight of local publications, and most good bookshops stock a variety of international (and super-pricey) magazines. *Cosmopolitan*, *Elle*, *Marie Claire* and *Glamour* all have local editions. If you're in the mood for a bit of celebrity gossip, look out for *Grazia* and *You*.

Newspapers

The Western Cape's newspapers focus mainly on local news, covering everything from sensationalist murder trials of high-profile musicians to the price of crude oil. If you're curious about the city's happenings, there's also a good selection of local community weekly newspapers available, such as the *Atlantic Sun* and *The Capetowner*.

Daily morning newspapers include *Cape Times & Business Day* (English), *Die Burger* (Afrikaans). *The Cape Argus* (English) is an afternoon newspaper. On Sundays there's the *Weekend Argus* Sunday edition (English), *Sunday Times* (English), and *Rapport* (Afrikaans).

Radio

Cape Talk (567 AM) broadcasts news, traffic reports, detailed weather information, and arts and entertainment updates – a great local resource for any tourist. Other local, largely music-oriented FM radio stations such as **5FM** (89.9 FM), **KFM** (94.5 FM), **Heart** (104.9 FM) and **Good Hope FM** (94-97 FM) give South African bands their fair share of

air time and also supply information on upcoming live performances. **Fine Music Radio** (101.3 FM) has a more classical line-up.

Television

SABC (South African Broadcasting Commission) owns SABC 1, 2 and 3. **SABC 1** caters almost exclusively to South Africa's black audience and has local shows, international sitcoms, news and soaps. **SABC 2** also has multilingual programmes, including in Afrikaans. **SABC 3** is an exclusively English channel and tries to cater for a higher income bracket, with much US and some British programmes.

e.tv is a privately owned station that tries to push the limits, but also has some not-so-great local shows alongside its big US series. Unfortunately, all these channels are renowned for their constant reruns of old films and TV series.

M-Net is a subscriber channel, big on sport, series and movies. **DStv** is South Africa's own digital satellite TV provider and offers local, American, British and European channels.

MONEY

Banks

ABSA *136 Adderley Street, City Bowl (021 480 1911).* **Map** p254 H4.

First National Bank *82 Adderley Street, City Bowl (087 575 9404).* **Map** p254 H4.

Nedbank *85 St George's Mall, City Bowl (021 469 9500).* **Map** p254 H3.

Standard Bank *Corner of Hans Strydom & Long Streets, City Bowl (086 012 3000).* **Map** p254 H3.

Bureaux de change

Foreign exchange facilities are found at large commercial banks, as well as at Cape Town Tourism Visitor Information Centre (see p237), the airport and bureaux de change such as American Express.

American Express *V&A Waterfront, Atlantic Seaboard (021 419 3917); Thibault House, Thibault Square, City Bowl (021 425 7991, www.americanexpress.co.za).* **Map** p253 H1.

Credit cards & ATMs

Most shops and hotels in Cape Town accept credit cards, including

international cards such as Visa and MasterCard (and to a lesser extent American Express and Diners Club). In far-flung towns the use of cards might be restricted. Always keep your card in your sight; new card machines are brought to your table so should never leave your sight. Automatic Teller Machines (ATMs) are widespread (and also often conveniently located in petrol stations) and accept most international cards. Most ATMs also offer the option to top up mobile phone credit.

Lost or stolen cards

American Express *0800 991 021.*
Diners Club *0860 346 377.*
MasterCard *0800 990 418.*
VISA *0800 990 475.*

Currency

The local currency is the South African rand. It's weak on international currency markets, which makes Cape Town a great destination for bargain luxury. (At the time of writing one US dollar was worth around R12, one British pound R18.50 and one euro R13.)

There are 100 South African cents in a rand. Coins in circulation are: 5c, 10c, 20c, 50c, R1, R2, and R5; and banknotes in circulation are R10, R20, R50, R100 and R200.

Tax

South Africa's VAT (Value Added Tax) is 14 per cent on purchases and services, and can be claimed back for purchases of R250 or more upon departure. You can't, however, reclaim on services. If you want to reclaim tax, go to the VAT office in the international departure hall at the airport, making sure to leave yourself plenty of time before your plane departs. You'll need to take along your passport and original tax-invoiced receipts together with the purchased goods. Once you've filled in the necessary paperwork and had your application processed, you can pick up a refund in your home currency from one of the banks in the departure lounge. For more information visit www.taxrefunds.co.za.

NATURAL HAZARDS

Local tap water is safe to drink. Visitors unaccustomed to South Africa's strong sun should cover up with factor 30 (or more) sunscreen and wear a hat, especially between

ESSENTIAL INFORMATION

noon and 3pm. Although reasonably rare in these parts, venomous snakes and spiders do sometimes make an appearance, especially on the mountains. If bitten, try to get a look at the culprit and then call the poison hotline (021 689 5227) for assistance.

OPENING HOURS

Most city shops (bar a few popular touristy hotspots in Kloof and Long Street) operate between 9am and 5pm during weekdays and until 1pm on Saturdays. Some shops also open on Sundays. Larger malls open daily from 9am to 9pm. On Sundays and public holidays things start up a bit later, usually from 10am. Banks are open from 9am to 3.30pm on weekdays and 8.30am to 11.30am on Saturdays. Muslim-owned businesses are closed for prayers between noon and 1pm on Fridays.

POLICE STATIONS

The police's national emergency number is **10111**. If you've been the victim of a crime, tell them what happened, where you're phoning from and what your contact details are. Always ask for the officer's name, rank and a case number.

When reporting a crime after the event, phone your nearest police station; they're listed in the blue section at the back of the telephone directory, or you can call directory enquiries at 1023.

Other useful contacts include:

Cape Town Charge Office
021 467 8000.
Cape Town International Airport Police Station *021 934 0707.*
Consumer Protector
0800 007 081.
Metrorail Protection Service
021 449 4336.

POSTAL SERVICES

The South African Post Office (Regional office 021 590 5400, track and trace 0860 111 502, www.postoffice.co.za) can't always guarantee safe and timely delivery with standard mail but, for a little bit extra, you could opt for the much more reliable registered mail and even add a tracking option. Recent postal strikes have caused massive delays in mailing.

Post offices are open 8.30am-4.30pm during the week and 8am-noon on Saturdays.

Smaller offices sometimes tend to vary their hours on certain days. PostNet (0860 767 8638, www.postnet.co.za) is a widely used private postal agency.

Postage stamps are available from post offices, newsagents and some retail outlets.

Never send money or important documents with standard mail. Send them with registered post, or use a courier or shipping company (*see p232*).

RELIGION

Buddhist Information
6 Morgenrood Road, Kenilworth, Southern Suburbs (021 761 2978, www.kagyu.org.za).

Cape Town Hebrew Congregation
88 Hatfield Street, City Bowl (021 465 1405). **Map** p254 G5.

Central Methodist Mission
Cnr Longmarket & Burg Streets, Greenmarket Square, City Bowl (021 422 2744, www.cmm.org.za). **Map** p254 H4.

Dutch Reformed Church
Groote Kerk, 39 Adderley Street, City Bowl (021 422 0569). **Map** p254 H4.

Greek Orthodox Church
75 Mountain Road, Woodstock (082 578 7415).

Hindu Temple Siva Aalayam
41 Ruth Road, Rylands, Southern Suburbs (083 794 2542, 021 638 2542).

Markaz Nurul Islam Mosque
134 Buitengracht Street, City Bowl (021 423 4202, www.nurulislammosque.org.za). **Map** p254 G4.

The Salvation Army
32 Prince Street, City Bowl (021 465 4846).

St George's Cathedral (Anglican)
Corner of Queen Victoria & Wale Streets, City Bowl (021 424 7360, www.stgeorgescathedral.com). **Map** p254 G4.

St Mary's Cathedral Parish (Roman Catholic)
Roeland Street, opposite Parliament, City Bowl (021 461 1167, www.stmaryscathedral.org.za). **Map** p254 H4.

Uniting Presbyterian Church
St Stephens Road, Southern Suburbs (021 531 8408, www.uniting presbyterian.org).

SAFETY & SECURITY

It's a sad fact that South Africa has a terrible reputation as far as crime is concerned. Cape Town's CCID (Central City Improvement District) has gone to great lengths in an attempt to make the Mother City a safer place. Security guards are visible throughout the inner city in their green uniforms. Long Street, especially, is experiencing some problems with crime and violence so keep your wits about you on this party street.

Cape Town Central Police Station
021 467 8001.
CCID *24-hour number 082 415 7127.*
Consumer Protector *0800 007 081.*
Metrorail Protection Service
021 449 4336.

For information on what to do if you get bitten by a poisonous animal, *see p235* Natural Hazards.

SMOKING

Smoking in enclosed public spaces in Cape Town is strictly prohibited. Some restaurants and bars do provide specially demarcated smoking sections for customers, however this is becoming rarer. Smoking is only allowed 10m outside a building entrance, but this is rarely enforced.

STUDY

Being such a cosmopolitan hub, there's a good selection of language schools dotted around the city where you can learn local or foreign languages. For more information contact the International School of Languages (021 674 4117).

TELEPHONES

Making a call

To make a phone call within South Africa, dial the area code followed by the phone number. To make an international call, dial 00 before the International Direct Dialling code, the area code and then the phone number. Cape Town's area code is 021, Johannesburg is 011, Pretoria is 012 and Durban is 031.

Phone Directory Enquiries (1023) if you're looking for a specific number that isn't listed in the phone book. Otherwise call the Talking Yellow Pages (10118) or try iFind (34600, www.ifind.co.za), a mobile directory service that you can call or SMS (text message) to find the required numbers of local shops and services.

Public phones

Green and blue public phone booths can be found all over the city. The blue phones are coin-operated, and the green ones work with a telephone card that can be bought at post offices, newsagents and Telkom offices, as well as selected grocery stores.

Mobile phones

All new mobile phones should operate in South Africa and SIM cards for all of the four national networks – Cell C (www.cellc.co.za), Vodacom (www.vodacom.co.za), MTN (www.mtn.co.za) and Virgin Mobile (www.virginmobile.co.za) – can be purchased at their respective outlets, at supermarkets like Pick n Pay and Spar, and also at newsagent chains such as CNA and PNA.

TIME

South Africa is two hours ahead of GMT, seven ahead of Eastern Standard Winter Time and ten ahead of Pacific Standard Time. There is no daylight saving time in summer.

TIPPING

The general guideline for tipping in restaurants is around 15 per cent of your total bill. Taxi drivers are usually tipped about ten per cent of the total fare, porters up to R10 a bag and petrol pump attendants R5 to R10. Car guards settle for about R5.

TOILETS

Public toilets in shopping malls and restaurants are generally clean and are preferable to the city centre's public facilities.

TOURIST INFORMATION

The **Cape Town Tourism Visitor Centre** is on the corner of Castle and Burg streets in the city centre (086 132 2223, www.capetown.travel). If you're having trouble deciding what to include on your itinerary, they'll help you make up your mind with a selection of maps, brochures, tour outings and other essential information on what's happening in the Mother City. Bookings and reservations can be made at the help desks.

The V&A Waterfront also has a visitor centre, the **V&A Waterfront Information Centre** (021 408 7600) located on Dock Road.

VISAS & IMMIGRATION

Visa requirements

Citizens from the UK, the Republic of Ireland, most European countries and Australia do not need visas, as long as they have a national passport valid for 30 days beyond the length of their trip, a return ticket and proof of accommodation.

Entry requirements can change at any time, so check carefully before you travel. For more information, visit www.home-affairs.gov.za.

WEIGHTS & MEASUREMENTS

South Africa uses the metric system. Useful conversions are given below.
1 kilometre = 0.62 miles
1 metre = 1.094 yards
1 centimetre = 0.39 inches
1 kilogram = 2.2 pounds
1 gram = 0.035 ounces
1 litre = 1.75 pints
$0°C = 32°F$

WHEN TO GO

Cape Town's climate is Mediterranean, with warm, dry summers and mild, moist winters. During summer (November to February) the temperature on the coast generally ranges between 15°C and 35°C (while inland it increases by around 3-5°C), although recent summers have seen temperatures in the City Bowl soaring to over 40°C. In winter (May to August) it ranges between 7°C and 18°C.

Cape Town's summer months are crammed with festivals, concerts and carnivals, with the weeks around Christmas and New Year being especially busy. The summer sun is no laughing matter, however, so make sure that you slap on plenty of strong sunscreen. The south-easterly wind known as the Cape Doctor also makes its appearance in summer, wreaking havoc on hairstyles and beach parties, but performing a vital service to the city by clearing it of smog.

The season starts getting slightly chillier around April. The lovely autumn colours draw people out of town to forests in Newlands and Constantia, as well as the Winelands, while winter is synonymous with rain showers.

Public holidays

New Year's Day (1 Jan)
Human Rights Day (21 Mar)
Good Friday (varies)
Easter Monday & Family Day (Monday after Easter Sunday)
Freedom Day (27 Apr)
Workers' Day (1 May)
Youth Day (16 June)
National Women's Day (9 Aug)
Heritage Day (24 Sept)
Day of Reconciliation (16 Dec)
Christmas Day (25 Dec)
Day of Goodwill (26 Dec)

WOMEN

While Cape Town is generally fairly safe in South African terms, violence against women is a serious problem in South Africa. Be wary of walking on your own, especially at night. Use reputable taxi services, be aware of your surrounds and trust your gut.

WORKING

Find information from your nearest Department of Home Affairs office (Private Bag X114, Pretoria 0001, 0800 601 190, www.home-affairs.gov. za) if you're in South Africa. If you're abroad, do so on the websites given under the Visa section (see p233).

LOCAL CLIMATE

Average temperatures and monthly rainfall in Cape Town.

	High (°C/°F)	Low (°C/°F)	Rainfall (mm/in)
Jan	26 / 79	16 / 61	15 / 0.6
Feb	27 / 81	16 / 61	17 / 0.7
Mar	25 / 77	14 / 57	20 / 0.8
Apr	23 / 73	12 / 54	41 / 1.6
May	20 / 68	9 / 48	68 / 2.7
June	18 / 64	8 / 46	93 / 3.7
July	18 / 64	7 / 45	82 / 3.2
Aug	18 / 64	8 / 46	77 / 3.0
Sept	19 / 66	9 / 48	40 / 1.6
Oct	21 / 70	11 / 52	30 / 1.2
Nov	24 / 75	13 / 55	14 / 0.5
Dec	25 / 77	15 / 59	17 / 0.7

Further Reference

BOOKS

Fiction & literature

Beukes, Lauren *Moxyland, Zoo City* The first is a gritty cyber-punk novel depicting a dystopian, corporation-run Cape Town of the future; the second, winner of the Arthur C Clarke Award 2011, mixes city crime with otherworldly elements.

Brink, André *Rumours of Rain, A Dry White Season* and *Praying Mantis* Intriguing politicised novels by one of South Africa's most acclaimed writers.

Brynard, Karin *Weeping Waters* Acclaimed thriller, in which the complex history of farming in South Africa is also explained.

Coetzee, JM *Disgrace, Waiting for the Barbarians, The Life and Times of Michael K* and *Dusklands* Winner of the Nobel prize for literature in 2003, Coetzee goes to the heart of the South African psyche and questions the country's political and social landscape.

Duiker, K Sello *The Quiet Violence of Dreams* and *Thirteen Cents* Duiker convincingly depicted the harsh realities of Cape Town's underbelly, exploring issues such as homelessness, mental illness, drug abuse, prostitution and the overwhelming sense of isolation to be found in any city. He committed suicide in 2005.

Fugard, Athol *Blood Knot, Boesman and Lena* and *A Lesson from Aloes* One of South Africa's most esteemed playwrights, most famous as a campaigning dramatist, tackling issues of apartheid.

Galgut, Damon *The Good Doctor* Short-listed for the 2003 Man Booker prize, Galgut's novel explores post-apartheid South Africa, where deep-rooted social and political tensions threaten shared dreams for the future.

Gordimer, Nadine *July's People, Burger's Daughter* and *Sport of Nature* Nobel prize-winning novelist dealing with the tensions of her racially divided country.

Khumalo, Sihle *Dark Continent My Black Arse* A humorous account of a womaniser's journey from the Cape to Cairo.

Matlwa, Kopano *Coconut* A novel about two young black women growing up in white, privileged suburbs and the social ostracism and identity struggles they experience.

Matthee, Dalene *Circles in a Forest* and *Fiela's Child* Historical novels with the lush Knysna Forest as a backdrop.

Mda, Jakes *Heart of Redness* and *Ways of Dying* Magic realism gets a contemporary African twist.

Meyer, Deon *Icarus, Cobra* and *7 Days* Highly acclaimed crime writer's novels mainly set in and around Cape Town. Troubled cop protagonist Bennie Griesel investigates chilling murders. Gripping stuff.

Orford, Margie *Water Music, Gallows Hill* and *Daddy's Girl* Excellent research and sinister Cape Town settings make for crime thrillers with social commentary, with Dr Clare Hart as investigative profiler.

Paton, Alan *Cry the Beloved Country* A South African classic, about families, racism, reconciliation and forgiveness.

Schreiner, Olive *The Story of an African Farm* An early South African classic, exploring themes around women and society.

Sleigh, Dan *Islands* The first years of the settlement of the Dutch colony in the Cape are documented through the accounts of seven historically based characters.

Van de Ruit, John *Spud* series Follow John 'Spud' Milton's coming of age at a private boy's school during the first days of democracy. Lovely schoolboy romp.

Van Niekerk, Marlene *Triomf* and *Agaat* Two multi-award winning books giving glimpses into the dark side of Afrikaner identity.

Vladislavić, Ivan *Missing Persons* and *101 Detectives* Well-known for his short stories, Vladislavić's books look at South Africa in its post-Apartheid state.

Non-fiction

Breytenbach, Breyten *The True Confessions of an Albino Terrorist* A memoir of the well-known poet's seven-year imprisonment in South Africa.

Cameron, Edwin *A Witness to AIDS* Constitutional Court Justice Edwin Cameron's extremely frank account of contracting and living with HIV/AIDS.

De Vries, Fred *The Fred de Vries Interviews: From Abdullah to Zille* A collection of insightful interviews by the renowned Dutch South African travel writer and journalist.

Dommisse, Ebbe *Anton Rupert: A Biography* The remarkable life story of one of the richest businessmen in the world, whose group of Rembrandt companies owns brands such as Cartier, Mont Blanc and Dunhill.

Du Preez, Max *Pale Native* Not known for mincing words, this roving reporter writes of his times in a troubled South Africa.

Gevisser, Mark *Thabo Mbeki: The Dream Deferred* A glimpse into the political and personal life of the man who followed in Nelson Mandela's footsteps as president.

Giliomee, Herman *The Afrikaners* Traces the history of the Afrikaner from Dutch settler to constructor of apartheid.

Gordin, Jeremy *Zuma: A Biography* Sheds some light on South Africa's president.

Kanfer, Stefan *The Last Empire: De Beers, Diamonds and the World* A story of cutthroat capitalism as well as the economic and racial development of South Africa.

Krog, Antjie *Country of My Skull, A Change of Tongue* and *Down to My Last Skin* Krog analyses the country and its people in an erudite manner.

Mandela, Nelson *Long Walk to Freedom* An inspiring and humbling autobiographical account of his life.

Marinovich, Greg & Silva, João *The Bang Bang Club: Snapshots from a Hidden War* The book shares frontline experiences of four photo-journalists during the tumultuous early nineties in South Africa.

Nicol, Mike *Mandela: The Authorised Biography* Sixty interviews with world leaders and friends, as well as previously unpublished photos and letters.

Pakenham, Thomas *The Scramble for Africa* A disturbing look at the colonisation of the African continent.

Tutu, Desmond *No Future Without Forgiveness* Essential reading on the transformation of the country in Tutu's lifetime.

Food & wine

Cheifitz, Phillippa *South Africa Eats* A showcase of the diverse peoples and foods of South Africa.

Essop, Sydda *Karoo Kitchen* Heritage and culture from South Africa's arid interior make a fascinating read, with recipes, home remedies and culinary tales.

Mouton, Maggie *Bo-Kaap Kitchen* Heritage and cooking combine to make a stunning book about the Cape's muslim community.
Platter's Wine Guide Annual guide to everything you need to know about South Africa's wine and wineries.
Riffel, Reuben *Braai – Reuben On Fire*, *Reuben Cooks – Local* Food by favourite local chef Reuben Riffel.
Snyman, Lannice *Tortoises and Tumbleweeds* South Africa's undisputed food doyenne takes readers on a journey through the history and cuisine of her homeland.

FILM

Amandla! – A revolution in four-part harmony *(Lee Hirsch 2002)* Stunning documentary tracking the history of South Africa protest music and the role it played in the struggle against apartheid.
Bunny Chow *(John Barker 2006)* A classic road trip movie about three stand-up comedians travelling to the annual music festival, Oppikoppi.
Country of My Skull *(John Boorman 2004)* Adapted from Antjie Krog's book about her time as a foreign journalist at the Truth and Reconciliation trials.
Cry Freedom *(Richard Attenborough 1987)* True story of an inspiring friendship in a politically turbulent time.
Cry, the Beloved Country *(Darrell James Roodt 1995)* A film adaptation of Alan Paton's novel, telling the heart-wrenching story of a father's love for his son.
District 9 *(Neill Blomkamp 2009)* Aliens forced to live in slums in Joburg get restless while a human becomes one of them.
Invictus *(Clint Eastwood 2009)* National pride and a new South Africa gain momentum over the 1995 Rugby World Cup.
Gandhi *(Richard Attenborough 1982)* Insight into Gandhi's experiences as a young lawyer in South Africa.
Promised Land *(Jason Xenopoulos 2002)* Adapted from the Afrikaans novel by Karel Schoeman, and winner of the best screenplay award at the Tokyo International Film Festival, it tells a story of hidden truths and near impossible quests.
Sarafina! *(Darrell James Roodt 1992)* In this film adaptation of Mbongeni Ngema's stage musical, Whoopi Goldberg plays an idealistic teacher who helps a teenage girl throw off the shackles of apartheid.
Silver Fez *(Lloyd Ross 2009)* A glimpse into the highly competitive world of Cape Malay choirs.

Stander *(Bronwen Hughes 2003)* Based on true events, this movie tells the tale of South African police officer Captain André Stander, who became a notorious bank robber.
Triomf *(Michael Raeburn 2008)* Based on Marlene van Niekerk's acclaimed novel, this disturbing movie follows the lives of one family living in the backwater of Triomf at the dawn of the 1994 elections.
Tsotsi *(Gavin Hood 2005)* A ruthless gang leader undergoes an existential crisis after finding a baby on the back seat of a car that he has hijacked. Winner of the Academy Award for Best Foreign-Language film in 2005.
U-Carmen eKhayelitsha *(Dimpho Di Kopan 2005)* George Bizet's 1875 opera is given a dramatic new guise in this Xhosa film adaptation set in Cape Town's densely populated township, Khayelitsha.
The Vula Connection *(Marion Edmunds 2014)* Fascinating documentary about the ANC's secret communication system during the struggle years.
White Wedding *(Jann Turner 2009)* A light-hearted feature film about love, race and the new South Africa.

MUSIC

Abdullah Ibrahim *African Magic, Senzo* The king of Cape Jazz, this pianist and composer is a living legend.
Brenda Fassie *Memeza, Mina Nawe* The late Fassie was hailed by many as Africa's queen of pop and had a string of hits to her name, including the infectious 'Weekend Special'.
Die Antwoord *Donker Mag, Ten$ion, O* Hard-core punk rap from Ninja, Yolandi Vi$$er and DJ Hi-Tek.
The Dirty Skirts *Daddy Don't Disco, Lost in the Fall* A quirky indie-pop act now with several hits to their name – think catchy hooks and vocals reminiscent of the Cure.
Freshlyground *Jika Jika, Nomvula, Ma Cherie, Radio Africa, Take Me to the Dance* Winner of the MTV Europe award for best African act 2006, this ensemble cast of talented musos will have you on your feet.
Goldfish *Caught in the Loop, Perceptions of Pacha, Get Busy Living, Goldfish* A talented Cape Town duo mixing their own distinctive brand of electro-jazz.
Jack Parow *Jack Parow, Eksie Ou, Nag van die Lang Pette* Rapper in Afrikaans and English, known for astute social observations and tongue-in-cheek commentary in his music.
Johnny Clegg *Third World Child, Shadowman, Cruel, Crazy Beautiful World* Known as the 'white Zulu',

Clegg has performed with groups Juluka and Suvuka since the apartheid years, combining Zulu and English lyrics with Celtic influences.
Ladysmith Black Mambazo *The Ultimate Collection* The Grammy Award-winning male choral group that performed on Paul Simon's *Graceland* album.
Locnville *Sun in my Pocket, Running to Midnight* Electronic hip hop music duo made up of identical twin brothers.
Lucky Dube *Soul Taker* South Africa's greatest reggae star was murdered in 2007 but the optimism of his music lives on.
Mafikizolo *Sibongile, Kwela, Six Mabone, Reunited* Award-winning *kwaito*-pop with retro Sophiatown influences.
Mi Casa *Mi Casa, Su Casa* House band based in Joburg with an authentic sound.
Nomfusi *Kwazibani, Take Me Home* This pint-sized Afro-soul singer certainly knows how to belt out some powerful tunes.
Parlotones *Antiques & Artifacts, Stand like Giants, Journey through the Shadows* Joburg rock group touring the world with their indie sounds.
Soweto String Quartet *Zebra Crossing, Renaissance* SSQ make their instruments sing, incorporating kwela and jazz rhythms.
Taxi Violence *Tenfold, Soul Shake, Unplugged: Long Way From Home* Modern rock band with a fantastic live act.
Yvonne Chaka Chaka *The Best of Yvonne Chaka Chaka* A leading figure in South African popular music.
Zola *Undiwembe, Khokuvula, Tsotsi* The undisputed king of *kwaito*.

WEBSITES

www.capetownetc.com
Events and activities as well as ideas for exploring further afield.
www.capetownkids.co.za
Packed with family-friendly ideas.
www.capetownmagazine.co.za
Keep a finger on the pulse of Cape Town's goings-on.
www.capetown.travel
Official tourism website filled with listings and resources.
www.eatout.co.za
A comprehensive directory of restaurants and reviews.
www.tablemountain.net
Check out all there is to know about the Cape's iconic mountain and book cable car tickets online.
www.weathersa.co.za
Cape Town weather is notoriously unpredictable, so keep an eye on the forecasts.

ESSENTIAL INFORMATION

Index

INDEX

INDEX

Maps

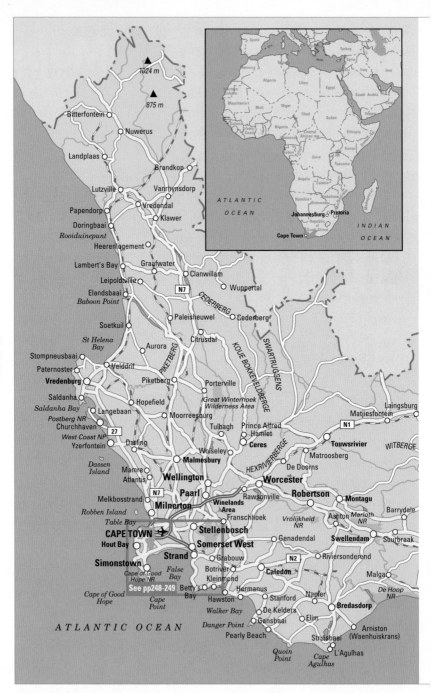

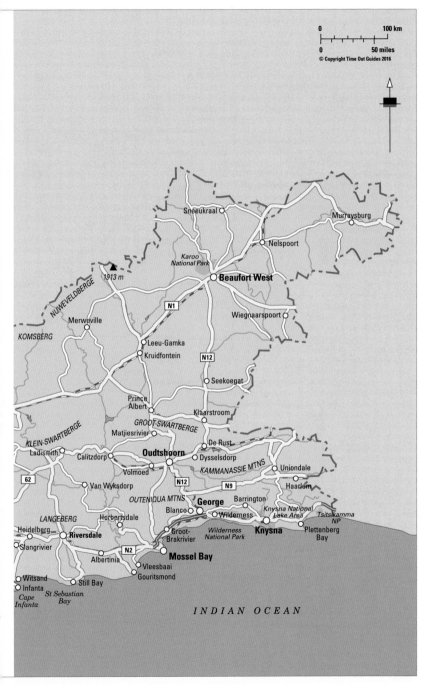

MAPS

0   100 km

0   50 miles

Murraysburg

Sneeukraal

Nelspoort

Karoo
National Park

▲ 1913 m

Beaufort West

NUWEVELDBERGE

Merweville

N1

Wiegnaarspoort

KOMSBERG

Leeu-Gamka

Kruidfontein

N12

Seekoegat

Prince
Albert

Klaarstroom

GROOT-SWARTBERGE

KLEIN-SWARTBERGE

Matjiesrivier

De Rust

Ladismith

Calitzdorp

Oudtshoorn

Dysselsdorp

Uniondale

62

Volmoed

KAMMANASSIE MTNS

Haarlem

Van Wyksdorp

N12

N9

OUTENIQUA MTNS

Blanco

George

Barrington

Knysna National
Lake Area

Tsitsikamma
NP

Herbertsdale

LANGEBERG

Wilderness

Wilderness
National Park

Knysna

Plettenberg
Bay

Heidelberg

Riversdale

Groot-
Brakrivier

Slangrivier

N2

Mossel Bay

Albertinia

Vleesbaai

Witsand

Still Bay

Gouritsmond

Infanta

Cape
Infanta

St Sebastian
Bay

INDIAN OCEAN

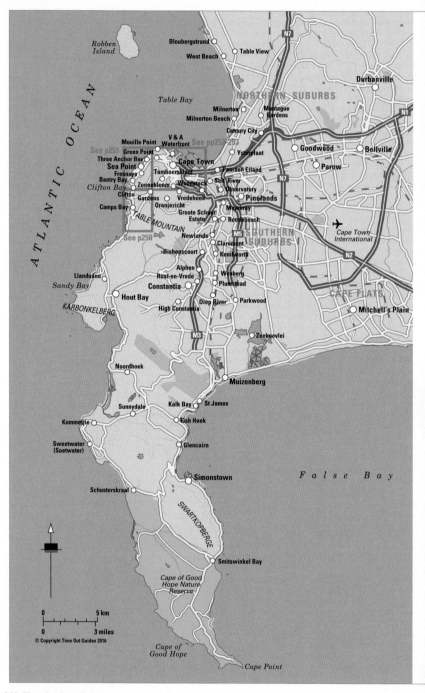

MAPS

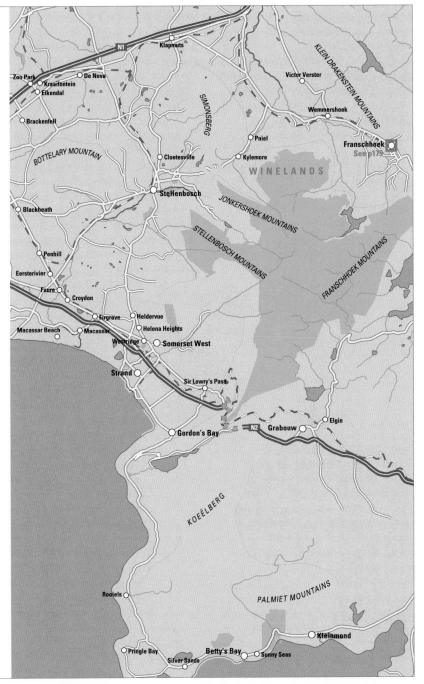

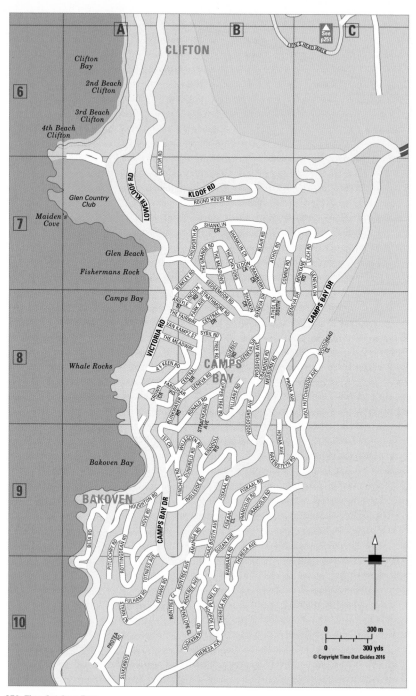

MAPS

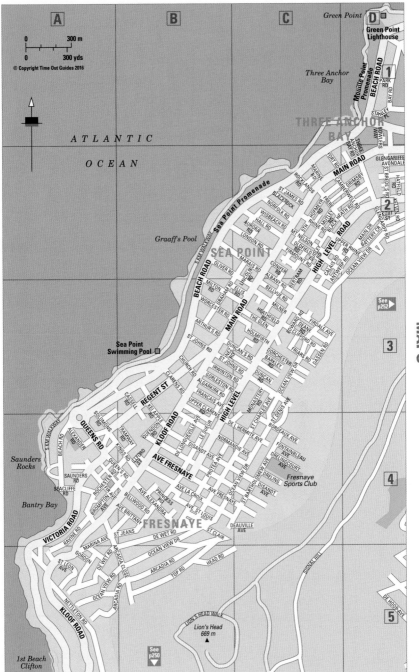

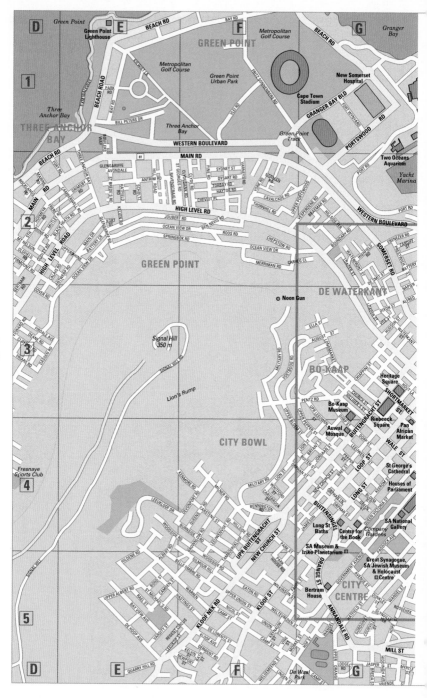

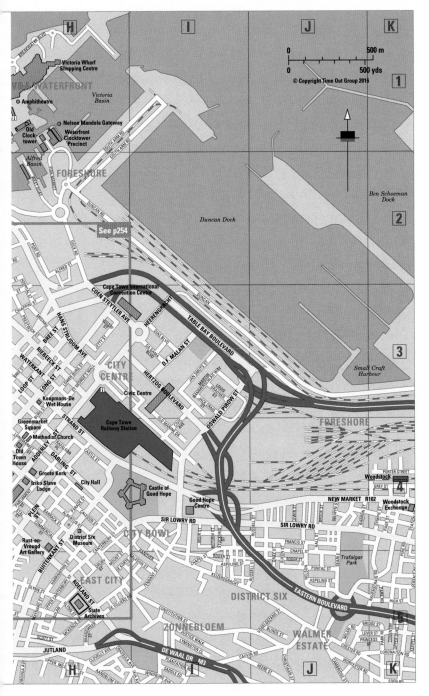

MAPS

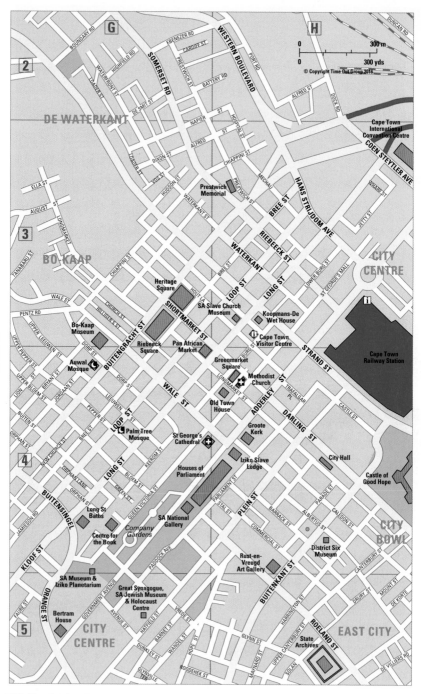

Street Index

STREET INDEX